Dou Dunning
263 Bradley
Battle Creek, Mi. 49017

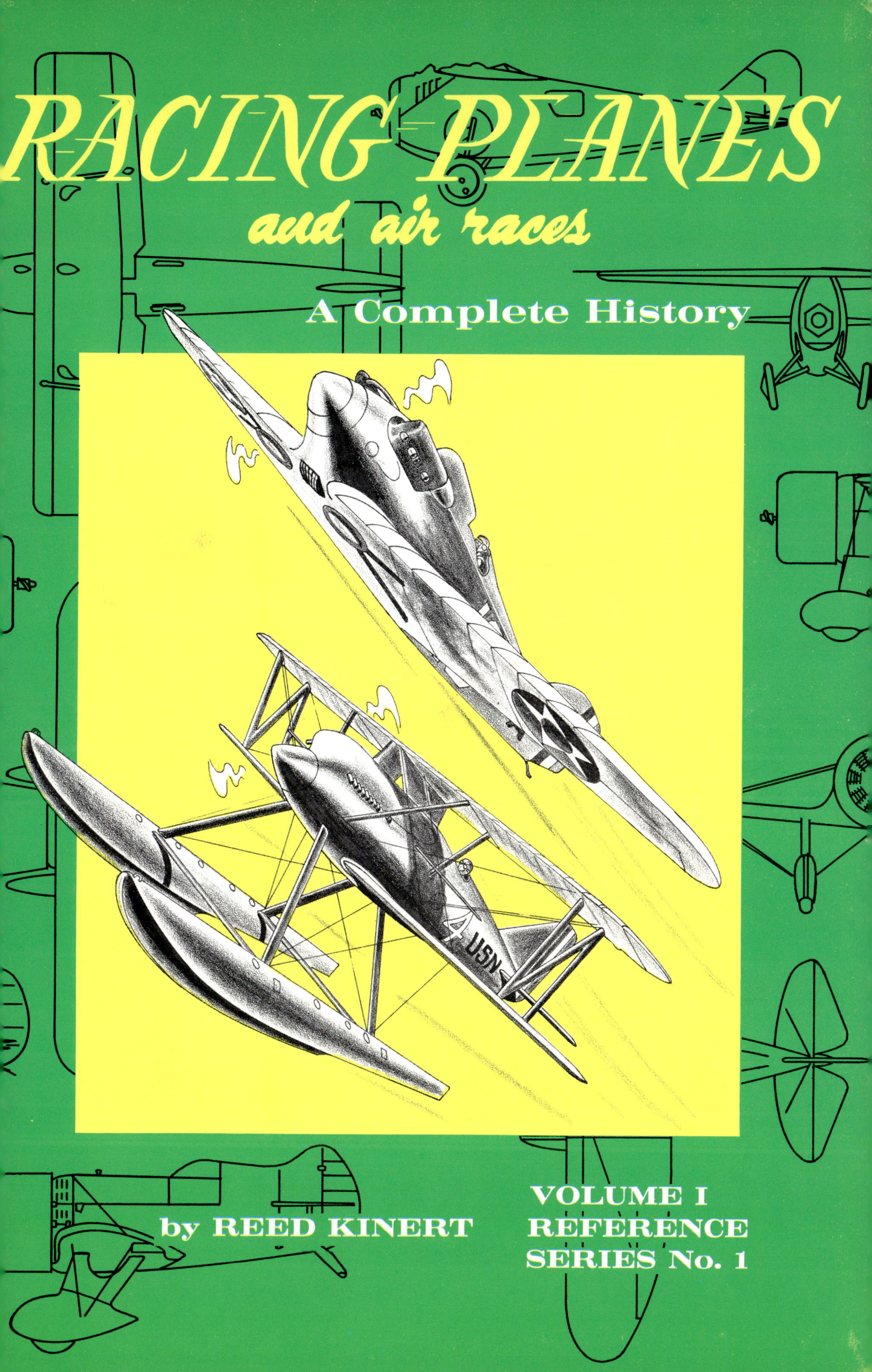

RACING PLANES
and air races
A Complete History
by REED KINERT
VOLUME I
REFERENCE
SERIES No. 1

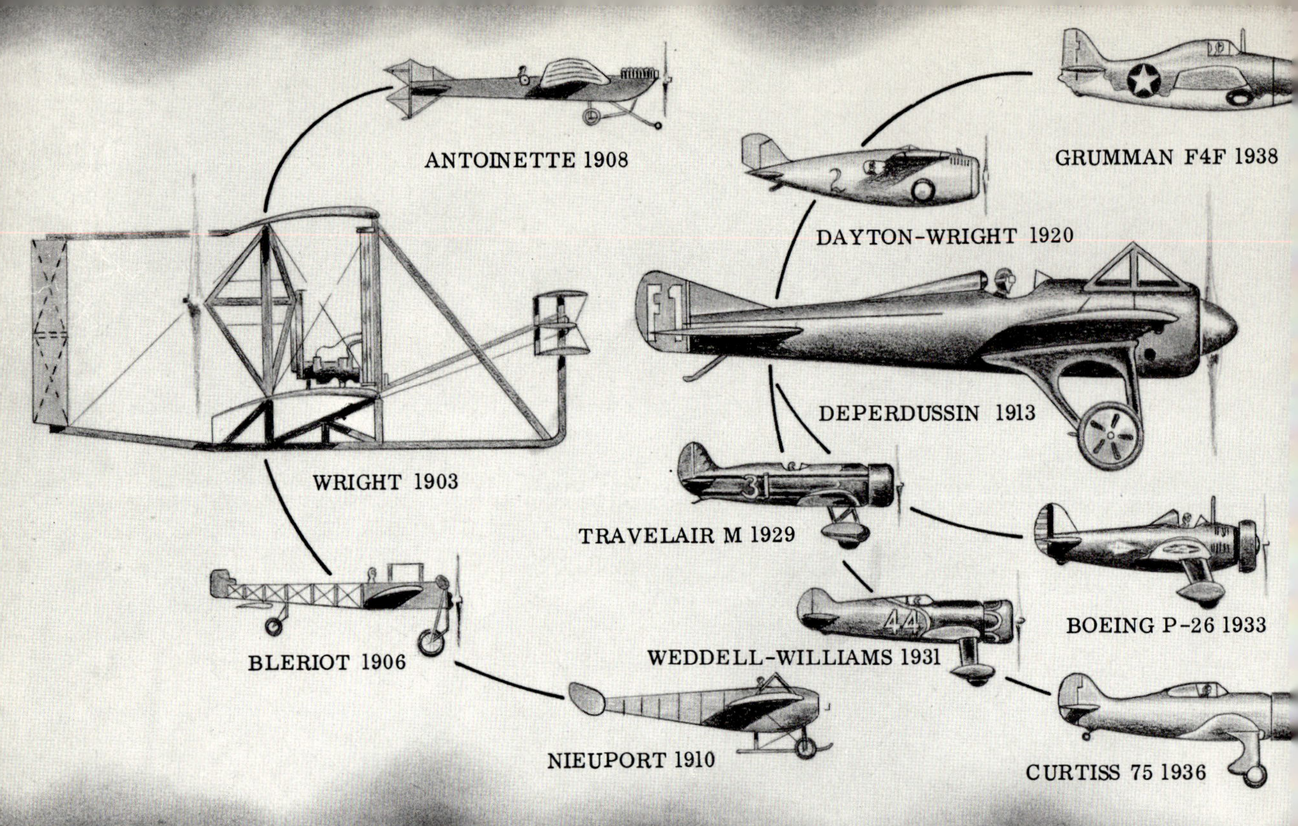

"Instead of the tardy conveyance of ships and chariots, man might use the swifter migration of wings, the fields of air are open to knowledge and only ignorance and idleness need crawl upon the ground."

—Rasselas, DR. SAMUEL JOHNSON, *1759*

Written and Illustrated by Reed Kinert

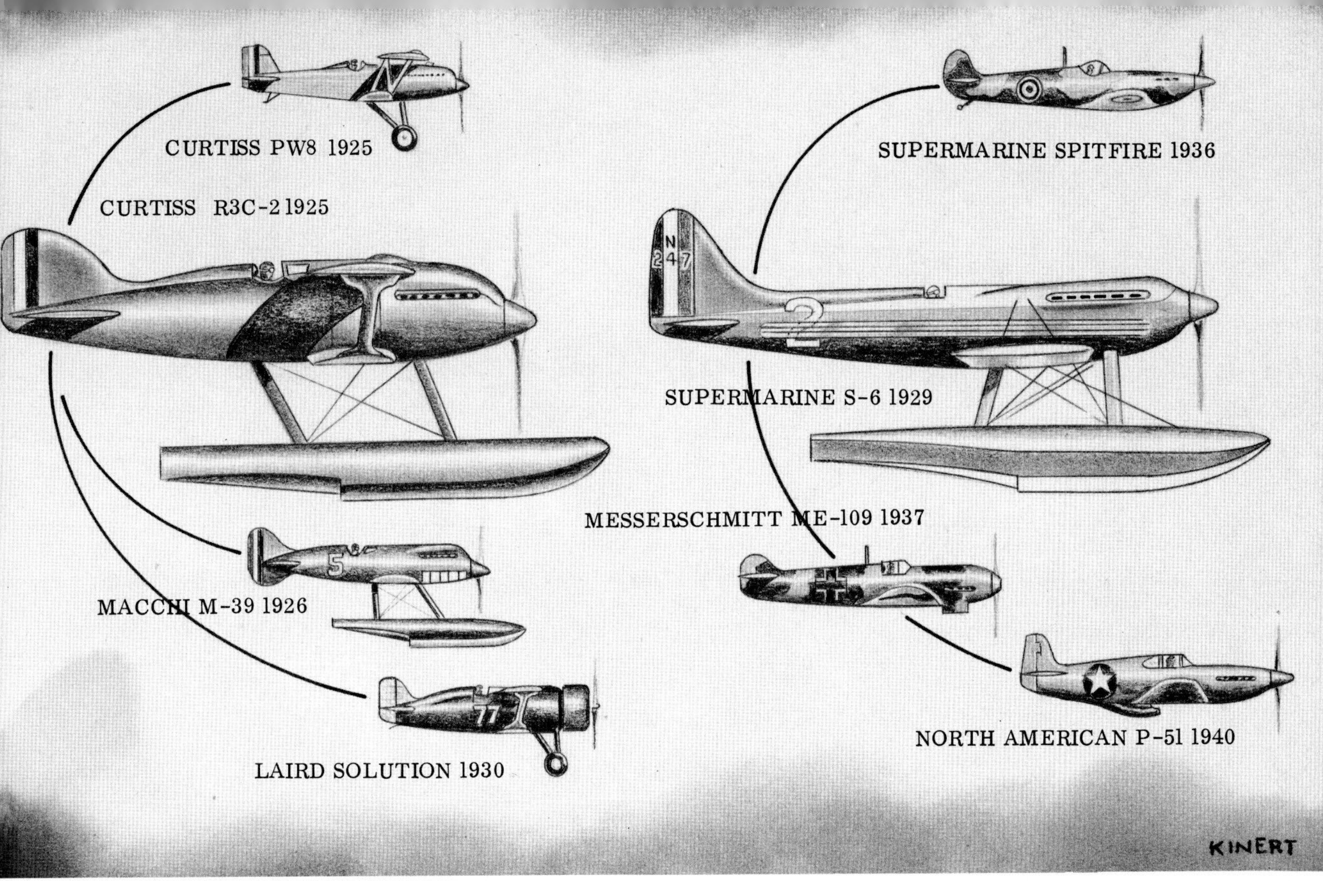

RACING-PLANES

and air races

A Complete History

VOLUME I
1909-1923

AERO PUBLISHERS, INC.

Fallbrook, California

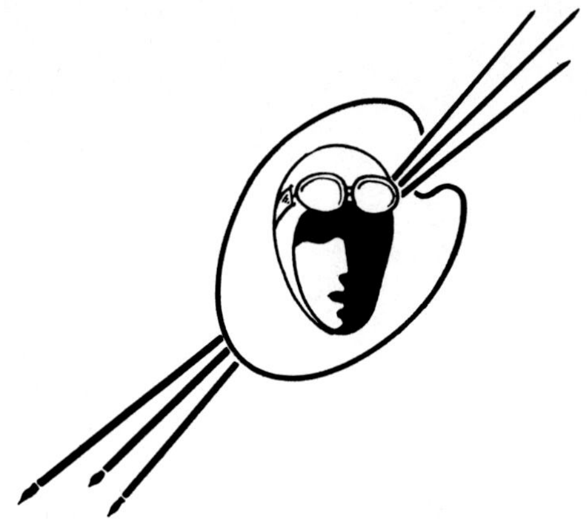

DEDICATION

To the designers, builders, and pilots of racing aircraft, for their contribution to the science of flight.

FIRST EDITION

SECOND PRINTING – REVISED – 1969

LIBRARY OF CONGRESS CATALOG CARD NUMBER
67-16455

Foreword

As a small boy I watched my first air race, if it could be called that — a race between an automobile and an airplane. The automobile won, at 40 miles an hour.

Since that day, closed-course racing speeds of airplanes have exceeded 600 miles per hour. The history of air racing — the events which made possible this tremendous advance during my lifetime — is the chronological record of the sacrifice and accomplishment of the men and women who made this history. Some of them you will meet in this book. Many others, however, are anonymous heroes: unfamiliar by name, known only through their work.

It is difficult for me to think of air racing as a sporting event. Men, not machines, indulge in sports. But to me, air racing is a contest between machines. It implies a conquest of speed, rather than a contest in speed.

The contest between men in air racing is largely the matching of wits in the design and building of the airplane and in its preparation for the race. Although I am sure that some will challenge my opinion, I feel that the pilot of a racing plane is not really the contestant. What he does or does not do has very little effect on the outcome of the race, provided, of course, that he uses everyday piloting skill and techniques and that he follows prescribed racing procedure. The two most perfect performances of race flying I can recall watching, one by a man and one by a woman, illustrate this point. In the case of the man, it was the first closed-course race he had ever flown; in the case of the woman, it was the first time she had ever touched the controls of a purely racing plane. They both won their races — because the planes were right!

I have found that if the flight characteristics of a racing airplane are tricky enough to require more than average skill in a race, it is very unlikely that it will ever be a winner. It certainly will never be a consistent one. Below-par design just can't be offset by above-par piloting.

The racecourse is a stern taskmaster for the airplane. It makes the pilot pay a high price for small deficiencies in original design or for laxity or incompetence in preparing the plane for the race. It is equally cruel and unforgiving of mistakes made by the pilot during the race.

The men and women who made air-racing history have been driven by an urge far more compelling than any instinct relating to sport, pleasure, or self-advancement. Yet it is hard to define this urge. I have been asked on many occasions, "What good is air racing? What has it done for aviation?" I find it difficult to answer specifically, for the benefits are numerous and varied. In groping for the answer, I find many more intangibles than tangibles and feel strongly that the intangibles are far more important.

The tangibles are more or less limited to the sort of thing that auto racing has done for the development of the automobile. The economic necessity or urge to "win" has in many instances prompted important developments in aircraft design considerably earlier than would have occurred in ordinary progress.

One intangible result of air racing, which indicates the gruelling tests imposed by the racecourse, occurred in the Jet Thompson Trophy Race of 1949. This was a race between three F-86's, our current high-speed fighters. These planes had passed all the stringent tests imposed on our Air Force jet fighters, but they found the racecourse still more exacting. All three planes suffered serious structural failure before the race was finished. The design corrections that resulted from these failures helped our flyers in Korean skies.

The intangible benefits of air racing are numerous. The chief one is that interest in air racing stimulates young people into technical study and eventually into the design and building of aircraft. Racing planes offer the best opportunity for designers to test their ideas and ingenuity. Usually only one racing plane of each design is built, and for that reason the hundred-odd racing planes built in this country in the four years for the Goodyear and Continental Trophy races alone represent a greater number of original and complete designs than has been produced by the entire aircraft industry in the same period. Less than a year after it was announced that races would be held for a new classification of "midget" airplane, thirteen new racers had been designed, built, tested, and raced.

This performance by the back-yard designers presents a real challenge to our great aircraft industry. The time factor in their accomplishments is particularly significant when you consider the accepted interval of several years between the time an airplane is designed and the day it can be flown away from the factory. In spite of the hundreds of millions of dollars spent on new aircraft designs following the attack on Pearl Harbor, only one, a Grumman F6F Hellcat, was ready for use in World War II. All the other planes used in that war were already in production or had entered the blueprint stage before Pearl Harbor.

From a monetary angle, I think that the achievements of these back-yard designers should provoke a complete analysis of the methods used by the engineering departments of large aircraft manufacturers, considering that dozens of original back-yard racers can be designed, engineered, built, and tested to exacting requirements for less than the cost of a *single* wind-tunnel model recently used by one of our large organizations as an aid in the design of a new aircraft!

In preparing this book, Reed Kinert has done aviation people the world over a real service. The accuracy and detail in which this exciting phase of the history of aviation is covered bespeaks much painstaking research.

It will be a treasured addition to my library as a reference aid from a technical standpoint, and as an aid to reminiscing. I will be reminded of many events, both happy and sad, of fine men I've raced against who are no longer here to read this, and of other fine men I've raced against who have since earned the gratitude of a nation for a different kind of flying. All have done their part in the advancement of aviation.

Benjamin O. Howard
Consulting Engineer
Consolidated-Vultee Aircraft
Fairchild Aircraft Corp.

AUTHOR'S NOTE

From the beginning of air racing in 1909 to the last pre-World War II races of 1939 the development of racing planes and their engines contributed directly to the technology applied to aircraft built in assembly-line quantity, both military and commercial craft.

Having wondered for years when and where air racing began I. went, one foggy morning while awaiting take-off from the local bean patch, to yon library for a bit of research.

Many libraries, hundreds of letters and thousands of books and magazines later I had to publish—in an effort to repay myself the time and effort spent!

Actually it has been fun. I have treasured letters in my files from famous, near-famous and unsung designers, builders, and pilots the world over. And many good friendships were made in my quest for the ever elusive last word or photograph of a particular aircraft or event.

Being a long time admirer of artist Clayton Knight, and remindful of how nicely his sketches dressed up so many aviation stories of WWI, I spent many hours on my drawing board embellishing the written word with action art, in hopes it would lend interest.

Dustin Carter, a fine scale drawing craftsman, has helped greatly to add book interest and the photo credits in our book are just that—in almost direct proportion to the number of photographs.

In these pages we depict but a few "stock" aircraft, military or civilian craft that, by having a number painted on, became racing planes. Rather we will use the valuable space to show, whenever possible, more than one view of each purely racing aircraft. When a particular production military or civilian aircraft was either extremely modified or as stock in appearance, did set a noteworthy record or win an important race we try to show that aircraft.

As I said—it has been fun and we hope you like it!

Reed C. Kinert
Commercial Pilot
No. 27006

Table of Contents

List of Illustrations

List of Three-Views

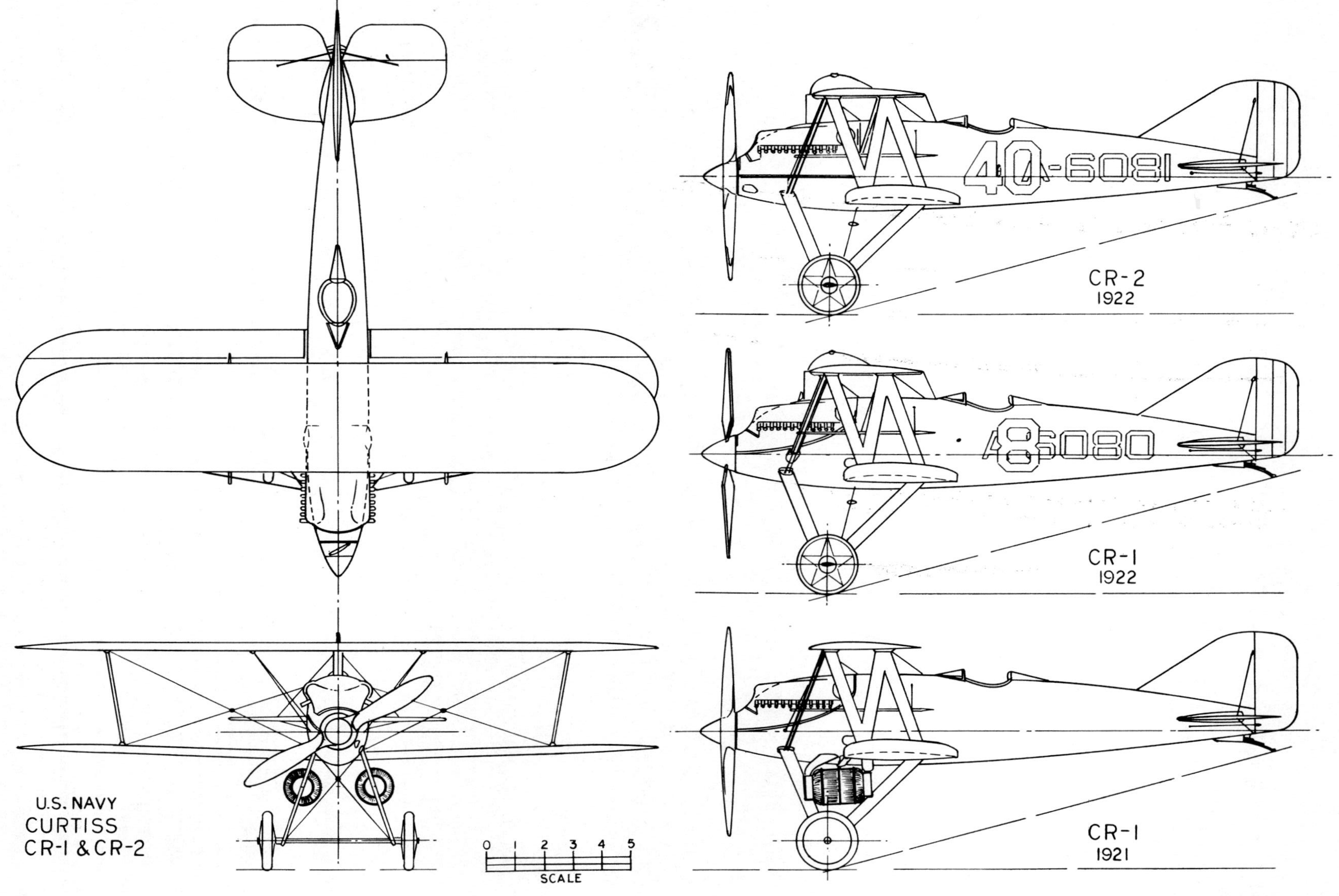

40-6081
CR-2
1922
A6080
CR-1
1922
CR-1
1921
U.S. NAVY
CURTISS
CR-1 & CR-2
SCALE
0 1 2 3 4 5
D.W. CARTER 7/66

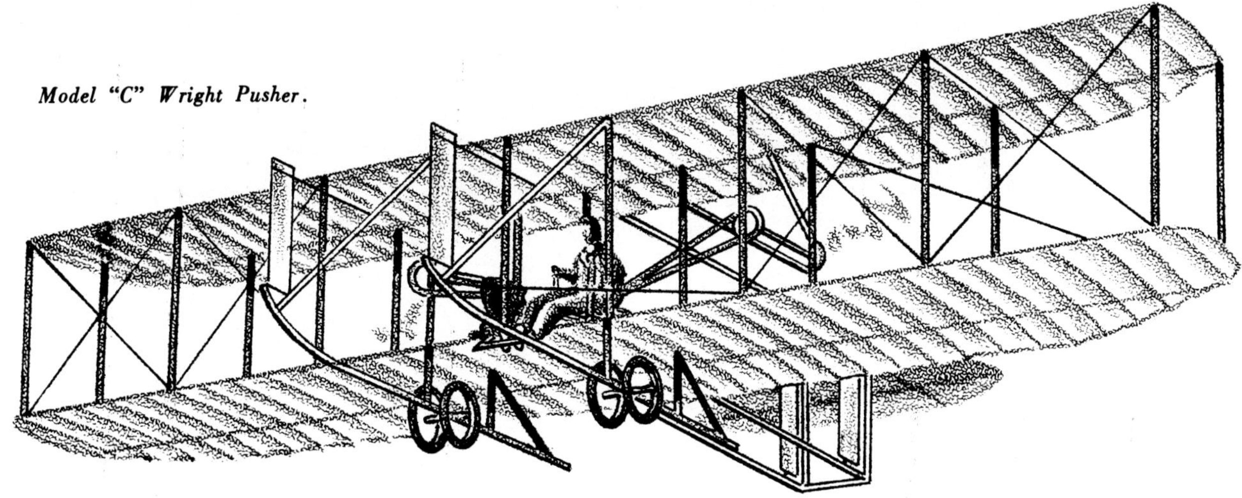

1909—The First International Air Meet

News of Orville Wright's first engine-driven flight at Kitty Hawk, N. C., Dec. 17, 1903, and the several flights made afterwards by both Orville and Wilbur, had traveled around the world, mostly in disbelief. Then on Sept. 26, 1905, Orville made the first officially recorded flight, when he flew 11.12 miles in 18 minutes, 9 seconds, at Dayton, Ohio. Disbelief changed to amazed wonder.

In France, Aug. 22, 1906, Brazilian-born Alberto Santos-Dumont made the first recorded European flight—in a boxkite-like biplane. The continental designers Leon Delegrange, and the brothers Farman and Voisin followed Santos-Dumont with their biplane aircraft in quick order. Bleriot in that same eventful year of 1906 had built and flown the world's first successful powered monoplane. Glenn Curtiss, like the Wright brothers, had manufactured bicycles, and followed the Wrights in the United States by building his biplane *June Bug* complete to its engine. He flew it June 21, 1908. The astonishing progress of aviation was on.

The newly formed Aero Clubs of France, England, and the United States soon decided to gather all the aviation clan together, realizing the tremendous boost it would give the newly born science, from both a public and an engineering viewpoint. Their plans culminated in 1909.

Just six years after the Wrights had made their powered flights, the first International Air Meet of heavier-than-air machines took place near the old cathedral town of Rheims, France, on the field of Bethany, where the troops of Joan of Arc had once camped.

Held August 22–29, the International races attracted over 100,000 people daily. The ancient little city seethed with excitement. A small hotel suite was $500 for the week, and the tiniest of rooms $10 a day. Dozens of special trains ran from Paris, and Paris itself was crowded by fans who worshiped their favorite flyers more fervently than movie stars are worshiped today.

Louis Bleriot, who had earlier that year been the first to fly the English Channel, and who was acknowledged the greatest flyer in France, was at Rheims with five machines of his own design. One, especially built for the feature speed event, the Bennett Cup race, was a big monoplane with a V-8 60-hp E.N.V. engine.

Hubert Latham's hangar held two Antoinettes, with widespread wings and pointed noses, powered by new Antoinette V-8 engines which delivered 50 hp. These aircraft were designed by Leon Levavasseur, designer of the Antoinette motorboats, and the nose of his aircraft looked much like a boat's prow. Even at this early date, streamlining appeared; the Antoinette was an example, with its sleek boatlike fuselage and copper tubing running along the fuselage sides for cooling the engine water.

In another hangar was young Bunau-Varilla's new Voisin, which looked like an oversize box kite. It had no ailerons; only the enclosed ends of the wings and the vertical planes between them gave it lateral stability, leaving it impossible to bank or maneuver properly in turns.

In the same hangar was Louis Paulhan's Voisin, powered by a 7-cyl. Gnome rotary motor, in which

At rest on one of its wing tip outrigger wheels the R.E.P. looked like a crackup but was an unusually clean aircraft except for its excessive tail surface. It was flown in the meet by its designer-builder, M. Robert Esnault-Pelterie. (Musée de l'Air)

Louis Bleriot awaiting a crank after tinkering with the engine in his Bleriot XII built especially for Rheims. Fabric is removed from wing trailing edge to gain access to wing warping mechanism which Bleriot used instead of ailerons. (Musée de l'Air)

The Antoinette No. 13 flown in 3rd place in the Bennett by Hubert Latham was, with its dragonfly grace, reminiscent of a Jules Verne dream come to life. Its configuration proved to be years ahead of both Bleriot and Curtiss. (Musée de l'Air)

Wright Model C, one of three appearing at Rheims. Seen rounding the home pylon it was flown to 4th place by Eugene Lefebvre of France. The Wright brothers were still launching aircraft by catapulting from wooden monorails, then landing on skids. (Musée de l'Air)

Remarkably sharp photo of a Curtiss Model D, for which the Golden Flyer became a prototype, taking off at Hammondsport, N.Y., in 1911. Photo reveals, more than any other we have located, the rickety bamboo construction and single-surface fabric covering typical of all early Curtiss aircraft. The only visible difference between this Model D and the Rheims Flyer is the absence of a fabric covered vertical stabilizer in and above the front elevators. Model D also carried a larger rudder.   *(Curtiss)*

the whole engine revolved with the propeller around the crankshaft. This ensured fine air-cooling of the cylinders, but the efficiency loss in spinning the engine was great.

Tissandier, de Lambert, and Lefebvre were there with Wright machines. Lefebvre's, a cut-down model built in France, was faster than the conventional Wright. All three of these machines had the advantage of not having to drag a landing gear through the air, as they were still launched from monorail trolleys, as the first Wright plane had been; they landed on their curved wooden runners.

The hangar of the French constructors Henri and Maurice Farman held two enormous biplanes. Their wing span stretched clear across the hangar. A single surface elevator jutted high out in front of the wings, while the broad boxed tail extended far rearward. The landing gear was a massive structure of struts and skids, which supported two pairs of wheels slung on thick rubber shock bands. The huge Farmans were powered by Gnome rotary engines; only 35 hp to drive that mass of wood, fabric, and wire through the air! They might fly a long time but certainly not very speedily.

Glenn Curtiss was the lone American entry, sponsored at the last moment by Courtlandt Bishop, President of the Aero Club of America. The Wrights had declined to enter, for they regarded themselves as scientists, ready for any risk essential to their experiments but not for mere glory. Curtiss knew that he was second choice, and had accepted only because he

sorely needed the possible prize money with which to continue his plane building.

Glenn's machine was the smallest there, a pusher biplane with but a 26-ft. wing span. The wings were covered with linen fabric and doped with a yellowish varnish which gave the plane a golden appearance and its name—*Golden Flyer.*

Curtiss had designed the 50-hp engine, his most powerful one to date. It was a V-8 water-cooled type and turned a 7-ft. propeller.

The most unique aircraft of the meet were three R.E.P. monoplanes, designed and built, complete to 35-hp radial engines, by M. Robert Esnault-Pelterie. The fuselage and wing were built up with steel tubing, the wing was full cantilever, there were no brace wires or struts showing on the aircraft, the propeller was 4-bladed, and the landing gear was bicycle type. Only their low-powered engines kept these R.E.P. planes from the winning ranks.

The Rheims meeting was a great success. There were prizes for time and distance covered, one for altitude, and a daily contest for speed (the *Tour de Piste*) flown over a 10-km course (6.21 miles). A balloon anchored in the center of the airdrome enabled spectators to judge the altitude of the contestants.

Hubert Latham (who later met his death while hunting big game in Africa) took the altitude prize and the world's record by ascending to the then terrific height of 503 feet. This was as daring a performance as any at the meet. Almost any of the machines present was capable of going higher, and many of them later ascended several thousand feet. It was the men themselves who were incapable of attaining altitude. They were still earthbound, venturing but a little way into the atmosphere, exploring it almost foot by foot. To them, flying high seemed not safer, as we now know it to be, but incredibly dangerous. Safety belts had not been thought of as yet, and who of us today would fly one of those crates in rough or even in smooth air, to any height, *with* a safety belt!

The planes were underpowered, unstable, many with no ailerons or other form of lateral control, with balky engines and novice pilots—yet how they flew! Thrill after thrill brought the spectators to their feet as records fell in rapid succession. Here was flying such as the world had dreamed of but had never seen before.

On the first day, despite a muddy field, six planes were in the air at once for the first time in history. As they landed, six more took their place. There were 38 "ships" at Rheims, and 36 of them actually flew.

The air was rough through most of the race meet —at one time 12 crashed aircraft lay scattered around the airdrome in mute warning. There were no deaths, for the machines were slow and the crash impact was lessened by the crumpling of the lightly constructed wood-and-fabric craft. Accidents seemed to spur the pilots on to further achievement and increased the admiration of the crowd.

Latham flew in heavy rain and nonchalantly rolled cigarettes in flight. Bunau-Varilla delighted the crowd by politely tipping his hat each time he flew by the grandstands. Fournier and Tissandier enthusiastically participated in every event, though they won none. The dirigibles, *Colonel Renard* and *Zodiac III*, droned across the sky and demonstrated to many the superiority of the airship over the airplane.

August 27 was the last day of competition for the time-distance race. Paulhan had bested the Wrights' incredible record of 124 km (77.04 miles) in 2 hrs. 20 min. 23 sec., made at Le Mans, France, in December 1908, and Latham had beaten that. Paulhan covered 134 km (83.26 miles) in 2 hrs. 43 min., and Latham did 159 km (99 miles) in 2 hrs. 13 min. At 4:25 the last afternoon H. Farman dragged his heavy plane into the air in quest of the record. Latham, Delegrange, Lefebvre, and others were aloft and after the record, too. Long after all the others had landed, Farman's huge machine rumbled on around the course into the dark of night. When he landed, he had won the contest, setting a new world's time-distance record of 3 hrs. 4 min. 56.4 sec., and 118.5 miles. Sitting on the front of his plane at 40 mph for three hours had made Farman so cold and stiff that he was virtually congealed. He could not walk, and a big fireman carried him to the warmth and gaiety of the celebration in his hangar.

Throughout the race meet Curtiss and Bleriot had seesawed in winning the daily *Tour de Piste* for best speed, one lap around the 10-km course. Then on August 28 came the major speed event, the Bennett Cup race, which caused great excitement. The contestants were to fly the course separately and against time, two laps around the 10-km course. First prize was $5,000 and a magnificent silver trophy, presented by Mr. James Gordon Bennett as a companion prize to his already famous Bennett Cup for an annual free-balloon race.

That morning Curtiss took off to try his engine first in the daily 1-lap speed race. He climbed into the hot, still, and cloudless sky hoping for a smooth flight. But he quickly found that the air was literally boiling; the little plane bucked and pitched like a wild bronco. Fighting the controls, Curtiss tried vainly to find a reason for this turbulence. No one knew as yet that air becomes a series of up and down drafts caused by absorption of the sun's heat by dark objects on the earth's surface and a reflection of the heat by lighter objects.

Curtiss landed to see the record signal flying and learned that he had bettered Bleriot's best time by nine seconds. Although exhausted by his rough flight, Curtiss reasoned that the weather would get no better and could change to the rains that had so hampered the first days of the meet, so decided to try at once for the Bennett Cup.

Roaring across the starting line at 45 feet, with his engine held wide open for the first time, the plane bounced so hard that Curtiss was flung from his seat. Having no safety belt, he grimly hooked his feet in the frame, flew the two laps at an average speed of 47.7 mph, and landed after a diving finish with the record signal again flying.

Hundreds of people dashed across the field to congratulate him, and to them Curtiss stated, "It's my opinion that the turbulent air helped me. It probably broke up the partial vacuum, which, forming behind the plane, holds it back." Such was the theory of flight in those days!

Cockburn of England, in his huge bumbling Farman, followed Curtiss into the air. Then in order came Lefebvre in a Wright, Latham in an Antoinette, and Bleriot in his own machine. Bleriot soon outsped the rest and in the first lap equalled Curtiss' best, but his speed fell off in the second lap. Curtiss had won over Bleriot by 5.4 seconds. The Gordon Bennett Cup now belonged to the United States, where it would be contested for one year hence.

Wing tenders duck under lower wing panels and the American Flag flutters behind the front elevator to act as a drift indicator as Curtiss makes his start in the daily Tour de Piste on August 26th. Glenn wore no goggles at Rheims, had ten hours' total flight time and none on the Golden Flyer when he arrived at Rheims. *(Musée de l'Air)*

Bleriot's Rheims Racer XLL was a rather large monoplane, as evidenced by the men standing by. The large wood-laminated, four-bladed propeller was tried by Bleriot before the race but was replaced by its original two-bladed prop for the race. Bleriot sat in shade under the wing directly in back of the noisy, oil-spewing hot engine, complete with blast from the chain-driven prop. *(U.S. Air Force)*

1910–James Gordon Bennett Cup Race

Born in America, aviation developed fastest in Europe, with France soon taking the lead. She wanted the Bennett Cup regained by her airmen, or at least by her aircraft, and so she was well represented at the 1910 meet. Just after the 1909 Bennett race, Bleriot had bettered Curtiss' time by seconds, setting a new record of 47.8 mph. Orders for Bleriot planes increased steadily, and he wanted this happy condition to continue.

The 1910 International Air Meet and return engagement for the Gordon Bennett Cup was held in October at Belmont Park (N.Y.) Race Track, where the world's finest thoroughbred horses still to this day are running at their 30-mph pace. Most of the world's great airmen were there, and again prizes were offered for duration, distance, speed, and altitude. Orville Wright demonstrated his new Baby Wright racer and was timed unofficially at 70 mph, his engine not wide open. Roland Garros, by then perhaps the most daring if not the most skillful of foreign pilots, gave startling exhibitions in a Demoiselle monoplane designed by Santos-Dumont. Capable of 51 mph, the plane had its engine mounted on the wing, and the pilot sat below on the landing gear. With characteristic generosity, Santos-Dumont gave the drawings of the plane to anyone who wished to duplicate his handy, well-performing craft.

Genial, smiling Captain Baldwin, balloonist, dirigible pilot, parachute jumper, and tightwire walker, who learned to fly heavier-than-air craft at the age of 60 years—first man to fly across the Mississippi River and first man to sell parachute-jumping altitude by the foot, his rate being one dollar per foot and altitude starting at 2,000 feet—waited until the wind died down at sunset to pilot his tricky, all-steel *Red Devil*, also called the *Tin Goose*, through the skies.

Hoxley and Johnstone, nicknamed "The Heavenly Twins," flying after the altitude record, encountered a wind so severe that it swept them tail first across the heavens, forcing them to land many miles away from Belmont. Before the meeting ended, Johnstone, a former trick bicycle rider in vaudeville, had climbed to the undreamed of altitude of 9,714 feet.

Glenn Curtiss had built a fast new monoplane for the Bennett race, but was not sponsored by the Aero Club of America because of what they considered his stupid insistence on exhibition flying. They did not realize the financial necessity, plus the advertising value, that drove Curtiss to this distasteful task.

Eight pilots competed in the Gordon Bennett race on Saturday, Oct. 29. Claude Grahame-White of England was first away on his Bleriot. He flew the required 20 laps of the 3.1-mi. course in 1 hr. 1 min. 4.47 sec., averaging 61 mph for the 62 miles. The development of aircraft during the preceding year was clearly indicated by the greatly increased distance over last year's race.

Leblanc of France was next off on his Bleriot at a fast rate. For 19 laps he bettered Grahame-White's time, setting a new world's speed record of 71 mph on one lap. Then suddenly his machine seemed to go out of control on a low pylon turn and flew head-on into a telegraph pole, completely demolishing the Bleriot. Leblanc was lucky enough to escape with severe contusions and three bad scratches across the face.

Ogilvie of England, flying a C-type Wright, tried next, and though he completed the course later, he was forced down for 54 minutes owing to ignition trouble. (The rules permitted only one try for the Cup by each pilot.) Deducting the delay time, his speed was 51.6 mph, a remarkable performance bearing in mind that his machine was fitted only with the ordi-

Claude Grahame-White finishing the course in his Bleriot. He won the 1910 Bennett race with an average speed of 61 mph. On the ground are Brookins' Baby Wright racer (foreground) and the Curtiss racer which did not race.

nary 35-hp Wright engine. Ogilvie's total time for the 62.1 miles was 2 hrs. 6 min. 36 sec. for an official speed of 29.4 mph.

Brookins of the United States was up next, in the fastest entry of the race, the Baby Wright racer. But on the very first lap, while passing in front of the grandstand at 200 feet, the engine stopped cold. Brookins was slow to drop the nose to maintain flying speed, the racer stalled and dropped like a dead duck in full view of the horrified crowd, and rolled up the homestretch with its tail wrapped around its wings. When the dust blew away, Brookins was miraculously intact but severely bruised.

Hubert Latham of France, on his mahogany-colored Antoinette, also completed the full course but made one very long stop because of engine trouble. His total time was 5 hrs. 48 min. 53 sec. J. Radley, third pilot of the British team, made his try but soon landed his Bleriot when the 14-cyl. Gnome rotary engine failed.

Just before the deadline ending the 7-hour period during which competitors could start for the prize, U. S. pilots Moisant and Drexel, both on Bleriots, started off in a last attempt to keep the Cup in America. Drexel was forced down after 7 laps. Moisant, however, completed the full course in the slow time of 1 hr. 57 min. and 44.85 sec., averaging 31.5 mph, thus securing second place in the races, Ogilvie taking third. By virtue of Grahame-White's victory, the Cup passed to England, and the next competition for it would take place there.

Seeing and hearing of the first International Air Meet to be held in the United States gave aviation here the impetus it needed. The Curtiss and Wright companies took many an order, as did Bleriot, who sold manufacturing rights to companies in England and the United States on a royalty basis. The U. S. Army and Navy, after viewing what was then an enormous increase in the speed-distance of the Bennett race, the new altitude record, and the general reliability of the aircraft, were influenced no little into expanding their viewpoint toward the airplane, and experts were predicting speeds of up to 100 mph!

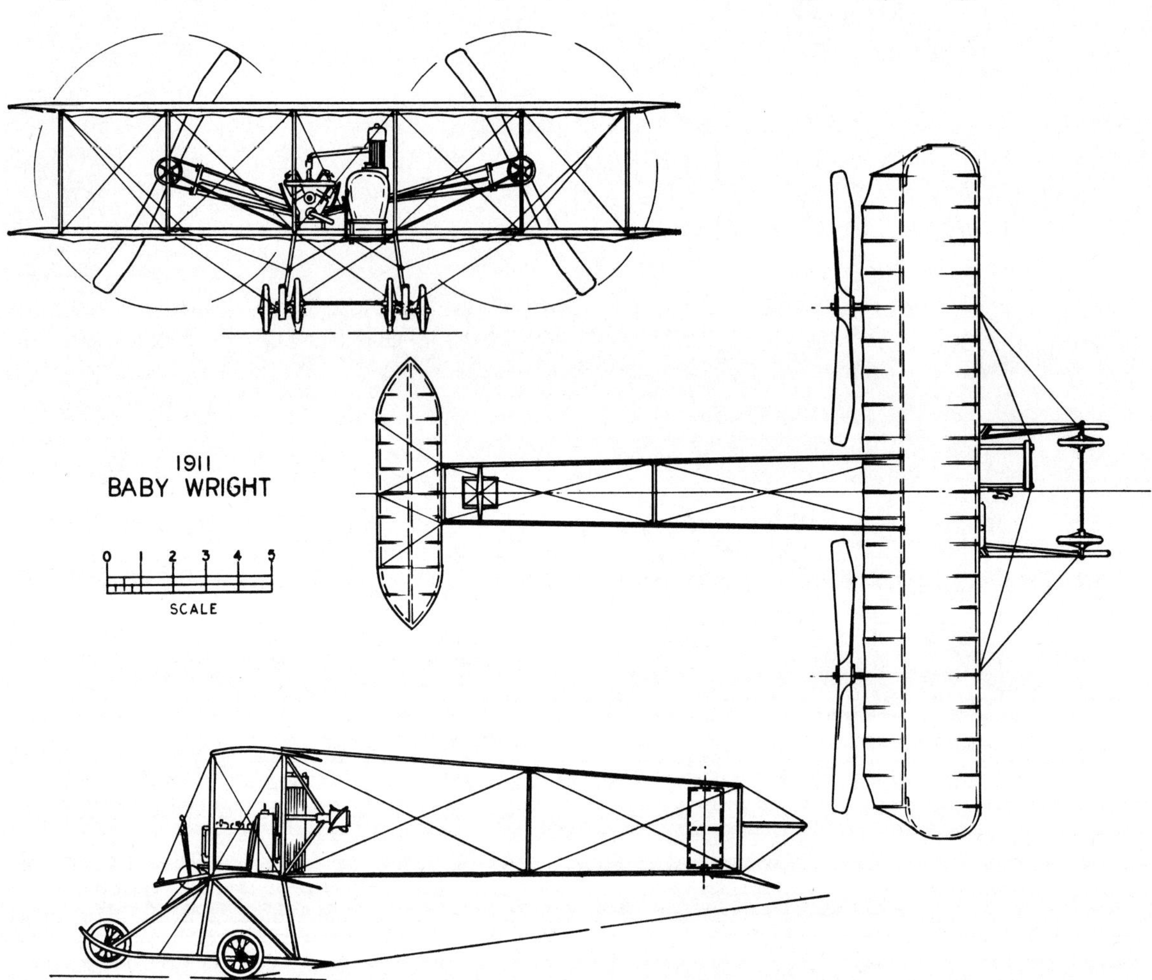

1911 – James Gordon Bennett Cup Race

By early 1911 over 1,000 aeroplanes had been successfully built and flown, covering a total distance of 150,000 miles. Bleriot alone had sold over 300 of his machines, which were in great demand because of their simplicity and fine showing at the race meets. Another French engineer, M. Nieuport, had studied Bleriot's monoplanes and compared them with biplanes. He was quick to see that the monoplane was cheaper to build because of the simplicity of structure, and that a higher speed was attainable through less head resistance. Nieuport also felt that the Bleriot design could be cleaned up, and proceeded to build the most streamlined planes of their time. Competition between Bleriot and Nieuport ran high as they moved into the third International Air Races, held at Eastchurch, England, during a 1-day race meet Saturday, July 1. There was exhibition flying and the Gordon Bennett Cup Race, the feature event.

An unexpected crowd of over 10,000 people made for out-of-the-way Eastchurch to see the events, going mostly by train, although 200 motorcars brought up to a thousand, and some journeyed by air.

The day prior to the race several of the pilots tried out their machines, and again early Saturday, the day of the race, Nieuport of France, Hamel and Ogilvie of England, and Weymann of the United States were all making tests. Weymann's 100-hp Gnome rotary engined Nieuport was timed faster than Hamel's Bleriot, which was powered by an identical engine; this showing prompted M. Louis Bleriot to clip the wing ends of Hamel's machine down to 17-ft. span in an effort to increase its speed.

At 2:50 P.M. Hamel of England was flagged off to be the first entrant in the Bennett race, which was 25 laps over a course about 3.75 miles around, for a total distance of nearly 94 miles. After passing the first mark tower (a scattering pylon placed outside the course to space the racers) too sharply, Hamel, in trying to get around to the racecourse before building up sufficient flying speed, was unable to recover from his steep bank. To the alarm of the onlookers, he came crashing to earth with such terrific force that the rotary engine, still revolving wide open, bounded along for some 60 feet, carrying and breaking up the machine on its way. By sheer luck, Hamel was thrown clear of the tangled wreckage. Beyond a severe shaking and bruising, he was none the worse for his smash!

Then at 3 P.M. Chevalier, one of the French champions, took off in his Nieuport No. 12. Although his 28-hp motor was cutting out at times, he kept up for 11 full laps and was just completing the 12th at 3:45 when he was forced down a quarter-mile from the finish line, breaking his undercarriage and wheels.

Barely three minutes before Chevalier went out of the running, America's Weymann, in his Nieuport, flew over the starting line. The increase in speed was instantly noticeable. By the time he had finished the race at about 4:56 P.M., it was believed that the winner was already found, for Weymann had flown over the course in 1 hr. 11 min. 36.2 sec., for an average speed of 78 mph.

In the meantime, Chevalier took off at 4:40 P.M. in another machine, but fared even worse than on his first mount, for within a few minutes he was forced down with engine trouble—in the same field and within 500 yards of the same spot where he landed with his first machine. He was thus completely out of the running. (They were now permitted two chances to complete the course.)

Just before 4:30, Alec Ogilvie of England brought out his Baby Wright powered with an N.E.C. water-cooled 50-hp engine, and was soon up to the starting line and away. The new note in the music of the two Wright propellers, and the fact that the machine was the only biplane in the race, created fresh interest amongst the crowd. But the "Baby" was soon passed by the cleaner monoplanes, first by Weymann's Nieuport and later by Leblanc's 100-hp Gnome-engined Bleriot and M. Nieuport's 70-hp Gnome-engined plane. (Leblanc on his start cautiously took a wide sweep around the mark towers, for, as on Hamel's machine, Louis Bleriot had cut down the span of Leblanc's monoplane, sacrificing some stability, control, and lift for more speed.)

As had been foreseen, no one bettered Weymann's speed, and the heartiest congratulations were accorded the American champion by both the French and the British competitors, amid cheers from the public. Finishing behind Weymann's winning 78 mph were Leblanc, Nieuport, and then Ogilvie with speeds of 75.8 mph, 75.1 mph, and 53.3 mph respectively.

At this meet, M. Nieuport's clean design and careful attention to small details had proven his planes' superiority over other craft of equal horsepower. Future aircraft design was to be greatly influenced by Nieuport's contribution to the science, and speeds of 100 mph were in the offing.

The Baby Wright Racer which Brookins was to fly in the Bennett Cup Race, shown here in early October 1910 at Simms Station near Dayton, Ohio, where it was constructed and test-flown prior to shipment by train to Belmont, N.Y., for the race.
(U.S. Air Force Museum)

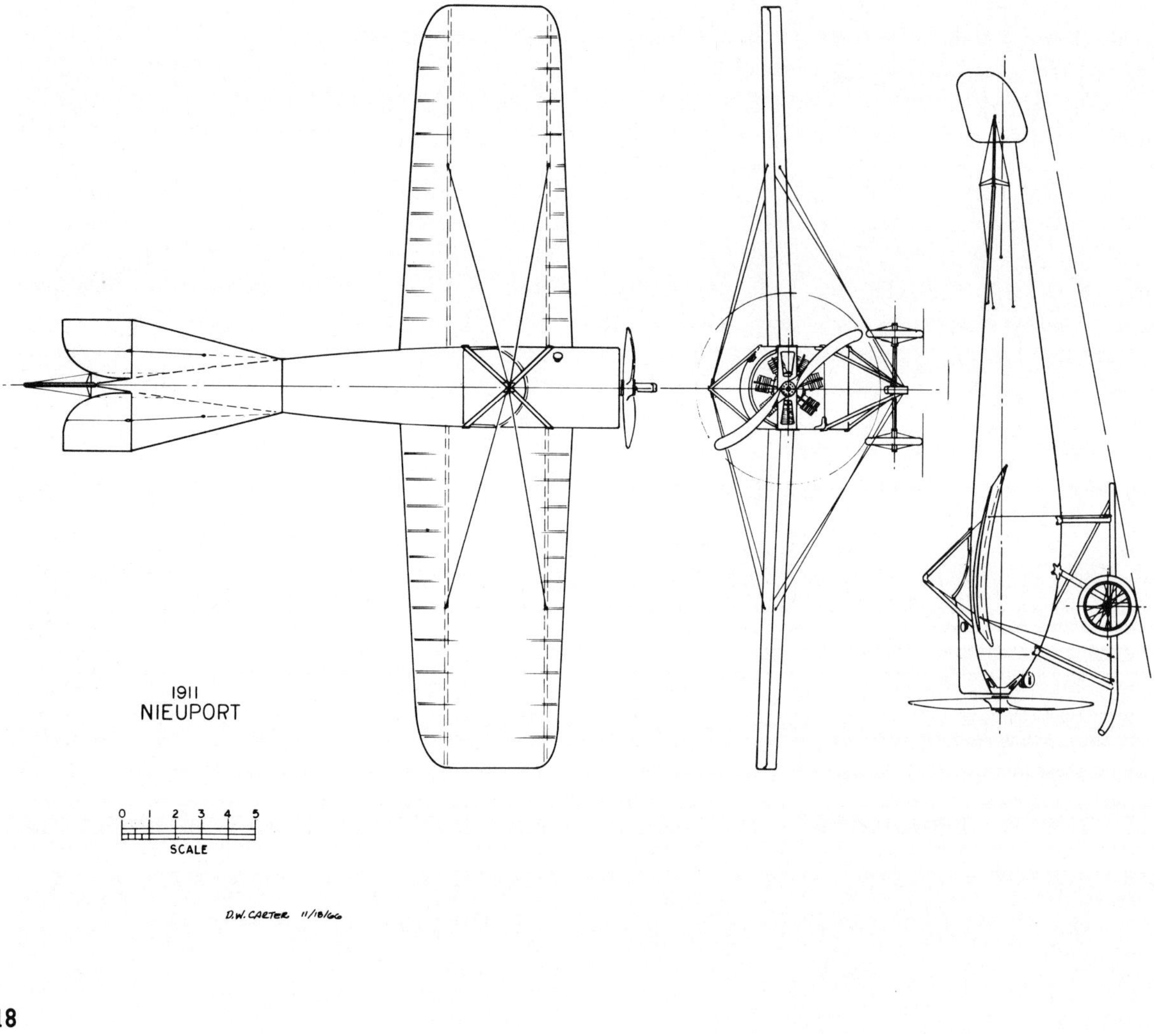

The Nieuport type monoplane that Charles Weymann flew to victory in the 1911 James Gordon Bennett Cup Race.
(Charles G. Mandrake)

The Baby Wright Racer of 1910, the first of several of its type, was one of the first Wright aircraft to be fitted with wheels. Although its pilot sat erect directly in the slipstream to add drag, the aircraft was quite fast for its 50 hp engine because of its low total frontal area. Photo taken at Simms Station in early October 1910. Pilot unidentified. Handlebar mustache probably acted as a drift indicator!
(U.S. Air Force Museum)

Ah, the sweetness of a propeller blast in one's face, the wonderful smell of burning alcohol and castor oil in the nostrils! What a feeling of achievement the pioneer aeronaut must have experienced flying his untrustworthy steed against the elements! Jules Vedrines of France is seen here about to make his start in the Paris-Madrid Race May 22, 1911, which he won in his Morane. Note whirling 7-cylinder Gnome rotary engine.
(U.S. Air Force)

1912 – James Gordon Bennett Cup Race

The rapid progress in practical applications of aerodynamics has been unparalleled in the history of science. In late 1911 a young French engineer, M. Bechereau, designed for the newly formed French firm of Deperdussin a monoplane that suddenly brought the speed of aircraft above that of the automobile and locomotive. Only above the speed of these earthbound forms of transportation could the airplane be truly useful.

M. Bechereau, only one year graduated from a Paris engineering school, had studied the Bleriot and Nieuport designs, and then improved on these by building a cigar-shaped fuselage, round like the Gnome rotary engine it wore, and cowling the engine to conform to the fuselage lines. By covering the spoke wheels with discs and streamlining the landing-gear legs to a minimum, he made his craft the cleanest of its day. Indeed, it was far ahead of its time, for many designers thought it too radical, mainly because of its landing speed of more than 60 mph. On Feb. 22, 1912, at Pau, France, pilot Jules Vedrines flew a Deperdussin over a straightaway course at the then amazing speed of 100.2 mph.

The Deperdussin firm built several fast ships, and then set about planning for the Gordon Bennett Cup, for only the fastest three ships could represent France. As was expected, Deperdussins piloted by Vedrines and Prevost were first and second in the competition, while Andre Frey was third in a Hanriot monoplane, copied from the Nieuport.

The French speed trio arrived in the United States with the world's three fastest aircraft, only to learn that they were to fly without competition. The English pilots, Claude Grahame-White and Hamel, were unable to come across the Atlantic, and the Burgess Company of the United States was unable to get their slower Nieuport-copied monoplane ready in time.

Glenn Curtiss and the Wright Company were still doggedly building biplanes and were busily filling orders for them, and so they did not build any race planes.

Vedrines' special Deperdussin was an exceptionally streamlined and neat craft for its day and had wheel and rudder foot bar controls — conventional, as we know them today. Ailerons, however, were still missing; the wing-tip trailing edges acted as ailerons and were warped up and down by turning

The 1912 Bennett winning Deperdussin was not as refined in finish as the 1913 models. Note crude seam weld in engine cowl that was not cleaned up for the race.
(National Archives)

The first Deperdussin built was powered by a Gnome rotary engine of only 50 hp. It became, after several tries by Jules Vedrines, the first aircraft to exceed 100 mph—speed 100.22 mph at Pau, France, February 22, 1912. First Deperdussins were easily identified as they carried only two struts on each of their two cabanes. *(Musée de l'Air)*

This Hanriot monoplane, flown in the 1912 Bennett by Andre Frey, was almost an exact copy of the 1911 Bennett-winning Nieuport. With this type landing gear the pilot had to make a four-point landing—two wheels and back end of skids, no tail skid being employed. Skids were turned up at the front like skis and extended well forward to prevent nose overs. *(Musée de l'Air)*

Built later in 1912 this Bennett-winning Deperdussin was powered by a 160 hp Gnome rotary engine. Note small rise headrest, two three-strut cabane braces, and still no windshield! Mechanic has just primed engine with raw petrol and Vedrines awaits crank for test hop at the factory. *(Musée de l'Air)*

Vedrines' Deperdussin overtaking Frey's Hanriot. He went on to win the 1912-Bennett race with an average speed of 105.5 mph.

the wheel control. The controls were the especial delight of Vedrines, for he said that he could maintain his flyer in perfect poise with the thumb and forefinger of his left hand.

The fuselage was built up of wood-lattice girders, covered with 3-ply wood veneer. The wing panels were built up of hickory spars, I-ribs of pine and ash, the leading edges plywood covered, and the whole wing covered with fabric treated with several coats of varnish. The wings were braced by stranded-steel cable.

Race day, September 9, was cloudless and hot but relieved by a fair breeze across the ground at Clearing in the neighborhood of Chicago, scene for the contest.

Vedrines made his start at 10:00 A.M. in his beautiful little Deperdussin, soon to be followed by Andre Frey in his Hanriot, and then Prevost, who flew a Deperdussin similar to that of Vedrines. Vedrines' plane was powered by a 160-hp 14-cyl. (twin rows of 7 cylinders each) Gnome rotary engine. The other two planes wore the same type of engine but were of only 100 horsepower.

Bumpy air kept the pilots busy as the planes tossed and rocked, often requiring a liberal margin in rounding the pylons. The turns, though 60° at each pylon, were made with suddenness. The planes would shoot like an arrow straight for the turning point, bank suddenly round the pylon, recover instantly, and then scoot on down the course only a few yards above the earth. When a lumbering biplane plodded over the racecourse, it seemed to stand still as the racers shot beneath.

Vedrines, with his engine running perfectly, finished the 30-lap 124.8-mile course in 1 hr. 10 min. and 56 sec., his speed averaging 105.5 mph.

Frey dropped out with engine trouble on the 24th lap, after averaging 94.3 mph. Prevost, of whom we will read more later, flying steadily, finished the racecourse with an average of 103.8 mph.

And so Vedrines of France was adjudged the winner with Prevost second. During his race for the Cup, Vedrines beat the world's speed record for 20 km (12.4 miles), covering the distance in 6 min. 56 sec. at a speed of 107 mph.

◆ ◆ ◆

Glenn Curtiss, after many trials, had in June, 1910, made the world's first take-off and alighting on water near his factory at Hammondsport, N. Y. His designs gave this nation the lead in seaplane development for many years, but France, which was leading the world in aviation, was quick to see the hydro-aeroplane's many advantages and jumped quickly into this new phase. However, by late 1912, Jacques Schneider, a wealthy French aviation enthusiast, felt that water aircraft were not being developed as speedily as they could be, and so he presented a trophy, the award designating an annual race over open water by seaworthy seaplanes. The nation winning the race three times in succession was to be permanent owner of the trophy, which was valued at £1,000. There was another £1,000 in cash prizes offered each year for the first three years.

Destined to become the world's most famous all-time air races, the first International hydro-aeroplane race for the Schneider Trophy was held during a water meet at Monaco, on the French Riviera, in April, 1913.

Qualifying tests began on April 3. Three French pilots and one American passed the tests. The French pilots were: Prevost flying a Deperdussin, Garros in a Morane-Saulnier, and Espanet in a Nieuport. The American pilot, Weymann, also flew a Nieuport. All four seaplanes were twin-float monoplanes, and were powered with Gnome 14-cyl. twin-row rotary engines that delivered 160 hp at 1,200 rpm. The Deperdussin was the least streamlined of the four aircraft, be-cause the alighting gear was a maze of bracing struts and wires. Certainly M. Bechereau, the Deperdussin designer, had not developed this gear!

The Schneider Trophy Race was held on Tuesday morning, April 6, over a 28-lap course for a total distance of 174 miles (280 km).

Prevost was the first away at 8:05, followed at 8:19 by Garros. Espanet started at 8:50, and Weymann at 9:14. Garros did not go very far, dropping out with engine trouble. Then Espanet was forced down, after his first lap, because of a fuel-line failure. The race therefore resolved itself into a duel between Prevost and Weymann. Weymann took the lead in the fourth lap, but after completing it — 200 km (124.27 miles) mark — he too encountered engine trouble and set his little Nieuport down safely. He had averaged 68.8 mph. This left Prevost to win as he liked. He skimmed low past the finish line and alighted. Then, however, at the request of the judges, he reflew part of the last lap, with the timers' watches still running, as there was some doubt as to whether he had turned outside one course marker.

Prevost had averaged only 45.8 mph to win the first Schneider Trophy Race, but his speed would have been closer to 60 mph had he not been timed during his refly of the last marker.

France now led the world in both sea- and land-plane types, and her experience provided designers with priceless data for building seaplanes with which to patrol her shores during the forthcoming war.

❖ ❖ ❖

Closeup of Charles Weymann's Nieuport as Weymann, right, and his mechanic await their turn in the Schneider Race. He flew a higher average speed than the winner before dropping out with engine trouble. (Musée de l'Air)

Weymann taking the lead in the fourth lap. He dropped out later with engine trouble, and Prevost (top) won the 1913 Schneider race with an average speed of 45.75 mph.

This beautifully clean Deperdussin seaplane was especially built and groomed for Prevost to fly in the 1913 Schneider Race but engine trouble prevented qualification. Setting is Monaco Harbor. *(Musée de l'Air)*

After French pilot Prevost learned that his special Deperdussin would be unable to fly, his race number 19 was quickly painted on this earlier vintage Deperdussin which the French team had been using to acquaint themselves with the race course. Prevost flew it to victory, braces, struts, wires and all! *(Musée de l'Air)*

Mechanic obligingly holds tail up for a good shot of the Nieuport (Race No. 3) flown by French pilot Espanet in the Schneider. Craft dropped out in 1st lap with a broken fuel line.
(Musée de l'Air)

Espanet in his Nieuport (Race No. 3) at bottom of ramp used to enter and leave water. Air-craft has just been towed to ramp by a rowboat after fuel line broke in the race.
(Musée de l'Air)

Morane-Saulnier (Race No. 1) piloted by Raymond Garros is seen dropping out of the Schneider in the first lap due to engine trouble. Small sailboat with two judges is moored to one of the race course marker buoys.
(Musée de l'Air)

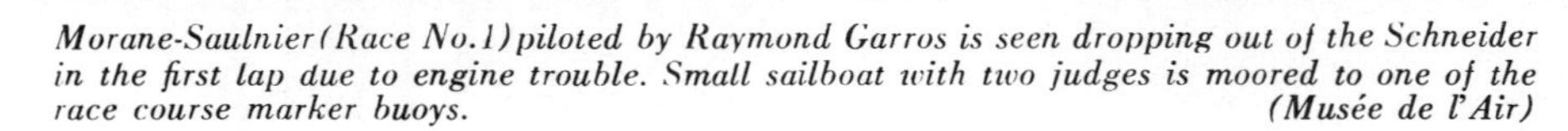

Weymann (Race No. 6 on rudder) flies near a Nieuport (Race No. 5) that is just taking off. Nieuport No. 5, pilot unknown, did not qualify but was not needed as France entered the race with their allowable three that did qualify.
(Musée de l'Air)

1913 – James Gordon Bennett Cup Race

Once again the International Air Races were held at Rheims, France, scene of the first important races.

The meeting opened on Saturday morning, September 27, with the French elimination trials to determine their three fastest entries for the Bennett Cup race. There were two afternoon events — one for height and the other for slow speed.

The altitude contest was held on each of the three days of the race meet. Gilbert of France led in all three sections for the three days, with 19,033 feet for pilot only, 14,265 feet with one passenger, and 11,936 feet with two passengers.

Sunday's program, September 28, included a speed test, the daily altitude contest, and a cross-country race. Then on Monday, September 29, came the high-speed event, the by now world-famous James Gordon Bennett Cup Race.

England, the United States, and Germany had withdrawn from the Bennett contest, probably because they could not equal the wonderful performance of France's aircraft. The only other country represented was Belgium, and her pilot, Crombez, flew a French Deperdussin. Prevost, Gilbert, and Vedrines flew for France, the first two pilots using Deperdussins and Vedrines a Ponnier, which followed the lines of its predecessor the Hanriot, which in turn had been copied from the Nieuport. All four entries were powered with identical 14-cyl. 160-hp Gnome rotary twin-row engines.

The Deperdussins designed by M. Bechereau for this race were the ultimate in streamlining for their day. A big propeller nose spinner graced the nose, and a tight-fitting cowl faired the engine into the fuselage. The landing gear was faired more cleanly into the fuselage, and so clean was the general design that it can be seen duplicated in the Travel-Air "Mystery" racer of 1929. Indeed, with equal horsepower, the Deperdussin of 1913 would outperform the U.S. Army Ryan PT-22 trainer of World War II!

The Bennett race was still flown against time, the pilots taking their planes off one by one, but individual piloting ability was, of course, a main factor.

Crombez was first away at 10 A.M. on Monday morning, but it was soon seen that, barring accidents, the Cup was not likely to leave France, for Crombez played his pylon turns very safe. Flying very regularly, he completed the full course of 20 laps with a time 1 minute and 3 seconds better than that of Jules Vedrines' in his winning flight at Chicago in 1912. But, as it turned out, Crombez' time was the slowest of the day, giving him fourth place in the race.

Prevost, who had earlier in the year won the Schneider Trophy Race, was next to go. At 11:15 he started off in his Deperdussin at "an alarming pace" and soon showed that the smaller wings installed just before the race (less than 20 feet) had materially assisted his speed. Flying very low, about 60 feet above the ground, and rising 15 feet or so at each pylon, Prevost banked steeply and dived around the corners nearly clipping the pylons, just as Curtiss had flown in winning the 1909 Bennett. This type of pylon turn was used for years until "groove" pilots flying at

Crombez of Belgium, race No. 17, about to be released by ground crew for his start in the Bennett. Crombez flew an early 1912 model Deperdussin in the race, did not take pylons closely, so finished 4th and last.   *(Musée de l'Air)*

This excellent view shows Prevost making pylon turn in Bennett. Photo shows aircraft to be no more than 25 feet above ground.   *(Warren M. Bodie)*

Emile Vedrines, seen banking around one of the course markers in his clean little Ponnier, flew the straightaways a bit high, dived as he turned pylons. Some early race pilots thought this method superior to steady altitude groove flying.   *(Musée de l'Air)*

Emile Vedrinès all fired up and ready for takeoff in the Bennett Race. Note absence of ailerons, wing warping being used, as on Deperdussin aircraft.   *(Musée de l'Air)*

Here is the Deperdussin brought to its sleekest refinement, complete with headrest and windshield. Gilbert, Race No. F2, seen here taking off for the Bennett Race, had a sour engine throughout the course, finished 3rd.   *(Musée de l'Air)*

Prevost flew entry F1 with no windshield as he felt it would slow his Deperdussin, wore a seat belt and shoulder harness. Prevost's ship is easily identified as it was fitted with the tallest headrest ever seen on any Deperdussin. This interesting photo was taken by a daring photographer from atop one of the pylons as Prevost began turn. Top of wheel control can be seen in cockpit just ahead of pilot. (U.S. Air Force)

Emile Vedrines has just warmed up his engine, shut it off, and now awaits his turn to take-off in the Bennett. What looks like a small opaque wind screen in front of Emile is in reality some person's hat. The silver Ponnier F-5 was an almost exact copy of the 1912 Hanriot racer which was, in turn, an almost identical ship to the 1911 racing Nieuport. (Musée de l'Air)

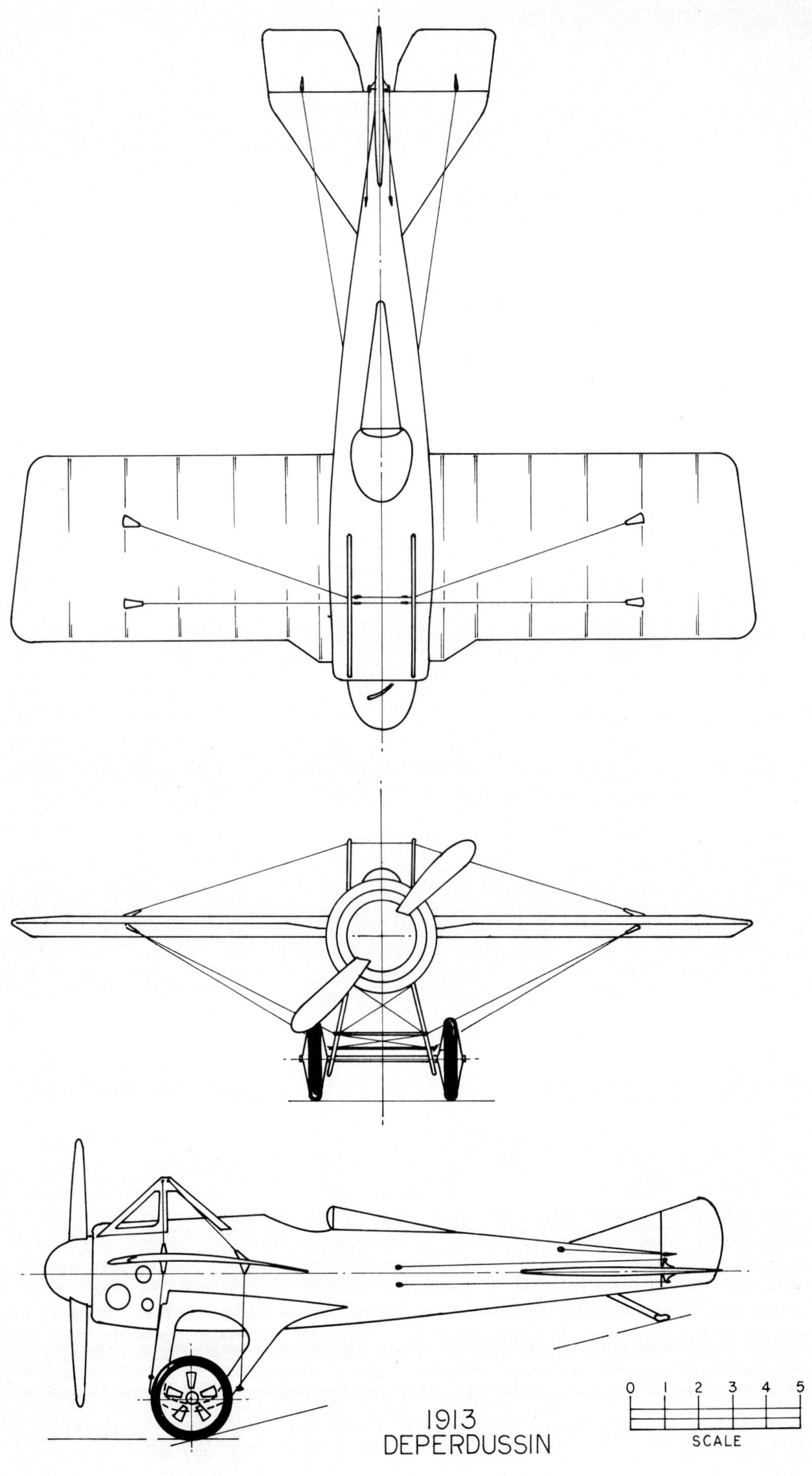

1913
DEPERDUSSIN
0 1 2 3 4 5
SCALE
D.W. CARTER 9/25/66

Monocoque fuselage of the Deperdussin was built up of 1/8" three-ply tulip wood covered on both sides with linen fabric which was glued on and then varnished several coats. Wing spars were of hickory and ash wood with pine ribs, and covering was doped linen. All Deperdussin aircraft were described as being chocolate in color.   (Musée de l'Air)

Fixed tail surfaces of all Deperdussins were built up of plywood covered on the outside with linen glued on, then varnished. Movable tail surfaces were built up of wood, then fabric covered. Bechereau obtained ultra-sleek finish on all his Deperdussin aircraft by using several coats of varnish and sandpapering the finish between each coat, like cabinet work.
(Musée de l'Air)

steady altitudes disproved the theory. The first round was completed at 127 mph; this and the sixth lap, which was covered in the same time, were the fastest in the race. Prevost covered the 124.3-mile course in 59 min. 45.6 sec., his average speed being 124.5 mph.

Gilbert started third in his Deperdussin, but his first lap took over three minutes and showed that his machine was a good deal slower than Prevost's. It took him 1 hr. 2 min. 55 sec., to cover the course for an average of 119.5 mph, which won third place in the race.

Emile Vedrines, no relation to Jules Vedrines, the fourth and last to start, "went off at a great pace" in a Ponnier monoplane. His speed during the first round was 125.5 mph. This proved to be his fastest lap, however. His average speed worked out to 123 mph to secure second place. Vedrines' little Ponnier racer was nearly as clean in design as the Deperdussins, and it seemed that the Ponnier was just as fast on the straightaway as the others, but Vedrines' pylon turns were very wide, losing possible first place, as his total time was but three seconds per lap slower than Prevost's.

Prevost won the race, and France had won the

Bennett for two years straight, almost without competition, with the fastest aircraft in the world. Winning the Schneider as well as the Bennett Trophy was to make 1913 France's best year in racing competition.

Once again the monoplane had proved itself superior, for with equal horsepower, no biplane could come close to it. However, the monoplane was falling into disfavor, for statistics showed that many more deaths were occurring in monoplanes. This was only logical — the monoplanes were faster, they were in greater quantity because of their speed and simplicity features, but they hit the earth from the then unexplainable stalls and spins with greater force. The biplanes, by their very mass, crumbled more on impact and so spared their pilots more often. England barred the monoplane from her military program entirely, and France soon followed. The clean features of the Deperdussin were, as far as possible, worked into the generally stronger-braced biplanes, and so it was that the Allies went into World War I almost entirely on biplanes. But no biplane of that war ever outsped a Deperdussin with near equal power, and few with twice the horsepower exceeded the Deperdussin.

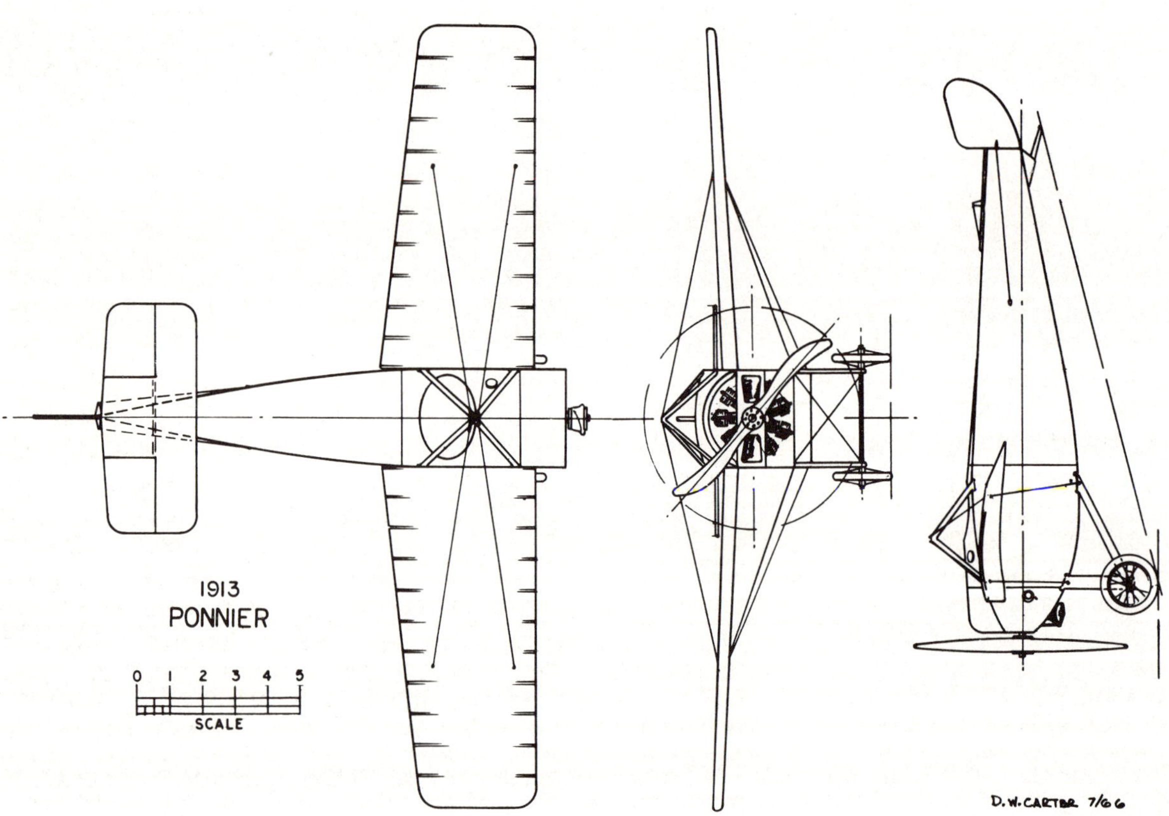

Although France now led the world in aviation, England was coming up fast, for she realized that her island was no longer isolated because of the English Channel. She was building Deperdussins and other French makes under license and buying French engines when her own did not fill the need. Also, England was building many planes of her own design, with Bristol, Roe, and Sopwith supplying many military models.

The United States was still lagging, while Germany was building up for the coming war, for she too realized that progress in military aviation was becoming a must. But neither Germany nor the United States was building the racing aircraft so necessary in the development of military planes.

So once again French entries led in numbers for the 1914 Schneider race, Monday, April 20, again held at Monaco on the French Riviera as France had won the previous Schneider. Competitors present were: Espanet and Pierre Levasseur, Nieuport monoplanes, and Garros, Morane monoplane, for France; C. H. Pixton, Sopwith Tabloid biplane, and Lord Carbery, Deperdussin monoplane, for Great Britain; Burri, F.B.A. biplane, for Switzerland; and Weymann, Nieuport monoplane, and Thaw, Deperdussin monoplane, for the United States. Stoeffler, Germany's entry, had a smash on the previous day, as did Lord Carbery in his Morane, but he borrowed a Deperdussin for the race. All entries were powered by French Gnome rotary air-cooled engines; the Sopwith and F.B.A. with 9-cyl. 100-hp Gnomes, and the others by 14-cyl. 160-hp twin-row Gnomes.

The rules specified that the individual starts must be made between 8 A.M. and sunset. When two bombs were fired at 8 A.M. on Monday, Levasseur, the Frenchman, took off from the calm waters of Monaco Bay into a strong easterly wind. His Nieuport monoplane took a 200-yard run. Next away was Espanet in a similar machine. He made a lightning take-off before the starter had given him the signal. Burri, the Swiss pilot, in his F.B.A. flying boat, the only boat in the races (all others were twin-float seaplanes), was next away. This seaplane had an inherent tendency to porpoise, and its take-off was a series of hops before the machine was airborne.

Pixton, in his Sopwith Tabloid, which had been converted into a single-seat racer, started about 15 minutes later and was into the air after a run of only 60 feet.

Rules of the contest decreed that the competitors be required to taxi across the line before taking off, then make two descents to the sea at specified points. Then they were to continue the flight proper, the starting line having been crossed in full flight. Total distance was 174 miles, or 280 km.

Pixton executed the rules superbly, but the other pilots had difficulty. Burri had to cope with a machine which bounced like a football every time it contacted the water, and his efforts caused great excitement.

Pixton's first lap lost him only 17 seconds, and as he roared around the course he turned the markers acutely in 70° banks.

The Continental spectators, accustomed to their own machines winning race after race, had never seen such flying and were loud in their praise.

For an hour or so the Sopwith kept buzzing round lap after lap with impressive regularity. During the 15th lap, the Gnome of the Sopwith began to misfire. Pixton kept going for the rest of the race, although the engine was running on only eight of its nine cylinders. Finally, at the end of the 28th (and last) lap, Pixton crossed the finishing line accompanied by the roar of an enthusiastic crowd. His time was 2 hrs. 13.4 sec., with an average speed of 86.8 mph.

Pixton then opened up his engine and tore around for another two laps at still higher speed. The little Sopwith responded magnificently and broke the world's record for seaplanes, with a speed of 92 mph for a total distance of 300 km.

Meanwhile, other competitors were crawling around. Lord Carbery, the other British pilot, flying a Deperdussin monoplane, got off all right, but after alighting in the first lap, could not get off again because of engine trouble. Espanet had to alight after 17 laps, and Levasseur had a similar fate after 18 laps. The rear banks of their twin-row rotary motors were overheating, a common source of trouble. Burri, in the bounding F.B.A. flying boat, completed 20 laps and then alighted to refuel. He had some trouble in taking off with full tanks, but eventually got off and finished the race, to win second place.

The rest of the competitors were dismayed by the Sopwith's performance and did not start, for only the winner received a prize.

The Sopwith was the most streamlined entry this year and justly deserved to win, for although a biplane, it was the smallest aircraft in the race; its wings were thin and its alighting gear was cleanest by far.

Repeated troubles with the twin-row engines influenced aircraft design throughout the coming war,

*The winning Sopwith Tabloid passing the F.B.A. flying boat. Espanet's Nieu-
port (No. 6) was forced down with engine trouble. C. H. Pixton piloted the
1914 Schneider winning plane at an average speed of 87.75 mph.*

for all rotary engines used in the conflict were single-row. Later, when more power was needed, water-cooled engines were developed.

Later this year events transpired which were to affect, directly and indirectly, the whole course of Allied aviation throughout the war. Armand Deperdussin, as farsighted as he was dishonest, went to jail on stock swindling charges. Louis Bleriot, in order to preserve the engineering talent of the Deperdussin firm and that of Bechereau in particular, took over the grounds and sheds near Paris and formed the now famous *Societé Pour Aviation et Derives* (S.P.A.D.). After war was declared, Papa Bleriot guided Bechereau in his wartime Spad designs, aircraft whose history will live forever.

◆　◆　◆

C. Howard Pixton's Schneider winning aircraft was practically a stock Sopwith Tabloid Scout, several of which were built, beginning in 1913. Twin main floats and a ventral tail float with a small rudder was fitted and the fuel capacity was increased by 30 gallons by fitting an extra tank beside the pilot's seat. The 100 hp Gnome Monosoupape nine-cylinder rotary engine had just appeared, so one was fitted to the Tabloid. (Musée de l'Air)

Pilot Burri being towed to a beaching ramp after finishing 2nd in the Schneider. His Franco-British Seaplane (F.B.A.) was the only seaplane in the race, also wore the new Monosoupape 100 hp engine which was lighter in weight to horsepower than previous rotary engines. (Musée de l'Air)

1920–Schneider Trophy Race

*The rugged Italian Savoia S-12, piloted by Lt. Luigi Bologna, won the 1920
Schneider race with an average speed of 107.2 mph.*

During World War I, Italy developed many fine military flying boats, and she appeared in Bournemouth, England, scene of the first postwar Schneider race, with the fastest entry. The race, on April 20, 1919, was flown in a dense fog, and the British and French contestants soon dropped out, unable to find their way around the water course. Italian pilot Janello, in his Savoia S-13 biplane flying boat, was the only pilot to finish the course, but unfortunately for him, he regularly flew around a buoy which he believed to be a course marker. The race was declared NO CONTEST. As reward for her effort, Italy was intrusted with the organization of the 1920 contest.

In 1920, only the Italian team survived the trials. The only pilot to undertake the navigability tests in the rough sea and winds of September 18 was Navy Lt. Luigi Bologna, flying a 500-hp Ansaldo-engined Savoia S-12 flying boat ruggedly built for bad-weather flying. He completed the tests and on the following day, the scheduled day for the races, attempted to fly over the triangular course that lay just outside Venice Lagoon. He gave up after 5 laps because of the squally winds. Bologna tried again on September 22, and covered the full course, 10 laps around the 22.2-mile course, averaging 107.2 mph, and was declared the winner of the race.

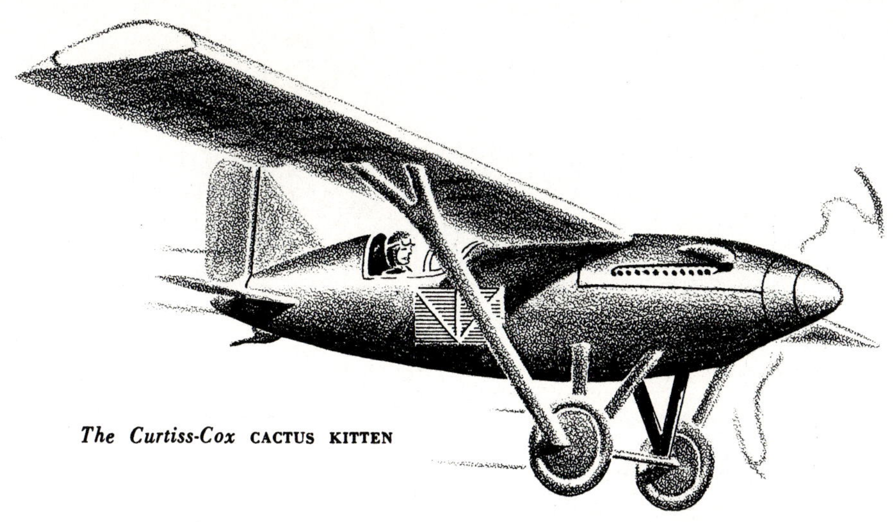

1920 – James Gordon Bennett Cup Race

The nation holding the world's speed record has invariably led the world in aviation, and so it was that France led the Allies to air supremacy during World War I, supplying not always the fastest but by far the most fighting planes. England contributed heavily too, but the United States rallied only in time to furnish training planes for her own pilots and, near the war's end, a relatively few English SE-5 fighters and two-place DeHavilland bomber-observation planes built under license.

Settling down from the effects of war, France was anxious to get on with the Gordon Bennett Cup Race, for she had made a poor showing in the 1920 Schneider race trials and had only to win the Bennett Cup once more to gain permanent possession. England and the United States took up the challenge, for they realized fully by now the importance of air power, and that today's racing craft became the pursuit plane of tomorrow.

The United States sent four aircraft abroad in quest of the Cup. Three of them were newly built pure racing craft, the only ones to appear, for all the rest were reworked pursuit types.

The Curtiss Company built two racers on order for Texas oilman S. E. J. Cox, and both were shipped to France for the race. The fuselages of both planes were identical, plywood in construction, powered with Curtiss V-12 435-hp engines, with rectangular water radiators along each side of the fuselage and the cockpits fully enclosed for the first time in history. One ship, the *Cactus Kitten*, was a thick-winged monoplane, and the other ship, the *Texas Wildcat*, was a biplane with double-cambered wings, the first ever used. Both were built without regard to landing speed, for the airfields of France were supposedly spacious. Such was not the case, however, and the faster landing *Cactus Kitten* was not assembled for the race. A hurried take-off without checking the airdrome at Morane-Saulnier Field just outside Paris, where the landing gear was weakened by an obstruction in the tall grass, caused the *Texas Wildcat* to roll into splinters upon landing at Etampes, scene of the races. Curtiss test pilot Roland Rohlfs escaped with only a dislocated shoulder, several cuts about the head, and a very black eye.

The U. S. Air Service entry and their first racing plane was a Verville Scout biplane VCP-1, with the usual Hispano-Suiza engine replaced by a new 12-cyl. V-type Packard engine rated at 638 hp at 2,000 rpm. The cooling radiator was of the honeycomb type, rectangular, and was placed under the lower wing's leading edge. The Verville was built entirely of wood and plywood, and the tapered wings and movable surfaces were fabric covered. This plane was by far the most powerful at the race meet.

The Dayton-Wright Airplane Company, with Orville Wright as consulting engineer, built and sent to France by far the most interesting plane of the races. This little craft was one of the first to have a retractable landing gear — a type the Grumman Aircraft Company many years later incorporated into their famous Navy biplane fighters and their later Wildcat monoplane fighter. The little plane's full-cantilever wing was built of solid balsa with chunks cut out, and the wing then covered with plywood. The wing leading and trailing edges were hinged so that the pilot could adjust the wing camber at will, an innovation that many years later gave aircraft wing flaps for faster take-offs and slower landings. The pilot was completely enclosed inside the cabin and could see only through windows at the side. For landing, the pilot could push the side windows open with

The Dayton-Wright drops out of the race as Sadi-Lecointe (No. 10), in his Nieuport, flies on to win the 1920 Bennett with an average speed of 168.5 mph, followed by de Romanet, who finished in second place.

The Dayton-Wright Racer, designed by Milton C. Baumann, was officially designated the RB Racer. View shows actuating rods for increasing wing camber on take-off and landing. Note leading and trailing edges depressed; mechanism was operated by hand crank on instrument panel which also actuated retractable landing gear. Original camber-change device, seen here, had two actuating arms on each side of wing top. *(U.S. Air Force Museum)*

Reports were various as to reason Dayton-Wright Racer dropped out of the race. One account stated the left rudder cable broke (doubtful), another that some scoundrel applied an acid to the left rudder cable which ate away the cable in flight (possible). A third account stated that its pilot, Howard Rinehart, was unable to crank the wing to its high-speed or flat contour and, of course, fully retract its landing gear which cranked up and down with wing camber change (probable). *(U.S. Air Force Museum)*

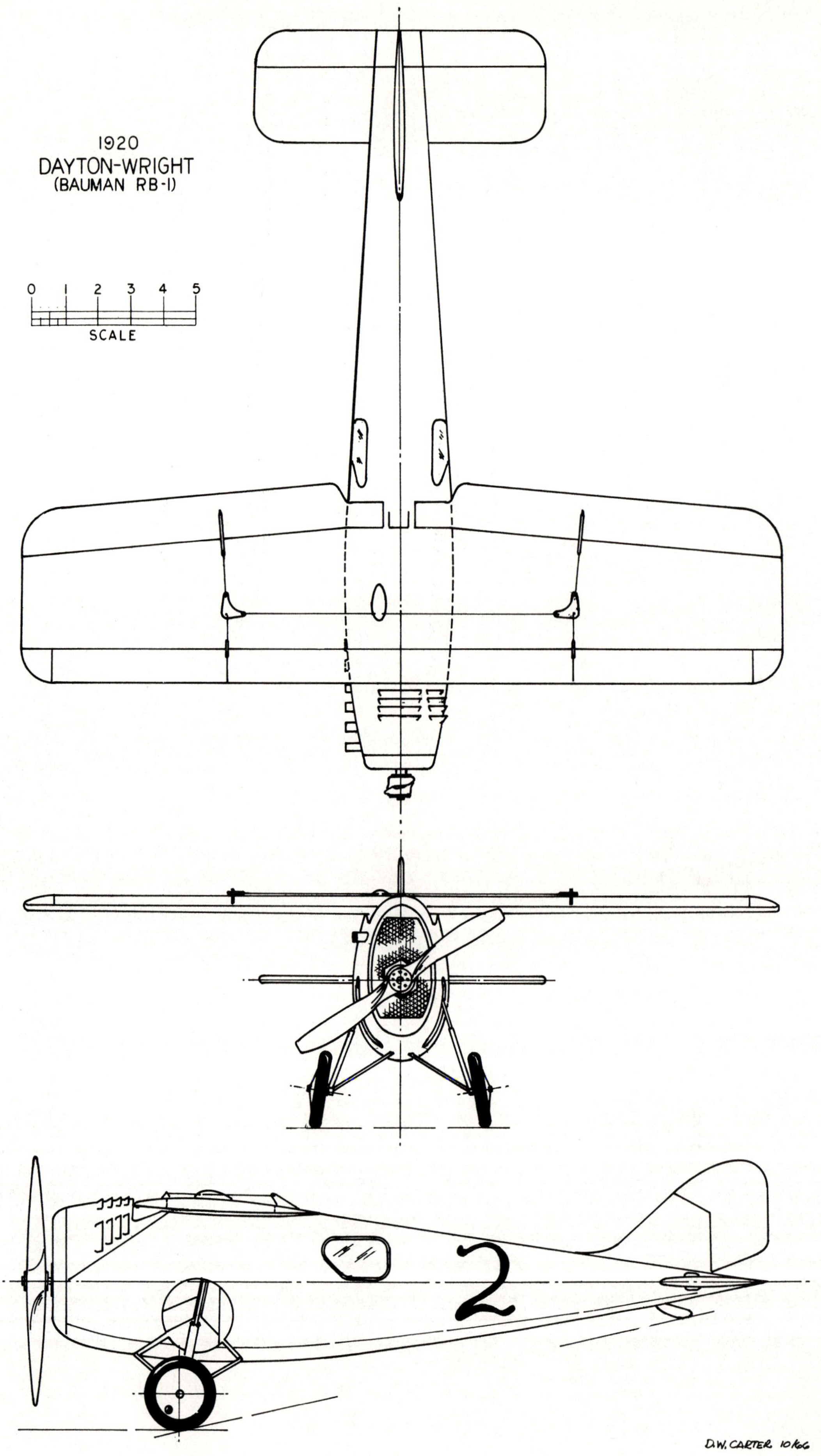

1920
DAYTON-WRIGHT
(BAUMAN RB-1)
0 1 2 3 4 5
SCALE
2
D.W. CARTER 10/66

This view also shows Dayton-Wright with two actuating rods on each side of wing top, its original configuration. Entire aircraft was covered with plywood, including movable control surfaces. Linen was then glued over the plywood, then varnished several coats, much like the pre-WWI Deperdussin aircraft. *(U.S. Air Force Museum)*

The Dayton-Wright did 165 mph on a practice lap of the Bennett course with engine not open, years ahead with features that were all eventually to be used on other aircraft. Reputedly it would do 200 mph with its 250-hp Hall-Scott Special engine. Actual aircraft can be seen today in the Henry Ford Museum at Dearbon, Mich. *(Musée de l'Air)*

Dayton-Wright Racer as it appeared at the Bennett Race with but one actuating rod on each side of wing top, which could account for possible failure to change camber properly. Pilot entered aircraft through trap door above cockpit, could open side windows by hand or, on landings, open them by leaning shoulder against back of frame and pushing forward, thus keeping hands free. *(Musée de l'Air)*

Borel biplane powered by a 320 hp Hispano engine and piloted by M. Barrault in French elimination trials, where it lost out to other entries. Small vertical fin and rudder must have presented control problems at slow speeds. *(Musée de l'Air)*

Martinsyde Semiquaver, a modified pursuit plane flown by Raynham, was the only English entry. Like all French entries it was powered by a 320 hp Hispano-Suiza V-8 engine. *(Musée de l'Air)*

Top wing was gulled into fuselage on this SPAD HERBEMONT for the race but ship, flown by M. Casale, failed to qualify. Wing and tail surfaces of both SPAD aircraft were built up of wood spars and ribs, fabric covered. Fuselages were of plywood, fabric covered. *(Musée de l'Air)*

Converted from a war-surplus DH9 as a test bed for a new Napier Lion engine of 450 hp, this DeHavilland DH9R achieved a closed circuit record of 145 mph at First Air Traffic Exhibition in Amsterdam in 1919. This speed was later raised to 149.43 mph. *(Napier)*

Curtiss-Cox Cactus Kitten was built with two sets of wings and is seen here with the long wing. Brace strut has initial fabric tape applied to hold balsa wood fairing in place for more complete wrap and fairing. Photo taken at Curtiss factory before final paint job—red fuselage and silver wings and tail—was applied. (Charles G. Mandrake)

This view of the Curtiss-Cox Cactus Kitten shows aircraft with its optional wing, of shorter span but quite a lot thicker in section, with extending ailerons. Note different wing brace strut than that used on the thinner winged Kitten. Wide-bladed wood propeller has extremely high pitch for top speed at expense of a long take-off run. (Charles G. Mandrake)

Here is the Nieuport Model 29 flown by Kirch, in its original and conventional configuration. Aircraft was stock in that several were built identical to each other on assembly lines as pursuit types.
(Musée de l'Air)

This post-WW1 SPAD HERBEMONT, flown by Bernard de Romanet in the Bennett, was practically a stock two-seater production line aircraft with the rear cockpit covered for the race. Race No. 8 was painted on fuselage after this photo was taken.
(Musée de l'Air)

This Nieuport 29 flown to victory by Sadi-Lecointe was a sister ship to No. 11 flown by Kirch and was powered by the 320 hp Hispano V8 water-cooled engines. All Nieuport entries wore Lamblin-type radiators to cool engine water.
(Musée de l'Air)

Sharp photo of a Nieuport Model 29 taken later in 1920, as it appeared for an annual French-held event, the Deutsch de la Meurthe Cup Race. Piloted by M. Lasne, the aircraft won the race.
(U.S. Air Force)

At first glance this Nieuport is a conventional open cockpit biplane. Closer inspection shows cockpit and a tear-drop shaped peephole below cockpit to be flush, covered with transparent material and its pilot, M. Kirch, is seen peering out the side! Musée de l'Air says Kirch flew this configuration in Bennett, which would account for its being faster than the winning ship before dropping out.   *(Musée de l'Air)*

The Curtiss-Cox Cactus Kitten monoplane and the Texas Wildcat biplane were probably the first aircraft with water-cooled engines that had a fuselage built up of plywood that ran its entire length. Only metal in the fuselage was the motor mount and engine top cowl. Craft were also the first to have transparent cockpit hatches, which had to be installed after pilot was in cockpit. This view shows neat wheel fairing which also acted as a mud scraper.   *(Dustin W. Carter)*

his head and could then see quite well. Very narrow but extremely deep, the fuselage was plywood. Powered by a 6-cyl. in-line Hall-Scott 250-hp engine with a nose radiator, this little ship was the only monoplane at the races and was by far the cleanest in design.

The English and French entries were all conventional pursuit biplanes, cleaned up for the race and powered with the 320-hp Hispano-Suiza V-type water-cooled engine.

It was a dull, misty morning at the Villesauvage airdrome of Etampes when, at 7 A.M. on September 28, the competitors arrived from their various hotels at Etampes and Paris. The clouds were low and visibility poor, weather that seemed the rule rather than the exception for European air races.

As time wore on, motorcars began to arrive from Paris, and one could see the famous French constructors Henri Farman, Louis Bleriot, Rene Caudron, Delage and Bazaine of Nieuports, Robert Morane, Louis Breguet, and young Marcel Hanriot; and famous pilots such as Weymann, Prevost, and Leblanc. They and other race pilots had been little heard of during World War I, for they saw little combat but were retained as test and consulting pilots.

At a little past 1 P.M. the sun broke through occasionally to improve the weather some, and there was a stirring about the machines at the far end of the airdrome. At 1:25, the Nieuport biplane, piloted by Kirch of France, came racing by the stands, took off, and cruised around for a few minutes. Having got his engine warmed up, Kirch approached the starting line and, with a dip salute of his wings, was off. About 20 minutes later he was followed by Bernard de Romanet of France in a Spad. Sadi-Lecointe of France was next off at 2:10 in his French Nieuport. A few minutes later Howard Rinehart, of the United States, got off in the little Dayton-Wright monoplane, and after circling the airdrome to retract his wheels into the fuselage, crossed the starting line and disappeared down the course. At 2:35 Maj. "Shorty" Schroeder of the U. S. team was off and roared over the line in his Army Verville-Packard.

In the meantime Kirch completed his first lap at 181.5 mph, which later proved to be the fastest lap of the day. Returning after the second lap, Kirch was forced to land because of "sooted-up" spark plugs. De Romanet in the Spad was next to complete his first lap and was around the marker and away on his second lap, averaging 162 mph.

The Dayton-Wright then flew into view, and, to the surprise of many and the dismay of all Americans, the landing wheels began to emerge. Rinehart made a beautiful landing and reported that he was unable to turn left. Examination showed that the left rudder cable was broken.

Soon afterward the Verville-Packard hove into sight and it too landed; with that America's last hopes were gone. It was later determined that the Verville did not carry enough radiator area to cool the 638-hp Packard engine, and the carburetor air intake was faulty at full throttle causing flames to pour out the exhaust pipes, with the danger of fire ever present.

On completion of his second lap, de Romanet landed, but after adjustments took off again, although by then the delay seemed too much. His total time for the 186.4 miles was 1 hr. 39 min. 6.6 sec., for an average speed of but 113.5 mph. During his last lap, an oil leak smothered him with oil. He had to raise his goggles and was blinded by the oil but somehow managed to make a safe landing. Certainly none begrudged plucky little de Romanet his second place.

Meanwhile Sadi-Lecointe of France was methodically flying the course, with beautiful turns at the pylons. He landed after completing the full course in 1 hr. 6 min. 17.2 sec. to average 168.5 mph.

It was not until about 4:30 that Raynham of England had his Martinsyde *Semiquaver* up to the starting line, wisely awaiting the cooler evening air, for he too had radiator-cooling trouble. He completed but one lap and landed with a broken oil pump, and England's only chance was gone.

And so Sadi-Lacointe had won the Gordon Bennett Cup for France's third consecutive win, to gain permanent possession of the Cup and thus end the first chapter in a glorious history of air racing.

This year's Bennett race again proved that the fastest plane alone does not win a race, but that a combination of mechanical perfection and piloting ability is necessary to victory. Sadi-Lacointe had flown his Nieuport over the course time after time until he knew every inch of it, and he and his mechanics had the Nieuport in top order.

Dayton-Wright racer showing landing gear extended.

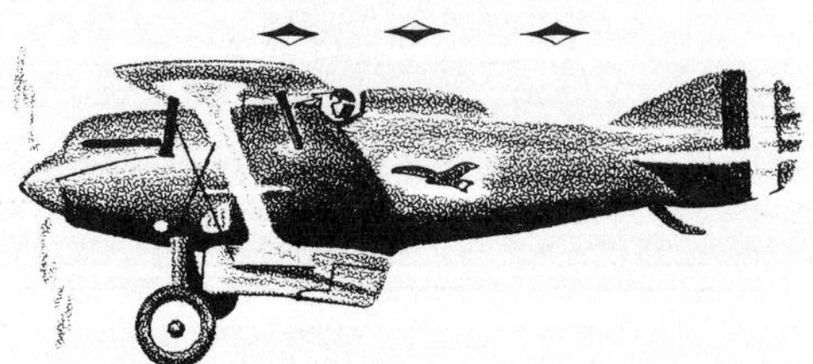

The U.S. Army's first purely racing craft, the Verville-Packard.

Since the dawn of history those people who possessed the best and fastest transportation — from horse to aircraft — have led the world. The United States was by now fully aware of this fact and was determined to improve her status, especially after her poor showing in the International Bennett races. Accordingly, newspaperman Ralph Pulitzer, after conferring with receptive U. S. Army and Navy officials, offered a trophy to promote high speed. Plaques and cash prizes were offered, and the race was to be an unlimited free-for-all, restricted only to landing speed, which could not, for safety's sake, exceed 75 mph. All nations were invited.

The first Pulitzer Trophy Race was held at Mitchel Field, Long Island, on Thanksgiving Day, November 27. The course was triangular, from Mitchel Field to Lufberry Field, then to Henry Damm Field, thence back to Mitchel. Entries were to fly four times around a 29.02-mile course for a total of 116.08 miles. The planes were sent off one after another, and each one timed separately.

More aircraft flew in this closed-course race than will ever bend throttles together again, for 37 started and 25 finished. Most of the aircraft were war-surplus or pursuits of postwar design. Of the 12 contestants who did not complete the race, one was disqualified for cutting inside a pylon, while 11 experienced power-plant troubles.

The race was witnessed by at least 25,000 people. The roads following the course were lined with parked cars, and large crowds gathered at the turning points.

Flying the fastest plane of the day with great skill, Army Capt. Corliss Mosely carefully threaded his way through the maze of racers to win the Pulitzer Trophy at a speed of 156.5 mph; then later flew the same machine over a measured mile at 186 mph. The 638-hp Verville-Packard which Mosely flew was the same machine entered in the Gordon Bennett race, with various small changes to improve its speed and reliability.

The Verville-Packard excited great interest, for its wing loading of 14.12 lbs. per sq. ft. was considered enormous, and it was doubtful if constructors, engineers, and military pilots would be converted to the use of such "very high powered" single-seaters. The practical limit for pursuits had previously been considered as being 300 hp.

Second place went to Harold Hartney, who flew a beautiful "groove" race in a Thomas-Morse MB-3 pursuit powered by a 300-hp Wright-Hispano engine. Hartney averaged 148 mph for the course. His plane was a standard military pursuit with only half the engine power of the winner. Manufactured in quantities for the Army Air Service, the MB-3 was all wood with fabric covering and was fairly clean in design. The engine was cooled by fuselage side radiators. In a later flight over a measured mile, Hartney, the famous American ace, succeeded in flying this machine at 177.3 mph.

Third place went to smooth-flying civilian pilot Bert Acosta, who averaged 134.5 mph in an Italian S. V. Ansaldo I Balilla, fitted with an SPA 220-hp engine. This single seater, one of the few entered by a private firm, was a single strutter of very clean design. It was powered by a 6-cyl. vertical in-line engine, cooled by a nose radiator, and the fuselage was deep and narrow with flat sides. Interplane struts were steel, and the plane was of conventional wood and fabric construction.

Lt. St. Clair Streett, commander of the famous Alaskan flying expedition, won fourth place, averaging 133 mph in an Orenco "D" pursuit fitted with a Wright-Hispano 300-hp engine. The Orenco was also a standard pursuit, conventional in construction, and was flown without alteration.

Fifth place went to Lt. (j.g.) A. Laverents at 125 mph in a Navy Vought VE-7 with a 180-hp Wright-Hispano engine. He far outclassed the other planes in the Vought class and so won the prize for that type.

Lt. John Roullot, USA, was sixth in a DH-4 De Havilland powered by a 400-hp Liberty engine. Averaging 124 mph, he led 12 other DH-4's in the race to win the special De Havilland class.

Following Lt. Roullot were six other DH-4's in order; then in 13th place was civilian pilot Willis Taylor in another Italian SVA, powered by a 220-hp SPA engine and similar in appearance, with the exception of W-type wing strut bracing, to the one flown by Acosta. Taylor flew at 117 mph, closely followed by Army Capt. Maxwell Kirby, who took 14th in a 180-hp Wright-Hispano engined SE-5, the only one in the race. Following the SE-5 were Vought VE-7's and De Havillands vying for the remaining places in the race; then, coming in 25th and last, was civilian Charles Colt in a French Morane-Saulnier, the only monoplane to finish the race, powered by a Le Rhone rotary engine of 110 hp, the smallest engine in the race.

U. S. Air Service Verville Scout biplane VCP-1 seen here with its Bennett race markings, top of engine cowl removed. Originally designed and flown with a 300-hp Wright-Hispano engine, this was removed and a new V-12 Packard engine of 638 hp was installed, and redesignated R-1. The original radiator was left on the aircraft, it being decided that the higher speed of the aircraft with its new big engine, would cool properly. *(U. S. Air Force)*

The Verville R-1 (Race No. 63) in its 1920 Pulitzer configuration and paint job. Radiator is greatly enlarged and water tank and vent placed high above the wing to prevent water from boiling out. Ducts were cut into leading edge of engine cowl top to furnish added engine cooling, exhaust stacks were streamlined with fairing that blended into engine cowling. *(U. S. Air Force)*

The Verville R-1 in its final configuration, as flown in the 1922 Pulizter by Captain Mosely. Seen here with engine cowling removed, the propeller spinner has been capped with a pointed cone and landing gear legs have been faired together and into fuselage with doped fabric to clean up ship. 		*(U. S. Air Force)*

Designed by Grover C. Loening, this unique Wright-Martin was flown in the 1920 Pulitzer Race by Lt. B. B. Bradley, USMC, and would have finished somewhere between 1st and 4th place had he not been forced out on the very last lap with a broken water connection hose. 		*(U. S. Air Force)*

This Curtiss 18-T Wasp triplane, powered by a new V-12 Kirkham engine of 400 hp, was one of two built in 1919 for the U. S. Navy as two-place fighter types. Both ships raced in the 1920 Pulitzer Race and proved to be quite fast but dropped out with engine trouble. Huge propeller and large radiator under center wing on fuselage side denotes high horsepower of the K-12 model engine. (U. S. Air Force)

Both Curtiss Wasp triplanes appeared at Detroit in 1922 mounted on floats and participated in the Curtiss Marine Trophy Race on October 8. This Wasp, flown by Lt. R. Irvine, USN, struck debris on the water during take-off, dropped out in the 5th lap because of excessive wind drag on the damaged portions. Lt. L. H. Sanderson, USMC, flying the sister ship, race No. 4, led the race, then ran out of fuel within sight of the finish markers. (Warren M. Bodie)

Two Navy Curtiss Wasp triplanes, each powered by a Curtiss-Kirkham V-type engine of 450 hp, started the race, but both developed engine trouble or they would probably have been up among the winners. Another interesting Navy entry was a Loening Special monoplane, which, after covering most of the course at 155–160 mph, was forced out one mile from the finish with a broken water connection; otherwise it would have finished between first and fourth.

Although the first Pulitzer race produced no record speeds, the absence of serious accidents and the highest speeds ever displayed in this country made a great impression on the spectators.

Designers, builders, and the military men left the scene with ideas for the next Pulitzer race; their competitive spirit had been thoroughly aroused and technical advancement thrives on competition.

Another view of the R-1 in its 1922 Pulitzer paint job. Designed for the Engineering Division by Fred Verville, there were two VCP-1's built, one retaining its original 300-hp engine built in the U.S. by Wright under license from the French firm Hispano-Suiza. (U. S. Air Force)

This Curtiss Wasp was photographed at the St. Louis Races October 6, 1923, just after engine warm-up. Flown by Ensign D. C. Allen, USN, it crashed during the second lap of the Liberty Engine Builders Trophy Race. (U. S. Navy)

The Savoia-13, flown by Italian pilot Janello, became known as unofficial winner of the 1919 Schneider race, which was called off because of dense fog. Why the race was not postponed until better weather prevailed was strictly a British decision.   (Savoia-Marchetti)

France entered in the 1920 Schneider race this conventional landplane pursuit type aircraft mounted on twin pontoons. Named the Monaco SPAD and flown by Casale, it failed to survive the rugged pre-race trials.   (Charles G. Mandrake)

This beautifully proportioned Savoia-21, built for the 1921 Schneider, was hailed as the fastest seaplane of her time, boasted a top speed of 160 mph with her Ansaldo San Giorgio engine of 300 hp. Span of lower wing was 20', length 25'4".   (National Archives/Mandrake)

The big Macchi-19 that caught fire while flying in the 1921 Schneider, the crew of two escaping unhurt. Quite large for racing, the hydroplane, seen here with engine cowl removed, was quite fast because of its powerful 720 hp engine.   (Warren M. Bodie)

1921 – Schneider Trophy Race

The Italian Macchi-7 flown by de Briganti, who won the 1921 Schneider with an average speed of 117.9 mph.

Held again at Venice, Italy, and over the same course as the 1920 race, the Schneider Trophy Race trials consisted of ten Italian reworked, pursuit-type flying-boat entries and one French entry. Sadi-Lecointe, the famous French speed pilot, flying a 300-hp Hispano-engined Nieuport bi-seaplane, damaged his undercarriage in alighting after a test flight and so was unable to compete.

Seven Italian entries including a Savoia S-21, the fastest seaplane of its time, were eliminated in the rugged trials, for it was a rule of the Schneider contest that only three planes be permitted to represent each country in the race.

The large number of planes dropping out during Schneider elimination trials and the races themselves, was due mostly to engine trouble — the result of constant efforts to raise engine power, mainly by higher compression and higher rpm, carried to extremes.

In the actual race, August 11, the three Italian flying boats took off separately to be timed around the course. Soon Lt. Zanetti's plane, a large Macchi-19 powered by a 720-hp Fiat 12-cyl. V-type engine, caught fire. He and his mechanic alighted and were rescued safely. Then Lt. Corniglio, flying a Macchi-7, ran out of fuel and alighted safely, leaving only de Briganti, who flew on to win the Schneider Trophy uncontested, flying his Macchi-7, with an Isotta V-type 12-cyl. water-cooled engine of 250 hp, at an average of 117.9 mph.

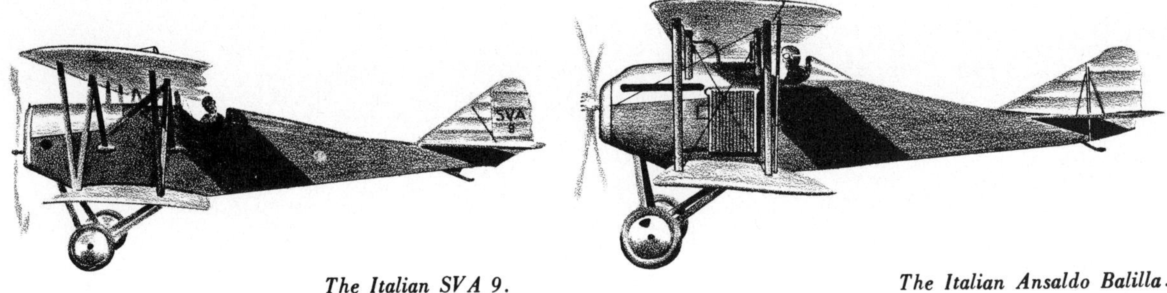

The Italian SVA 9. *The Italian Ansaldo Balilla.*

1921 – Pulitzer Trophy Race

The second annual contest for the Pulitzer Trophy was the main attraction of an aviation meeting, held at Omaha, Neb., November 3, 4, and 5. Only six entrants appeared as against last year's large array, but the aircraft were more specialized: two were of pure race design built specifically for this race, and three were pursuit studies also built with the race in mind, leaving only one stock entrant.

Earlier this year the U. S. Navy had placed an order with the Curtiss Corporation for a special race plane that would further the development of military fighters and engines. The racer was conceived about the 1st of June, 1921; one machine was completed on August 1; another identical racer was finished August 8. These craft, the cleanest biplanes of their time, were flown early in August, with Bert Acosta as test pilot, at Curtiss Field, Mineola, L.I., and tests continued up to race time. Constructed mostly of plywood, these racers were fitted with Curtiss direct-drive CD-12 engines of 405 hp, cooled by Lamblin-type radiators fitted to the landing gear struts. When it was decided that the Navy and Army Air Services would not compete for the Pulitzer Trophy, the Curtiss Corporation requested and received the loan of one of the Navy racers for the race.

The Curtiss Corporation also designed and built a racer for oilman S. E. J. Cox of Houston, Tex., who was still anxious to get a racing aircraft into the win- column. The fuselage, engine, etc., were those of the 1920 *Cactus Kitten* monoplane now fitted with a set of triplane wings, which brought the landing speed down to about 70 mph. Tested in October by Acosta, the new Curtiss-Cox *Cactus Kitten* triplane showed a top speed of 196 mph with its Curtiss C-12 geared engine of 435 hp.

Mr. Cox had also entered in the Pulitzer his repaired Curtiss *Texas Wildcat* biplane of 1920, but this machine was ruled out because of its "unduly high" landing speed of 95.5 mph.

Italy, whose aircraft sales were world-wide because of her fine seaplanes and her stock landplanes of the first Pulitzer race, was again represented this year through the Aero Import Corporation which entered two aircraft: the Ansaldo Balilla, which had won third place in the previous Pulitzer, now fitted with a 400-hp K-12 engine as a pursuit study; and an SVA-9 two-place stock machine like that which placed 13th in the 1920 Pulitzer.

The Thomas-Morse firm of Ithaca, N. Y., anxious for more military orders, entered two single-seat fighters; one a newly designed fabric-covered parasol MB-7 monoplane; and a clip-winged MB-3 biplane, now designated an MB-6. Both were powered by Wright 400-hp V-8 engines.

On the day of the Pulitzer race, November 3, the weather was all any speed pilot could ask. The sky was clear with a bright sun, visibility was splendid, and there was but a light breeze with smooth air.

Bert Acosta won the toss-up and the privilege of starting first over the 31.07-mile triangular course, which the contestants had to cover five times. He crossed the starting line, in his new Curtiss Navy racer, at a "terrific speed" estimated at more than 200 mph and was out of sight behind the hills in a moment.

Lloyd Bertaud, in the Ansaldo Balilla, followed Acosta three minutes later. Bertaud flew high, whereas Acosta barely skimmed the line of trees on the hills.

The third pilot off was Clarence Coombs, flying the Curtiss-Cox triplane *Cactus Kitten*. When Coombs crossed the line, roaring wide open to get the very limit of speed from his red-and-silver machine, he was cheered by the spectators as their favorite. Before Coombs had got out of sight, Acosta was back, having covered the first lap in 9 min. 40 sec. He was off on the second lap before the fourth and fifth men took the air.

Harold Hartney was to follow Coombs, but be-

The Curtiss triplane CACTUS KITTEN *flown by Coombs was faster on the straightaways, while Acosta made his gains with better pylon turns in the Navy Curtiss racer and won the 1921 Pulitzer with an average speed of 176.7 mph. Note the fuselage-side radiator on the* KITTEN *and the Lamblin radiator on the Navy racer's landing gear struts. Bottom: Macready's Thomas-Morse MB-6, a modified MB-3 with shorter wings (left). The Thomas-Morse MB-7 in which Hartney crashed (right).*

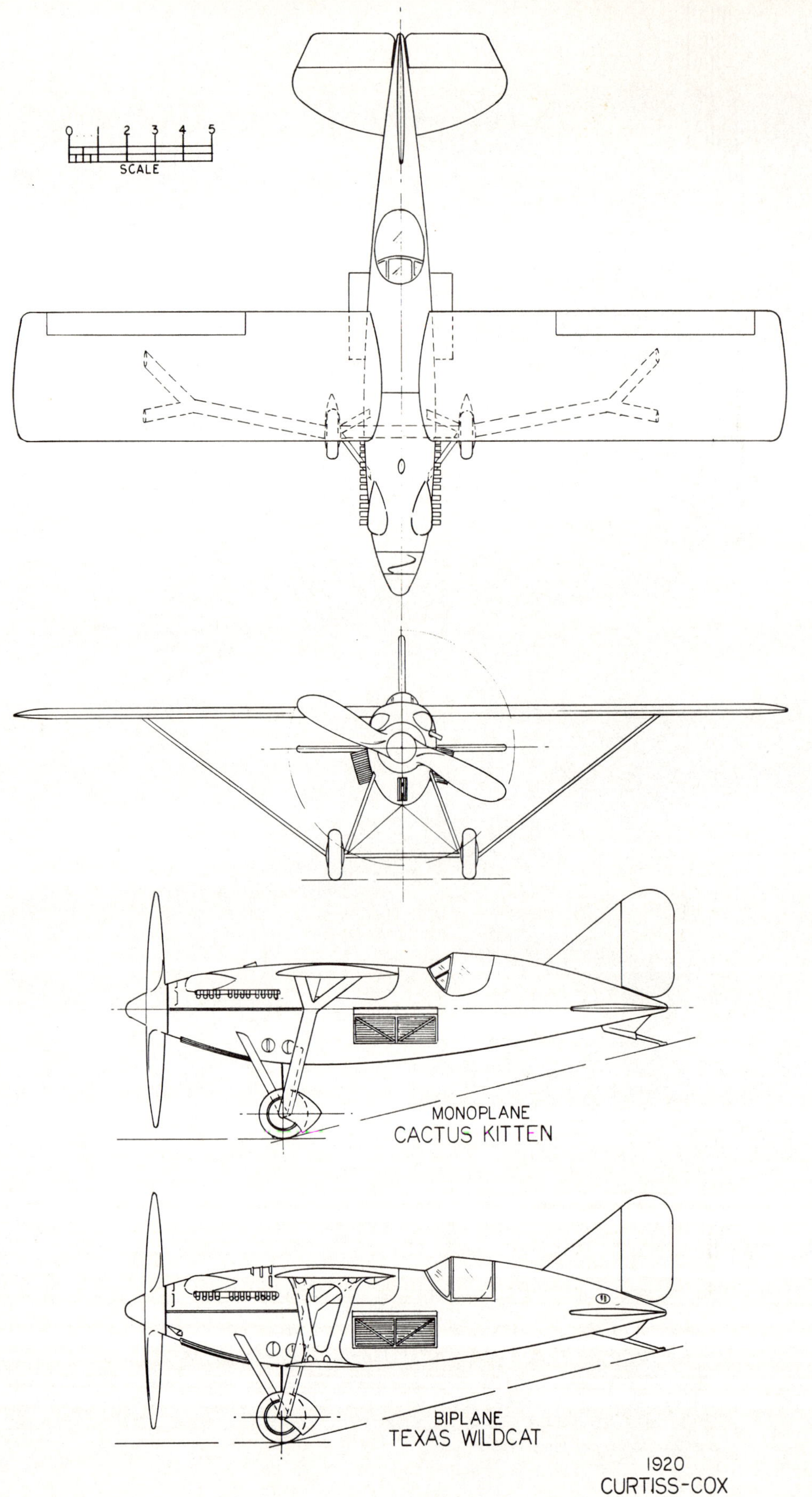
0 1 2 3 4 5
SCALE
MONOPLANE
CACTUS KITTEN
BIPLANE
TEXAS WILDCAT
1920
CURTISS-COX
D.W. CARTER

The Cactus Kitten triplane was composed of the fuselage, engine and other usable parts from the original monoplane Cactus Kitten, and a newly designed set of triplane wings of 20-foot span. After the 1921 Pulitzer, S. E. J. Cox, to whose order the Kitten was developed and raced, decided this race-plane sponsoring was getting out of hand and, in a grand gesture of patriotism, donated the Kitten to the U. S. Navy for a one dollar transfer of title fee.   (Warren M. Bodie)

Cactus Kitten, still painted red and silver but with its new owner's name painted on the vertical fin. Young Ensign Alford J. Williams, in cockpit, flew the Kitten, gathered valuable test data on the unique craft.   (Curtiss-Wright)

Cactus Kitten triplane had 175 sq. ft. of wing area, was quite clean in design except for the big rectangular unstreamlined brass radiators mounted on the fuselage sides. Ensign Williams poses alongside. (Warren M. Bodie)

The Cactus Kitten as it appeared at the Curtiss factory during flight tests, and before cleanup for train shipment to Omaha for the race. Bert Acosta. Curtiss chief test pilot, in cockpit, did all initial testwork on the Kitten. (Curtiss-Wright)

Bert Acosta poses with his winning ship and the coveted Pulitzer Trophy. Acosta and Bernt Balchen later flew Adm. Richard E. Byrd and his radioman Noville across the Atlantic in a Fokker triplane to earn Byrd and Noville only.the Navy DFC. (U.S. Air Force)

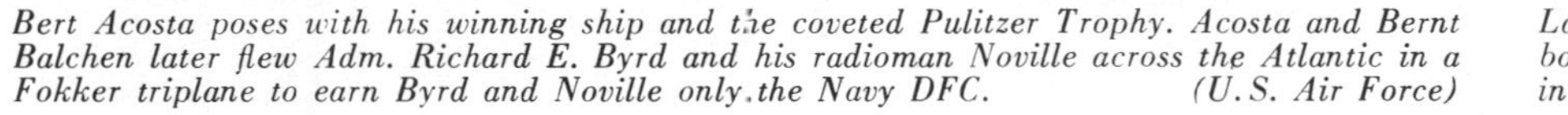

Landing gear shock absorbers on the Curtiss racers were rubber shock cord built into the bottom of gear struts. This photo of Acosta, and the one alongside. were taken on the lawn in front of the Curtiss factory on Long Island. (Curtiss-Wright)

The two Navy Curtiss racers, later designated R-2 and R-3, were the cleanest biplanes built up to their time and the first to be fitted with the newly developed streamlined brace wires. Cockpit cowl is removed in side view.   (Curtiss-Wright)

The Thomas-Morse MB-6 was essentially an MB-3 pursuit ship with seven feet cut off its wing span. It was fitted with single-bay interplane struts and wore a Wright V-8 engine of 400 hp, 100 hp more than the MB-3, giving it a wing loading of slightly over 5 pounds per hp. Water cooling radiator was carried on left side of fuselage only, between wings; straightaway speed was estimated at 185 mph.

(U. S. Air Force)

cause of trouble with his gasoline pump, gave place to James Curran, in the Italian SVA-9, who was followed by J. A. Macready, flying the silver Thomas-Morse MB-6.

For the next 45 minutes the course was full of racing airplanes, as many as three coming down the straightaway at the same time.

On the third lap Curran's engine developed trouble. Forced out of the race, he made a perfect landing on the field.

From the start, the race was between Acosta and Coombs. The latter's machine, the *Cactus Kitten,* gained on straightaways, while Acosta made his gains with pylon-dusting turns. It was Coombs' first time in the strange triplane, and he wisely flew a cautious race.

Having finished his fifth lap, Acosta brought his hot-landing, little grey Curtiss biplane in smoothly, his average speed 176.7 mph, a new world speed record for a closed-course race.

Then Coombs roared over the finish line, but his time was slower, 170.3 mph, which insured second.

Macready finished in third place, averaging 160.7 mph, and then came Bertaud with 149.8 mph.

When all the other entrants had completed the course, Hartney finally took off. It was a close squeak, as the Contest Committee had given him 20 minutes in which to be off. With two minutes to spare, Hartney crossed the starting line. When 15 minutes passed and the MB-7 had not returned, anxiety became intense. Various airplanes were making ready to take off and look for him when a farmer on the course telephoned in that an airplane had crashed near Loveland, Iowa, and that the pilot was injured. Hartney was rushed to a farmhouse and treated by a physician. Although he suffered internal injuries and a fractured hip, Hartney told that his gasoline pump had failed to work, and that when he attempted to change to his reserve tank the switch stuck and he crash-landed. The Omaha Hospital later announced that Hartney was not in danger, and his recovery was expected in two months.

And so Bert Acosta, flying the Navy's beautiful little Curtiss racer, was adjudged the winner. Although he did not know it at the time, Acosta had started a chain of victories for Curtiss planes that was to place the United States in commanding lead over all nations for several years.

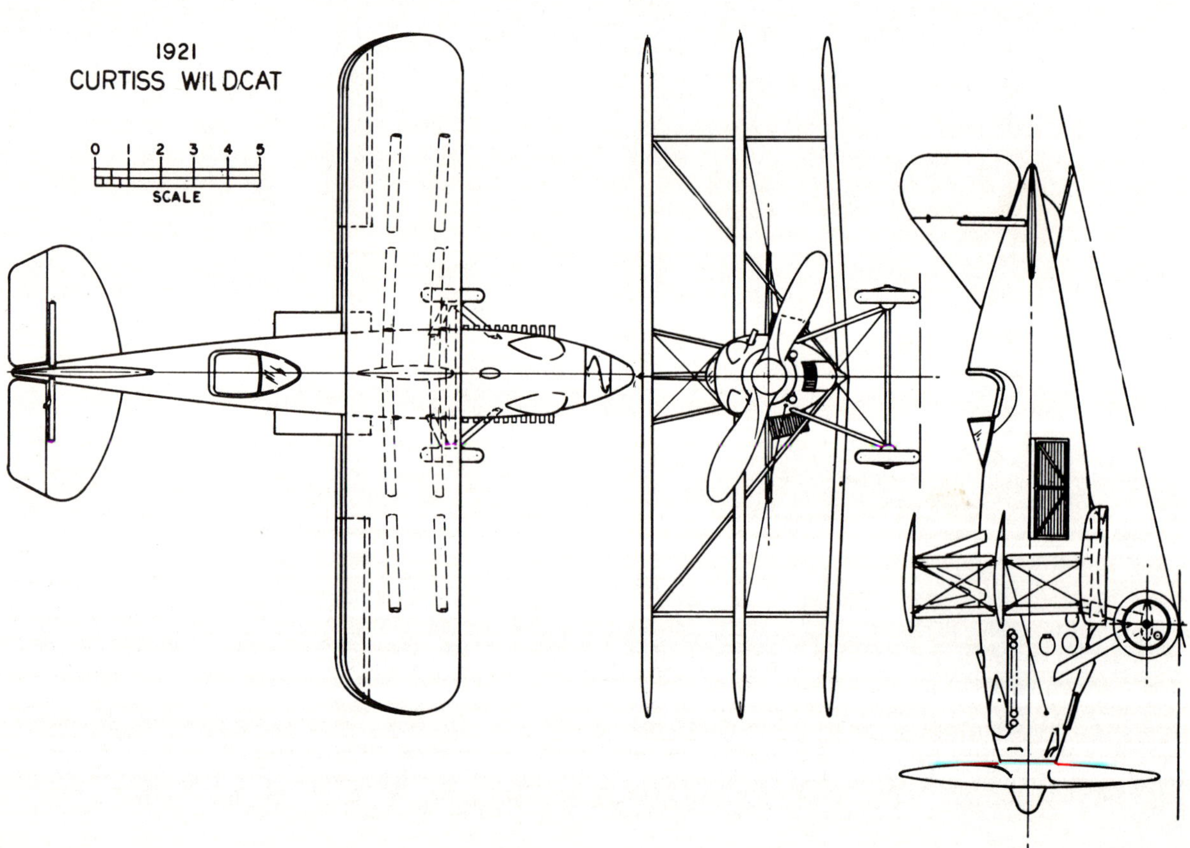

England's Supermarine Sea Lion III passing Italy's Macchi-17 (center), which finished in third place, and the clean Savoia S-51 (lower right) that finished second despite a badly damaged prop. Capt. H. C. Baird, flying the Sea Lion III, won the 1922 Schneider with an average speed of 145.7 mph.

To describe in detail the 8-day aviation meet held at Naples, Italy, Sunday, August 6, to Sunday the 13th, would fill many pages. Therefore, we shall deal with only the Schneider Trophy Race, the most important event of the meet.

Held on Sunday, August 13, over a triangular course, the race was 13 laps around for a total of 200 nautical miles (230.3 statute miles). The planes, as in all Schneider races, were sent off one at a time and were clocked separately to determine the winners.

Four machines started, all flying boats with pusher-type engines, three being Italian. Capt. H. C. Baird, the lone English entry, flying a Supermarine Sea Lion III (450-hp Napier Lion engine), took off first and was followed at intervals by the three Italian ships. Capt. Baird did his first lap at more than 160 mph and held this speed for six laps, during which time he overtook and passed two of the Italian ma-

chines. From the seventh to the eleventh laps he nursed his engine a bit, and the Italian planes reduced the lead.

Then, on the 13th and last lap, Baird opened his engine and crossed the finish line, having covered the course in 1 hr. 34 min. 57.6 sec., averaging 145.7 mph, which won the trophy for England. Before alighting Baird flew two extra "insurance laps."

Passaleva of Italy, flying the cleanest entry, was handicapped early in the race when some of the laminations of his wood propeller came unstuck, setting up a terrific vibration and forcing him to throttle back. He managed, however, to fly his trim Savoia S-51 into second place averaging 143.5 mph, while third place went to Zanetti in a Macchi M-17 at 133 mph. Fourth and last place went to Corniglio in a Macchi M-7 at 90.6 mph.

◆　◆　◆

1922 – Pulitzer Trophy Race

General William "Billy" Mitchell, aviation leader during World War I and our greatest advocate of air power, finally convinced the stubborn land- and sea-locked Congress and military leaders of the vital necessity for aircraft development. Pointing out, among other facts, that air speeds had jumped from a 130-mph top speed in 1918 to 205 mph (France) in late 1921, solely through special racing craft, Mitchell wheedled more and more funds for experimental purposes. Spurred by orders and with ever-rising speed marks to aim for, U. S. manufacturers built the world's most advanced aircraft designs for the 1922 Pulitzer Trophy Race, held on the last day of a 3-day aviation meet near Detroit, Mich., October 12, 13, and 14. On the 12th and 13th there were the usual "class" races for various aircraft types, with but a few civilian planes appearing to compete with the military.

Just before the Pulitzer race, six Thomas-Morse MB-3 airplanes were flagged off to fly four laps, about 125 miles, over the Pulitzer course. The planes and pilots were of the First Pursuit Group, Selfridge Field, and were competing in the first annual John L. Mitchell Trophy Race, donated by Brig. Gen. "Billy" Mitchell in honor of his brother who was killed in World War I. Restricted to the First Pursuit Group, the race was won by ship No. 54 piloted by Lt. Stace at an average of 148 mph. Fine piloting was seen in all contestants, especially at the pylons, and increased the interest in the later Pulitzer race on the part of the crowd of 25,000, who had flocked to Selfridge since early morning.

The Pulitzer course was over a circuit of 31.07 miles, which the contestants had to cover five times for a total of 155.35 miles, and was measured in kilometers for easier registry if new world's records were set. The course was mostly over the waters of Lake St. Clair: from Selfridge Field, Mount Clemens, Mich., along the shore line to Gaukler Point, then to a kite balloon anchored to a barge, thence back to Selfridge, a triangular course with roughly ten miles to a side.

At 1:00 P.M. the first four planes were flagged off into a hazy sky of moderate wind for the Pulitzer race. The contest was a free-for-all open to airplanes having an air speed greater than 140 mph and a landing speed not exceeding 75 mph. The racers were sent off in three separate groups (heats) so as to not have too many ships on the course at one time.

The first group to be flagged off in the race consisted of a Navy Thomas-Morse MB-7 similar to last year's ship (Navy Capt. Mulcahy), one Bee-Line BR-1 Navy racer (Lt. Callaway), and two Army Verville-Sperry racers.

The two Verville-Sperry planes and the Bee-Line racer wore the first retractable landing gears to be

The 1921 Navy Curtiss Racers No. 1 and 2 were both fitted with flush wing radiators, top wing only, for the 1922 Pulitzer. An additional brace strut on each side of the fuselage, which ran to the top wing between gaps in the radiator, was fitted to carry the higher loaded wing. This is Navy Curtiss No. 2 flown by Lt. Harold J. Brow. (Curtiss-Wright)

Navy Curtiss No. 2 as Lt. Brow raced it in 1922, with race No. 40 on fuselage side. Race numerals were often of a water soluble paint that could be readily washed off after racing. Later day race planes were painted well ahead of the races when possible, with numbers that were permanent, with a sleek finish that would not cause parasite drag.

(Warren M. Bodie)

Navy Lt. Brow poses in front of Navy Curtiss No. 2. Streamlining wheels with doped fabric was highly perfected by 1922, as evidenced in this view. Added strut between middle of fuselage side and wing is clearly seen, as well as skin radiator and water expansion tank atop wing.

(Curtiss-Wright)

USMC Capt. F. P. Mulcahy poses in front of Navy Curtiss No. 1 just before craft was returned to Curtiss factory for removal of Lamblin-type radiators under fuselage nose and addition of top wing skin radiator. Mulcahy was later assigned to race the Thomas-Morse MB-7 in the 1922 Pulitzer instead of this ship. *(Curtiss-Wright)*

Navy Curtiss No. 1 raced in the 1922 Pulitzer, flown by Lt. Al Williams, race No. 8 under cockpit. This ship was modified at the factory like ship No. 2. The added brace strut was placed differently in this ship, ran from top of forward landing gear strut at fuselage to just back of leading edge of wing, between gap in wing radiator. In each instance, the strut replaced a brace wire, the rear wire of ship No. 2 and the front wire on No. 1, seen here. *(Warren M. Bodie)*

Three Verville-Sperry R-3 racers, designed by Alfred Verville and built at the Sperry plant, were procured by the Army Air Service for the 1922 Pulitzer race. All three ships wore Lamblin-type water radiators slung under their wing at the center and were fitted with retractable landing gear, with no wheel-well covers provided, thus causing undue drag. Ships were built as pursuit studies and needed only leak-proof gas tanks to convert them.   (U. S. Air Force)

Another view of Verville-Sperry R-3 A.S. 23-326, race No. 49, flown to 5th place by Army Lt. E. H. Barksdale in the 1922 Pulitzer. One of the sister ships, A.S. 23-328, which took 7th place, flown by F. B. Johnson, is parked alongside. Third R-3, article A.S. 23-327, race No. 50 (not shown) flown by Captain St. Clair Street in the Pulitzer, dropped out in the fifth lap with a frozen engine. All three craft were painted olive drab overall except for markings. Hangars in background are Selfridge Field, Mt. Clemens, Mich.   (U. S. Air Force Museum)

The Navy NW-1 Mystery was the first aircraft to wear full wheel pants and attracted a lot of attention because of its unusual design. (Dustin W. Carter)

Combined drag of the many and long struts of the landing gear, plus its twin Lamblin radiators, presented tremendous drag on the N-W1 aircraft. Tail stand was necessary for access to engine and propeller for hand cranking. (Warren M. Bodie)

Air Service serial No. A.S. 6856, Curtiss R-6 racer designation and procurement number P-278 are clearly visible in this side view of Lt. Maitland's ship. The fuselage, struts, stabilizer and fin of both R-6 racers were painted a dull black. (U.S. Air Force)

Trim little Gloster Mars 1 won the English Aerial Derby race in 1921-22 and set an official world speed record of 212.15 mph on October 4, 1922. Nicknamed "Bamel" by her crew, this well-proportioned ship was powered by a 450 hp Napier Lion engine. (Gloster)

Two Navy-Wright sesquiplane racers were built in 1922 as flying test beds for a new 650-hp V-12 Packard T-2 engine. Designated NW-1, the first of the two ships, nicknamed "Mystery" (above), was completed in time for the 1922 Pulitzer. Racer No. 9, Navy serial A-6543, was dunked and turned over in four feet of Lake St. Clair water when its engine failed. USMC pilot Lt. Sandy Sanderson was barely able to scramble through bottom muck and swim ashore.   (U.S. Navy)

The second Navy-Wright NW-1 aircraft, A-6544 above, did not race but carried on its duties as an engine test bed. This craft was later rebuilt as a twin-float bi-seaplane, entered by the Navy in the 1923 Schneider race, and designated an NW-2.
(U.S. Navy)

Navy Lt. Callaway awaits a crank for his BR-1 on the race starting line. Oil radiator is seen under fuselage at wing leading edge root. None of the aircraft at the 1922 race meet were fitted with wheel brakes, still depending on tail skid to stop.   (U.S. Air Force)

Streamlined water expansion tank mounted atop fuselage in front of the cockpit of the Bee Line racers, acted as a wind screen in lieu of a transparent shield. Sister ship, BR-2, is seen in background, over rudder of BR-1.   (U.S. Air Force Museum)

In design theory the R-4 was supposed to be rugged in construction and the thick wing was to give the ship good take-off and landing characteristics. The big bore 600 hp Packard engine was, hopefully, to pull it through the air at good speed.   (U.S. Air Force Museum)

Army Lt. D. F. Stace, winner of the 1922 John L. Mitchell Race, standing alongside his trim little MB-3 pursuit in which he averaged 148 mph.   (U.S. Air Force)

The Navy ordered two Bee Line low-wing monoplane racers for the 1922 Pulitzer race and they were identical except for their radiators. One, the BR-1, was fitted with flush-type radiators built into the top of the wing surface and the sister ship, the BR-2, wore a Lamblin-type radiator on each side of its fuselage at the wing root. Above ship was flown in Pulitzer by Navy Lt. Callaway. (U. S. Navy/Bodie)

Navy Lt. Rittenhouse in front of the BR-2 which did not race because of mechanical trouble. The Bee Line aircraft were designed by Booth and Thurston of the Aerial Engineering Corp. of Hammondsport, N. Y., an outfit newly formed by ex-Curtiss employees. (U. S. Air Force Museum)

publicly demonstrated in the United States. The cold mention of this fact does little justice to the emotion the onlookers felt when the three pilots actually did crank their landing gears into the fuselage.

The Navy Bee-Line racer designed by Booth and Thurston, former Curtiss engineers, who had worked on the 1921 Navy Curtiss racers, was not sufficiently flight tested before the races, but in design was the most promising of all, with many new ideas that were to survive the race. Powered by a Wright H-3 engine of 380 hp, the entire wing was covered with a thin sheet of copper, under which the cooling water circulated so that the copper acted as a radiator as well as wing structure. The retractable landing-gear legs wore full skirts, so when the wheels retracted into the wing the wheel wells were completely covered.

The Verville-Sperry planes were pursuit studies, powered by 380-hp Wright H-3 engines. They were full cantilever in construction and very clean, except that the wheel wells were uncovered, certainly causing quite a lot of air drag.

The story of this race was brief, for the Bee-Line racer dropped out in the second lap due to radiator trouble, and the Navy Thomas-Morse MB-7 followed suit with lubrication trouble. This left only the two Verville-Sperry ships, and both finished, Lt. Barksdale making an average speed of 181 mph and Lt. Johnson 178 mph, which was good for only fifth and seventh places in the final results.

The second group of Pulitzer racers sent off was comprised of two new Army Curtiss biplane racers, two identical Navy Curtiss biplane racers, one of which had won first place in the 1921 Pulitzer, plus a Navy "Mystery" ship. The latter had been completed only shortly before the race, and its hurried assembling and testing handicapped its chances.

The Navy "Mystery" racer was built as a flying test bed for a new 650-hp Packard T-2 engine, the most powerful of its day. A sesquiplane of unusual appearance, her pilot, Lt. Sanderson, reported her to be admirably controllable and most satisfactory to fly.

The Curtiss racers, and in particular the two clean Army ships, were naturally the favorites, for it was known that Lt. Maughan in one of these ships had attained in unofficial tests at Garden City, N. Y., a speed of 222 mph, a new record. The question most discussed was whether these fast ships would prove maneuverable enough on the turns to hold the speed they would make on the straightaways.

Despite the "terrific" speed of their ships, the Army's Lt. Maughan and Lt. Maitland swung them around in perfect banks at the pylons with no more visible difficulty than the standard pursuit ships had

had a few hours previously. Lt. Maughan was banking his turns at least 80° and clearing the pylons by a few feet.

Lt. Sanderson handled the brand-new Navy "Mystery" plane like a veteran, cutting the pylons even a bit sharper than Maughan. He made one lap at 187 mph but was forced out in the fourth lap by engine trouble, setting the "Mystery" down in water at 90 mph and swimming ashore uninjured. Sanderson seemed pursued by ill luck, for he had a week previously lost what seemed to be a sure victory in the Curtiss Marine Trophy Race (restricted to Navy service types), when his Curtiss triplane ran out of gas while within sight of the finish line.

Lt. Maughan broke all world's records for speed in a closed circuit for 100 and 200 km to win the heat, averaging 205.8 mph. Lt. L. J. Maitland, flying a sister ship to Maughan's Curtiss, finished second with an average of 198.8 mph, and Navy Lt. Brow was third with his Curtiss R-2 averaging 193.2 mph.

Lt. Alford Williams, in the fourth Curtiss racer, the Navy R-1, had a thrilling experience when a fire extinguisher in his cockpit exploded, a piece of it knocking his helmet off. He had great difficulty arranging his helmet while plunging on at better than three miles a minute, and though fumes from the extinguisher sickened him, he succeeded in finishing fourth at 188 mph. Speeds of the four Curtiss racers proved to be the fastest of the day, winning first, second, third, and fourth places in the race.

Lt. Maughan was exhausted by the race and leaned against his plane for a few minutes until he had revived. "I got lost four times in the haze," Maughan said. "I was stunned (blacked out) more or less at each of the fifteen turns. On the straightaway I came to. Another trouble I had was with my feet going to sleep." We know today that Maughan was making his turns too abruptly — it was estimated that he was pulling at least 7G's (seven times gravity) in his turns!

The last group of Pulitzer racers, which was sent off at 3:46 P.M., was comprised of the Verville-Packard VCP-1 biplane, with which Capt. Mosely won the 1920 Pulitzer race, and which he again piloted in this year's race; two new Army Loening low-wing racers, piloted by Lts. Whitehead and Schulz; two Army Thomas-Morse TM-22 raised-wing (parasol) monoplanes, piloted by Capt. Hunter and Lt. Bissell; and the third remaining low-wing Verville-Sperry with retractable gear, piloted by Capt. St. Clair Streett.

The Loening racers were powered by new 600-hp V-12 Packard engines, but were handicapped by thick wings and a fixed and not very streamlined

Both MB-7 aircraft wore a 320-hp Wright V-8 engine in a shapely fuselage but were handicapped by a weird wing that sat too close to the fuselage. Top speed was estimated to be 180 mph, landing speed 80. Capt. F. P. Mulcahy, USMC, who piloted the MB-7 in Pulitzer, poses above.

(U. S. Navy)

Another homely product of the Thomas-Morse Aircraft Corp. was this MB-7 fabric-covered parasol monoplane, two of which were hopefully built in 1921 for possible sale as pursuit studies. Only one was finished in time for the 1921 Pulitzer and ex-military pilot Harold Hartney cracked it up in a forced landing during the race. The second MB-7, above, was purchased by the Navy for the 1922 Pulitzer.

(U. S. Air Force)

Nieuport-Delage monoplane flown to 1st place in the 1922 Deutsch de la Meurthe Cup Race, an annual French event, by Sadi Lacointe. He set a new world speed record in the same ship in 1923, traveling 234.66 mph. Engine is a 420 hp Hispano V-8. (U.S. Air Force)

Nieuport-Delage full-cantilever sesquiplane was built for the 1922 Deutsch de la Meurthe Cup Race. Windshield and headrest of open cockpit can be seen above the wing. Engine is a 380 hp Hispano V-8. (U.S. Air Force)

Landing gear of the R-4 was rugged, with big wheels for rough field operation, such as pursuit ship might encounter in normal operation. Landing brace wire running from wheel outside center to wing prevented wing vibration on Whitehead's ship. (U.S. Air Force)

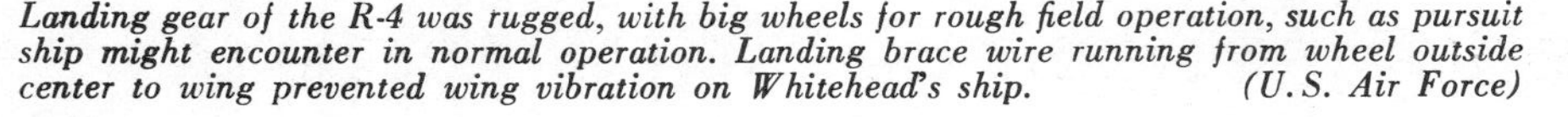

One of the two TM-22 R-5 racers sitting on a ridge near the Thomas-Morse factory at Ithaca, N.Y. Fuel tank was fitted into wing at the middle. The wing itself was built into two panels, left and right, and had no center section. (U.S. Air Force)

Two Loening R-4 low-wing monoplanes, with fixed landing gears, designed as pursuit studies, were built for the 1922 Pulitzer in 60 days before race time. Lt. Ennis Whitehead test flew the R-4 (race No. 46) that he was to pilot in the Pulitzer and reported that at full speed the wing tips vibrated at least two feet vertically and he was sure they would come off. Radiator area also proved inadequate so the fuselage back of the engine was faired and both ships were flown minus cowls.

(U. S. Air Force)

With the race only a few days off there was no time to build new wings for the R-4 racers, so a dedicated crew worked around the clock giving the wings torsional strength by veneer covering in the case of Lt. Whitehead's plane, and external struts (above) on Lt. Schultz's craft (race No. 45). Both R-4's were condemned after the race, almost total flops.

(Warren M. Bodie)

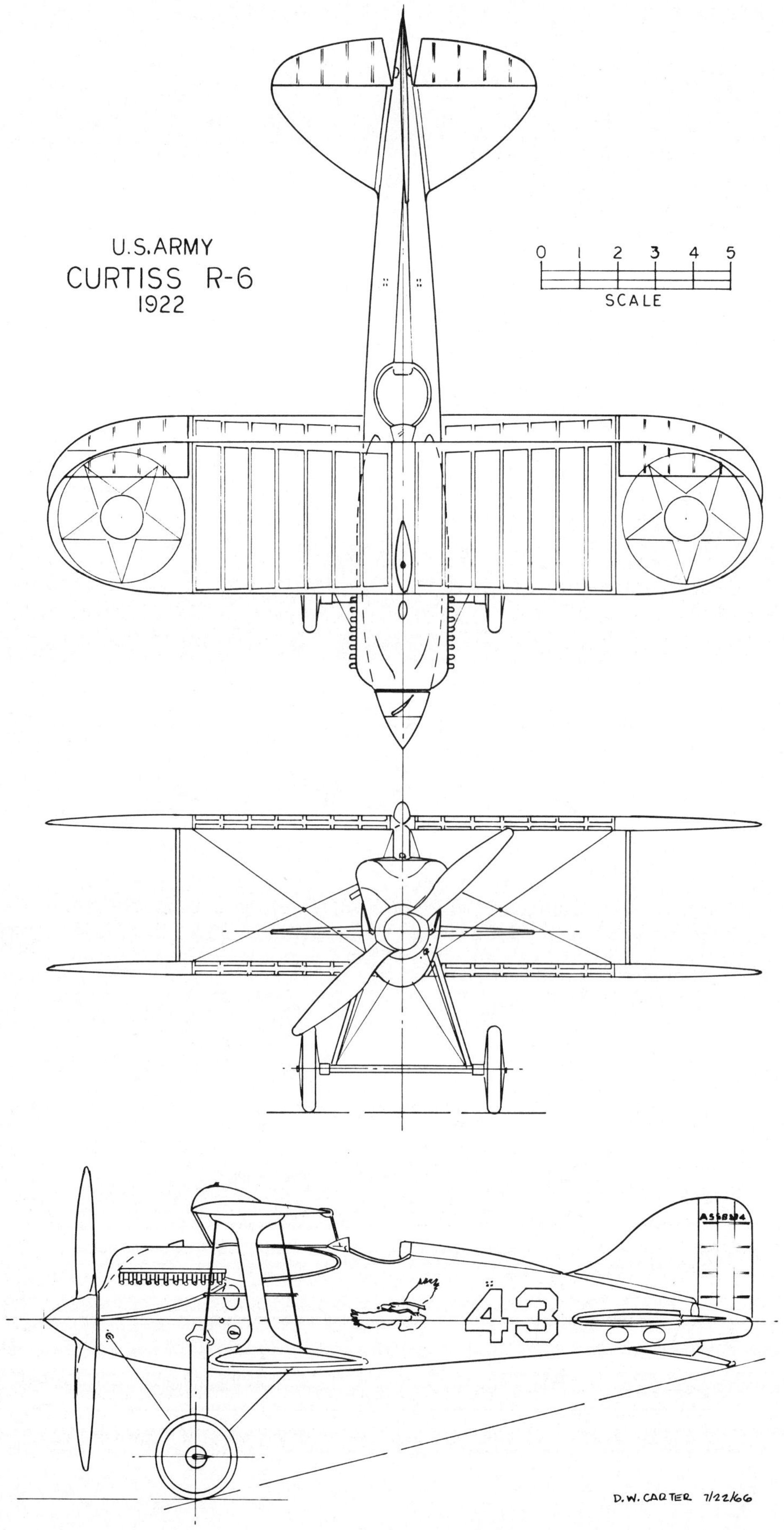

U.S. ARMY
CURTISS R-6
1922
0 1 2 3 4 5
SCALE
A6584
43
D.W. CARTER 7/22/66

The exquisite Curtiss R-6, is considered by many Curtiss racer fans to be the most beautiful aircraft ever built. Two were built under contract No. 552, dated May 27, 1922, between the Army and Curtiss. Contract required a sea level top speed of 175 mph, and landing speed not over 75 mph. The craft bore procurement Nos. 278 and 279. Lt. Russell L. Maughan poses with R-6 No. 2, P-279, in which he won Pulitzer. (Curtiss-Wright)

Army Lt. L. J. Maitland poses with R 6 No. 1 (P-278) in which he finished second in the Pulitzer. Both aircraft were re-worked during the winter, and between March 21 and 29, 1923, new speed trials were made at McCook Field, Dayton, Ohio. Racer No. 2 (P-279) established a new record of 236.598 mph. In September both ships were plagued by mishaps and did not do well in the October 1923 Pulitzer despite new and more powerful engines. (Curtiss-Wright)

Denied sufficient funds for purchase of research aircraft, Air Services frequently bought racing craft under the guise of pursuit studies. Two Thomas-Morse TM-22 parasol monoplanes similar to model above, were acquired in 1922 and designated R-5 racers. Homely in appearance, it was ahead of its time in having all-metal construction and wore a big Packard V-12 engine of 600 hp in a clean fuselage but was handicapped by an awkward and thick wing. (U. S. Air Force)

A thick wing section was used on the R-5's in an effort to give the aircraft shorter take-off and landing rolls, plus good climb—desirable characteristics for pursuit ships. Several propellers were tried on the TM-22's. the one above used on No. 48 necessitated an almost 3-point take-off because of its length. (Warren M. Bodie)

landing gear, which held the planes' speed down.

The three Thomas-Morse planes, two Army TM-22's and one MB-7, were specially built by the Ithaco firm for the race and were very similar to the MB-7 of last year's race. The TM-22 racers were entirely of metal construction, covered with corrugated sheet aluminum. The TM-22's were powered by 12-cyl. Packard engines of 600 hp, and the MB-7 wore a 380-hp Wright H-3.

In contrast with speeds of the previous racers, it was at once apparent that none of these ships could make the time of the Curtiss racers. The old Verville-Packard, piloted by Mosely, made the best time of this group, averaging 179 mph to take sixth place in the race. (Lt. Barksdale having won fifth place in the first heat.)

Capt. Streett, after doing the fourth lap at 169 mph, developed engine trouble on the fifth and last lap and landed safely just outside Selfridge Field.

Lt. Whitehead and Lt. Schulz, in their Packard-engined Loenings, took second and third in the heat and eighth and ninth places in the race, averaging 170.2 and 160.9 mph respectively. Then came Lt. Bissell and Capt. Hunter in their TM-22's, to finish in the last places in the heat and the race. Capt. Hunter, unfortunately, got lost in the haze on the first lap and wasted about five minutes, but thereafter made better time than two of those who were credited with finishing ahead of him.

When the last ship had landed, and the timers' stand announced the victory of Lt. Maughan, a great volume of cheers broke out, for the victory had placed America in the front rank of military aviation.

Four days later, amplifying his plea for air power development through racing craft, Gen. "Billy" Mitchell flew the winning Curtiss plane four runs over a 3-km course, averaging 224.4 mph to break the world's speed record.

The four Curtiss racers, particularly the two Army Curtiss planes, still hold title as being the most beautiful and streamlined biplanes ever built, as well as the fastest for their power. The success of these craft was to cause U. S. pursuit and fighter planes to be predominantly biplane through the 20's and into the 30's.

The two Army Curtiss planes were faster than the Navy's, for they were designed from knowledge gleaned in building and flying the two Navy racers.

Designed and built in but 90 days, the Army Curtiss planes were the first to have oil and water radiators built into the wings. Curtiss designed, they were made of corrugated brass and were the ultimate in streamline cooling for water-cooled engines.

The wings, fuselage, and fixed tail sections were constructed of wood, then plywood covered; the ailerons, elevators, and rudder of metal, then fabric covered. The engine cowling was metal. The Army Curtiss planes were of shorter span than the Navy's, had I interplane struts instead of the Navy's N type, and were powered by Curtiss V-12 engines (D-12) of 460 hp.

The Navy Curtiss planes were further streamlined for this year's race and had wing radiators (top wing only) instead of the old Lamblin type.

Direct front view of the Thomas-Morse TM-22 (R-5). Water-coolant radiator suspended under fuselage was encased in a metal shell in an effort to streamline it.
(U. S. Air Force/Bodie)

1923 – Schneider Trophy Race

Though the Schneider races had contributed little to technical progress, they had increased interest in aviation. The entries from 1919 to 1922 had been reworked single-seat pursuit seaplanes. From 1913 to 1922 the Schneider races had remained a field of activity for the sportsman pilot and the aircraft manufacturer. Technical development was slow and systematic preparation at a minimum until the respective governments took an active interest in the races.

Pure racing craft appeared in the 1923 Schneider, when the United States was represented by a full team for the first time. The team, entered by the U. S. Navy, consisted of four pilots: Lt. David Rittenhouse and Lt. Rutledge Irvine, both flying float versions of the Navy's two Curtiss racers (465-hp D-12 engines) of 1921-22 Pulitzer fame; Lt. Frank Wead, whose biplane Navy Wright NW-2 seaplane, powered by a Wright T-3 700-hp engine, was eliminated before the trials by a broken propeller blade which ripped open the floats and caused the machine to crash on alighting; and Lt. A. W. Gorton, flying a TR-3A biplane, the reworked Navy TR-1 in which he had won first place in the Curtiss Marine Trophy Race in 1922.

The TR-3A was fitted with wing radiators and a 265-hp Wright water-cooled engine in place of its regular 200-hp radial air-cooled Wright. This plane was entered as an alternate and was used by the U. S. pilots to familiarize themselves with the racecourse.

The British Schneider Cup team originally consisted of three planes, but two of them were crashed by their pilots during tests, leaving only H. C. Baird to fly a Supermarine Sea Lion III flying boat with a Napier Lion engine. This plane was the same that won the Schneider Cup in 1922 at Naples, Italy, but the engine was boosted to 575 hp, new wings were fitted, and the design was cleaned up.

The French team consisted of four biplane machines; two CAMS flying boats, each with a 360-hp Hispano-Suiza engine; and two Latham LI flying boats, each with two 400-hp Lorraine-Dietrich tandem-pusher and tractor engines.

The CAMS boats differed in that the CAMS 36 had a tractor propeller, while the CAMS 38, fitted with a pusher prop, was 10 mph the faster of the two.

The two Latham flying boats were the French "bad weather" chance, of very sturdy construction, and would have made a showing only on a windy day with choppy water. One of these was so damaged by shore helpers that it had to be withdrawn.

Large crowds watched the qualifying tests held the day before the race. Each machine was required to taxi over the starting line, take off and alight three times, and then lie at anchor unattended for six hours.

These provisions called for a rugged and seaworthy plane, and the American machines, being pontoon type, were watched with much interest, as it was believed that they would "porpoise." They behaved well, however, taxiing fast and getting off quickly.

The race proper was held on Friday, September 28, over the triangular Cowes-Selsey-Southsea course, which measured 42.86 statute miles, five times around for a total distance of 214 miles. The weather was fine, with bright sunshine and calm sea, though the wind freshened later.

At 11:00 A.M. the starting signal was given to Lt. Irvine, who quickly left his spray path behind and took-off in his sleek grey Navy Curtiss. He was soon followed by his teammate Lt. Rittenhouse in the other Curtiss, but engine trouble prevented the third plane of the American team, the TR-3A, from starting.

Fifteen minutes later and just as Lt. Irvine roared by to finish his first lap, Baird of England, in his Supermarine, crossed the starting line. Then the start was given to the three French machines, but only the fastest one, the CAMS 38 piloted by M. Hurel, crossed the starting line. The CAMS 36 fouled a mooring buoy on its take-off run, while the Latham did not get away at all because of trouble with its tandem engines.

The two Curtiss ships streaked by, to be followed by the Supermarine. Hurel developed engine trouble early in the second lap and alighted off Selsey, his speed for the first lap but 130.4 mph.

It was soon evident that the U. S. Curtiss planes were much faster than England's fastest entry, and that, barring engine trouble, the Cup would go to the United States.

And so it did. Rittenhouse worked up to first place and finished with an average speed of 177.4 mph. Lt. Irvine finished second with 173.5 mph, and Baird, in the Supermarine, secured third place with 157.2 mph. Then Lt. Rittenhouse roared around the course once more on his "insurance" lap and was clocked at a new high of 188.2 mph for seaplanes.

It was a great day for American aviation. For the first time an American plane and engine flown by an American pilot had won the famous Schneider.

The British and French paid warm tribute to the efficiency of the American team and said the Curtiss planes were the cleanest and most perfect racing

Both U. S. Navy Curtiss racers of 1921-22 Pulitzer fame (A-6080 and A-6081) were fitted with twin pontoons for entry in the 1923 Schneider Trophy race. Additional weight was carried by new Curtiss D-12 engines delivering 450 hp at 2300 rpm. Designations were changed again. In 1921 the ships were CR-1, in 1922 CR-2 and now were CR-3 as seaplanes. Both photos on this page are of CR-3 A-6081, with Lt. David Rittenhouse, Schneider winner, in cockpit.   *(Curtiss-Wright)*

Several changes were visible in the Curtiss racers as seaplanes. Struts were substituted for the remaining double-brace wires that ran from inboard section of the top wing to the lower fuselage. Wing radiators were added outboard of the N struts on the top wing to cool the larger engines, and the newly developed Curtiss-Reed metal propellers were installed on both craft. Fuel tanks were placd in the floats, a feature to be much copied abroad.   *(Curtiss-Wright/Brodie)*

Interesting TR-3A bi-seaplane was re-worked Navy TR-1 which had won the 1922 Curtiss Marine Trophy race for service craft. Plane went to England in 1923 as an alternate and was used by the U.S. team for practice. (U.S. Navy)

The rather large and awkward Navy-Wright NW-2 which was a rebuild of the 1922 Navy-Wright NW-1 sesquiplane. Craft suffered a pre-race accident so did not race. All four Navy racers went to England by cruiser in 1923. (Curtiss-Wright)

The Supermarine Sea Lion III flying boat of 1923 was a re-work of the 1922 Schneider winner cleaned up and wearing a new big engine of 575 hp. It was designed for seaworthiness, had struts and wires galore. (U.S. Navy)

This unique and promising English entry, a Blackburn "Pellet," G-EBHF race No. 6, powered by a 450 hp Napier Lion engine, crashed before the 1923 Schneider race. Lamblin radiator and oversize wing tip floats were its only poor features. (Charles G. Mandrake)

aircraft yet seen in Europe. Of special interest to them were the Curtiss-Reed metal propellers on the Curtiss racers (the first metal props ever flown) and the wing radiators of all our entries.

Partly through increased horsepower, but mainly by its use of wing radiators and metal prop, the winning Curtiss traveled faster as a seaplane than the same ship had in winning the 1921 Pulitzer when fitted with wheels.

The Curtiss racers, foreground and upper left, finished easily in first and second place over England's Supermarine Sea Lion III (upper right). Lt. Rittenhouse, No. 4, worked up to first place and set a new speed record for seaplanes, winning the 1923 Schneider race with an average speed of 177.4 mph. Bottom: The TR-3A, reworked Thomas-Morse Navy Scout (left). The 700-hp Navy Wright NW-2, damaged by broken prop, crashed (second from left). The French CAMS 36 fouled a mooring buoy on take-off (second from right). The French Latham (right).

Direct rear view of the Curtiss R2C-1, photographed on September 9, 1923, shows wing skin radiators on both wings, fabric covered ailerons and elevators.
(Curtiss-Wright)

1923 – Pulitzer Trophy Race

The St. Louis Air Meet, held October 4, 5, and 6, was by far the biggest and best aeronautical demonstration in the world up to this time, with 125,000 persons witnessing the last day's events. Over 300,000 miles were flown without a serious accident. To describe the whole meet would require a volume in itself, and so we will stick to the most important event, the Pulitzer Trophy Race, which did so much to develop our nation's military and racing aircraft.

Held on the last day of the meet, the Pulitzer Trophy Race was comprised of seven highly developed racing craft, all of them constructed mainly of wood, with plywood-covered wings and fuselages and the movable surfaces fabric .covered. Water-cooled engines and wing radiators were installed on all seven planes. The Navy had spent a lot of money on monoplanes for last year's race, only to see biplanes take the first four places. Justly believing biplanes more suitable for her newly converted carrier, the U.S.S. *Langley,* and anxious to win over the Army, she placed her bets on a proven builder by ordering two new and improved Curtiss biplanes (R2C-1) for this race. Perfectly streamlined, they differed from previous Curtiss racers in that their fuselages were smaller, the top wings were flush with the fuselage, and the landing gear simplified. Powered by Curtiss D-12 Special engines of 500 hp, both planes wore the newly invented Curtiss-Reed metal propellers, which had been proven in the Schneider race eight days earlier.

In an effort to exploit biplanes to their fullest, the Navy also ordered two biplane racers from the Wright Company. Although powered by Wright T-3 engines of 700 hp, the highest horsepower in the world at this time, the Wright F2W racers were poor copies of the Curtiss racers and not as clean in streamline.

The Army Air Service spent little money this year on its Pulitzer entries. Two of them were the Curtiss ships which took first and second in last year's race, one even having the same engine, while the other had the new 500-hp D-12 Special engine. A third Army entry, the Verville-Sperry, the low-wing monoplane which had flown in the 1922 race (see illustration on page 53) now fitted with a 500-hp D-12 Special engine, was the only monoplane of the race.

To reduce possibilities of accident, it was decided, as in past Pulitzer races, to pair the contestants and run the race in heats over the 124.28-mile 4-lap course.

THE FIRST HEAT

Lt. Lawson "Sandy" Sanderson of the Marines was first into the clear blue sky with his red Navy Wright. He did a climbing turn over the field beyond the starting point and, after reaching 4,000 feet, swung far into the sun and then dived straight for the first pylon. He flashed by the timers at 2:31 P.M. and, rounding the pylon, left a smoky trail in the eastern horizon as he streaked out of sight.

Only one of the original three Verville-Sperry R-2 (A.S. 22-328) appeared at St. Louis for the 1923 Pulitzer race. Fitted with a special D-12 engine of 500 hp, it wore a new streamlined engine cowl complementing its enlarged propeller spinner. Spinner nose cone became loose, setting up a vibration that forced Lt. Alex Pearson to drop out in the first lap. The R-3, with full cantilever low-wing configuration and retractable landing gear, was ahead of its time.   (U. S. Air Force)

The elegantly beautiful Curtiss R2C-1 racers of 1923 were the epitome of biplane streamlining, had only one main landing gear leg on each side and used streamline wires from the axles as side braces to absorb extra loads. Above is A-6691 with Lt. Harold J. Brow in the cockpit. This ship was first test-flown by Lt. Brow with a wooden propeller while its sister ship wore one of S. Albert Reed's forged one-piece duraluminum props from the first.   (Curtiss-Wright)

As in the R-6 Curtiss racers, the R2C (with Lt. Williams) had a semi-monocoque wood fuselage with "Curtiss ply" 2-ply spruce veneer, glued and tacked in strips two inches wide diagonally to the frame, fabric covered, doped and waxed to a high lustre. Entire water supply, about 12 gallons, was circulated through the wing radiator, top and bottom wings, over five times a minute. Radiator skin was fabricated with corrugated brass sheet of only .004" thickness. (U.S. Air Force)

Lt. Sanderson alongside his F2W which wore a 3-bladed wooden propeller in the Pulitzer. Sling with wooden pole handles over fuselage just forward of vertical stabilizer was used by ground crew to hold tail skid in its dolly when moving aircraft about.
(U.S. Navy)

R2C-1 A-6692 in which Lt. Alford J. Williams won the 1923 Pulitzer race. Design of the two R2C's was largely the work of Curtiss' chief engineer William L. Gilmore, who created all the Curtiss racing craft, from the Wildcat to the R3C-1 of 1925. Power loading of the R2C-1, only 4.17 lbs/hp, gave the ships a then fantastic climb to 5,000 feet in 1.6 minutes, 10,000 feet in 3.6 minutes, 15,000 feet in 5.8 minutes and 20,900 feet in 10 minutes. (U. S. Air Force)

The two 1923 Navy Wright F2W racers were practically enlarged copies of the Curtiss R-6 Army racers of 1922 fame, their larger size necessary to handle the huge 700-hp V-12 Wright T-3 Tornado engines fitted to both ships. On the rudder of both F2W aircraft were the words "NAVY WRIGHT FIGHTER" to justify their purchase to a penny-pinching Congress. No. 8, above, was test-flown with a two-bladed propeller, raced with the three-bladed one. (U. S. Navy)

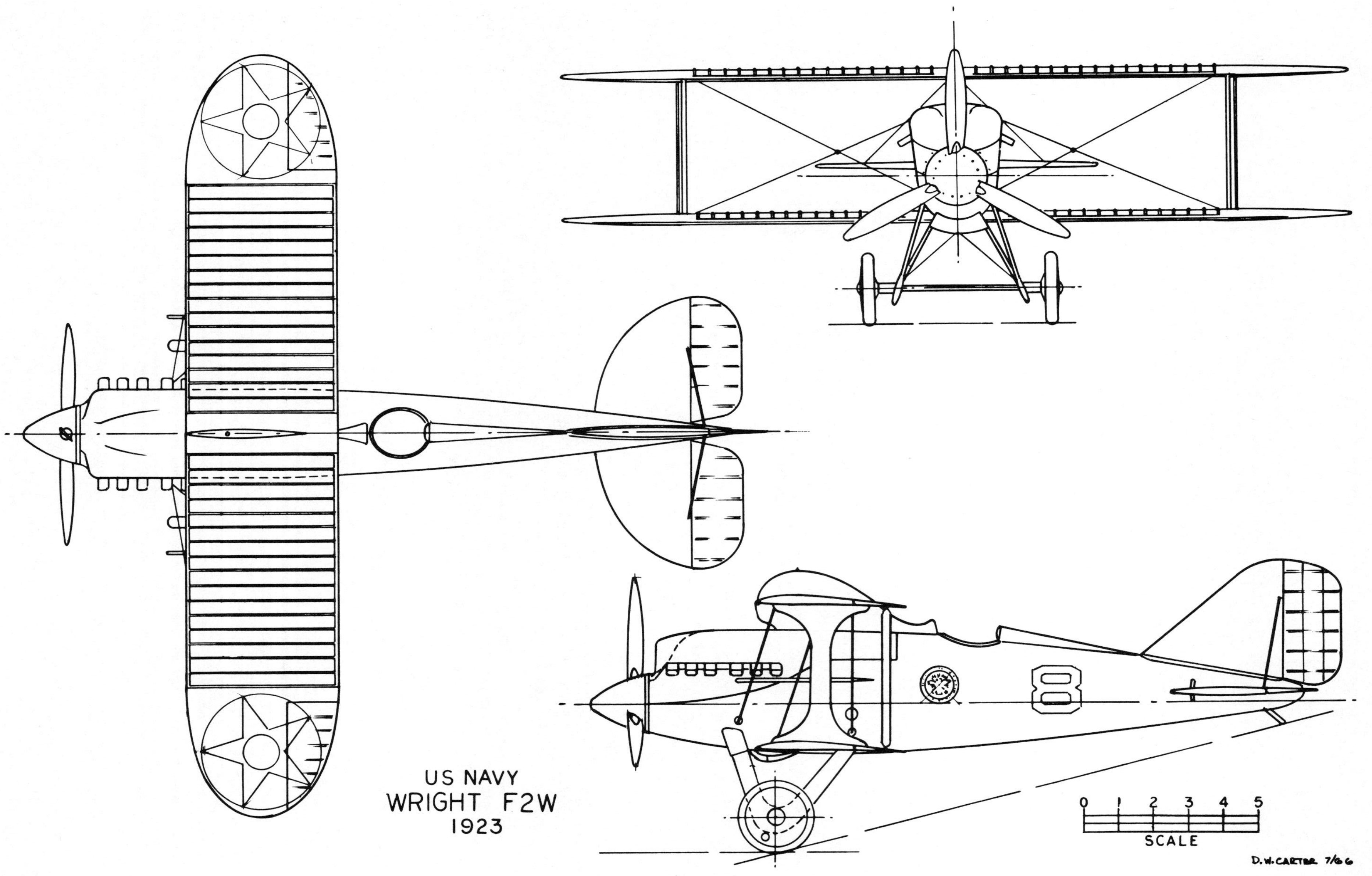
US NAVY
WRIGHT F2W
1923
0 1 2 3 4 5
SCALE
D.W.CARTER 7/66

Although seen here with a three-bladed propeller, F2W No. 7 was flown in the 1923 Pulitzer with a two-bladed propeller —and both ships finished only seconds apart in the Pulitzer. (Warren M. Bodie)

Navy Wright F2W-1 as it rolled out of the factory for initial test flights, and before being final-painted with fire engine red fuselage, white wings and tail surfaces. Fuselage of the F2W was unique in that its entire length was built up of wood, then plywood and fabric covered, the only metal being in its motor mount and the top front of the fuselage which streamlined the cylinder banks. (Curtiss-Wright)

Although larger than the earlier R-6 racers, the R2C-1 was still quite small as view shows, with Lt. Williams alongside. Aileron and empennage control surfaces had metal frames and doped linen covering. No control cables or horns protruding. *(Curtiss/Bodie)*

Lt. Harold Brow took R2C-1 A-6691 on its first test flight at Mitchel Field on September 9, 1923, and four days later piloted this ship to 244.3 mph in level flight to set an unofficial first in exceeding four miles per minute. *(U.S. Air Force)*

Lt. L. Sanderson, USMC, in his Navy Wright F2W No. 8 awaiting starter's flag for Pulitzer Race, October 6, 1923. *(U.S. Navy)*

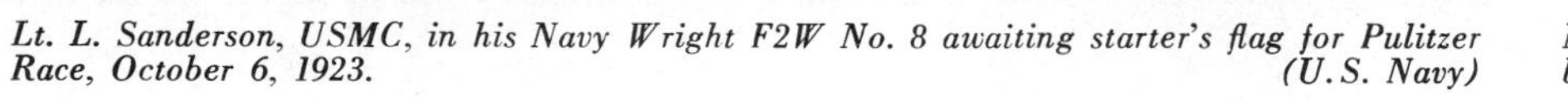

Navy Lt. S. W. Callaway taking off in his Navy Wright F2W No. 7 for a practice flight just before race day. *(U.S. Navy)*

Sharp, revealing view of the 1923 modified Verville-Sperry R-3 shows, over its tail, a Fokker XCO-4 and DH-4 aircraft in the background that flew in the then annual Liberty Engine Builders Trophy Race.   (U. S. Air Force Museum)

Just before race time the Verville-Sperry R-3 was fitted with wheel-well covers that had been made earlier. This view was taken just after the R-3 had dropped out of the Pulitzer. Note missing spinner nose cone.   (U. S. Navy)

Lt. Lawson H. M. (Sandy) Sanderson, USMC, left, poses with Lt. S. W. Calloway, USN, alongside Calloway's F2W just before race time. Note two-bladed propeller. Neither F2W wore transparent windshields but were fitted with half-conical windbreaks in front of cockpit. (U. S. Navy)

One of the Navy Wright F2W ships as it left the Wright factory for delivery to Navy where it would receive its red and white paint job, complete to insignia and race number. Large size of F2W is seen here as aircraft seems to dwarf its pilot. (U. S. Navy)

A moment later Lt. Corkill took off in the black Army Curtiss racer. He made a steep dive on the pylon from 3,000 feet, turning it so closely that there were doubts as to whether he went around it, but the judges ruled the race on.

Soon Lt. Sanderson was swinging wide around the home pylon to turn in 240.3 mph for his first and fastest lap, and then Corkill, a bit off course, flew by at a 210 mph clip. Corkill was troubled by loose glasses in his goggles, and the earth "seemed to quiver" until finally, on the third lap, he succeeded in readjusting them and picked up speed. His plane, fitted with a crash pad but with no windshield to protect him, flew at such speed that the wind stripped the top of his leather helmet off. Corkill whirled around the triangular course to average 216.5 mph for the race, not enough to overcome the steady pounding of his Marine opponent, who finished well ahead with an average speed of 230.1 mph.

Zooming over the finish line, Sanderson climbed to 2,000 feet like a rocket, his luck finally allowing him to finish a race. His luck gave out just then though, for in his gliding turn around the field his gas tank went dry, and he disappeared behind a railroad embankment in a fast glide. Seeing a soft haystack, Sandy headed for it. The crash came and when Sandy came to, his first thought was to get clear of the wreck before it burned. He felt quickly for his safety belt and then, brushing the straw from his eyes, found that he was far from his mangled ship but still strapped to his seat, and was wearing a new collar — the leather cockpit ring! Sandy had suffered only a sprained ankle and abrasions on his face and hands.

THE SECOND HEAT

Lt. Al Williams took off in his new blue R2C-1 Navy Curtiss racer, with an engine bark that was loud beyond belief and, after his climbing turn, dived past the starting line with a whine like that of a high explosive shell. The terrific roar of a D-12 engine, either in a climb, level flight, or dive, has never been equaled to this day.

Then Lt. Pearson took off, climbed, and dived across the starting line in his slate-colored Army R-3 Verville-Sperry. But the low–wing monoplane didn't get a chance to prove its worth, for hardly had Pearson reached the far end of the field when he was forced to turn back and land. The propeller spinner had come loose, unbalancing the prop and setting up a terrific vibration.

And now Williams was roaring over the timers' stand at 245.3 mph, a mark unprecedented in the annals of aviation.

THE THIRD HEAT

With Pearson out, the third and last heat was flagged off with Williams still in the air. Lt. S. Callaway, in the red Navy Wright racer, took off first, followed by Lt. H. J. Brow in the blue Navy Curtiss, a sister ship to Williams' racer, trailed by Lt. W. Miller in the black Army Curtiss racer, a twin ship to Corkill's racer.

Williams, meanwhile, had been flying his beautiful little Curtiss around the course with exact precision and finished the race with an average speed of 243.7 mph.

It then remained to be seen whether Williams' time could be beaten by the three pilots entered in the last heat. It was not, and Lt. Al Williams had set new speed records for the 100- and 200-km distances, and had bettered last year's winning speed by more than 37 mph.

Navy Lt. Brow finished second with 241.8 mph, and all six planes exceeded last year's record. America was leading the way for all future aircraft design!

In November, Lts. Williams and Brow engaged at Mitchel Field, N. Y., in dive starts from thousands of feet in the air, flying their Curtiss racers low over a 3-km course in competition for the world's speed record. This contest ended with the speed mark being raised by Lt. Williams to 266.6 mph on November 4, when the Secretary of War called a halt to their dramatic but extremely dangerous duel.

Lt. Calloway making his start in the Pulitzer race.

(U. S. Navy)

Wing load is in lbs. per sq. ft. throughout

JAMES GORDON BENNETT CUP 1909—1920

YEAR	COURSE and PLACE		PILOT	NATION	RACE NO.	AIRCRAFT	ENGINE (*w*) water-cooled	HP	SPAN	LENGTH	EMPTY	GROSS	WING LOAD	AV. SPEED	REMARKS
1909	2 laps—12.43 mi. Rheims, France	1	Glenn Curtiss	U.S.	8	Curtiss *Golden Flyer*	Curtiss V-8 (w)	50	26′3″	25′	470	690	3	47.65	*Pusher type. Level top 60 mph.*
		2	Louis Bleriot	France	22	Bleriot XI	E.N.V. V-8 (w)	60	31′2″	27′10″	510	720	4.5	46.83	*Tractor type.*
		3	Hubert Latham	France	13	Antoinette	Antoinette V-8 (w)	50	46′	40′	990	1200	3.03	42.5	*Tractor type.*
		4	Eugene Lefebvre	France	2	Wright	Wright 4 cyl. (w)	25	41′	32′6″	750	1100	2.05	35.7	*Level top speed 52 mph.*
			Cockburn	England		H. Earman	Gnome rotary 7 cyl.	35	32′6″	39′	975	1212	3		*Level top speed 37 mph.*
1910	20 laps—62.137 mi. Belmont Park, Long Island	1	Grahame-White	England		Bleriot XI bis	Gnome 14 cyl. 2 row	100	23′9″	26′6″	530	750	5.76	61	
		2	Moisant	U.S.		Bleriot XI	Gnome rotary 7 cyl.	50	28′2″	26′6″	510	720	4.5	31.5	
		3	Alec Ogilvie	England		Wright "C"	Wright 4 cyl. (w)	35	38′	29′9″	800	1150	2.63	29.4	*Landed for 54 min.*
		4	Hubert Latham	France		Antoinette	Antoinette V-16 (w)	100	49′3″	43′	1050	1350	3.33	17.8	*Landed for 4 hrs.*
			Leblanc	France		Bleriot	Gnome 14 cyl. 2 row	100	23′9″	26′6″	530	750	5.76		*Crashed 19th lap. 1 lap 71 mph.*
			Drexel	U.S.		Bleriot XI	Gnome rotary 7 cyl.	50	28′2″	26′6″	510	720	4.5		*Out 8th lap, engine trouble.*
			J. Radley	England		Bleriot XI bis	Gnome 14 cyl. 2 row	100	23′9″	26′6″	530	750	5.76		*Out 2nd lap, engine trouble.*
			Walter Brookins	U.S.		Baby Wright racer	Wright V-8 (w)	50	21′5″	24′	685	860	5.92		*Stalled on take-off, crashed.*
1911	25 laps—94 mi. Eastchurch, Eng.	1	Chas. Weymann	U.S.		Nieuport	Gnome 7 cyl.	100	27′6″	23′	700	925	5.3	78	
		2	A. Leblanc	France		Bleriot	Gnome 7 cyl.	100	16′6″	26′6″	750	948	6.2	75.83	
		3	M. Nieuport	France		Nieuport	Gnome 7 cyl.	70	27′6″	23′	700	890	4.9	75.07	
		4	Alec Ogilvie	England		Baby Wright	N.E.C. V-8 (w)	50	21′5″	24′	685	860	5.92	53.31	
			M. Chevalier	France	12	Nieuport	Nieuport 7 cyl.	28	27′6″	23′	520	740			*Out 12th lap. Av. 48 mph.*
			Hamel	England	4	Bleriot	Gnome rotary 7 cyl.	100	17′	26′6″	750	948	6.2		*Crashed on 1st turn.*
1912	30 laps—124.8 mi. Chicago, Ill.	1	Jules Vedrines	France		Deperdussin	All entries	160	19′6″	21′	710	1040	11.7	105.5	*Fastest laps 107 mph.*
		2	Prevost	France		Deperdussin	Gnome 14-cyl. 2 row	100	23′	20′6″	700	1030	10.3	103.8	
			Andre Frey	France		Hanriot	Air-cooled rotary	100							*Out 24th lap. Av. 94.3 mph.*
1913	20 laps—124.3 mi. Rheims, France	1	Prevost	France	1	Deperdussin		160	19′6″	20′	992	1411	10.24	124.5	*Fastest lap 127 mph.*
		2	Emile Vedrines	France	5	Ponnier	All entries	160	23′	17′	1006	1425	9.89	123	*Fastest lap 125.5 mph.*
		3	Gilbert	France	2	Deperdussin	Gnome 14-cyl. 2 row	160	21′10″	20′	1001	1421	10.1	119.5	
		4	Crombez	Belgium	17	Deperdussin	Air-cooled rotary	160	21′10″	20′	1001	1421	10.1	106.9	
1920	3 laps—186.4 mi. Etampes, France	1	Sadi-Lecointe	France	10	Nieuport	Hispano-Suiza V-8	320	19′6″	20′3″	1521	2060	15.6	168.5	*All engines in this race water-cooled.*
		2	Bernard de Romanet	France	8	Spad	Hispano-Suiza V-8	320	28′6″	21′9″	1950	2875	10.5	113.5	*Landed once. 1st lap 162 mph.*
			Kirch	France	11	Nieuport	Hispano-Suiza V-8	320	19′6″	20′3″	1521	2060	15.6		*Out 3rd lap. 1st lap 181.5 mph.*
			Raynham	England	4	Martinsyde *Semiquaver*	Hispano-Suiza V-8	320	20′2″	19′3″		2025	6.7		*Out 2nd lap. Broken oil pump.*
			Maj. R. W. Schroeder	U.S.	1	Verville-Packard	Packard V-12	638	28′2″	24′2″	2485	3233	14.12		*Out 1st lap. VCP-1.*
			Howard Rinehart	U.S.	2	Dayton-Wright	Hall-Scott 6 cyl.	250	21′	22′8″	1400	1850	18		*Top speed 200 mph. Out 1st lap.*
			Roland Rohlfs	U.S.	3	Curtiss *Texas Wildcat*	Curtiss C-12 V-12	435	26′	19′3″		2300	25.5		*Top speed 215 mph. Pre-race crash.*

YEAR	COURSE and PLACE		PILOT	NATION	RACE NO.	AIRCRAFT	ENGINE	HP	SPAN	LENGTH	EMPTY	GROSS	WING LOAD	AV. SPEED	REMARKS
1913	Monaco	1	Prevost	France	19	Deperdussin	Gnome 14 cyl. twin	160	44'3"		2095	2646	8.8	45.75	*Av. 60 mph—reflew marker.*
	28 laps—174 mi.		Weymann	U.S.	6	Nieuport	row, all entries	160	39 7"	28 7"	1323	1874	7.27		*Out 5th lap. Av. 68.8 mph.*
1914	Monaco	1	C. H. Pixton	England	3	Sopwith Tabloid	Gnome 9 cyl. rotary	100	24'7"		992	1433	5.7	86.75	
	28 Laps—174 mi.	2	Burri	Switzerland	7	F.B.A.	both entries	100			1323	1874	9.2	62	
1920	Venice, Italy	1	Lt. Luigi Bologna	Italy	7	Savoia S-12	Ansaldo V-12	500	36'5"			4784	20.62	107.2	*Only contestant—bad weather.*
	10 laps—222 mi.														
1921	Venice, Italy	1	Lt. Briganti	Italy		Macchi M-7	Isotta V-12	250	32'8"		1720	2382	9.4	117.859	*Only ship of 3 to finish.*
	10 laps—222 mi.		Lt. Zanetti	Italy		Macchi M-19	Fiat V-12	720	51'7"		5489	6150			*Forced out, fire. Did 141 mph.*
1922	Naples, Italy	1	Capt. H. C. Baird	England		Supermarine Sea Lion III	Napier Lion V-12	450	31'10"	27'6"	2381	3163	9	145.7	
	13 laps—230.3 mi.	2	Passaleva	Italy		Savoia S-51	Itala (Hispano) V-12	300	32'9"	26'1"	1716	2376	9.2	143.5	*Fastest entry—prop vibration.*
		3	Zanetti	Italy		Macchi M-17	Isotta V-12	250						133	
		4	Corniglio	Italy		Macchi M-7	Isotta V-12	250						90.6	
1923	Cowes, England	1	Lt. D. Rittenhouse	U.S.	4	Curtiss R-3 Navy	Curtiss D-12 V-12	465	22'8"	25'	2119	2747	16.35	177.38	*1 lap 188.17 mph, seaplane record.*
	5 laps—214 mi.	2	Lt. R. Irvine	U.S.	8	Curtiss R-3 Navy	Curtiss D-12 V-12	465	22'8"	25'	2119	2747	16.35	173.46	*Sister ship to winner.*
		3	Capt. H. C. Baird	England	7	Supermarine Sea Lion III	Napier Lion V-12	575	32'	27'6"	2403	3240	9.24	157.17	*Reworked 1922 Sea Lion II.*
			M. Hurel	France	10	CAMS 38	Hispano-Suiza V-12	360	28'2"	25'5"	1675	3200	10.2		*Out 2nd lap. 1st lap 130.4 mph.*
			Lt. Frank Wead	U.S.		Navy Wright NW-2	Wright T-3 V-12	700	28'	28'5"		4447	16.7		*Damaged floats—crashed in trial.*
1925	Baltimore, Md.	1	Lt. James Doolittle	U.S.	3	Army Curtiss R3C-2	Curtiss V-1400	619	22'	20'2"		2738	19.04	232.573	*Set 4 records. 3 km 245.713 mph.*
	7 laps—217.49 mi.	2	Capt. Hubert Broad	England	5	Gloster III	Napier Lion VII	700	20'		2028	2650	18	199.169	*Fastest lap 201.536 mph.*
		3	G. de Briganti	Italy	7	Macchi M-33	Curtiss D-12	435	32'	27'4"	2073	2777	17	168.444	*Fastest lap 173.858 mph.*
			Lt. George Cuddihy	U.S.	2	Navy Curtiss R3C-2	Curtiss V-1400	619	22'	20'2"		2738	19.04		*Out 7th lap.*
			Lt. Ralph Ofstie	U.S.	6	Navy Curtiss R3C-2	Curtiss V-1400	619	22'	20'2"		2738	19.04		*Out 7th lap.*
			Capt. H. C. Baird	England		Supermarine S-4	Napier Lion VII D	675	30'6"	27'	2425	3150	23.1		*Crashed in trials. 226.6 mph.*
1926	Hampton Roads, Va.	1	Maj. de Bernardi	Italy	5	Macchi M-39	Fiat A.S. II V-12	800	30'4"	22'1"	2760	3263	22.52	246.496	*1 lap 248.520 mph.*
	7 laps—217.49 mi.	2	Lt. Christian Schilt	U.S.	6	Curtiss R3C-2	Curtiss V-1400	619	22'	20'2"	2050	2738	19.04	231.363	*1 lap 233.164 mph. Same as 1925.*
		3	Lt. Bacula	Italy		Macchi M-39	Fiat A.S. II V-12	800	30'4"	22'1"	2760	3263	22.52	218.006	*Sister ship to winner.*
		4	Lt. T. Tomlinson	U.S.		Curtiss F6C-1 Navy	Curtiss D-12	435						136.953	
			Lt. Geo. Cuddihy	U.S.	4	Curtiss R3C-4 Navy	Curtiss V-1570	700	22'	20'					*Out 7th lap. 1 lap 242.16 mph.*
1927	Venice, Italy	1	Flt. Lt. S. N. Webster	England	6	Supermarine S-5	Napier Lion VII G	875	26'9"		2536	3197	27.85	281.65	*Record 319.5 mph Nov. 4, 1928.*
	7 laps—217.49 mi.	2	Flt. Lt. O. F. Worsley	England	4	Supermarine S-5	Napier Lion VII D	875	26'9"		2602	3043	26.62	273.07	
			Capt. Guazzetti	Italy	7	Macchi M-52	Fiat A.S. III V-12	1030	28'10"			3439.2	27.99		*Out 6th lap. Record 318.4 mph March, 1928.*
			Flt. Lt. S. M. Kinkead	England	1	Gloster IV B	Napier VII G	875	22'8"	26'4"	2415	3085	22.19		*Out 4th lap. 1 lap 277.14 mph.*
			Maj. de Bernardi	Italy	5	Macchi M-52	Fiat A.S. III V-12	1030	29'5"			3160	23.9		*Out 2nd lap.*

Year	Course and Place	#	Pilot	Country	No.	Aircraft	Engine	HP	Span	Length	Empty	Gross	Wing Load	Av. Speed	Remarks
1929	Cowes, England — 7 laps—217.49 mi.	1	Flt. Off. Waghorn	England	2	Supermarine S-6	Rolls-Royce R V-12	1920	30'	28'8"	4471	5250	36.2	328.63	Full wt. 5771 lbs. Wing load 39.8.
		2	Qtrmstr. T. Dal Molin	Italy		Macchi M-52R	Fiat A.S. III V-12	1030	25'9"			3263	29.69	284.20	1927 model. One lap 287.78.
		3	Flt. Lt. d'Arcy Greig	England		Supermarine S-5	Napier Lion VII G	875	26'9"		2536	3197	27.85	282.11	World record 1928.
			Flt. Off. R. Atcherly	England	4	Supermarine S-6	Rolls-Royce R V-12	1920	30'	28 8"	4471	5250	36.2		Cut pylon. Rec. 100 km 331.75, 50 km 332.49.
			Lt. Remo Cadringher	Italy	7	Macchi M-67	Isotta-Fraschini V-18	1400	29'6"			4740	32.8		Out 2nd lap. 1st lap 283.88.
			Monti	Italy	10	Macchi M-67	Isotta-Fraschini V-18	1400	29'6"			4740	32.8		Out 2nd lap. 1st lap 301.47.
1931	Lee on Solent, England — 7 laps—217.49 mi.	1	Lt. J. H. Boothman	England		Supermarine S-6B	Rolls-Royce Buzzard V-12	2350	30	28'10"	4590	6086	41.3	340.1	Record 406.997 mph Sept. 29, 1931, by Lt. Stainforth in a S-68. The engine developed more than 2600 hp.

PULITZER TROPHY RACE 1920—1925

Year	Course and Place	#	Pilot	Race No.	Aircraft	Engine Air-cooled (a)	HP	Span	Length	Empty	Gross	Wing Load	Av. Speed	Remarks	New
1920 4 laps—116.08 mi. Mitchel Field, Long Island		1	Capt. Corliss Mosely	63	Verville-Packard	Packard 1A-2025, V-12	638	28'2"	24'2"	2485	3233	14.12	156.5	186 mph. Normal top.	
		2	Harold E. Hartney		Thomas-Morse MB-3	Wright-Hispano V-8	300	26'	19'11"	1360	2037	8.1	148	171.25 mph. Normal top.	
		3	Bert Acosta		Italian SVA A-1	SPA 6 cyl. in-line	220	25'	21'8"	1470	1965	8.7	134.5	147 mph. Normal top. Balilla.	
		4	Lt. St. Clair Streett		Orenco "D"	Wright-Hispano V-8	300	30'	21'6"	1666	2432	9.3	133	147 mph. Normal top.	
		5	Lt. A. Laverents		Vought VE-7	Wright-Hispano V-8	180	34'1"	24'5"	1560	2100	7.35	125		
		6	Lt. John Roullot	16	De Havilland DH-4	Liberty V-12	400	42'6"	21'11"	2390	3600	8.2	124	DH-4's placed 6th to 12th.	
		13	Willis Taylor		Italian SVA 9	SPA 6 cyl. in-line	220	22'11"	19'8"	1600	2144	8.5	117		
		14	Capt. Maxwell Kirby		SE-5A	Wright-Hispano V-8	180	26'9"	20'10"	1570	2060	8.7	116.7	DH-4's and VE-7's placed 15th to 24th.	
		25	Charles Colt		Morane-Saulnier	LeRhone rotary (a)	110	28'7"	18'8"		1155		95	Pursuit trainer.	
			Lt. B. G. Bradley, USMC	46	Loening Special	Wright-Hispano V-8	300	30'5"	24'2"	1450	1850	12.5	150	Out last lap.	
1921 5 laps—155.35 mi. Omaha, Nebraska		1	Bert Acosta		Navy Curtiss R-1	Curtiss CD-12	405	22'8"	21'	1735	2165	12.5	176.7	Straight top 200 mph.	New
		2	Clarence Coombs	3	Curtiss-Cox	Curtiss C-12	435	20'	19'3"	1936	2406	13.75	170.26	1920 Cactus Kitten fuselage.	
		3	J. A. Macready		Thomas-Morse MB-6	Wright V-8	400	19'	18'6"	1512	2023	12.3	160.71	Army R-2 racer.	
		4	Lloyd Bertaud		Ansaldo Balilla	Curtiss K-12, V-12	400	26'	22'6"	1823	2367	10.5	149.78	1920 reworked New eng., 4 blade prop.	
			Harold E. Hartney		Thomas-Morse MB-7	Wright V-8	400	24'	18'6"	1502	1975	17.6		Crashed 1st lap. Straight top 179 mph.	
			James Curran		Italia SVA-9	SPA 6 cyl. in-line	220	22'11"	19'8"	1600	2144	8.5		Out 3rd lap. Engine trouble.	
1922 5 laps—155.35 mi. Detroit, Michigan		1	Lt. R. Maughan	43	Army Curtiss R-6	Curtiss CD-12	460	19'	18'11"	1454	1950	14.1	205.8	Best lap 207 mph.	New
		2	Lt. L. J. Maitland	42	Army Curtiss R-6	Curtiss CD-12	460	19'	18'11"	1454	1950	14.1	198.8	Best lap 203 mph.	New
		3	Lt. H. J. Brow	40	Navy Curtiss R-2	Curtiss CD-12	405	22'8"	21'	1735	2165	12.5	193.2	Best lap 196 mph. Built 1921.	
		4	Lt. Alford Williams	8	Navy Curtiss R-1	Curtiss CD-12	405	22'8"	21'	1735	2165	12.5	188	Best lap 190 mph. Winner 1921.	
		5	Lt. E. H. Barksdale	49	Verville-Sperry R-3	Wright H-3, V-8	380	32'4"	22'5"	1795	2225	14.83	181	Normal top 191 mph. Low-mono.	New
		6	Capt. Corliss Mosely	42	Verville-Packard R-1	Packard 1A-2025, V-12	638	27'6"	24'7"	2763	3511	15.04	179	Reworked 1920 winner.	
		7	Lt. F. B. Johnson	48	Verville-Sperry R-3	Wright H-3, V-8	380	32'4"	22'5"	1795	2225	14.83	178		New
		8	Lt. E. C. Whitehead	45	Loening R-4	Packard 1A-2025, V-12	600	27'	21'	2102	2700	15.5	170.2	Condemned after race. Wing flutter.	
		9	Lt. L. D. Schulz	46	Loening R-4	Packard 1A-2025, V-12	600	27'	21'	2102	2700	15.5	160.9	Condemned after race. Low-mono.	

YEAR	COURSE and PLACE		PILOT	RACE NO.	AIRCRAFT	ENGINE Air-cooled (a)	HP	SPAN	LENGTH	EMPTY	GROSS	WING LOAD	AV. SPEED	REMARKS	
		1	Lt. Alford Williams	9	Navy Curtiss R2C-1	Curtiss D-12 Spl., V-12	500	22'	19'8"	1565	2071	14	243.67	*Best lap 245.27 mph.*	*New*
1923	4 laps—124.28 mi.	2	Lt. H. J. Brow	10	Navy Curtiss R2C-1	Curtiss D-12 Spl., V-12	500	22'	19'8"	1565	2071	14	241.78	*Sister ship to winner.*	*New*
	St. Louis, Missouri	3	Lt. L. H. Sanderson, USMC	8	Navy Wright F2W	Wright T-3, V-12	700	22'6"	21'4"	2420	3000	17.2	230.06	*Top 240.3 mph.*	*New*
		4	Lt. S. W. Callaway	7	Navy Wright F2W	Wright T-3, V-12	700	22'6"	21'4"	2420	3000	17.2	230		*New*
		5	Lt. W. Miller	49	Army Curtiss R-6	Curtiss D-12 Spl., V-12	500	19'	18'11"	1465	1961	14.2	218.91	*Winner 1922. New engine.*	
		6	Lt. J. D. Corkill	50	Army Curtiss R-6	Curtiss D-12, V-12	460	19'	18'11"	1454	1950	14.1	216.45	*Took 2nd 1922.*	
			Lt. A. Pearson	48	Verville-Sperry R-3	Curtiss D-12 Spl., V-12	500	30'6"	23'5"	1950	2475	16.9		*Out 1st lap. Spinner loose.*	*1922*
1924	4 laps—124.28 mi.	1	Lt. H. H. Mills	70	Verville-Sperry R-3	Curtiss D-12 Spl., V-12	500	30'6"	23'5"	1955	2475	16.9	215.72	*Raced 1922-23.*	
	Dayton, Ohio	2	Lt. W. H. Brookley	69	Army Curtiss R-6	Curtiss D-12 Spl., V-12	500	19'	18'11"	1465	1961	14.2	214.75	*Winner 1922.*	
		3	Lt. Rex Stoner		Curtiss Hawk PW-8A	Curtiss D-12, V-12	460	30'	22'2"	1986	2819	11.05	167.95		
			Capt. Burt Skeel		Army Curtiss R-6	Curtiss D-12 Spl., V-12	500	19'	18'11"	1465	1961	14.2		*Crash dived. Ship placed 2nd 1922.*	
1925	4 laps—124.28 mi.	1	Lt. Cyrus Bettis	43	Army Curtiss R3C-1	Curtiss V-1400, V-12	619	21'9"	19'10"	1792	2182	15.1	248.975	*New joint Army-Navy design.*	
	Mitchel Field,	2	Lt. Alford Williams		Navy Curtiss R3C-1	Curtiss V-1400, V-12	619	21'9"	19'10"	1792	2182	15.1	241.695	*New joint Army-Navy design.*	
	Long Island	3	Lt. Dawson		Curtiss Hawk P-1	Curtiss V-1150-1, V-12	435	31'6"	22'6"	2041	2841	11.36	169.9	*New production pursuit. Taperwing.*	
	(*Last Pulitzer Race*)	4	Lt. Norton	50	Curtiss Hawk PW-8	Curtiss D-12, V-12	460	32'	22'10"	1865	2761	10.4	168.8	*Production pursuit.*	
		5	Capt. Cook		Curtiss Hawk PW-8	Curtiss D-12, V-12	460	32'	22'10"	1865	2761	10.4	167.4		
			Lt. C. T. Cuddihy		Curtiss Hawk PW-8	Curtiss D-12, V-12	460	32'	22'10"	1865	2761	10.4		*Out 4th lap, engine.*	

Index

RACING PLANES
and air races

A Complete History

by REED KINERT

VOLUME II
REFERENCE
SERIES No. 1

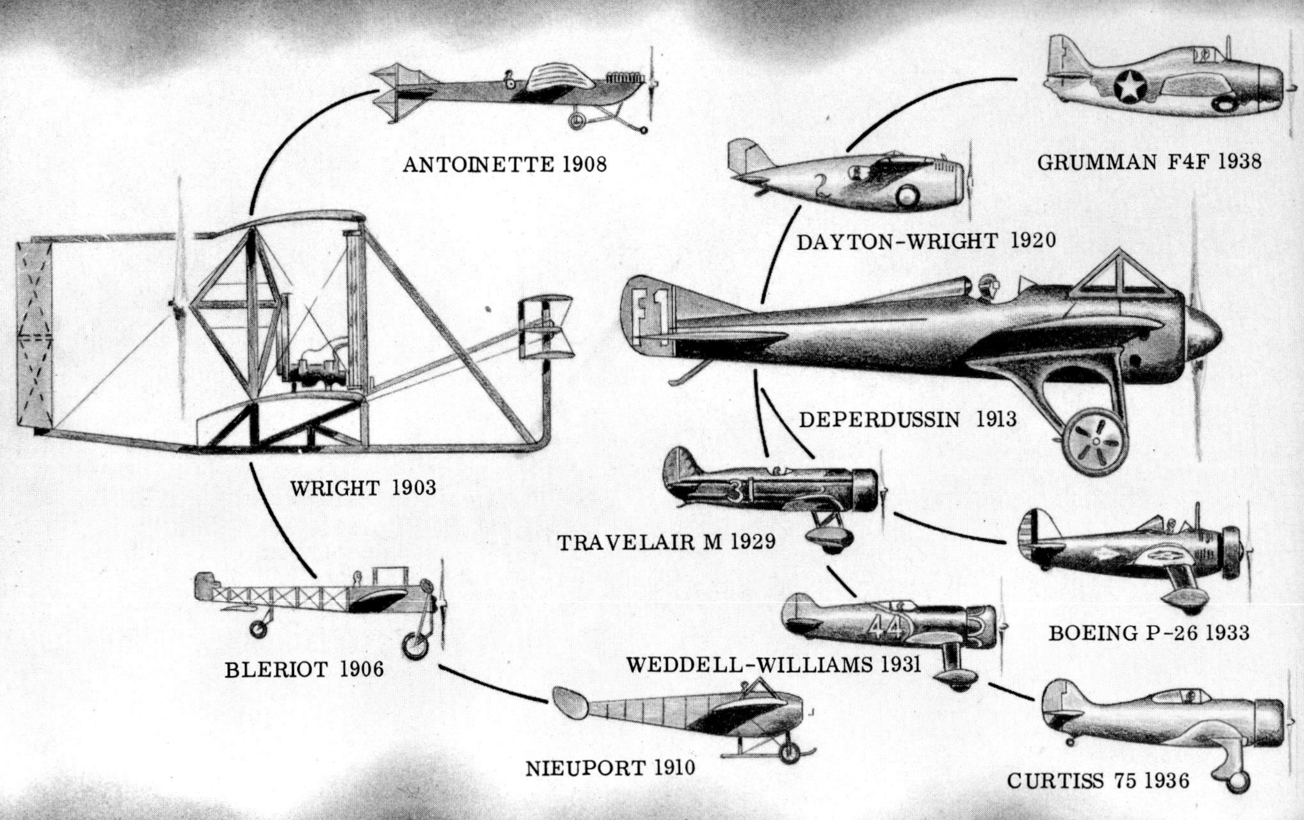

Written and Illustrated by Reed Kinert

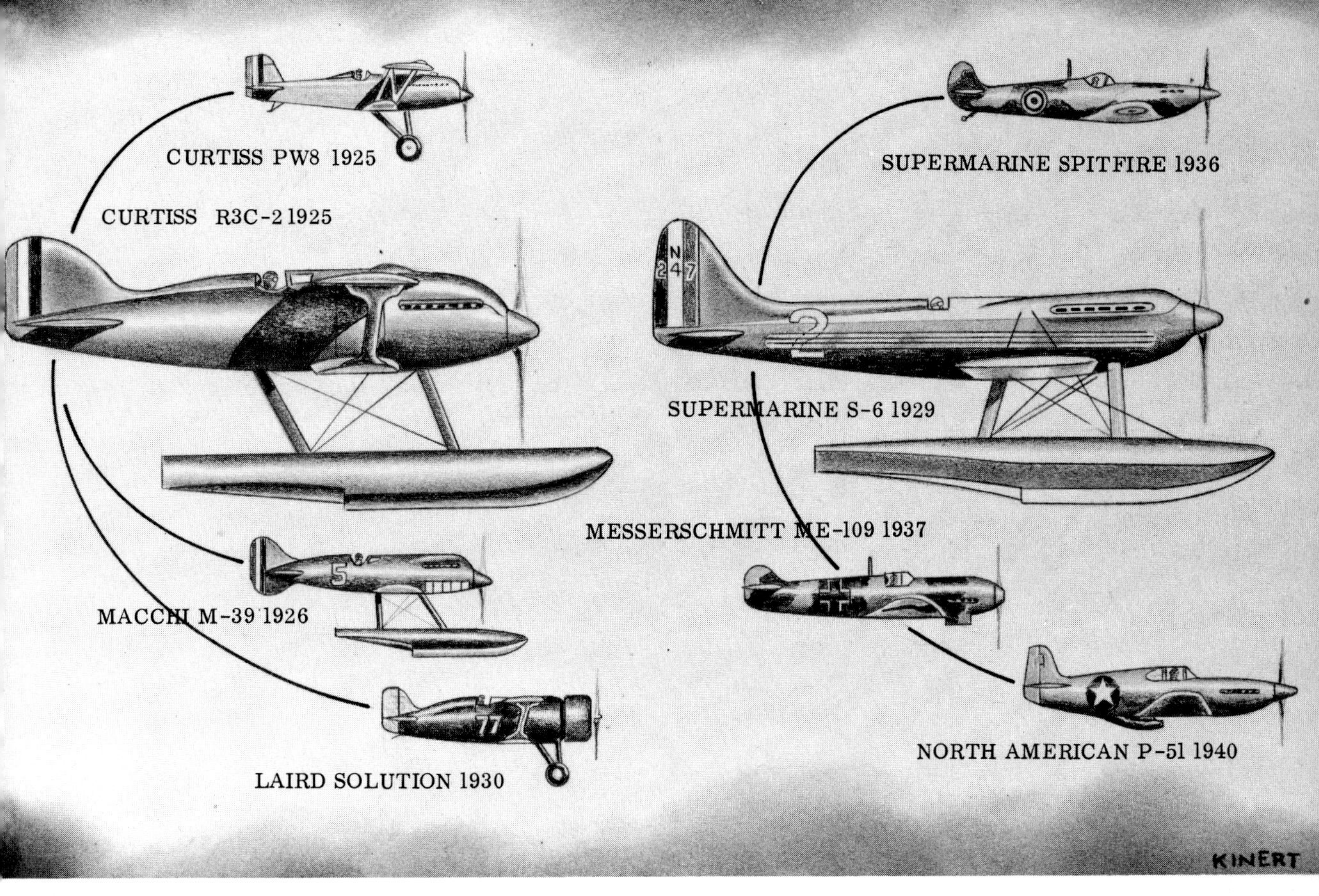

RACING PLANES

and air races

A Complete History

VOLUME II
1924-1931

AERO PUBLISHERS, INC.

Fallbrook, California

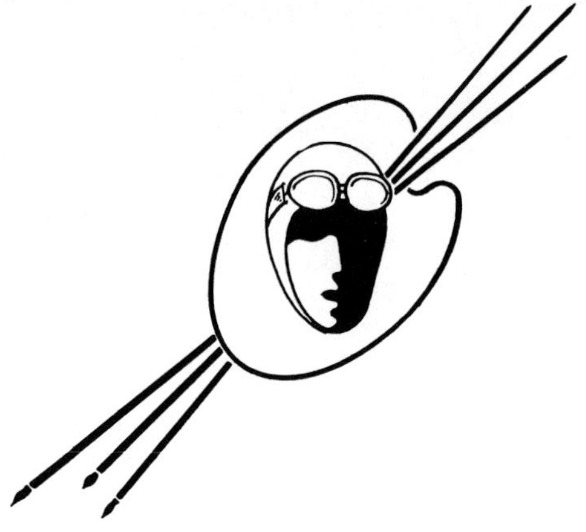

DEDICATION

To the designers, builders, and pilots of racing air-craft, for their contribution to the science of flight.

FIRST EDITION

SECOND PRINTING - REVISED - 1969

LIBRARY OF CONGRESS CATALOG CARD NUMBER

67-16455

ALL RIGHTS RESERVED

COPYRIGHT© 1967 AERO PUBLISHERS, INC.

Table of Contents

List of Illustrations

List of Three-Views

The fourth annual National Air Races were held at Dayton, Ohio, October 2, 3, and 4. For the first time there were more civilian planes entered than military, 63 as against 32. There were six civilian races and four military races, but the military planes dominated the speed events.

The third annual John L. Mitchell Trophy Race was by far the most exciting to watch, as all 11 entries, new Curtiss PW-8 pursuits, were strictly service types and evenly matched. Regarded as the world's finest fighting plane, the Curtiss PW-8 (see illustration, page 10) was evolved directly from the Curtiss racers and fitted with a race-developed Curtiss D-12 460-hp engine.

MITCHELL RACE

The Mitchell race distance was 124.28 miles and consisted of four laps, the same course and distance as the Pulitzer. Unusually good speed was made because of the diving start allowed. It was the first race of the three days in which the pilots circled for altitude and then dived to the starting line, right in front of the grandstands.

Down they came at steep angles, all 11 planes in evenly spaced intervals, the air shrieking around their streamlined wires, and their roaring D-12 engines an inferno of noise. It was an awe-inspiring sight.

Lt. Cyrus Bettis was in first place and stayed there throughout, to win with an average of 175.5 mph. Close behind during the entire race were Lts. Don Stace and Tom Matthews, who contested throughout the race for second place, which was barely taken by Stace at 173.7 mph, only .4 mph ahead of Matthews. Lt. Reuben Moffat was last at 164.2 mph.

PULITZER RACE

For the first time the Pulitzer race, with no new planes entered, failed to dominate the race meet. Only four planes, all Army, lined up for the starter's flag; the two Curtiss R-6 racers which finished first and second in the 1922 Pulitzer; the Verville-Sperry racer which had dropped out of last year's race, now fitted with wheel-well fairing; and a new Curtiss PW-8A pursuit plane, identical to the PW-8 except that it

had a tunnel radiator slung under the engine instead of wing radiators, and had single interplane struts. The Army had borrowed one of the Navy's faster R2C-1 Curtiss racers for the Pulitzer, but crashed it before the race. The Navy was busily preparing for the Schneider Trophy Race (later cancelled for lack of foreign entries) so did not enter this Pulitzer.

The four ships took off from Wright Field in the above order, climbing high to dive into the course, and as usual, the pilots wore no parachutes. Then tragedy struck. The first Curtiss racer, piloted by Capt. Burt Skeel, was just nearing the starting line in a steep dive when suddenly it seemed to disintegrate, and the fuselage dived vertically into the ground, embedding its pilot in ten feet of muck beside a creek. The cause of the accident was never determined, but it was felt that the high engine speed had been too much for the wood prop (which the Air Service had decreed be used on all four planes), and losing a tip, the prop had set up a terrific vibration, tearing the engine and ship apart.

Undaunted by the crash of their teammate, the three remaining pilots dived on and flew in the race, watched by thousands of anxious eyes, for it was known that two of the racers were three years old, that they had been flown and stunted often, and that they had been built for one race, not for indefinite racing.

Lt. H. H. Mills flew his Verville-Sperry (500-hp D-12) to victory at a speed of but 215.7 mph, and Lt. Brookley, in the other Curtiss R-6, was a close second at 214.8 mph, which was about 10 mph faster than the same ship made in winning the 1922 Pulitzer. Lt. Rex Stoner was third in the PW-8A averaging 168 mph.

If metal propellers had been used the speeds would have been greater this day but still would have fallen a bit short of last year's. Capt. Skeel's accident caused the Army to decree metal props for all but their trainers, parachutes were compulsory hereafter in all aircraft, and of course, dive starts, which contributed nothing to race plane development, were banned forever.

◆　◆　◆

Capt. Skeel's old (1922) Curtiss racer disintegrated as he neared the starting line. Undaunted, the other pilots dived on. Leading is the twin ship to Skeel's, followed by the 1924 Pulitzer winning Verville-Sperry low-wing, piloted by Lt. H. H. Mills at an average 215.7 mph, and the Curtiss PW-8A.

Although the Verville-Sperry R-3 won the 1924 Pulitzer over a Curtiss biplane racer (which was fitted with an equal 500 hp engine), the U. S. Army Air Corps would not consider purchase of monoplanes in quantity for pursuit duties, claiming superior climb and maneuverability of the biplane made it more desirable. (Warren M. Bodie)

This Verville-Sperry R-3 showed up for its third Pulitzer race in a row and won the event. The ship was cleaned up a bit more than during its 1923 appearance, sported a white paint job which set off its brass wing radiators in contrast. Nicely proportioned, the R-3 was full cantilever in construction except for a brace strut on the undersides of its stabilizer. (Air Force Museum)

The Curtiss R-6 (P-278, 68564), which Air Corps Lt. W. H. Brookley flew to 2nd place in the 1924 Pulitzer. This craft, which won the 1922 Pulitzer, is seen before race minus propeller spinner and fabric wheel covers.
(Dustin W. Carter)

Lt. Harry H. Mills with his 1924 Pulitzer winning R-3. Note clean leading edge of the wing radiators which contrast quite distinctly with the radiators used on the same ship in 1922. Blur in air above cockpit is a diving aircraft.
(U. S. Air Force)

Curtiss R-6 (P-279, 68563), in which Capt. Burt Skeel died. Both R-6 aircraft were flown by every Corps pilot who could wrangle a hop, and had been used and abused for two years before this year's race.
(Warren M. Bodie)

Eleven shiny new Curtiss PW-8 Hawks of the 1st Pursuit Group, Selfridge Field, lined up for start of the 1924 John L. Mitchell Race. The Hawks were painted standard olive drab overall, except for brass wing radiators and markings.
(Warren M. Bodie)

Navy Curtiss R2C A-6691 (1923 race No. 10) was acquired by the Air Corps for $1.00 transfer fee, redesignated R-8 and was groomed for the 1924 Pulitzer. On September 2, 1924, Lt. Alex Pearson, while flattening out from a dive onto a 3 km course near Wright Field, had the wings collapse at 300 ft. The I interplane struts had been lightened by removal of inner wood laminates and one of these struts had failed. Pearson was killed. (Warren M. Bodie)

JAMES HAROLD DOOLITTLE

Jimmy Doolittle, after winning the 1925 Schneider Trophy at Baltimore.

JIMMY DOOLITTLE *was born in Alameda, Calif., Dec. 14, 1896. He lived in Alaska as a child, returning to California to attend and graduate from Manual Arts High School, Los Angeles. He then attended the University of California's College of Mining, completing three years' work.*

Small of stature, Jimmy learned early in life to take care of himself with his fists, and during college won the Bantamweight championship of the Pacific coast.

Jimmy entered the School of Military Aeronautics, Berkeley, in November of 1917, and was sent to Rockwell Field, San Diego, for flight training. His unusual ability and patience were soon discovered, and Jimmy was ordered to Dallas, where he taught cadets until early 1919, although constantly requesting combat duty. His modest, quiet, unassuming personality endeared him to everyone.

Flying a specially reworked Army DH biplane, Doolittle took off from Pablo Beach, Fla., early Sept. 4, 1922, and landed 35 minutes for fuel, oil, and water at San Antonio, Texas. He then flew on to land at Rockwell Field, San Diego, September 5, setting a coast-to-coast record of 22 hours and 34 minutes elapsed time and averaging 101 mph. It was the first time the United States had been spanned in less than a day and a night. This flight set off a chain of events that was to establish Jimmy as the Army's finest pilot for all time.

After winning the 1925 Schneider Trophy Race for seaplanes, Jimmy was loaned to the Curtiss factory and went to Chile to demonstrate a Hawk pursuit. Performing the night before his scheduled air show, Jimmy fell from a second story balcony railing while doing a handstand and broke both ankles. Though wearing plaster casts, he took off the next day, flew a competing German pilot out of the sky, and took a big order for pursuit ships. Later he flew his Hawk over the Andes mountains, history's first such flight, although his feet were still trussed up.

On May 25, 1927, in furtherance of his Army flight research work, Jimmy performed history's first outside loop. Then, on Sept. 24, 1929, he completed the first blind take-off and landing.

In 1930 Jimmy resigned from the Army Air Corps to become manager of the Aviation Department, Shell Petroleum Corporation. He remained with Shell until 1940. Promotions in the Air Services through the 20's and 30's caused many good pilots to go into civilian flying. Jimmy Doolittle and Al Williams (USN) were only lieutenants after 13 years of service, though they were the nation's top pilots.

While flying for Shell, Jimmy won the Bendix Trophy in 1931 and the Thompson Trophy in 1932. In qualifying for the 1932 Thompson, Jimmy flew his Gee Bee to a new landplane speed record of 296.3 mph and, characteristically, left at least 5 mph in the Gee-Bee so its owner, Russell Boardman, recovering from a crash, could later try for a 300+ mph record.

Jimmy was appointed major in the Army Air Corps July, 1940. He was promoted to brigadier general in 1942, then to major general later the same year, and to lieutenant general in 1944. He commanded the Twelfth Air Force in North Africa, the Northwest Africa Strategic Air Force, and then the Fifteenth and Eighth Air Forces. He returned to the Shell Oil Corporation in 1946 as a vice-president, and is with them today.

The highlight of Jimmy's World War II career was, of course, his historic bombing attack on Japan, April 18, 1942. Leading 16 B-25 medium bombers from the deck of the U.S.S. HORNET aircraft carrier, Jimmy and his squadron made pin-point bomb drops on vital targets in Tokyo and other Japanese cities.

1925—Pulitzer Trophy Race

The National Air Races were held at Mitchel Field, Long Island, N. Y., beginning on Thursday, October 8, and ending on October 13, two extra days being necessary because of unfavorable weather. There were six civilian and four military events — 122 civilian and 41 military planes entered — but again the main attractions were the Mitchell and Pulitzer Trophy races held on the last day.

Notable features of the race meet were the splendid formation flying of the Army DH's and pursuit planes and the wonderful stunt flying of Lt. James H. Doolittle, who flew his new Curtiss P-1 through the acrobatic book in an amazing exhibition of upside down flight, slow roll variations, loops, snaps, etc.

MITCHELL RACE

The Mitchell race was again the tightest of all, being limited to ten identical Curtiss PW-8 pursuit planes, which took off at 10-sec. intervals. Lt. T. K. Matthews moved from fifth to first place, finishing with an average of 161.5 mph. Lt. Schulgen flew from last place up to second with an average of 158.7 mph, and Lt. Lyon finished third. The speed this year was slower by nearly 4 mph because the racecourse was only 12 miles around as compared to last year's 31.07 miles, and dive starts were forbidden.

PULITZER RACE

With the finish of the Mitchell race, the crowd, which had grown steadily in size, waited expectantly for the Pulitzer race, the great event of the whole meet. The atmosphere was clearing, and the clouds, which during the earlier part of the day hung like a solid blanket over the sky, began to break up. This was fortunate indeed for the haze would have been a great obstacle in piloting the high-speed planes four times around the 31.07-mile course, a total of 124.28 miles.

For this race, the Army and Navy each ordered a new Curtiss racer (R3C-1) from the factory, and these two planes were built as nearly alike as was possible, embodying improvements over previous Curtiss racers. They were powered by a new Curtiss V-12 engine of 619 hp, but retained the appearance of the sleek Navy Curtiss racers of 1923.

In addition to the new Curtiss racers there were two Curtiss PW-8 planes piloted by Lts. Cuddihy and Norton of the Navy, a Curtiss PW-8 piloted by Capt. Cook, and a Curtiss P-1 piloted by Lt. Dawson of the Army, thus making it an all Curtiss race. The P-1 was a new production pursuit, retaining the PW-8 fuselage but fitted with tapered wings. All four were powered by D-12 engines.

With possible trouble resulting from the continual overtaking of the slower planes by the Curtiss racers, it was decided to send the two faster planes off first, and then send the four slower planes off in a second heat.

Shortly after 3 P.M. Lt. Al Williams took off smoothly in the Navy Curtiss racer and flew around the field to bring his engine temperatures up. Two minutes later Lt. Cyrus Bettis took off in the Army Curtiss. Pilots were forbidden diving starts over the starting line after last year's disaster, so Williams approached the field from a far corner to cut down his pylon-turn angle and, flying at full throttle, passed the timers' stand and on around the home pylon. Bettis did not follow for some few minutes later, so the race lost all recognition as such and resolved itself into a speed trial. With both pilots flying a smooth groove course at 300 feet, it was noticed that Bettis was beating his own speed at each lap, while Williams' laps were getting slower. At the end of the 4-lap race, Bettis had closed up toward Williams and had reached an average of 249 mph, while Williams made 241.7 mph.

Then the four pursuits were flagged off to compete for third place in the race. This was far more of a race, since the planes took off in close succession and chased each other during the entire contest.

As the planes went into their third lap, Dawson, in the faster P-1, was leading, with Navy pilots Norton and Cuddihy following closely, and Cook coming up fourth. The PW-8's flown by Norton and Cook were flown in the earlier Mitchell race, but they were making better speeds due mostly to the different course lengths. Cuddihy was forced to land with engine trouble, and the heat ended with Lt. Dawson finishing first in his Curtiss P-1 at 169.9 mph, Lt. Norton a close second at 168.8 mph (placing third and fourth in the Pulitzer), and Capt. Cook coming in a few seconds later.

Although the Curtiss R3C-1 racers were faster than any previous Pulitzer winners, their speed in the race was somewhat disappointing; but one must remember that dive starts were banned, and too, the windy weather plus one very sharp pylon turn did much to keep all the contestant's speeds down.

And thus ended the second great era of air racing, for although Army pilot Bettis, in the world's fastest aircraft, had set a new world's record for a closed course, the United States decreed that no money be spent on future racing craft.

◆   ◆   ◆

Lt. Cy Bettis in the Army's new Curtiss R3C-1 racer leads
Lt. Al Williams in the Navy R3C-1 over the airport in a low
turn after winning the 1925 Pulitzer Trophy with an average
speed of 248 mph. On the ground warming up for the second
heat is the Army PW-8 in which Army Lt. Matthews had
earlier won the Mitchell Trophy and which was flown to
fourth place in the Pulitzer by Navy Lt. Norton.

Lt. Alford Williams' R3C which finished second in 1925 Pulitzer despite a faltering engine that decreased in rpm throughout the race. Ship was painted light blue with chrome yellow wings, radiators were natural brass. U. S. Navy Bureau of Aeronautics Seal is prominent below cockpit.
(Warren M. Bodie)

Lt. Bettis warming up his R3C just prior to race start. The roar of Curtiss V-12 engines at high rpm, combined with propeller tip slap, filled the air for miles around with a crescendo of sound that was unbelievably loud.
(U. S. Air Force)

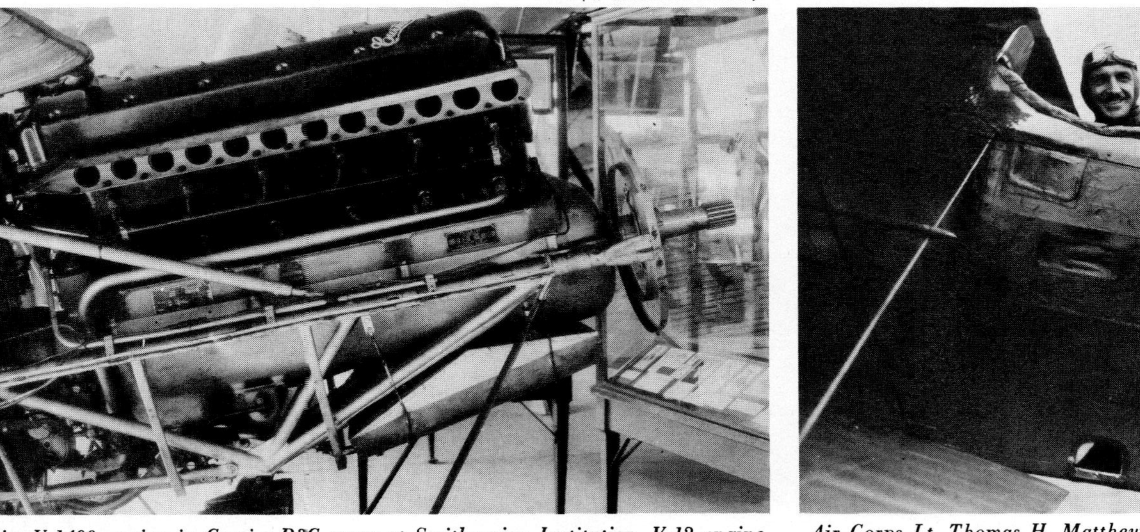

View of Curtiss V-1400 engine in Curtiss R3C racer at Smithsonian Institution. V-12 engine delivered 619 hp at 2450 rpm and was unique in that it had four valves per cylinder, two intake, two exhaust. Note oil tank under front of engine.
(Warren M. Bodie)

Air Corps Lt. Thomas H. Matthews, winner of the 1925 John L. Mitchell Trophy race. Note "ringworm" effect in dope paint on fuselage side. A rejuvenating paint was later developed that restored smoothness to finish. Windshield was plate glass.
(U. S. Air Force)

Air Corps Lt. Cyrus Bettis and his new Curtiss racer in which he won the 1925 Pulitzer Trophy and set a world's closed course record of 248.975 mph. The three R3C aircraft of 1925, one Army and two Navy, were the last and largest of the Curtiss racers to be built, were also the most powerful. Note single strut landing gear and wire bracing fore and aft of struts.
(Warren M. Bodie)

This view of Bettis' ship clearly shows wing radiators and water expansion tank atop fuselage which was utilized as fairing for the windshield. Two weeks after winning the 1925 Pulitzer race this same ship, fitted with pontoons won the Schneider Trophy race. Craft now reposes in the Smithsonian Institution, the only Curtiss racer to survive. Fuselage and tail surfaces are black, wings chrome yellow, the brass radiators natural. Rudder was the usual red, white and blue stripe, the blue being forward.
(Curtiss-Wright)

1925 – Schneider Trophy Race

One of the most interesting races ever held in the United States was the contest for the Schneider Trophy held at Bay Shore Park, Md., near Baltimore, on Monday, Oct. 26, 1925. There was no contest in 1924 due to a lack of foreign entries.

The U. S. Navy team's 1923 victory had acted as a stimulus for the English and Italian Air Ministries, and so by Saturday morning, October 24, two Italian, one British, and three United States planes had qualified for the race to be held that afternoon. The race, however, had to be postponed for two days. Winds and rains swept into Chesapeake Bay and wrecked 17 visiting Martin-TS Navy seaplanes.

THE TRIALS

Qualifying tests were the same as the 1923 Schneider trials. In a trial flight England's fastest entry, a graceful blue and white midwing Supermarine Napier S-4 monoplane, was stalled out by its pilot at high speed and fell a hundred feet into the bay. The pilot was uninjured, but the plane, though intact, was rendered useless by salt water.

Bert Hinkler of England, flying a new Gloster-Napier III biplane, broke a landing wire in the trials and tried again Monday morning just before the race. He failed to qualify. Rough water bent a float strut causing the entire undercarriage to collapse.

England's newly formed high-speed research program called for both monoplane and biplane seaplanes in an effort to explore both types to their fullest. Italy concentrated on monoplanes, while the United States, denied additional funds, used her new biplanes.

The U. S. Army entered the new Curtiss R3C-1 racer, with which Lt. Cyrus Bettis had won the Pulitzer earlier in the month. Converted to a twin-float seaplane, it was to be flown by Lt. Jimmy Doolittle. The U. S. Navy entered the new Curtiss R3C-1 that Lt. Al Williams had flown to second place in the Pulitzer and a third new R3C-1 racer that had been built for the Pulitzer but not flown in that race. Thus all three U. S. entries, now designated R3C-2 with pontoons, were alike, having been built from the same plans, and Curtiss engines of 619 hp powered all three. The Navy entries were to be flown by Lts. George Cuddihy and Ralph Ofstie.

The remaining British entry, another new Gloster-Napier III, was similar to the Curtiss Schneider racers of 1923 but not nearly as clean. There were many external fittings and control horns showing themselves to the airstream. The tail surfaces were externally braced with wires, two of which were not streamlined. Lamblin external water radiators were fitted on the lower wings on both sides, and an exposed oil radiator hung under the engine. Though very efficient, they were not as clean as the Curtiss wing radiators. The duralumin pontoons on the Gloster were very clean and simple in comparison to the wooden floats on the Curtiss planes. The Gloster was powered by a Napier Lion 12-cyl. W-type 700-hp engine and was to be flown by Capt. Hubert Broad.

The Italian Macchi flying boat, designed by Mario Castoldi, was the most original plane in the race. The Macchi was clean in details, except for its exposed engine radiators. It was much heavier than the other entries and was powered by an older Curtiss D-12 engine of only 435 hp, and the propeller was wood.

By 10 A.M. on race day, all remaining contestants were testing their engines and getting their planes ready for the afternoon race. No difficulty was experienced by the three American entries, nor by Capt. Broad with his Gloster-Napier III, but when the engines of the two identical Macchi planes were started, one was not functioning properly. The rules required that all engines be sealed after navigability trials, and as the plane would have been disqualified had the engine been adjusted, the Italian team gave their full attention to the remaining Macchi.

The five remaining planes were put in the water about 2 P.M. and prepared to start.

The conditions of the course had by this time become nearly perfect, the water choppy but not rough, the wind from the right direction, and the morning haze had burned off. The course was triangular, 31.07 miles around, and seven laps were required for a total of 217.5 miles.

THE RACE

Promptly at 2:30 P.M. Lt. Doolittle left the hangars and taxied to the starting line. As he reached the rougher water, spray was thrown up on all sides and it appeared that he was going to have trouble, but he opened his engine wide and made a perfect

Busy scene with Macchi 33, race No. 7, discloses, in background, an ever faithful Curtiss F6C-1 Hawk fitted with twin floats that American pilots used to acquaint themselves with the racecourse and, further back, is the Curtiss R3C-2 flown by Ralph Ofstie in the 1925 Schneider. This latter ship is not to be confused with the R2C-2 that had crashed in September, 1925, although it wears the same race number. The R2C-2 was totaled in the crash. (Mario Castoldi)

Direct front view of Macchi M-33 has been much reproduced but is, as it serenely rests on placid waters of Lake Verese in Italy, a study in hydro-aerodynamic simplicity. This design concept was never fully exploited although it had much merit. M-33 craft were constructed of wood and plywood covered. The wing was full cantilever while the tail surfaces employed a single continuous brace wire. (Macchi)

CURTISS R3C-2 ARMY RACER
1925
0 1 2 3 4 5 6
SCALE
U.S. ARMY
3
U.S. ARMY
43
D.W. CARTER

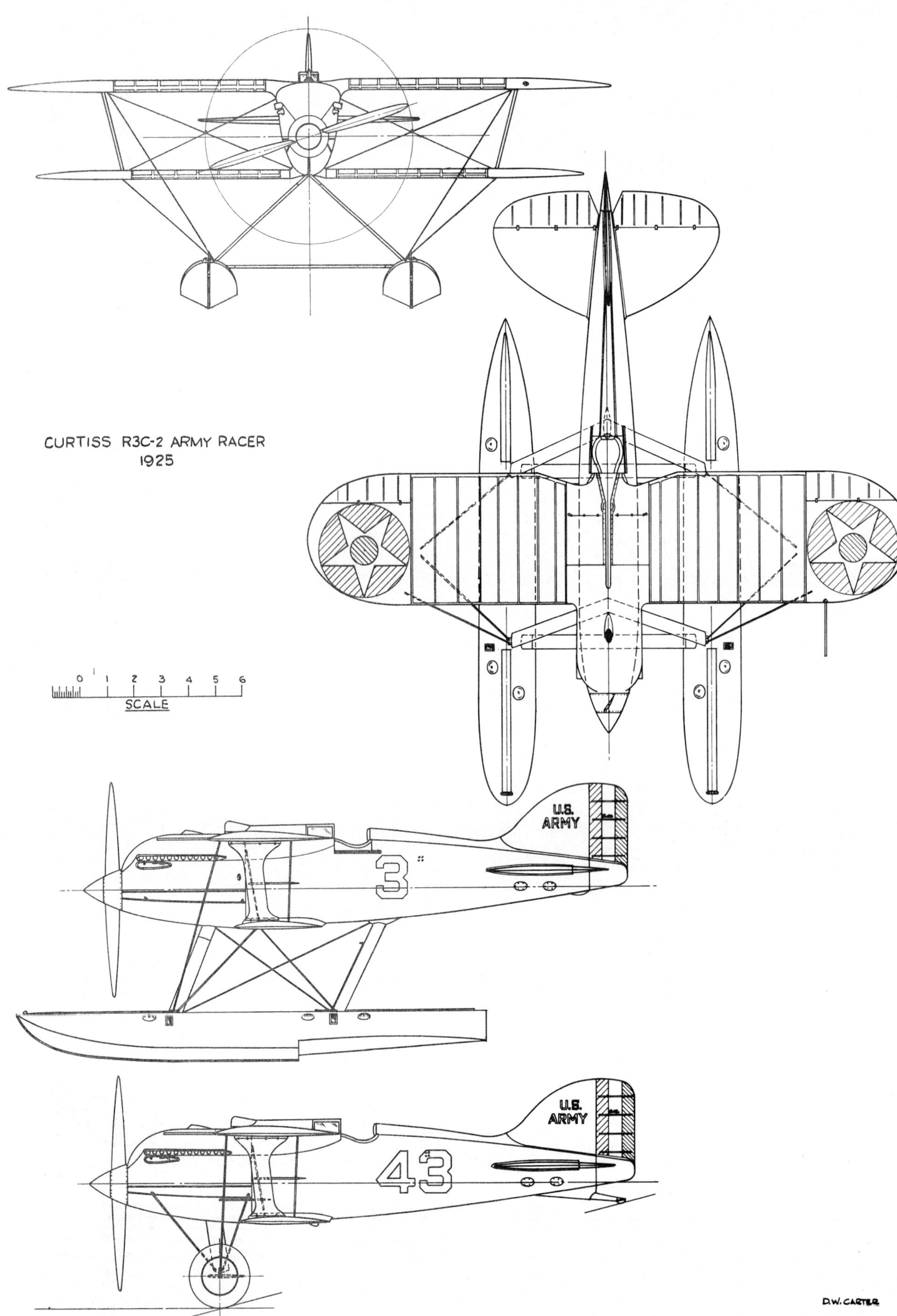

18

Lt. Ralph Ofstie in one of the Navy R3C-2 craft. Tail skid was built integral to fuselage structure so was left in place for later conversion back to landplane. Engines of R3C-2 aircraft were started with hand-cranked inertia starters located on left rear of engine. Cockpit instruments were Pioneer 0-350 mph airspeed, tachometer, water temperature, oil temperature, oil gauge, and a clock. Photo was taken before race number was applied. All Navy racers also carried Navy Bureau of Aeronautics seal below cockpit on both sides. *(Curtiss-Wright)*

Doolittle's 1925 Schneider-winning R3C-2 poised atop her crude launching cradle. Beautifully proportioned, all the Curtiss racers were extremely photogenic from any angle—and the Curtiss photographer was a master of his art This view was taken at Bay Shore Park, Maryland. Doolittle beat all seaplane records from 3 km to 350 km by 47 to 65 mph in the last biplane to win the Schneider. Although metal in appearance the twin pontoons were built of wood and were plywood covered. *(Curtiss-Wright)*

The Gloster biplanes were not as clean in detail as the Curtiss racers. Note double brace wires on tail surfaces of the Gloster IIIA, seen here undergoing her mooring floatation test period, canvas covering radiators on lower wing leading edge. (U. S. Air Force)

James H. Doolittle, still Number One pilot of many enthusiasts, seated in the Army R3C-1 at Mitchel Field in 1925. Denied piloting honors in several big military races, Doolittle did a lot of research and pleasure flying in the Curtiss racers. (Warren M. Bodie)

One of the Navy Wright F2W racers was vastly improved for the cancelled 1924 Schneider race and was redesignated F2W-2. Pictured on October 10, 1924, the F2W-2 lost out to the faster Curtiss racers in the 1925 trials. Lt. Wead poses in cockpit. (U. S. Navy/Bodie)

Here is one of the two Navy R3C-2 Curtiss racers in all her glory, complete to racing numeral and Navy seal on fuselage sides, being taxied out to make its start in the 1925 Schneider by Lt. George Cuddihy. (U. S. Air Force)

Doolittle's R3C-2 was, like all Curtiss racers, fitted with shoulder straps as well as waist belts. Some of the engine fuel was carried in the starboard or right float but fuselage main tank back of fire wall carried 42 gallons; the oil tank under engine crankcase held 4 gallons. The Curtiss R3C, as a landplane, could zoom from ground level to 5,000 feet in less than one minute and was, like all the Curtiss racers, extremely agile in response to all controls. *(Curtiss-Wright)*

Curtiss R2C (A6692), wore race No. 9 as winner of the 1923 Pulitzer, was fitted with floats and renumbered 6 for the 1924 Schneider, which was canceled. It was relegated to role of alternate for the 1925 Schneider, being superseded by the three new R3C craft. On September 13, 1926, 1st Lt. Harmon J. Norton, USMC, in attempting to slow the R2C-2 down and formate with two Army aircraft at 2,000 feet, stalled and fatally crashed into six feet of water near Anacostia, D.C. *(Warren M. Bodie)*

Direct side view of Gloster IIIA shows likeness to 1923 Curtiss racers. W type engine, three banks of four cylinders, delivered 700 hp, 81 hp more than the winning Curtiss racer, was the highest horsepowered craft in the race. (Gloster)

Pert little Gloster II, with its radiators at top of front float struts canvas covered, was built for the 1924 Schneider. Craft did 250 mph, became prototype for the 1925 Gloster III ships, differed mainly in floats and their struts, and in rudder fin area. (Gloster)

This view of Gloster IIIB also shows its clearer lines as compared to her sister ship. Large expansion tank atop wing center section was necessary for critical amount of water carried for such a large engine. Note windshield difference from that of IIIA. (Gloster)

One of the Macchi M-33 racers on Lake Varese, Italy, after a test flight. These beautiful craft, designed by Mario Castoldi, were powered by Curtiss D-12 engines of only 435 hp. lacked only more power and metal propellers to be serious contenders. (Mario Castoldi)

The Gloster IIIA was a mixture of sleekness and awkwardness in streamline. Except for the cumbersome radiators set in the lower inboard wing leading edge, and the round-wire braced tail surfaces, she was quite trim and did finish second in the 1925 Schneider. Float struts appear flimsy, as proved to be the case on sister ship below. Note external aileron control cable horn on lower wing. Control horns for rudder and elevator were also exposed.   (Gloster)

This Gloster IIIB, sister ship to the above craft, was a more polished example of Gloster workmanship—and looked very much like the Curtiss racers that had visited England in 1923 to win the Schneider. IIIB wore flush skin wing radiators, had full cantilever tail surfaces, and all control actuating mechanism was built internal. Both the IIIA and IIIB provided Gloster with a wealth of test data for their future military aircraft—and an outstanding twin-float seaplane to come.

(Gloster)

The promising Supermarine S-4 mid-wing monoplane, seen here in a backdrop of her builder's shops, utilized its outboard banks of cylinders (W type Napier Lion VII, three banks of 4 cylinders each, 700 hp) as fairings for its wing roots. The S-4 was extremly clean in design and was full cantilever in construction throughout. Note water core radiator on underside of wing which extended from the fuselage outward. Cockpit is covered in this view and two rope tiedowns encircle fuselage.

(Supermarine/Mandrake)

Supermarine S-4 was constructed entirely of wood with plywood covering except for her pontoon legs, engine mount and cowl. Cockpit was quite large and the windshield stuck upward at an awkward angle to add unnecessary drag, the only mar to her beautiful streamlined shape. A high-speed stall by her pilot at 100 feet altitude wiped the S-4, England's fastest entry, out of the contest. She had attained 226.6 mph in one of her test flights.

(Supermarine/Mandrake)

take-off. At five minute intervals he was followed by Capt. Broad in the Gloster-Napier III and Lts. Cuddihy and Ofstie in their Curtiss racers. Giovanni de Briganti followed in his Macchi flying boat. All made their take-offs before their five minute time limits, the low monoplane wings of the Macchi, with only a 2-foot clearance above the water, giving the crowd a thrill by its long run before taking off.

By this time Jimmy Doolittle had become the hero of the crowd, which marveled at his perfect flying. He had made his first lap at 223.2 mph from a taxiing start and was cutting the pylons at almost vertical banks with his engine full out. Only Briganti was turning the pylons as sharply as Doolittle, but he was not flying at as high a speed.

With a new world's record in sight all eyes watched for the British contender, but when his time for the first lap was announced as 194.3 mph it seemed certain that the Schneider Cup would remain in the United States another year. With Capt. Broad off on his second lap the interest centered on Lt. Cuddihy, but his first lap was only 211.6 mph. Lt. Ofstie then roared past, and Navy partisans cheered. Their enthusiasm was cut short, however, when 208 mph was marked up. Both Navy pilots were flying their pylon turns very wide.

Toward the end of the race, after it had become certain that Lt. Doolittle, barring trouble, would break all world's seaplane records up to 350 km, the onlookers were further excited when neither Cuddihy nor Ofstie appeared. It was soon learned, however, that Lt. Ofstie was down safely with engine trouble, and that Lt. Cuddihy had his engine catch fire almost within sight of the finish mark. He put out the blaze with his hand extinguisher and alighted safely, to be towed, along with Ofstie, to the Bay Shore hangars.

By this time, Doolittle had finished, winning the race at 232.6 mph for a new record and setting new records for 100 and 200 km at better than 234 mph. His seventh and last lap was the fastest, 235 mph, and as he rounded the last pylon he zoomed up several thousand feet before gliding in to alight. He received a tremendous ovation from the thrilled spectators, who had seen as fine a job of speed flying as had ever been witnessed.

Capt. Broad soon finished, with an average speed of 199.2 mph, to ensure second place, and then de Briganti finished with 168.4 mph.

Later Doolittle set his fourth world seaplane speed record by flying four times over a measured 3-km straightaway, in rough air and with a brisk crosswind, at an average speed of 245.7 mph.

ALFORD JOSEPH WILLIAMS

Alford Williams, during his 1927 flight tests of the Packard-Kirkham racing seaplane.

AL WILLIAMS was born in New York City, July 26, 1896, and was educated in P.S. No. 8 (the Bronx) and Fordham University. He was graduated in 1915 with an A.B. degree and a marked prowess as a baseball pitcher, and joined the New York Giants baseball club. He was farmed out to Tennessee to improve his finesse.

Coming up fast in 1917, his second year as a Giant recruit, Al enlisted as a Naval aviator when the United States entered the War. Giant Manager John McGraw later said that baseball lost a pitching ace when the Navy gained its greatest flier.

A keen analytical pilot, Al was not permitted to go into combat during World War I. He remained in the Navy until 1930 as a research test pilot and combat tactic instructor. During this time, Al managed to attend Georgetown University's evening law school, graduating with a bachelor of law degree in 1925. He was admitted to the New York bar in 1926.

During his 13-year Navy hitch, Williams turned in complete flight characteristic reports on more than 80 different types of aircraft, specializing in high-speed research (fourth place in the 1922 Pulitzer, first place in 1923) and inverted flight. With the aid of recording instruments in a standard fighting plane, Lt. Williams obtained for the aeronautical world the first definite load factors for all forms of inverted flight, including the outside loop, inverted loop, inverted tail spin, and vertical figure "S," and their application to fighter combat tactics. In recognition of his feats he was awarded, in 1929, the Distinguished Flying Cross.

After becoming highly critical of the Navy's shortsighted aviation policy, which was dominated by battleship-loving admirals, Williams resigned in 1930. In 1933 he was made manager of the Aviation Department, Gulf Oil Corporation, a post he held until 1951.

Although a rugged individualist, Al gave his all unstintingly throughout his flying career to the advancement of U.S. aviation, with no consideration for monetary reward.

Through most of World War II, while on leave from Gulf, he toured the United States as a technical consultant to the Army Air Forces, lecturing and demonstrating fighter technique to pilots and cadets. He refused payment for this great service!

1926 — National Air Races

Early in the afternoon of Saturday, September 4, with a thick overcast sky which later proved ideal for air racing, the National Air Races started at Model Farms Field, Philadelphia, just southwest of the Sesquicentennial Exposition grounds. Scheduled for seven days, the air meet lasted nine days because of heavy rains.

The entry list for the 19 race events of the week totaled no less than 215 entrants, and there were numerous other contests, and many parachute jumps.

Waco, Travel-Air, Swallow, Eaglerock, Buhl, and Ford all had planes in the civilian races, but tricked-up planes or planes designed specially for the event were beginning to win the big prize money.

The racing events were mostly restricted to engines of a certain cubic inch cylinder displacement with Curtiss OX-5 war surplus engines of 90 hp predominating. There was even a race for Curtiss Jennys, the National Guard Trophy Race, won by Carl Rach of New York, flying a JN-11 at 93.1 mph to win over ten other entrants.

The Liberty Engine Builders Trophy Race for observation planes was held on Thursday, September 9, and the surprise of the race was the speed made by a Packard 600-hp engined Special DH (De Havilland) built up by Navy Machinist Mate Leo Mohme at Anacostia. On the first lap Lt. G. T. Owens, USN, pilot of the plane with Mohme as mechanic, made better time than any of the 11 other entrants. On the fourth lap he was still leading, but he narrowly avoided a collision on the home pylon and never regained the lead. The winner of the race was Capt. Ira Eaker, AC, who averaged 142.2 mph in his new production Curtiss O-1 Falcon fitted with a D-12 435-hp engine. Capt. Aubrey Hornsby, also in an O-1, came in second at 141.8 mph, and Lt. Owens was third in the Special DH at 140.5 mph, beating out eight new Curtiss O-1 and Douglas O-2 (Liberty 400-hp engine) planes.

Friday, September 10, dawned bright and clear after two days of heavy rains, and that afternoon the *Los Angeles*, the world's largest airship, arrived on the horizon, circled the field in majestic splendor, and was brought to ground for about 40 minutes — the first time it had touched ground other than her home station at Lakehurst, N. J.

MITCHELL RACE

The last event on Friday was one of the feature races of the meet, the fifth annual John L. Mitchell Trophy Race. The nine planes entered in this race, which it will be remembered was a closed event for First Pursuit Group pilots, flew overhead at 6 P.M. in a very tight 3-group V formation. Then at a signal from their leader, Maj. Tom C. Lamphier, the pilots went into a single line and, keeping perfect distance in a wide sweeping curve, came roaring down over the starting line.

The race was a close contest, for all the planes, Curtiss P-1 Hawk pursuits with Curtiss D-12 435-hp engines and Curtiss-Reed metal propellers, were identical, and the pilots were among the finest in the world, with the result that there was but 3 mph between the winner and the last in. Each pilot took very fine close turns at the pylons, and the race was won by Lt. L. G. Elliott at 160.4 mph.

KANSAS CITY ROTARY CLUB TROPHY RACE

The Pulitzer races had ended last year after six years of competition which did much to make U. S. military planes the finest in the world. This year the trophy was replaced by a Kansas City Rotary Club Trophy Race, which proved to be the fastest of the air meet. Held on Saturday, September 11, the event was open to both Army and Navy pilots and all pursuit-type planes, over a distance of 120 miles.

There were twelve entrants, eight being Air Corps, three Navy, and one Marine Corps. The race was a close match and proved exciting because of the intense competition between the services.

Flying a new Boeing FB-3 Navy fighter (similar in appearance to a Curtiss P-1) powered by the highest hp production engine to date, Lt. George Cuddihy, flagged off tenth in a field of twelve, steadily forged ahead past plane after plane to win the trophy and establish a new world's speed record of 180.5 mph for standard pursuit ships. His Packard 2A-1,500 engine, developed from the racing Packard engine, delivered 600 hp.

The Air Corps took second place, Lt. L. G. Elliott, winner of the Mitchell Trophy, averaging 178.6 in a Curtiss Hawk P-2, which was identical in appearance to a Curtiss P-1 but had more horsepower. Lt. Sandy Sanderson, USMC, our hard-luck pilot, flew in this race without any mishap whatsoever, but because of a faulty engine, had to be satisfied with seventh place.

The aircraft of exceptional interest in the race,

in addition to the winning type, were the Navy's new Wright Apache F3W-1, powered by a Pratt and Whitney Wasp air-cooled radial engine, and the Air Corps' Curtiss P-1, fitted with an inverted air-cooled Liberty engine. Both of these planes were of the same power, each engine rated at 410 hp, the highest horse-power ever developed by air-cooled engines to date. The Wright Apache made one lap at better than 173 mph, forecasting a later trend to air-cooled engines for fighter planes.

The Wright Apache (top) was disqualified for pylon cutting, as was the Curtiss P-1 with the inverted Liberty engine (bottom of page). Lead plane is Cuddihy's 1926 Kansas City Rotary Club Trophy Race winning Navy Boeing FB-3, flown at an average speed of 180.5 mph, followed by Elliott and Hoyt in their Curtiss P-2 Hawks.

1926 – Schneider Trophy Race

Italy and the United States contested this year for the speed honors of the world at Hampton Roads, Va.; in November—England's entries not being ready in time. The race was held over a 31.07-mile course, seven laps around for a total of 217.5 miles.

Italy was represented by three new Mario Castoldi designed Macchi M-39 low-wing monoplanes with wing water radiators and twin pontoons. Powered by Fiat V-12 type engines of 800 hp, the cylinder banks were well streamlined and faired into the smooth lines of the slim fuselage. The flush–type oil radiator was mounted smoothly under the engine. In design the Macchi was the last word in cleanness and streamlining, with a fuselage not unlike the Curtiss racer, and had the lines of England's Supermarine S-4, which met with an accident before the race last year. The Italian pilots were Maj. Mario de Bernardi, Capt. Arturo Farrarini, and Lt. Adriano Bacula, all of the Royal Italian Air Force.

From the close of World War I until the end of 1925 the United States was out front, holding most of the air records, foremost among these being the land- and seaplane speed records. We built planes which could show their tails to those produced abroad, could carry heavier loads faster, and could reach higher altitudes. The home of the Wrights led the world. Then the government refused to spend money on research race planes, little realizing that, economically, high-speed development was actually a saving because of the shorter time necessary to attain technical perfection. So this year the United States was represented by U. S. Navy pilots flying the same three Curtiss R3C planes flown in winning the Schneider last year, two of which, it will be remembered, took first and second places in the Pulitzer last year. The Army Curtiss racer that had won last year's Schneider race had been borrowed by the Navy for this year's event. A fourth plane, a standard Navy Curtiss F6C-1 Hawk powered by a D-12 engine, was entered as a reserve. The only material difference between the three Curtiss racers were their engines. One was fitted with a geared Packard V-12 engine of 700 hp and the plane designated as R3C-3. A second Curtiss racer, an R3C-4, was fitted with a new Curtiss V-12 engine of 700 hp, and the third racer, the R3C-2 that had won the Schneider last year with a Curtiss V-12 engine of 619 hp, was unaltered.

The U. S. race team consisted of Lts. George Cuddihy and William G. Tomlinson, both of the U. S. Navy, and Lt. Christian F. Schilt, USMC. Lt. Frank Conant, USN, who was to have flown the R3C-3, had been killed in a service-type seaplane a few days before.

The navigability tests were held on Thursday and Friday, November 11 and 12. On Friday morning Lt. Tomlinson bounced badly in taking the R3C-3 off the water and nearly overturned. Although he had flown fighter planes, Tomlinson was unaccustomed to this

Major Mario de Barnardi and his red and white Macchi M-39 with which he won the 1926 Schneider Trophy. Plywood covered aircraft were prone to wrinkling in damp weather, as can be seen aft of cockpit in this view. In low humidity conditions or in full sunlight plywood smoothed out. M-39 is seen here during flight test and shake-down period, before her race No. 5 was painted on.
(Warren M. Bodie)

Excellent view of R3C-4, taken October 28, 1926, just after being reworked for the Schneider race. As seaplane speeds rose, skin friction between bottom of plywood covered floatation gear and surface of the water became a critical factor. Excessive speed upon contact with the water could actually peel plywood off so an extra sleek finish was applied to bottom of pontoons on all Curtiss racers, as seen here. (Curtiss-Wright)

Lt. Frank H. Conant, USN, photographed October 26, 1926, in the Curtiss R3C-4 which he was to have flown in Schneider race. Unfortunately Conant was killed in a service-type seaplane before the race. The Navy did not always identify their racing craft with external markings so it was often impossible to pin down the exact aircraft depicted in a photograph, when two or more of them were built, as is the case with this aircraft. This ship wore either race No. 4 or 6 in the Schneider. (Curtiss-Wright)

The three M-39's were the most functional liquid-cooled racing seaplanes built to date, had a sleek hand-rubbed finish that was a joy to behold. Radiator beneath engine was for oil cooling. Like the Curtiss V-12 engines, the Fiat V-12 engines had two intake and two exhaust valves per cylinder. Engines in all three M-39's were set up loose to prevent seizure so trailed quite a heavy wake of oil smoke in flight.   (U. S. Air Force)

Beautifully proportioned Macchi 39 was graceful from all angles. Mario Castoldi, who designed all the Macchi monoplane racers, will go down in history as one of the world's finest all-time aircraft designers. He never turned out an ugly aircraft. All three M-39 craft were identical in construction, being built up of wood, plywood covered, except for engine mount, engine cowl and float struts. Gentleman facing camera in felt hat is Mario Castoldi.   (U. S. Air Force)

Here is a former R3C-2 now fitted with a geared Packard 1A-1500 V-12 engine of 700 hp and redesignated R3C-3. Note reverse direction propeller. Gears and gear cases were designed to raise propeller axis to center of fuselage so engine could wear an almost symmetrical cowling. Aircraft, which test-flew faster than the winning Macchi, is seen here before receiving final paint job. The 2-inch strips of laminated plywood construction is plainly visible on starboard float.

(Warren M. Bodie)

Lt. Wm. G. Tomlinson USN, being lowered onto water day before the Schneider for a test flight which proved to be the last for this beautiful Packard engined R3C-3. Although fin had been offset to correct the reverse engine torque, this ship was almost uncontrollable in certain attitudes, had a tendency to bury its right wing up to nearly take-off speed. Windshield was carried well aft and the cockpit cowl was fitted around the pilot's neck so only his head protruded from cockpit.

(Charles G. Mandrake)

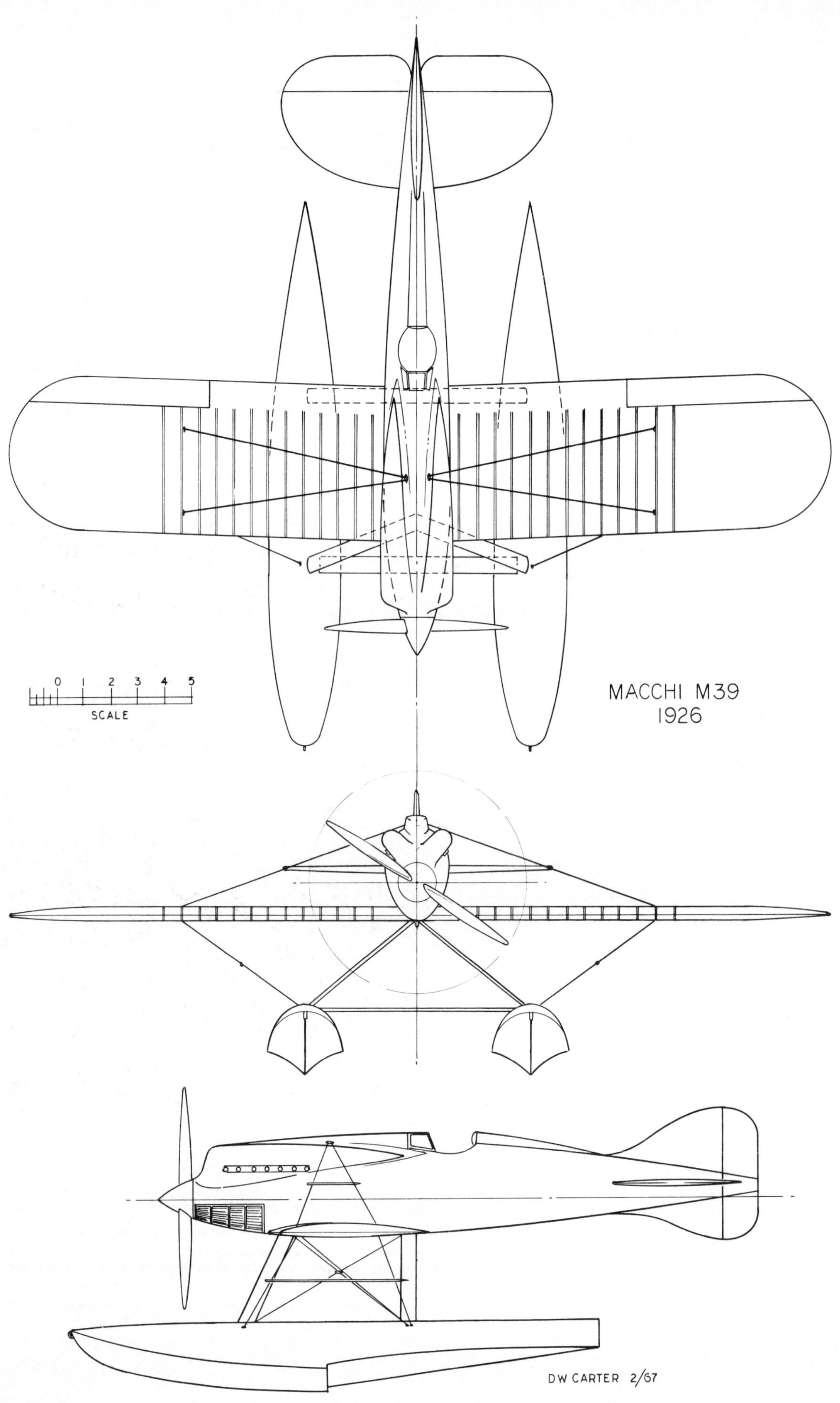

SCALE
0 1 2 3 4 5
MACCHI M39
1926
DW CARTER 2/67

racing plane. The propeller direction was reversed as compared to other planes, due to the gearing on the Packard engine. Once in the air he flew perfectly for about 30 minutes, then came in to alight, misjudged his distance and "alighted" a few feet above the water. The plane dropped and bounced, and when it again touched the water it began to sink to the right, for there was by now a large hole in the bottom of the starboard pontoon. Tomlinson still had a 50- or 60-mph headway and in an effort to pick up the right wing, over-controlled, and the little seaplane did a left side somersault, ending up with only its pontoon bottomsides visible above the water's surface. Tomlinson swam up unhurt, but the fastest U. S. race plane went to the junkheap.

That afternoon Tomlinson qualified the F6C Curtiss Hawk, to make three entries for the United States. The three Italian pilots had already qualified their three little scarlet Macchi planes with excellent displays of piloting.

The Schneider Trophy Race was flown on Saturday afternoon, November 13, under perfect weather conditions. Thousands of people had gathered at the Norfolk Air Base to view the race at the home pylon, which was 100 yards off shore and mounted on a barge. There were large crowds at Newport News, one of the turning points, and Old Point Comfort, over which the machines flew on the longest leg of the course.

Lt. Bacula was let down the slipway at 2:35 P.M. and, taxiing rapidly across the starting line, quickly climbed his Macchi into the air. The second plane to leave was the slow Curtiss Hawk piloted by Lt. Tomlinson. Due to leave next, under the schedule of one machine each five minutes, was Capt Farrarini. However, as he was having trouble warming up his engine, Lt. Cuddihy took off in the R3C-4 racer. One minute later Farrarini took off. By this time Lt. Bacula had completed his first lap at only 209.6 mph, causing surprise among the spectators. Bacula, however, had planned to hold back and conserve his engine.

Lt. Tomlinson completed his first lap, averaging but 137 mph, and was quickly followed by Cuddihy flying at 232.4 mph. Bacula's time on the second lap increased to 213.4 mph, but then Capt. Farrarini came roaring around the home pylon, his first lap speed being 234.6 mph, 2 mph faster than that of the R3C-4, the United States' best plane.

Maj. de Bernardi, captain of the Italian team, took off at 3 P.M. and was followed a minute later by Lt. Schilt of the Marines, flying last year's winner, the Curtiss R3C-2. The Italian planes were taking off the water in 20 to 30 seconds, while the U. S. planes took a little longer.

Almost at the instant of Bernardi's take-off, Capt. Farrarini turned the home pylon at 200 feet on the start of his third lap, streaming dark smoke from his engine exhaust, a characteristic of the three Italian planes. Lt. Cuddihy, completing his second lap, chalked up 236.2 mph, which raised the hopes of the United States, for it was 4 mph faster than his first lap. However, when Capt. Farrarini's time was computed it was found that he too had increased his speed by 4 mph, increasing the enthusiasm and excitement of the spectators.

Then around the home pylon came Bernardi, and his speed went up on the scoreboard — 239.4 mph for his first lap! In the meantime Lt. Cuddihy was increasing his speed average by about 1 mph on each lap, while Lt. Schilt was doing around 230 mph.

Capt. Farrarini rounded the home pylon after averaging 238.4 mph for three laps, but his engine was giving trouble so he left the course and alighted on the water, his engine still ticking over. An oil line had broken. Around came Bernardi doing 248.5 mph on his third and fastest lap to send his average up to 244.9 mph. Lt. Cuddihy completed his fifth lap to average 238.8 mph, flying the fifth lap at 242.2 mph, the fastest speed of the U. S. team.

The Italians were taking the pylons much wider than the American pilots, who were cutting the home pylon, which was the widest on the course, very close; Lt. Tomlinson, in the Hawk, naturally cutting closer. Lt. Schilt, flying a steady race with his engine wide open, completed his sixth lap to average 231.2 mph. Then Lt. Cuddihy, after flying a perfect course throughout the race, and when within sight of the finish line and an easy second place, was forced to alight dead-stick when his fuel pump failed to pump gasoline up from the pontoon tank. He had averaged 239.2 mph. Lt. Bacula, the first to start, finished the race at an average of 218 mph, which later proved to be third in the race. Maj. de Bernardi gradually increased his speed lap by lap. On his sixth lap Bernardi climbed to 600 feet in an effort to cool his engine-oil temperature, which had gone quite high, but on his seventh and last lap he came down low again and shot across the finish line at 247.2 mph and an average of 246.5 mph to win the Schneider Trophy.

Lt. Schilt finished with an average speed of 231.4 mph to take second place in last year's winning plane. Then Lt. Tomlinson, almost a full lap behind, finished fourth and last with 137 mph.

Italy's win was the result of the superior design of her planes over the American entries and the excellent teamwork of the entire Italian race team. It was a well-flown race and a well-deserved victory.

❖   ❖   ❖

1927 – National Air Races

For the first and only time the National Air Races were held at Spokane, Wash. Highly interesting and exceptionally well conducted, the races were held at Felts Field, Spokane, during the week of September 19–25. The races attracted Indians from nearby reservations, broad-hatted cattlemen, ranchers, and thousands of residents from faraway towns. There were four civilian "on to Spokane" races, five civilian closed-course races, and six military closed-course races, with the military furnishing, as usual, the highest speeds.

Something new, however, was shown in the free-for-all race for commercial planes, when pilot James Ray pushed a Pitcairn Sesquiwing around the 10-lap course, averaging 136.1 mph for the 80-mile race, and doing one lap at better than 141 mph. The Pitcairn was powered by a C-6 Curtiss 6-cyl. in-line engine of 180-hp, and was the only plane in the race which did not have a Wright J-4-5 Whirlwind 225-hp engine. Ray flew a splendid race, crowding the pylons just enough and banking his little plane around them in a style equalled by few of the pursuit pilots. Ten of the twelve planes entered were 3-place open-cockpit biplanes; the other two were cabin monoplanes.

Charles "Speed" Holman won the New York to Spokane Class "A" Air Derby in his Laird biplane at an elapsed time of 19 hrs. 47 min. 47 sec. All eight planes in the derby were powered by the new Wright 225-hp J-5 Whirlwind engine.

Charles A. Lindberg's solo flight in May of this year, when he flew a Wright J-5 engined Ryan cabin plane across the Atlantic, had proven the reliability of this new hp-class engine, so it was only natural that most designers had adopted it at once, replacing World War I surplus water-cooled types.

The Liberty Engine Builders' Trophy Race for 2-place observation-type planes was contested by one model XO-13 and one model XO-13A, Curtiss Falcon biplanes, and three O-2C Douglas biplanes. Both Falcons wore Conquerer high-compression 700-hp engines and differed only in that the XO-13 had a standard tunnel radiator, while the XO-13A wore wing radiators. The O-2C Douglas planes had Liberty engines of 435 hp.

Taking an early lead and flying a perfect race,

Lt. Harry A. Johnson flew the specially groomed XO-13A into first place over the 100-mile course at an average of 170.2 mph. Lt. George A. McHenry, flying the other Falcon, was second at 162 mph.

SPOKANE SPOKESMAN-REVIEW TROPHY

This free-for-all military-pursuit race was to mark the next-to-last time in U. S. military-racing history that the Army and Navy competed against each other on a closed course, and as seemed fitting, it furnished the highest speeds of the air races. Six Army and four Navy planes were entered. Two of the planes, both Army, were experimental types, while all the others were standard service types.

Denied funds for new racing craft, the Army's Experimental Section at Wright Field, Ohio, built, as a race project, an XP-6A Curtiss Hawk with straight wings and a standard Hawk fuselage, powered by a 700-hp Curtiss V-1,570 Conqueror engine, which was by far the cleanest entry of the race. This semi-race plane was the only entry fitted with wing radiators. Three Curtiss P-1B standard Army Hawks, with D-12 435-hp engines, tapered wings, and tunnel radiators, were entered; and an XP-6 Hawk, identical in appearance to the standard P-1B Hawks but powered by a 700-hp engine like that of the XP-6A, was entered in the race. Also entered by the Army was a standard Boeing PW-9C pursuit, powered by a D-12 engine.

The Navy entries were three Boeing FB-5 shipboard fighter planes that were identical to the PW-9C excepting their engines, which were Packards of 600 hp. The fourth Navy plane was a Curtiss Hawk F6C-4 shipboard fighter fitted with a 435-hp Pratt & Whitney Wasp, the only air-cooled engine in the race.

The planes were flagged off one at a time, and from the first lap it was evident that there would be no great competition for Lt. Batten if the thin-skinned brass radiators of his XP-6A Hawk stood the strain. He overtook plane after plane, the sun glittering on his wings as he hurtled through the air. The noise of the Hawk's 700 hp was deafening, as Batten roared on to win first place at an average speed of 201.2 mph.

The only pilot flying close to Batten was Lt. A. J. Lyon in his souped-up Curtiss XP-6 Hawk with the tunnel radiator under its nose, and he averaged 189.6

Lt. Batten's XP-6A Hawk roars ahead to win the 1927 Spokane SPOKESMAN-REVIEW *Trophy Race with an average speed of 201.2 mph. Lt. Jeter, who finished third in his Boeing FB-5 (top), and Lt. Rogers (center), who finished seventh with his F6C-4 Hawk, follow Batten.*

mph through the race to win second place. Navy Lts. Thomas Jeter, H. E. Regan, and Gerald Bogan finished third, fourth and fifth in their standard Boeing FB-5 fighters. Lt. Beverly took sixth place in his Boeing PW-9C, averaging 169.7 mph, and Navy Lt. F. C. Rogers, in his Wasp-powered F6C-4 Hawk, averaged 161.6 mph to nose out all three Army P-1B Hawks for seventh place.

Although Lt. Batten once again proved the speed superiority of built-in wing radiators, the military declined to adopt them for their newer pursuits, contending that they presented too large a target and that maintenance and repair problems had been too great on their earlier PW-8 pursuits, which had worn wing radiators.

This XP-6A Curtiss Hawk was built up from a P-1A fuselage and XPW-8A single-bay wings, complete to wing radiators, for the 1927 National Air races. Its pilot, Air Corps Lt. Earl C. Batten proudly wore his E for excellence in gunnery competition on the vertical fin which gave the aircraft a pursuit flavor—which was the intent. The wheels were not cleaned up with fabric covering nor was the step indent on bottom left of fuselage, below cockpit, covered for the race.

(Warren M. Bodie)

This Curtiss XO-13A Falcon was, like the Hawk above, reworked by Air Corps Experimental Section, and fitted with a 700 hp engine and wing radiators for the annual Liberty Engine Builders' Trophy Race, which it won handily. Falcon flew the race as seen here, with engine hand crank exposed to the wind, and the wheels not fabric covered. Note water line for wing radiator just above left landing gear struts at fuselage. Winning Pilot Lt. Harry A. Johnson sits in front cockpit, his observer in rear.

(Curtiss-Wright)

1927 – Schneider Trophy Race

The ninth competition for the famous Schneider Trophy was held off Lido Beach, Venice, Italy, on Sept. 26, 1927. England and Italy each qualified three race planes for the contest. The lone private U. S. entry, Al Williams, was unable to get his special Packard-Kirkham biplane of 1,250 hp ready in time.

Air power in Europe was regarded with great seriousness so Venice was *en fête* — flags, banners, tapestries, and posters were everywhere. The canals were crowded with gondolas and other small boats of every type. Thousands of Italian, English, German, and American tourists overran the narrow streets, while St. Mark's Piazza was filled both day and night with a joyous, happy throng.

England was represented by two S-5 Supermarine-Napier low-wing monoplanes and one new Gloster-Napier IV biplane. The S-5 planes were improved developments of the S-4 Supermarine of the 1925 races, while the Gloster IV was an improved version of the Gloster III that finished second in the 1925 contest. All three of England's entries were powered with Napier Lion 12-cyl. W-type water-cooled engines of 875 hp. Fuselage construction of the S-5 was all metal, while the wings, almost completely covered with smooth-surface brass water radiators, were built up of wood. The engine oil was cooled by passing it along both sides of the fuselage inside the skin. The S-5 fuselage was probably smaller in cross section than had ever been designed before. The pilots had to be specially fitted to the machines, the fuselage top being rounded off to fit over the shoulders of the pilot. His head was thus in line with the center-engine cylinder block. Air ducts from the leading edge of the wing to the cockpit ensured fresh air to the pilot, preventing exhaust gas and engine heat from becoming unbearable, a feature used on all later single-seat pursuits. Engine fuel was carried in the starboard float, as on most later Schneider racers, to offset engine torque.

The Gloster IV biplane was built of wood and plywood, except for the engine mount, cowling, and floats, which were duralumin. Curtiss-type wing radiators of thin corrugated copper and brass were fitted, and additional surface radiators were built into the float decks. Main fuel tanks were carried in the fuselage.

England had also brought a unique air-cooled-engined low-wing racer to Venice for the contest. Designed and built to test the possibilities of an air-cooled radial engine in a high-speed machine, this Short Crusader was powered by a 9-cyl. Bristol-Mercury engine of extremely low weight per horsepower. The engine cylinders were individually cowled, developing 800–900 hp, and the airplane very clean in design. The Crusader crashed during a take-off due to its ailerons having been crossed by an assembly mechanic, but fortunately the pilot was uninjured.

Italy was again represented by three identical scarlet low-wing monoplanes, Macchi M-52 racers which were new and improved versions of the M-39 that had won the 1926 Schneider race. Construction was of wood, excepting the metal wing radiators, engine mount, and cowl.

The M-52 model looked very much like the earlier M-39 except that its floats were shorter and the wings had a slight sweep-back. Other modifications included removal of the streamlined spreader bars between the floats, the substitution of streamlined wires, and a reduction of wingspan. All three Italian Macchi's were powered by V-12 1,030-hp Fiat engines like those used in the M-39 racers.

The race was to be seven laps around a 31.07-mile course for a total distance of 217.5 miles, and the course was, as it had been in previous years, a very narrow triangle with two almost 180° hairpin turns to negotiate, which cut down the speeds considerably.

Precisely at 2:30 P.M., Flt. Lt. Kinkead, in his Gloster IV, flashed past the start at a speed that showed his biplane to be extremely fast. Maj. de Bernardi followed at 2:35 in his red Macchi. Flt. Lt. Webster, flying the first Supermarine S-5, took off next.

At five minute intervals Capt. Guazzetti in the

Flight Lt. S. N. Webster, 1927 Schneider winner, being towed to landing ramp in his magnificent little Supermarine S-5 after a practice flight. This ship, N219, had a geared Napier Lion engine to slow propeller rpm's and proved to be 10 mph faster than the direct drive engine in S-5 N220 which took 2nd place in the race. Several aluminum propellers were made by the Fairey Aviation Co. and tested on all three S-5 aircraft until the fastest were found. This ship carries race No. 5.

(Supermarine)

S-5 floats, built of aluminum, were very lightweight, and were anodized to resist sea water corrosive action. An engine driven pump sucked fuel from starboard main float tank and delivered it to a small gravity tank in fairing of starboard engine cylinder block. Fuel then ran to carburetors and an overflow carried excess fuel back to main tank. A similar header tank in fairing aft of center row of cylinders contained engine cooling water which was circulated through wing radiators by an engine driven pump.

(Napier)

From many angles the Kirkham-Williams looked like a king-size Curtiss racer, as well it might, being designed and engineered by men who had or were still working for Curtiss. Ship was, like the Curtiss racers, all wood in construction, plywood covered. Lift section built into landing gear axle seemed unnecessary as craft carried 142 sq. ft. of area in the top wing and 75 in the bottom panels. Radiator, which cooled 15 gallons of oil, was in outboard section of lower right wing. 　　　　　　　　　　　　　　　　　　　　　　　　　　　　　　　　*(U. S. Air Force)*

One of the Macchi M-52's taxiing slowly as its engine warms up for a test hop. Fascist insignia plainly visible on fuselage side above swept-back wing. All the Italian seaplanes did their test work off fresh water lakes to avoid sea water corrosion. 　　　　　　　　　　　　　　　　　　　　　　　　　　　　　　*(Macchi)*

Top wing of the Kirkham-Williams seemed too large in proportion to rest of aircraft, both in span and chord. Williams, who was over six feet tall, appears small alongside craft. Wingspan, top, was 29 feet 10 inches, length overall (including floats) was 26 feet 9 inches. (Dustin W. Carter)

Al Williams, who never allowed anyone but himself in the cockpit, is seen here after a flight over Port Washington, where all test work was done. Packard X type engine delivered 1250 hp at 2700, weighed only 1400 lbs. Propeller diameter was 8 feet six inches. (Stephen J. Hudek)

Finish of the Kirkham-Williams was in two tones—the body, floats, struts, fin and stabilizer were flag blue while the wings, elevators and rudder were gold. The wing radiators were natural brass. 12,000 feet of brass radiator tubes carried 35 gallons of water through the radiators. (Peter M. Bowers)

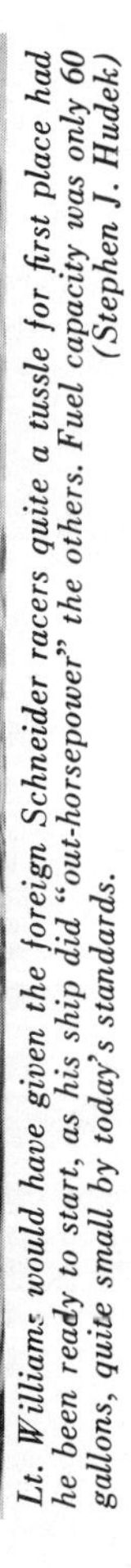

Lt. Williams would have given the foreign Schneider racers quite a tussle for first place had he been ready to start, as his ship did "out-horsepower" the others. Fuel capacity was only 60 gallons, quite small by today's standards. (Stephen J. Hudek)

The Kirkham-Williams seaplane was built on Long Island by the Kirkham Products Corp. Alford Williams put every dime he owned or could scrape up, along with his heart, into the project. Packard donated the engine; a lot of parts and accessories and many hundreds of manhours were donated by selfless individuals in their attempt to have America represented in the 1927 Schneider. A win would have gained permanent possession of the trophy for the U.S.

(Charles G. Mandrake)

Unable to ready his Kirkham seaplane in time for the 1927 Schneider, Al Williams converted his ship to a landplane, reportedly flew to an unofficial world's speed record of 322.6 mph. Why Williams never tried for an official record is not known. The new and more streamlined nose cowl was made for the Kirkham when it was converted to a landplane, greatly enhancing its appearance. Direct side view was one of its best camera angles. Number X-648 on rudder was added after conversion.

(Charles G. Mandrake)

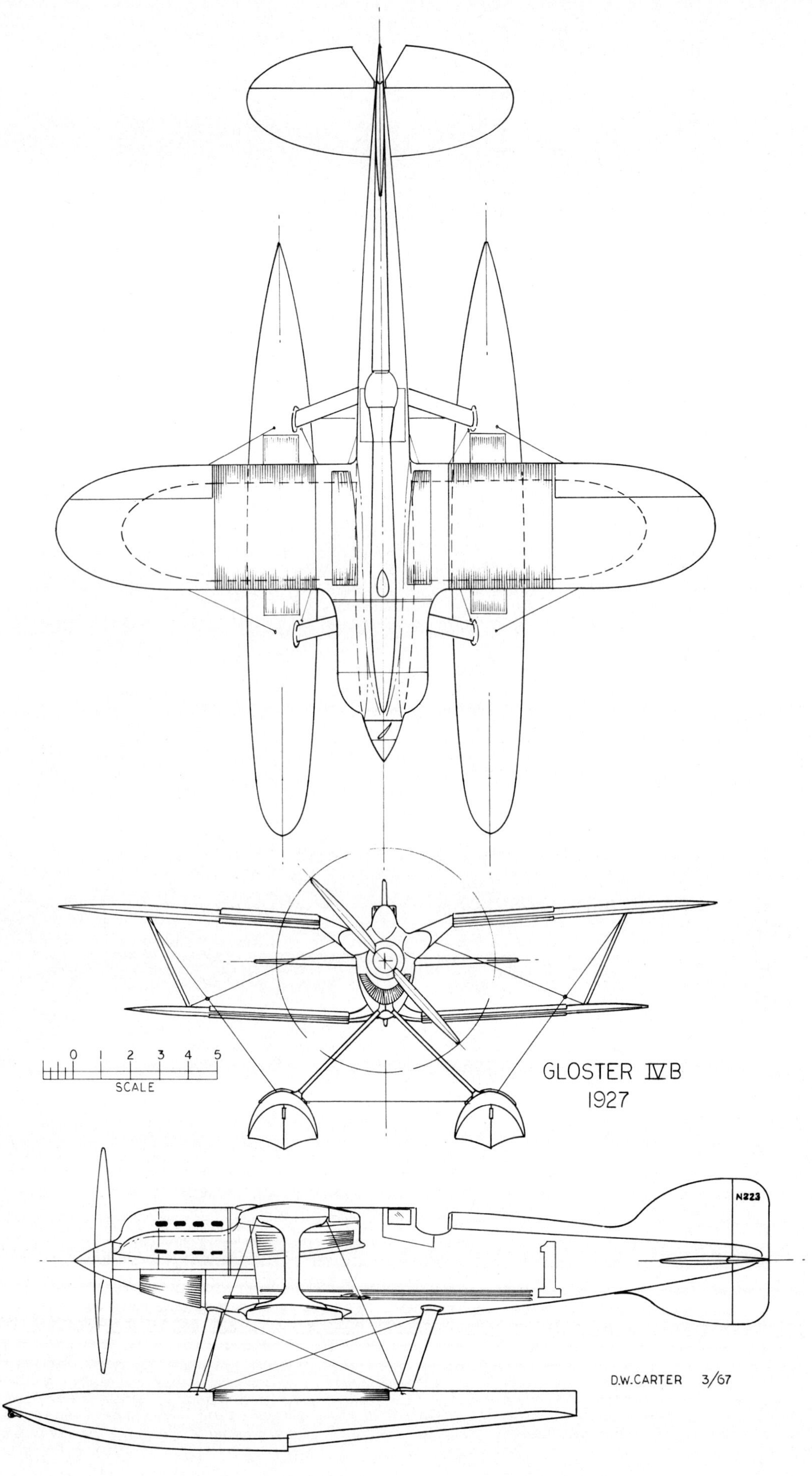

GLOSTER IVB
1927
0 1 2 3 4 5
SCALE
N223
1
D.W.CARTER 3/67

Superb Gloster IV was one of the most gracefully beautiful biplanes ever constructed. Top wing panels extended outward from the side engine block fairing, giving a gull-wing effect—and the lower wing panels did gull inverted from the fuselage bottom. Wing surface radiators were made of thin corrugated copper sheet, with brass leading and trailing edges. Additional surface radiators were built on the float decks for a total of 125 sq. ft. cooling area. Lower surface of oil tank under engine was ribbed to aid cooling.   _(Gloster)_

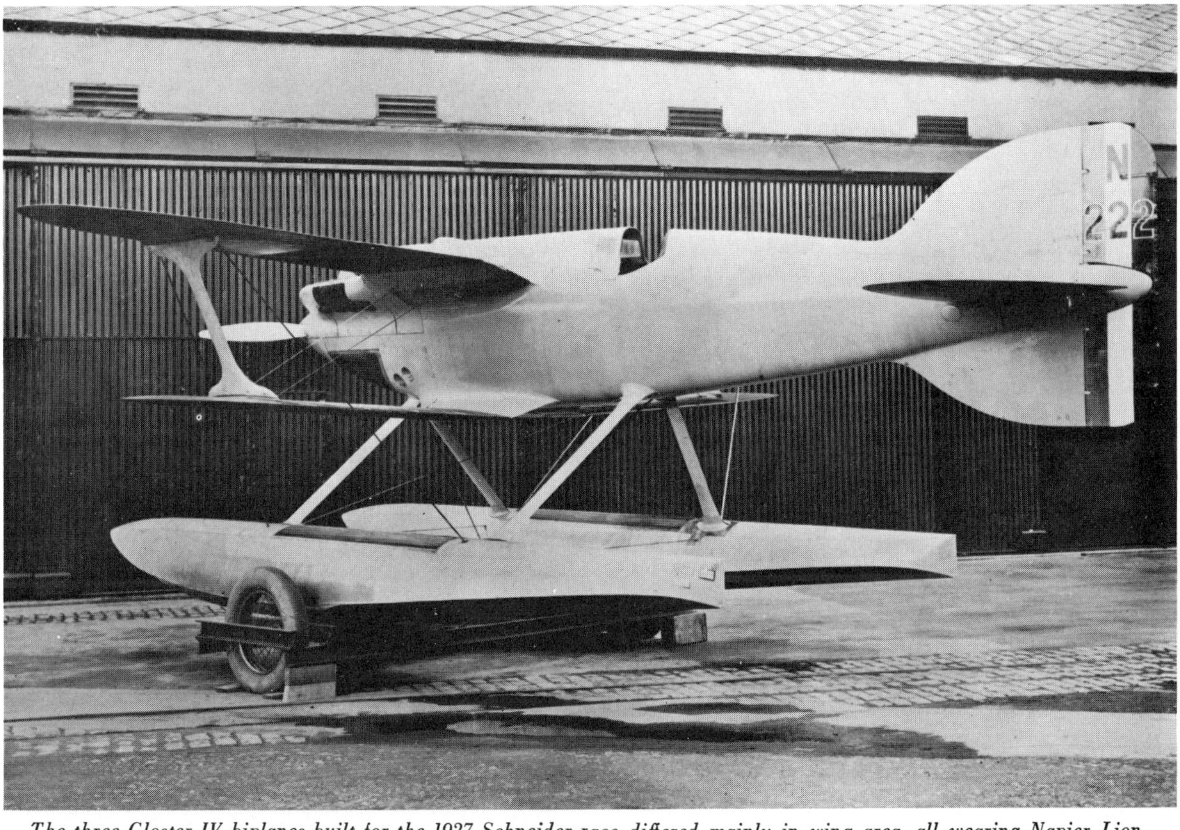

The three Gloster IV biplanes built for the 1927 Schneider race differed mainly in wing area, all wearing Napier Lion W-12 engines. The IV had 104 sq. ft., the IVa and IVb 139 ft. The IV turned in a disappointing 265 mph in flight tests, the IVa 289 mph and the IVb depicted on this page, with the only geared engine, did 295. Top and bottom tail fins were built of wood integral with fuselage and plywood covered. Plywood covered horizontal tail plane was adjustable on ground.   _(Gloster)_

Short Brothers 1927 Crusader aircraft wore the most unusual fairing ever fitted to a radial engine. This nicely proportioned craft was quite small overall, was sleek in design and finish, features which made it quite fast despite its radial engine. Unique wing was the thickest in section midway between the root and tip, also had its widest chord midway, being quite thin in section and short in chord at the root. The aircraft was totally wrecked before exact performance figures could be obtained, but top speed approximated 280 mph. (Short Bros.)

Bristol-Mercury engine was geared, which allowed a more streamlined nose. Test wooden propeller turned clockwise. Top engine cylinder cowling was carried rearward to the vertical tail fin with a break halfway back for windshield and small cockpit. 1927 was an extravagant race year for England. She showed up at Venice, Italy, for the Schneider with three Supermarine S-5 craft, three Gloster IV's and this Crusader, the most aircraft ever built for a single air race by one nation. (Short Bros.)

Another view of Flt. Lt. S. N. Webster and his S-5 after a test flight. Although three S-5 Supermarine aircraft were built, only two raced in 1927 Schneider, one giving up its place so the graceful Gloster IVb could race. After the race Flt. Lt. D. D'Arcy A. Grieg set a new world record 319 mph in an S-5. The S-5 carried 55 gallons of fuel, had an endurance of 1.15 hours. Landing speed was 90 mph. The S-5 ships were used by the 1929 British Schneider team as practice machines.
(Dustin W. Carter)

Wing structure of the Gloster IV aircraft consisted of a series of spruce spars, with intermediate contour-pieces instead of the usual ribs, then was plywood covered. I interplane struts were of forged steel. Floats were aluminum. Main fuel tanks were in fuselage with a header-tank in streamlining behind center engine cylinder block. Tanks held 59 gallons, sufficient for 1 hour, plus 10%. Wing flaps had not yet been developed so that the Gloster IV landed at 97 mph, quite fast for a biplane.
(Gloster)

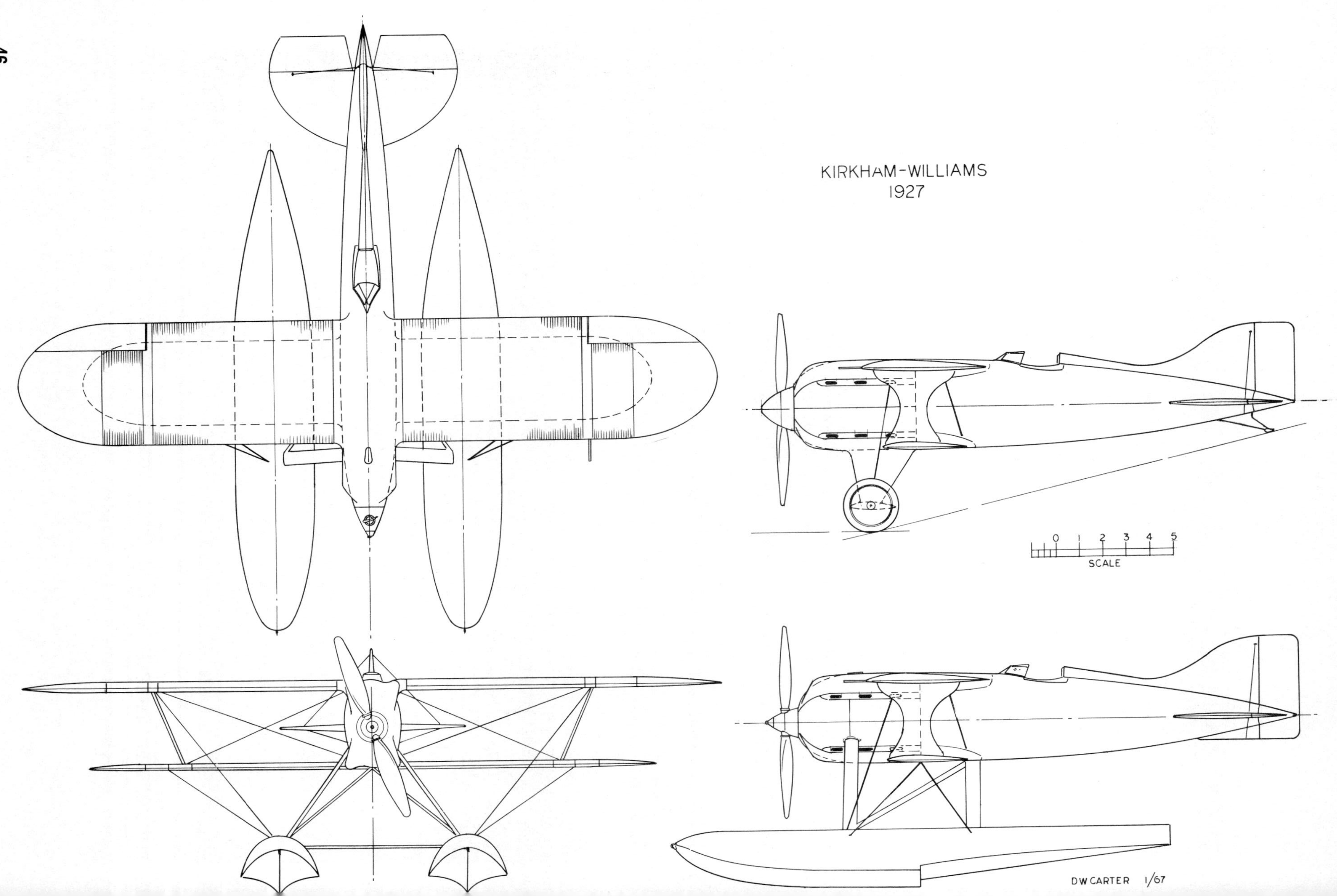

KIRKHAM-WILLIAMS
1927
0 1 2 3 4 5
SCALE
D W CARTER 1/67

second Macchi, Flt. Lt. Worsley in the second Supermarine S-5, and Capt. Farrarini in the third Macchi crossed the starting line.

The first surprise came when the first lap speeds were being posted. It was immediately apparent that the planes were roaring around the course faster than any aircraft of any kind had ever flown before. Further, it was obvious that all the British entries were faster than the Italian Macchis.

Speed in aircraft comes from two major sources: excellence in airplane design and superiority in engine development. It took many thousand parts and hundreds of accessories to make those racing craft the marvelous mechanisms they were. If but one of these component parts had been defective, it could have meant the difference between victory and defeat. This was severely pointed out later, for the usual disappointments of Schneider Trophy races commenced at this stage of the race. Maj. de Bernardi dropped out on his second lap. Almost immediately after Capt. Farrarini flew over the starting line he turned back and alighted near the Italian team's hangar. The throng of Italians on the Lido beach were stunned. Capt. Guazzetti, the only Italian pilot left in the race, was flying 20 mph slower than the English planes, although this speed was almost 20 mph faster than Maj. de Bernardi's winning speed at Norfolk the year previous. The astonishing speed of all thrèe British planes cast a spell over everyone, for when Kinkead's first lap over the difficult scissor-point course was posted at 277.1 mph, it was evident to all that a speed of over 300 mph was being attained on the straightaway.

After three laps, Flt. Lt. Kinkead was forced to alight, his prop shaft sheared, leaving the two Supermarine S-5's and one Macchi in the race. At the end of the sixth lap, however, Capt. Guazzetti was forced to alight because of engine trouble. All three Macchis were later found to have defective alloy in their engine pistons, and Mario Castoldi, designer of last year's winning M-39's, was heartbroken as he saw his new creations drop out through no fault of his own. The M-52 speeds, from the first part of the race, had probably been impaired by the faulty pistons.

Flt. Lt. Webster flashed over the finish line to win first place with an average of 281.7 mph, having flown each of his seven laps within a second or two of each other. Flt. Lt. Worsley was second and last at 273.1 mph. After the race Webster reported that during the race his engine cowling became loosened, and he dropped his motor revs back, but strangely enough his speed did not decrease. His S-5 was fitted with a geared engine as was the Gloster IV biplane, while Worsley's S-5 had a direct drive engine.

This race marked the last appearance of a biplane in the Schneider races, but the Gloster had turned one lap at 277.1 mph to set an all-time record for biplane types.

Increasingly complex racing craft made longer preparation time necessary, and it was decided after the 1927 Schneider to hold the races every other year.

Supermarine S-5 No. 220 which finished 2nd in 1927 Schneider. Running up engines on land was quite a chore as witness the dolly plus pontoon cradles to steady the aircraft. Note also the rubber topped cockpit access ladder. Floats equalled fuselage in size, as seen here.

(Dustin W. Carter)

1928 — National Air Races

General William "Billy" Mitchell had been court-martialed Dec. 17, 1925, for overzealously advocating air power. He had built our Air Corps into the world's finest and fastest, and, to the horror of the Navy admirals, his bomber pilots in tests sank, in addition to other ships, an "unsinkable" captured German battleship. During Mitchell's post-war tour of duty, our pursuit planes, in any given year, were patterned from last year's racing planes. The pursuit had to be built stronger to carry military loads, and had more wing added to carry the weight to altitude.

When the United States stopped building racing planes, pursuit-plane development stopped as though on orders forbidding any further experimentation.

This fact was seen repeatedly during the National Air Races held at Mines Field, Los Angeles, September 8–16. The field, now the Los Angeles International Airport, was especially built for the event, and 100,000 people attended each of the last three days, coming early and staying late. Just 18 years earlier the first National Air Meet had been held at Los Angeles, but the events were mostly of local interest while this year's races were truly national.

Three transcontinental derbies from Roosevelt Field, N. Y., for engines of different categories, were outstanding events on the program. These races focused the attention of millions on flying, and thousands gathered at Mines Field to see the finish of these races. The fastest speed was turned in by Robert Cantwell when he flew his orange-colored Lockheed Vega coast to coast in 24 hrs. 9 min. elapsed time, averaging a little more than 100 mph including gas stops.

The John L. Mitchell Trophy Race was held for the seventh straight year, and for the fourth consecutive year the winning speed dropped.

The ten starters this year were all Curtiss P-1A and B pursuits, and the race was, as usual, close, with Lt. E. H. Lawson winning at 154.7 mph.

The closed-course races were still being separated, civilian or military, and this year the Army and Navy did not fly against each other. Event No. 12, held on Sunday the 16th, was open to all military planes, but only the Navy participated, probably because their first new Boeing XF4B fighter was known to be faster than any Army standard pursuit.

Lt. Treadwell, in a Boeing Packard FB-5, led the first two laps but was forced out after blowing two sparkplugs. Winner was Lt. Jeter, flying the XF4B against the remaining F2B-1 Boeings. He set the fastest speed of the races—172.3 mph average—for the 60-mile 6-lap course. All finishers were powered by P&W Wasp engines. The Navy was beginning to equip all her fighters with lighter weight, easier maintained air-cooled engines, shunning the more streamlined water-cooled types.

Most popular of all the flying events was the daily performance of the Army's "Three Musketeers," Lts. J. J. Williams, Cornelius, and Woodring, in their Boeing PW-9D planes; and the Navy's "Three Sea Hawks," Lts. Tomlinson, Davis, and Storrs, in Boeing F2B-1's. The "Sea Hawks" stole the show when each day they took to the air in a breathless series of tight formation acrobatics, often inverted and at altitudes of less than 100 feet.

On the fourth day of the races, Lt. Williams, leader of the "Three Musketeers," flew into the ground while diving inverted across the airport in emulation of the "Three Sea Hawks," and was instantly killed. Army Reserve Lt. Charles A. Lindbergh, who had, the year previous, flown the Atlantic Ocean solo, led the "Musketeers" very ably for the remaining days of the races.

The 19 closed-course races, seven civilian and twelve military, were run off with pleasing regularity. While no unusual speeds were made, the commercial ships generally showed a higher speed level than the year before, mainly because of Lockheed's Vega, which attracted great attention. Here was a 6-passenger cabin plane that was cleaner and faster than any previous commercial aircraft. It was designed by John Northrop and the first one was built in 1927. The Vega ships were somewhat similar in appearances to the Dayton-Wright racer of 1920, but were fitted with a fixed landing gear. Construction was of plywood covered with linen, which was doped and polished to a high luster, cutting wind-drag to a minimum.

In the unlimited free-for-all race for civilians, Robert Cantwell again showed his skill and his Wasp-engined Lockheed Vega's speed when he won the Detroit News Trophy by turning in a speed of 140.3 mph.

Arthur Goebel was second in an identical Vega at 139.7 mph, and Roscoe Turner was eighth and last at 90.7 mph, flying a Menasco-engined Timm.

Navy's famous "Three Sea Hawks" (Boeing F2B-1's) fly inverted over the airport as Bob Cantwell pulls his Lockheed Vega out of the way as he finishes first in the coast-to-coast race. On the ground (left) is Lindbergh's Boeing PW9-D and to the right is the new Boeing XF4B.

1929 — National Air Races

Again breaking all attendance records, the National Air Races, held at Cleveland, Ohio, August 24 to September 2, drew over half-a-million paid admissions. Many more thousands of outside-the-fence watchers saw the finish of nine "on to Cleveland" derbies and twenty-seven closed-course races, for planes of every type from tiny light single-seaters with motorcycle engines on up to a trimotor race. And then, too, there were the exhibition flights.

Charles "Speed" Holman looped a Wasp-engined Ford trimotor close to the ground several times, then amazed everyone by doing a half-loop and flying the elephantine monster on its back across the airport!

Al Williams and Jimmy Doolittle, not to be outdone, put on skillful exhibitions in specially equipped stunt ships. Williams' very slow, slow rolls seemed one of the most beautiful and graceful maneuvers possible. He climbed, banked, and flew around the airport upside down, and at the finish would glide inverted as if to land in this position, then half-roll out just in time to make an eggshell-smooth, three-point landing.

Doolittle took a P-1 Curtiss Hawk five miles behind the airport grandstand for a little practice, and the Hawk shed its wings. He bailed out, went back to the Army building for another airplane, and shortly after put on his usual dazzling exhibition.

For the first time there were events for the ladies. Louise Thaden flew her Wright J-5 220-hp biplane Travel-Air from Santa Monica, Calif., to Cleveland in 20 hrs. 2 min. (flying time) to win the Women's Derby. Gladys O'Donnell was second in a straight-wing Waco biplane 41 minutes later, and Amelia Earhart came in third flying a Lockheed Vega. The first five places went to J-5 powered planes.

The first successful nonstop race from Los Angeles to Cleveland drew but two entries. Henry Brown, flying a P & W Hornet 525-hp Lockheed Air Express, glided into the Cleveland Airport with a sputtering engine and rolled over the finish line completely out of gas to win the race in 13 hrs. 15 min., having averaged 186 mph through and around adverse weather. Lee Shoenhair finished 36 minutes later in a P & W Wasp C engined Lockheed Vega.

At last most of the closed-course races were "race-horse" starts. All entries for each event were flagged off at once, and the planes flew straight ahead and then around a "scattering" pylon before entering the racecourse proper.

From complete domination by the military, the skies of America were now filled with private and commercial aircraft and pilots. And so it was at the races. There were but five military races, and the fastest speed was made by Lt. Wurtsmith when he flew his D-12 engined P-1B Curtiss Hawk around the 10-mile 12-lap course at 152.2 mph to win the eighth annual Mitchell Trophy Race. The winning speed had dropped for the fifth consecutive year.

Robert Cantwell bettered this speed slightly in the Civilian Cabin Ship Race, when he won over four other entries at an average speed of 152.3 mph, flying his 6-passenger Wasp-engined Lockheed Vega. Cantwell's speed was nearly 10 mph faster than that of Lt. Boyden, who won the U. S. Marine Squadron Race in a Wasp-engined Curtiss Sea Hawk fighter at 142.9 mph. The Vega's speed increase this year was mainly due to a newly added close-fitted engine cowling.

The multi-motored race was won by Waldo Waterman flying a 10-passenger Bach Air Yacht, powered by one P & W Hornet and two Wright J-5's, at an average speed of 136.4 mph. William Brock was second at 134.5 mph in another Bach, while M. Gorton was third and last in a Fokker F-10, powered by three P & W Wasps, at a speed of 123 mph.

Gladys O'Donnell won the women's race with 137.6 mph, in her J-5 powered taperwing Waco, and flew like a veteran. In fact, Miss O'Donnell took the home pylon on several occasions in less time than was caught for any other competitor at the meet.

Then came the big surprise of the race meet. The feature event for Labor Day was to be a free-for-all race over a 50-mile 5-lap course, in which seven planes, including one Army and one Navy plane, were entered. For seven years military and civilian planes and pilots had not competed against each other.

The Army entered a Curtiss P-3A Hawk fitted with an N.A.C.A. cowled Wasp engine, and the Navy entry was a Prestone-cooled D-12 Hawk, with the radiators built into the fuselage sides. The best civilian entry was a Travel-Air model-R "Mystery" ship, a wire-braced low-wing monoplane powered by a 400-hp supercharged Wright Whirlwind J-6-9 fitted with an N.A.C.A. cowling. This ship was flown from the Wichita factory into Cleveland Airport, where it was hangared at once and hidden by canvas curtains until race time, hence its "Mystery" name.

Seven planes started in the race, but from its beginning, the race lay between Lt. R. G. Breene in the P-3A Hawk and Douglas Davis flying the Travel-Air "Mystery" ship. In the first three laps Breene had passed three competitors, and Davis had passed two

This Travel Air Mystery, fitted with a Chevrolair 6-cylinder inverted and in-line air-cooled engine of 250 hp, was built in 1929. Carrying license R613K this ship was flown to first place in event 3 by Doug Davis at the 1929 Nationals, averaging only 113.38 mph with a sick engine. Craft was also entered in the Free-For-All but its engine ills could not be cured. Engine, built by the Chevrolet Brothers of Indianapolis, had faults but a future until depression wiped it out. (Beech)

Sharp photo shows extremely graceful lines of Chevrolair powered Mystery as it appeared at the 1929 Nationals. Craft was completed just in time to fly into Cleveland for the races so color separation stripe could not be applied. This ship could have won several class races and placed well in others, competing against aircraft of equal or more horsepower, had the engine functioned properly. (Peter M. Bowers)

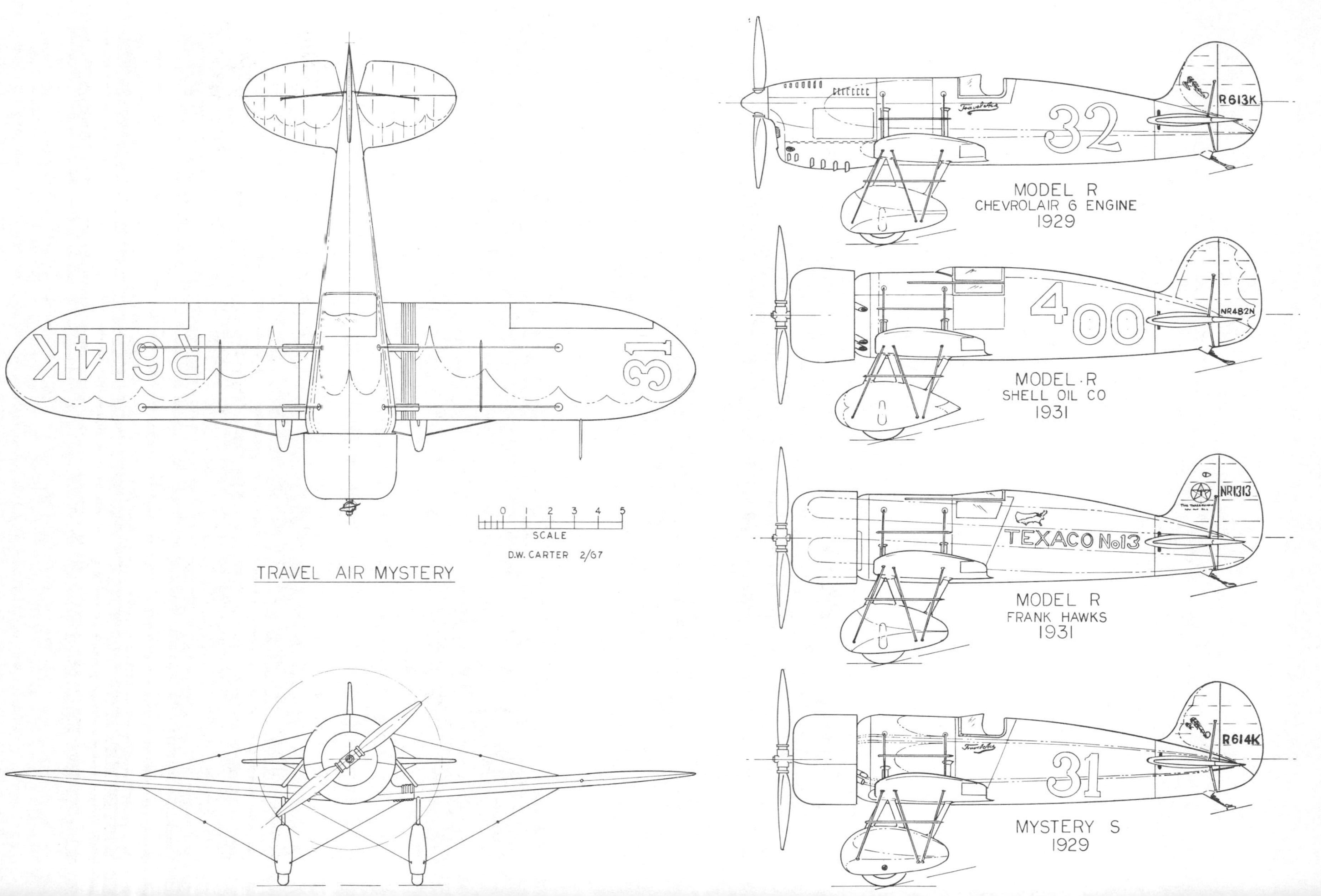
R613K
32
MODEL R
CHEVROLAIR 6 ENGINE
1929
NR482N
400
MODEL·R
SHELL OIL CO
1931
NR1313
TEXACO No 13
MODEL R
FRANK HAWKS
1931
R614K
31
MYSTERY S
1929
R614K
31
SCALE
0 1 2 3 4 5
D.W. CARTER 2/67
TRAVEL AIR MYSTERY

The trim little Travel Air Model R Mystery Ship, winner of event 26, the Free-For-All speed contest of the 1929 Nationals, was the first landplane to exceed 200 mph with an air-cooled "waffle iron" radial engine. Its special Wright R-975 9-cylinder Whirlwind engine developed about 400 hp at 2300 rpm. Its increase in power over the stock 300 hp Whirlwind was obtained by increasing the compression ratio, rpm's and supercharger speed. (Peter M. Bowers)

The Mystery Ship was designed by two of Walter Beech's young engineers, Herbert Rawdon and Walter Burnhan, as a sport and racing plane. Work began on the craft in the summer of 1928 and was built rigidly to design specs. Completed and testflown in August, 1929, the aircraft performed in excess of predictions. Top speed was 235 mph and climb rate 3200 ft/min. Range, with 47 gallons of fuel and 6 gallons of oil aboard. was 525 miles. (Beech)

Curtiss F6C-3 Hawk being fitted with unique Prestone radiators in fuselage sides, just in rear of engine. No "X" prefix to model designation was assigned to aircraft although modifications were extensive. Aircraft was restored to its original configuration after the race. (U.S. Navy)

Curtiss F6C-3 Hawk after a test hop. Great Lakes Navy BG-1 biplane dive bomber wheel pants were fitted to the Hawk just before the 1929 Thompson in an effort to eke out a few more miles per hour out of the ship.
(U.S. Navy/Bowers)

Heath Baby Bullet was world's first successful midget racer. Ed Heath did 109.5 mph in one 1929 Nationals race with his tiny ship which was powered by a 2-cylinder opposed Bristol Cherub engine of only 27 hp!
(R. E. Lorenzen)

Ed B. Heath of Chicago, in the late 20's and early 30's, designed and sold drawings and kits for a small parasol and midwing monoplane. Engines were optional, furnished either by Heath or the customer, and included a modified 4-cylinder in-line Henderson motorcycle engine.
(R. E. Lorenzen)

This extensively modified Curtiss XP-3A Hawk was fitted with a 450 hp P & W Wasp engine to compare performance with its Curtiss D-12 engined counterpart—just in time for the 1929 Nationals! Its flat-sided fuselage was rounded, back of its full NACA cowl, with formed aluminum to smooth the air flow. A rounded windshield replaced the flat-sided military type for the Thompson Products sponsored Free-For-All race. All struts and wires were faired at their connector points and smaller wheels seen here were worn in the race. (U. S. Air Force)

This Navy Curtiss F6C-3 Hawk was also highly modified for the 1929 Free-For-All. Its Curtiss D-12 engine was cooled by Prestone radiators which were fitted on both sides of the fuselage, between rear of engine and front of cockpit in area usually occupied by machine guns and ammunition. All struts and wires were faired at connections and the landing gear was simplified by using wire instead of center brace struts. Engine malfunction during race prevented Hawk from showing its true capability. (U. S. Navy)

Doug Davis poses at Cleveland with his Mystery which greatly influenced trend towards low-wing monoplanes. Ship wore no flaps, was painted red with engine cowl, stripes and scallops painted black. Landing gear shock springs were built inside of wheel pants, a novel method.
(Peter M. Bowers)

Curtiss-Wright bought out Walter Beech shortly before the 1929 stock market crash and sent this Mystery Ship, along with other Curtiss aircraft on a wide demonstration tour. Cy Young-love, in his flashy exhibitions, featured a mile around loop with the ship to show its agility.
(Beech)

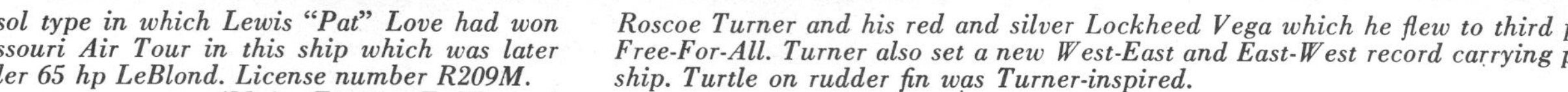

Davis high-wing monoplane was re-worked parasol type in which Lewis "Pat" Love had won 1929 All-Ohio Derby. Pat won the 1929 All-Missouri Air Tour in this ship which was later destroyed by a factory fire. Engine was a 5-cylinder 65 hp LeBlond. License number R209M.
(Major Truman T. Weaver)

Roscoe Turner and his red and silver Lockheed Vega which he flew to third place in the 1929 Free-For-All. Turner also set a new West-East and East-West record carrying passengers in this ship. Turtle on rudder fin was Turner-inspired.
(Lockheed)

in spite of having to turn back and recircle a pylon he had missed. Both pilots flew rather high, between 200 and 300 feet, but their turns were a little better than the other pilots.

Davis soon led the field and finished well ahead at an average speed of 194.9 mph, his fastest lap being 208.7 mph. Lt. Breene was second at 186.8 mph, and Roscoe Turner, flying a Wasp-engined Lockheed Vega, was third at 163.8 mph. Comdr. J. J. Clark, USN, finished fourth in a Curtiss Hawk F6C-6, averaging 153.4 mph.

In winning, Doug Davis had made the highest speed ever achieved by a commercial plane, and it was also the first time in the history of American air racing that a commercial plane had defeated both the Army and Navy in a free-for-all. And Roscoe Turner had bested a cleaned-up Navy fighter in a 6-passenger cabin plane!

This race and the appearance of the Travel-Air "Mystery," which was capable of 235 mph on the straight-away, 70 mph faster than the Army's standard P-1 ships and 50 mph above the Navy's new F4B fighters, heralded the beginning of a new era in racing history.

Frank Hawks' famous record-setting Lockheed Air Express was built for possible air line use. Ship was purchased by Texaco after Hawks flew it non-stop Los Angeles to New York in 18 hours 21 minutes on February 5, 1929, the second non-stop coast-to-coast flight ever made. Hawks later, on June 27/28, set a new East-West record of 19 hrs., 10 min. He rested for 7 hours, then flew West-to-East in 17 hrs., 38 min., 16 seconds. (Lockheed)

Black and white Lockheed Air Express was purchased by the General Tire & Rubber Co. for entry in the 1929 Non-Stop-Derby, Los Angeles to Cleveland. Flown by National Air Transport mail pilot Henry J. Brown, the "Black Hornet" consumed all of its 550 gallons of fuel and sputtered across finish line to win. Originally fitted with a P&W 450 Wasp engine the craft wore a 525 hp P&W Hornet in the Derby but gained only slightly in top speed with the larger engine. (Stephen J. Hudek)

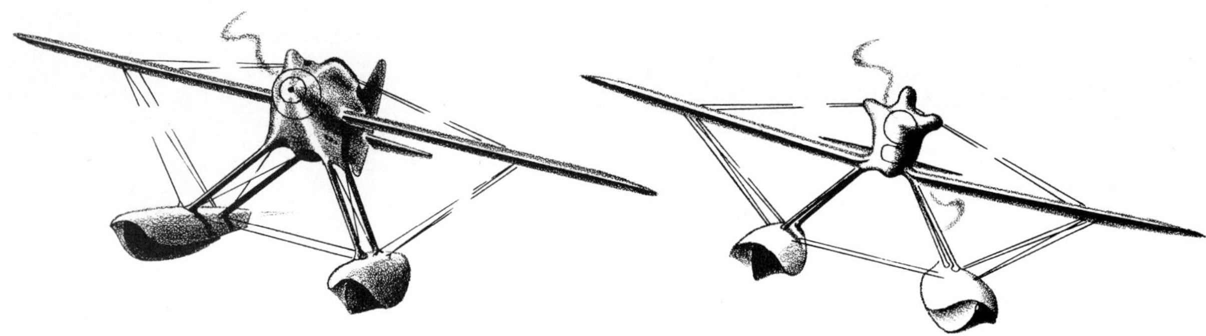

<table>
<tr><td>Lt. Al Williams' Mercury racer, which did not race.</td><td>The Gloster VI which set a record of 336.3 mph.</td></tr>
</table>

1929 – Schneider Trophy Race

When the first Schneider Trophy contest was organized in 1913, nothing of the magnitude of the later Schneider races could have been visualized. Schneider Trophy winners, from 1927 to 1931, traveled faster than any other human beings had before them and contributed more to the advancement of speed than any single factor in the history of aviation.

Originally, ten machines were entered in this year's race: one by America, three by France, three by Italy, and three by England. Then France announced that her entries would not be ready in time. The lone American entry, Lt. Alford Williams with his new Mercury midwing racer, built largely by private donations, saw the Navy withdraw its cooperation, and he was forced to remain at home.

Italy lost several (including her fastest) racing seaplanes in accidents and lost Capt. Motta, one of her best racing pilots, during early tests. He was killed while testing a Macchi-67, a single-engined seaplane capable of doing 351 mph. Italy, however, announced that she would fly in the race as a sporting gesture, without much hope of victory, to make the race possible.

The Italian race team was selected and trained in the manner of a team of championship swimmers or boxers. Some 50 good pilots were examined, and from these about 20 were chosen for further tests on fast seaplanes. Finally the number was cut down to the six who arrived at Calshot, England. Their doctor dogged each man's footsteps constantly: no man could drink coffee, special cooks from sunny Italy prepared spaghetti in just the right manner, and no man on the Italian team was allowed social visits with Calshot girls.

The British team, called the High-Speed Flight, was kept more or less intact from year to year. Each pilot was a graduate of special instruction courses and each was a qualified flight instructor. Britain flew three machines in this year's race; two new wire-braced Supermarine S-6 low-wing monoplanes, each powered by a Rolls-Royce supercharged V-12 geared engine of 1,920 hp at 3,050 rpm; and a Supermarine S-5 plane that had flown in the 1927 Schneider.

The Gloster Works had built a beautiful low-wing monoplane, powered by a W-type engine, for this race, but it could not be readied in time.

The Supermarine S-6 was a direct descendant of of the S-4, which in 1925 set the world's seaplane record of 236.6 mph, and of the S-5, which in 1927 won the Schneider Trophy at 281.6 mph and in 1928 averaged 319.5 mph over a 3-km course, the fastest speed ever recorded for land or seaplanes.

All metal, the S-6 weighed nearly twice as much as the S-5 and was larger because of the engine weight and size, but its engine power was more than doubled, improving the power-weight ratio a little. Designed by R. J. Mitchell, the S-6 had many novel features. The wing radiators, consisting of two sheets of dur-alumin with water space between, were made as a wing covering to take torsional loads. Perfectly flat, the radiators had no wind resistance and saved weight over other types. Twenty-four gallons of water filled the cooling system. The engine-oil tanks were located in the tail fin, the surface providing radiation for cooling. Hot oil from the engine passed through external corrugated radiators along the fuselage sides to the tank and returned to the engine through ducts under the fuselage. Eleven gallons of castor oil circulated through the system at the rate of eight gallons per minute. The pontoons carried 115 gallons of gasoline.

The engine was not run at full throttle for long because of insufficient cooling, and the gas tanks did not carry enough fuel to cover the course at top power.

The 1929 Schneider-winning Supermarine S-6 looked very much like a larger edition of the 1927 Supermarine S-5, which it was. Main difference included a V-type engine instead of W-type, which changed appearance of nose considerably, and larger overall size apparent mainly in floats. Corrugated oil radiators on fuselage sides were of greater capacity to handle heat of larger engine. S-6 was all metal in construction. Note huge butter-knife propeller necessary to absorb 1,920 hp delivered by the geared Rolls-Royce engine. (Supermarine)

Flying Officer Henry R. D. Waghorn being towed to ramp after winning 1929 Schneider. Huge size of propeller blade is again apparent. Waghorn said the S-6 aircraft was extremely sensitive on its controls. "A very slight movement on the stick back and you feel as though you were being shoved through the seat; while if, after a climb, you inadvertently ease the stick forward too quickly, you feel as if no straps on earth would hold you in." (Warren M. Bodie)

Two beautiful Macchi 67 twin-float seaplanes arrived in England for the 1929 Schneider race without sufficient shake-down test flights. A third M-67 had crashed earlier in Italy, killing its pilot. The aircraft were extremely well streamlined and depended on their sleekness rather than horsepower to compete in the race. Engine power was absorbed by a three-bladed metal propeller of fixed pitch. One of the Mario Castoldi designed Macchi M-67's officially flew over a 3 km course at 347.984 mph after the Schneider. (Macchi)

Mario Castoldi still relied on plywood construction in his M-67 design, varnished and polished like a fine piano or violin. All engine water was cooled by flush wing radiators while the engine oil was cooled by radiators set flush under the engine and on fuselage sides, as seen here. All Italian racers were painted white and vivid red in later years, England wore white or aluminum and light blue for her racing colors, while the U.S. wore navy blue and gold or chrome yellow. (Warren M. Bodie)

The Gloster VI was this firm's first monoplane and was a jewel of detailed refinement. All metal in construction, it had not a projecting rivet anywhere. Plagued by various troubles the ship was not ready for the 1929 Schneider but showed off her trim form on September 10 by establishing a new world's speed record of 336.31 mph. This record was, in turn, broken on September 12 by Sqn. Leader A. H. Orlebar when he flew one of the Supermarine S-6 bombs to 357.7 mph.

(Gloster)

Wing shape of the Gloster VI was a unique effort to combine the lower drag of a thin wing with the higher lift of a thick section, much like the Short Crusader of 1927 employed. As this view and the one above shows, the wing thickens towards the outer portion thus increasing lateral control at low speeds, as the inner portion would begin to lose its lift before the outer part. Maximum chord also occurred at the maximum thickness.

(Gloster)

Italian Lt. Remo Cadringher's Macchi 67 being beached after a 15-minute test flight, the only hop made before going to England for the 1929 Schneider. The other Macchi 67 had never flown when it reached England. Note protective canvas on pontoon struts, and handling slings draped on pontoons fore and aft of struts. This particular M-67 was fitted with radiators between the fore and aft struts atop the pontoons. (Aeroplane)

The Supermarine S-6 was rigidly limited to flying in winds between 5 and 15 mph. It refused to take-off from either a glassy or oily sea and was dangerous to handle in the slightest swell or white caps on the other limit. Such had become the delicate art of seaplane racing, a condition found in most Schneider planes of that era. Just five days after the 1929 Schneider race, weather conditions permitted Squadron Leader A. H. Orlebar to fly an S-6 to a new world's record 357.7 mph. (Supermarine)

The Gloster Napier VI carried its fuel in the floats and wing radiators cooled the engine water. Main oil tank was located behind the pilot and was flush with the fuselage sides, acting as radiator. Extension pipes led to flat-tube oil radiators atop the floats, as seen here. Water temperatures proved to be excessive so an extra oil radiator was installed on each side of the cockpit, spoiling the fine body lines somewhat, and the float radiators were switched over from oil to water. (Gloster)

Eversharp-nosed Gloster VI flew but one minute on its maiden flight. Taxiing tests were completely successful but when pilot Orlebar took the machine off its engine showed signs of starvation. Napier men worked day and night revising the fuel system; then, pressed for time, Orlebar made a spectacular flight so late that as he took off lights were aglow in the Yacht cabins on the Solent and the navigation buoys in the channel. Never had a high-speed flight been made under such poor light conditions.

(R. R. Martin)

The beautifully proportioned Mercury racer was designed in the Bureau of Aeronautics, Navy Department and was built at the Naval Aircraft Factory, Philadelphia under extreme secrecy. A non-profit firm, the Mercury Flying Corp. was formed to provide funds for the enterprise. Again Lt. Alford Williams was the guiding spirit and most of his personal funds went into the effort. Wind tunnel models were tested at the Washington Navy Yard and aeronautical engineer John S. Kean supervised construction of the Mercury. (Anthony W. Yusken, Jr.)

Mercury fuselage, wing and fixed tail surfaces were built of wood, then plywood covered. Control surfaces and floats were aluminum. Water radiators were placed in the wing and on the float bottoms, the latter to provide cooler water while taxiing. The Mercury was powered by the same 1100-1200 hp geared 24-cylinder X-type Packard engine that carried the 1927 Williams-Kirkham biplane to 290 mph as a seaplane. Photos were taken on Santee Wharf, Annapolis Military Academy, where all test work was done. (Anthony W. Yusken, Jr.)

One of the nicest proportioned aircraft ever built, the Mercury was extremely photogenic from any angle. Much publicity attended its many mishaps and all Americans suffered with Lt. Williams in his frustrating attempts to become airborne. Engineering data was reviewed and the craft was found to be 400 lbs. too heavy. A more powerful Packard X engine of about 1300-1500 hp was to be installed while the aircraft journeyed to England aboard a destroyer but the Navy declined help at the last instant. (Associated Press)

Dejected Al Williams is seen here being towed after another futile take-off attempt. Mercury's pontoons sat quite low in the water and had a tendency to bury the left wing while taxiing below "hump" speeds. In this case the use of rudder and ailerons increased drag loads which prevented getting on the step. As a last resort the controls were kept in neutral and it was found the craft would right itself due to water reaction on the submerged float bottom. (Anthony W. Yusken, Jr.)

Propeller damage from spray occurred on take-off attempts, also when the engine was throttled back after a taxiing run on the water. To overcome the latter, Williams would cut the switch so the surge of water washed through a stopped or slowly turning propeller.   (U. S. Navy)

Richard Carroll, an avowed spectator, stated that on August 18, 1929, Williams finally lifted the Mercury into the air for a few hundred yards, her only flight. Keeping about four feet off the water he set down again because of low gasoline pressure—and another bent prop.

(Anthony W. Yusken, Jr.)

Four crewmen on starboard pontoon while portable starter was about to be engaged to nose caused this near-capsize mishap. A few loud and blue words by Williams cleared the pontoon except for this tenacious fellow who finally let go. Testing ended for that day!

(Robert F. Pauley)

Spray was so bad on take-off attempts that Williams covered his goggles with a handkerchief until sufficient speed was attained to blow spray clear of cockpit, a dangerous but necessary procedure. Roar of the wide open and laboring Packard was incredibly loud.   (U. S. Navy)

In the race the engine was held to 2,950 rpm, at which speed it developed 1,850 hp. At full throttle the engine burned about two gallons of fuel per minute.

Italy was represented by two new red Macchi-67 monoplanes, each powered by a W-type 18-cyl. Isotta-Fraschini engine of 1,400 hp; and one Macchi-52, which had flown in the 1927 race, now fitted with shorter wings.

The M-67 machines were improved versions of the M-52. The wings were wood, covered almost entirely with flattened tube water radiators, and the remainder of the wing was covered with plywood.

The fuselage engine section was of metal construction, the after part being wood covered with plywood. The plywood-covered floats were built up of metal and carried the fuel. Oil radiators were built into the fuselage sides and float tops.

The contest was held in the Solent, a body of water between the Isle of Wight and Isle of Solent. A greater number of persons gathered to see this year's Schneider race than had witnessed any single activity in recent history. The water was covered with yachts and a line of large ocean steamships that had made a special cruise of the event. In addition, two British aircraft carriers and several battleships lined the course. Every space of land on each side of the course teemed with people.

The course consisted of four marker-buoys, with two of the four turns being almost hairpin angles. The course was 31.07 miles around, and seven laps were to be flown for a total of 217.5 miles.

Navigability trials had been completed the day before, and on September 7 the contestants, three Italian and three British, were lined up off Ryde Pier, Isle of Wight, for the start. Promptly at 2 P.M. Flying Officer Waghorn, in his new S-6, took off, after only a 28-sec. run, in an ideal 10-mph wind, which gently ruffled the water. He turned the first pylon off Sea View at a wide angle and promptly broke the world's speed record by rounding the first lap at 324 mph.

Dal Molin, with his engine making three times the roar of the S-6, started later in the Macchi-52, his take-off hampered by sudden rough water. Waghorn flashed by on his fourth lap before Dal Molin started, for the contestants were taking off at 15-minute intervals.

The Italian pilots Monti and Cadringher took off in their new and almost untried Macchi-67's, Atcherly roared away in the second new Supermarine S-6, and Greig crossed the starting line in the old S-5 Supermarine.

The British pilots Waghorn and Atcherly, in the S-6 planes, made their turns alike, starting their bank gradually long before approaching the pylon, throttling back their engines very distinctly, and keeping a full 80° bank, after which they leveled off, opened up their throttles, and roared down the course. Dal Molin, the Italian, made his turns in about the same manner, but skidded upwards and then dived to regain speed.

The millions watching the race had the feeling that they were being bombarded by shells everytime the fliers zipped past. A roar, a scream of wires, a flash of color, and they were gone again, almost before the watchers could see them.

Monti did 301.5 mph on his first lap, only to have an oil line burst and shower him with burning oil. He set down his M-67 magnificently at well over 100 mph although suffering acute agony, and was fighting for his life when help arrived.

Cadringher, making his first turn at the Cowes pylon at well over 300 mph, started to skid badly after his bank had reached 20°. During the skid, he seemed to be trying for more bank out of the plane with no success, and kept on sliding outward. Just when it seemed he would high-speed spin into the water, Cadringher leveled out and headed straight inland for Cowes, actually passing over Somerton Airdrome, some three miles from the shore, after which he very slowly made a wide turn and proceeded onto the course. Even so he made the first lap at 283.9 mph, but then was forced to alight, nearly suffocated because of engine fumes which filled his cockpit. This was no mean feat, for wing flaps had not been invented, and the racers landed with great care even at 100 mph. Cadringher stated that the M-67 controls were not balanced and that the exhaust fumes blew in his face making it very hard to see any reference points. Dal Molin, in his 2-year-old M-52, was now Italy's last hope.

Atcherly, in his S-6, did the first lap at 302.4 mph and, after his third lap, gained on Waghorn in the other S-6 but was disqualified for cutting a pylon. Greig, poking along at 282 mph in his 1927 S-5, provided a backing for his teammates in case of trouble with their S-6 machines.

Waghorn, first to start, turned his third and fastest lap at 331 mph and led the field throughout the race, winning first place and the coveted Schneider Trophy with an average of 328.6 mph. Dal Molin, the only Italian to finish, took second place with a speed of 284.2 mph and rounded his second lap at 287.8 mph. Greig, in the old Supermarine S-5, flew the most consistent race, varying only 2 mph in his laps, and seemed able to take his pylons sharper. He was surprised to find that he had placed third, with an average of 282.1 mph, because of Atcherly's disqualification.

Atcherly explained that his goggles had become oiled during the first lap, and in trying to remove them and reach for another pair, he had lost sight of the pylon. He was, however, officially credited with the fastest single lap time and fastest speed at which man had ever traveled, 332.5 mph.

This gem-like little Fiat C-29 had a wing-span of only 21.72 feet, while its fuselage length was but 18.88 ft. Powered by a Fiat AS 5 V-12 engine of only 1000 hp the ship once flew 347.98 mph. The craft was extremely sensitive on its controls and two sister ships were lost in earlier flights due to this characteristic. Frontal area was quite small on the sleekly finished craft and the pilot was completely enclosed by a sliding windshield. Built in 1929, did not race. (Fiat)

This unique Italian Piaggio, built in 1929, had a conventional propeller on the nose—plus a hydro propeller at the fuselage tail. Fitted with watervanes like duck feet, on struts below engine on fuselage, the idea was to get nose propeller clear by use of tail propeller; then, by use of clutch mechanisms, disengage tail prop and apply full engine power to nose propeller. Craft never flew. Note exhaust ports of Fiat 1000 hp engine atop fuselage and wing radiators which covered all but tips of wing. (Piaggio)

This Savoia Marchetti S-65 was one of the most unique aircraft ever built. A central nacelle housed two engines with the pilot sandwiched between—and an oil radiator was placed on either side of the cockpit, keeping the pilot quite warm! The wing was rather thick in section and was nearly all corrugated radiator. The pontoons were nearly flat-bottomed and made quite narrow and very long to extend far rearward and thus support the outriggers which provided clearance for the rear propeller and supported the tail surfaces. *(Warren M. Bodie)*

Extremely bold in concept the S-65 was plagued by endless troubles and was worked on from 1929 to 1931 in an effort to get it into the last two Schneider races, but to no avail. One of the new features of the aircraft were the engine crankcases of the two 1000 hp Isotta Fraschini engines. The lower half was especially molded to an elongated shape to provide a good streamline and act as the engine mount. It was ribbed and stiffened, then bolted directly to the fireproof bulkhead. *(Savoia)*

1930 – National Air Races

The 1930 National Air Races were held at Curtiss-Reynolds Airport, 17 miles out of Chicago, August 23 to September 1. There were seven derbies flown from various cities to Chicago, 34 closed-course races, and for the first time, there were closed-course events for women.

Each day Army, Navy, and Marine Squadrons displayed their beautiful formation flying, and Jimmy Doolittle, in his fast Shell Travel-Air "Mystery" ship, and Al Williams, in his special stunting Gulf Hawk rigged for inverted flight, dazzled the crowd with acrobatic flying. Williams won the trophy for the most meritorious flying of the meet.

Globe-girdling Wiley Post flew his famous *Win-nie Mae* nonstop from Los Angeles in 9 hrs. 9 min., to win this second annual event. The first four pilots flew Wasp-engined Lockheed Vega's, and Roscoe Turner was fifth and last in his slower Hornet-powered Lockheed Air Express.

Of the three military races, the fastest speed was turned in by Marine Lt. Sandy Sanderson, who had had so many harrowing experiences in his racing career. Flying a perfect race, Sandy won the U. S. Marine Race averaging only 142.4 mph. All entries were Wasp-engined Curtiss Sea Hawk fighters.

In contrast to the Marine race speed, "Benny" O. Howard, then an air mail pilot, won the civilian free-for-all race for 350 cu. in. engines by flying his

Wiley Post with his Lockheed Vega "Winnie Mae" shortly after he set a round the world solo flight record in 1933, cutting the time to 7 days, 18 hours, 49 minutes. In 1931 he and Harold Gatty had used the same plane to establish the earlier round the world record of 8 days, 15 hours, 51 min. Wiley started his climb to fame by winning the 1930 2nd annual race from Los Angeles to Chicago.

(Lockheed)

Roscoe Turner, in early 1930, talked Earl Gilmore of the California-based Gilmore Oil Company into purchasing the General Tire "Black Hornet" Lockheed Air Express for publicity. Repainted cream with red and gold trim, and complete to a 5-month-old lion cub as mascot, Roscoe set many inter-city records and, in May 1930, he and "Gilmore" (lying on ground below window) set a new East-West record of 19 hours, 42 minutes, 30 seconds, stopping once in Wichita for fuel.

(Lockheed)

Captain Arthur Page, USMC, with the specially groomed F6C-3 Curtiss Hawk in which he won the 11th and last Curtiss Marine Trophy Race May 31, 1930, at Anacosta. Engine was a stock Curtiss D-12 of 435 hp. Note forward scoop extension on bottom of radiator, streamline cover over gas filler-cap back of exhaust stacks, fairing back of radiator and elongated head rest. Lower wing roots were faired into fuselage—and all struts and wires were faired at their fitting points with putty. Engine cowl seams were taped over. (Warren M. Brodie)

Here is the same Curtiss Hawk as the seaplane above it, converted to an extensively modified parasol monoplane and redesignated XF6C-6. Newly fitted with a 700 hp supercharged Curtiss Conqueror engine and wing radiators the craft wore a sleek new engine cowling, had the gas filler cap indented and flush-covered and entire fuselage was carefully cleaned up, with no breaks for access as the stock service Hawks had. Special wheel pants were made for the craft and all struts were carefully filleted. (Kinert)

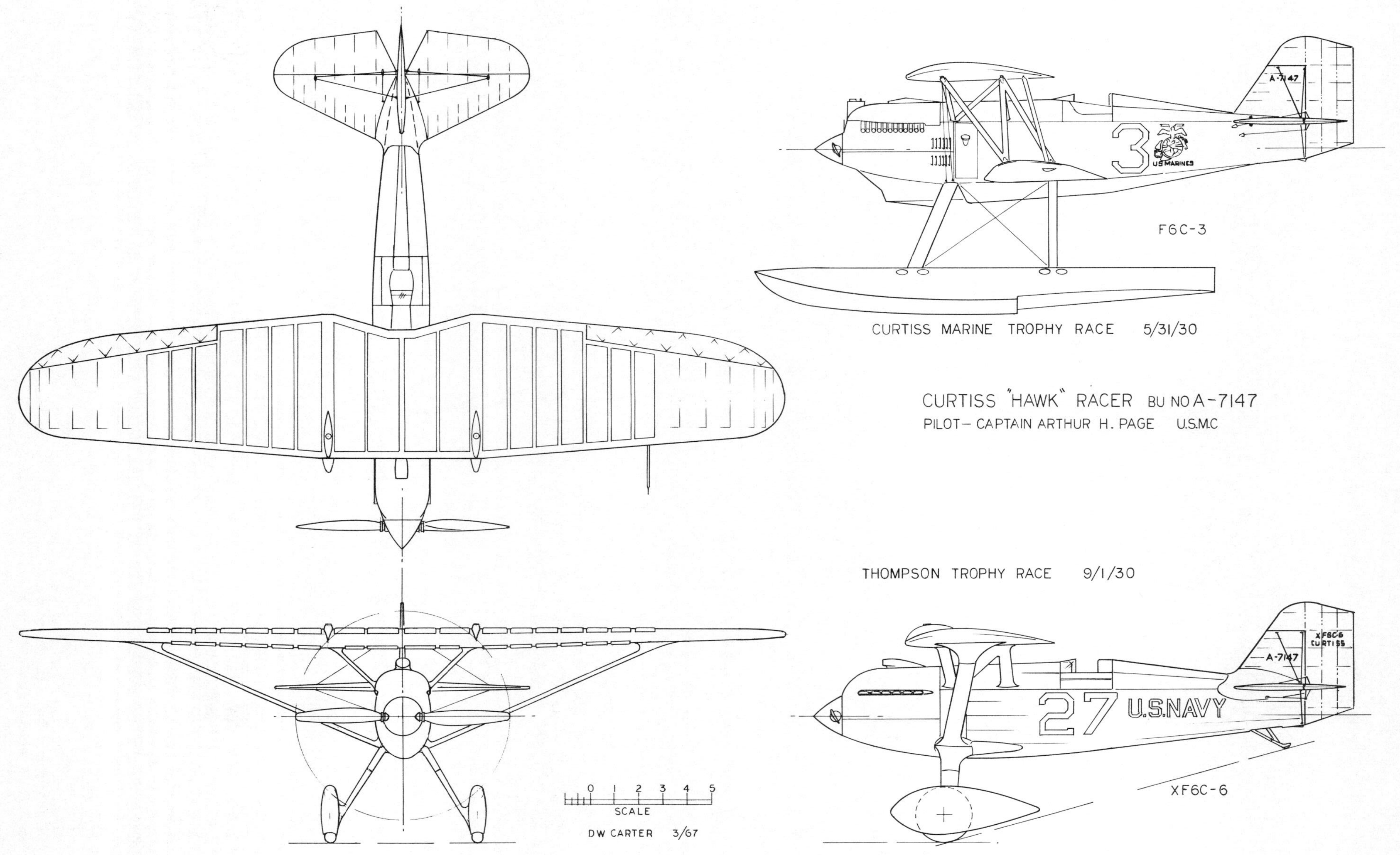
A-7147
3
U.S.MARINES
F6C-3
CURTISS MARINE TROPHY RACE   5/31/30
CURTISS "HAWK" RACER BU NO A-7147
PILOT- CAPTAIN ARTHUR H. PAGE   U.S.M.C
THOMPSON TROPHY RACE   9/1/30
XF6C6
CURTISS
A-7147
27 U.S.NAVY
XF6C-6
0 1 2 3 4 5
SCALE
DW CARTER   3/67

Captain Page poses for publicity shot, wheel pants propped into place before attach fittings were completed. Carburetor air intake atop engine was removed in trials making cowl smooth but was replaced for the race. Before the Thompson, Page stated his top speed as being about 210 mph but he averaged 219 for 17 laps from a standing start and the engine sounded as though it was not being pushed. Racer would probably true out to about 250 mph at its best altitude.　　　*(U. S. Navy)*

Rare view of Page Racer shows specially-built carburetor intake scoop atop engine cowl which was tried but later removed in favor of conventional scoop. Engine starter was moved to right rear of engine to make way for supercharger installation on left side. Starter crank and its shadow is seen below rear of engine exhaust ports. Wing radiators were natural brass finish, balance of wing was chrome yellow while balance of aircraft was a high-gloss Navy blue finish. Service stars were worn on top of wing only.　　　　　　　　　　　　　　　　　　　　　　　　　　　　　　*(U. S. Navy)*

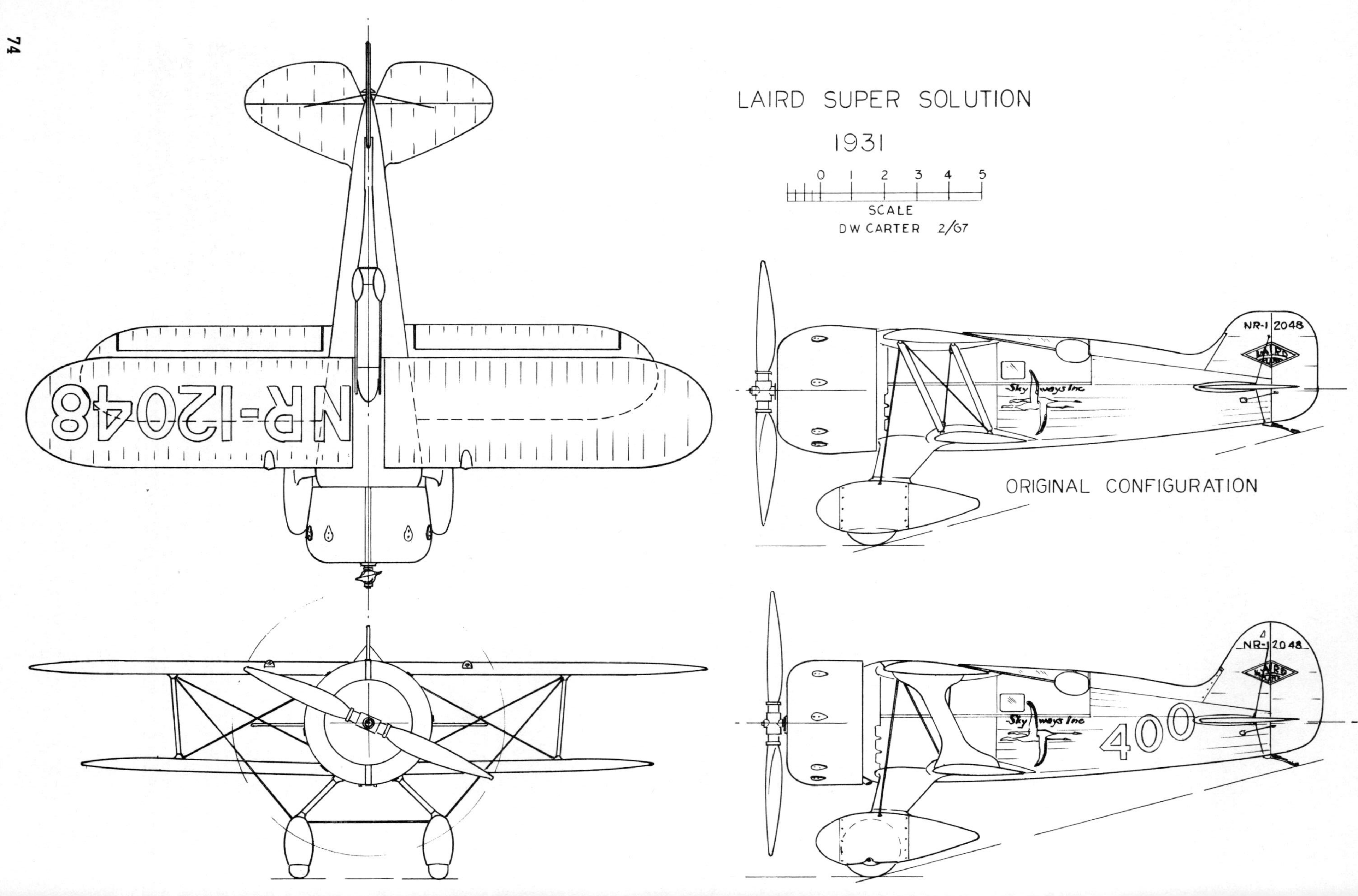

LAIRD SUPER SOLUTION
1931
SCALE
D W CARTER 2/67
0 1 2 3 4 5
NR-12048
LAIRD
Sky ways Inc
ORIGINAL CONFIGURATION
NR-12048
LAIRD
400
Sky ways Inc
NR-12048

Laird Solution after its return to factory after winning 1930 Thompson Trophy race. Charles "Speed" Holman, its pilot in the race would ordinarily dust pylons with the best but flew a cautious race as there had not been time to properly shake the ship down. Craft actually changed rig in flight to scene of the races and also in the race itself. Race number was hurriedly applied with water soluble white wash which was used at the races to mark off aircraft parking area.
(E. M. "Matty" Laird)

Contract between Mathew Laird and engine builders Pratt and Whitney called for prominent display of engine make and type on both sides of cowling.The words PandW WaspJunior were hastily and incorrectly hand painted on cowl just before ship left factory for the races. It should have read P&W Wasp Jr. as per the builder's trademark. This aircraft is being restored to its original 1930 configuration and should be on display at Hebron, Conn., by the time you read this.
(Charles G. Mandrake)

Cessna GC-1 built for the 1930 5541-mile Cirrus All-American Air Derby. Stan Stanton, above, flew entire Derby with a sick Cirrus, finished 7th out of 10 finishers. Earl Smith flew GC-1 to 4th place in 1000 cu. in. event at 1930 Nationals, did 137.4 mph.　　　　(Cessna)

Cessna GC-2, sister ship to the GC-1 except for its 110 hp Warner engine, was built for the 1930 Nationals. Bill Ong flew it to two 2nd places and one 3rd place while Mary Haizlip tooled it to 2nd in the Women's Free-For-All.　　　　(Cessna)

Direct front view of the 1930 Solution shows enormous size of its P&W Wasp Jr. engine as compared to wing span. Solution was only biplane to ever win Thompson. Wings and tail surfaces were painted gold, I interplane struts and fuselage were glossy black.
(Dustin W. Carter)

Paul Adams, who finished 4th and last in the 1930 Thompson, is seen here getting a crank for his 300 hp Wright engined Travel Air. Two-seat front cockpit was cowled over for the race, the only clean up of an otherwise stock assembly line aircraft.　　　　(Kinert)

Jimmy Doolittle standing alongside Shell Oil Company red and yellow Travel Air Mystery S which Jimmie Haizlip, also of Shell, flew to 2nd place in the 1930 Thompson, just over 2 mph slower than winner Holman. Haizlip flew a much tighter race than Holman but was out-horsepowered. Five Mystery ships were built by Travel Air and this ex-ample was the only one not fitted with exposed diagonal brace struts between wing stubs and fuselage. Note large fillet at wing root. *(Beech)*

Frank Hawks and his famous red and white Travel Air Mystery Ship in which he logged well over 200 hours at an average speed of better than 200 mph. Hawks and No. 13 set and broke many inter-city speed records both in the U. S. and abroad—and sold a lot of gasoline with the publicity. Mystery wore a water-soluble white race number 28 in 1930 Thompson. Aircraft is on display at Museum of Science and Industry, Chicago. *(Texaco)*

Florence Barnes and her Mystery Ship. Florence, a female Wallace Beery type, purchased her ship with money earned operating a real swinging motel on the Mojave Desert above Los Angeles. Many a pilot availed themselves of the landing strip near her fun place.
(Charles G. Mandrake)

Another view of Florence Barnes' Mystery Ship with new 7-cylinder Wright Whirlwind and before final striping had been applied. The engine alone cost $3,000, a lot of money in a 1930 depression year, but the motel continued to flourish.
(Beech)

Jimmy Doolittle with modified Shell Mystery as it appeared in 1931. Note higher head-rest and new canopy which made cockpit more comfortable and increased visibility. Wheel pants are slightly different shape than those on other Mystery Ships.
(Beech)

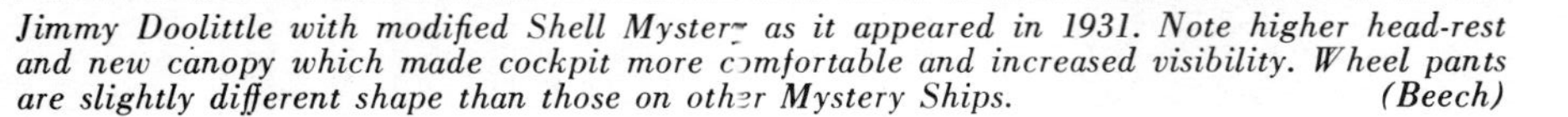

Frank Hawks poses in flight with his flashy Mystery. New canopy which covered entire cockpit had not yet been installed. Hawks was killed attempting to take-off down wind in demonstration of a Gwinn Air Car biplane, crashed into trees at end of a short field.
(National Archives)

Here is the 1930 Travel Air Mystery that originally wore a Chevrolair in-line and inverted air-cooled engine, now wearing a J-6-7 Wright engine of 225 hp, the only Mystery to be so fitted. Striping to delineate new red and black re-paint job had not yet been applied. This is the aircraft that Florence Lowe Barnes purchased and had a Townend short chord ring cowl fitted, the only Mystery not to wear a full NACA cowl. Fuselage of the Mystery Ships was oval in shape although appearing round. (Beech)

Florence Barnes, on the 5th of August, 1930, set a new world's record for women by flying this Mystery over a 3-kilometer course at Grand Central Airport, Glendale, California, at an average 196.19 mph. This is how ship appeared in late 30's after Paul Mantz had flown it in countless movies and re-painted it several times. Ring cowl is the original, although quite beat up. Engine wears an exhaust collector ring, an addition. Parts of this ship still exist. (Paul Mantz)

Frank Hawks' Mystery rolled out of the factory painted red and yellow, as seen above, soon wore the more traditional Texaco red and white, below. Hawks, who once flew a towed open cockpit glider from coast-to-coast in stages as a publicity stunt, was one of the first well-known pilots to "come inside" from the elements, quickly grew to love the comforts of an enclosed and heated cockpit. No. 13 was the first of two Mysteries to have cockpit enclosed, Shell following suit later. (Beech)

Texaco 13 as she appeared just before retirement and well-deserved rest. Hawks, in his record setting attempts had to fly No. 13 wide open practically wherever he went so ship quickly grew tired. Hawks established more than 200 speed records in America and Europe with No. 13, and the maps of U. S. and Europe painted on fuselage sides pinpoint the record paths. Air speed pitot tube on left wing tip seems bent a bit out of shape! (Warren M. Bodie)

Ben Howard's little jewel-like Pete was painted snow white and its black numerals were edged in gold striping. Howard had found the Wright Gypsy engine in storage in St. Louis, talked the owner into loaning it to him, then built Pete around the engine. Howard, then a United Air Lines pilot, built Pete in his spare time, won enough money the first year to more than pay for Pete and picked up extra money endorsing products because of his and Pete's new-found fame. (Dustin W. Carter)

Pete was the first aircraft of 100 hp or less to exceed 150 mph. Fuselage was built up of steel tubing with wood formers and stringers, fabric covered. Wing and tail surfaces were wood, fabric covered. Wright Gypsy 4-cylinder engine weighed 285 lbs. dry, was supposed to deliver 100 hp at 2100 rpm's but Howard expressed doubts as to its ability to give 90 hp at any rpm. Engine displacement was 318 cu. in. and compression ratio was a low 5 to 1. (Dustin W. Carter)

tiny new home-made low-wing racer *Pete* at 163 mph.
Ben's beautiful vertical pylon turns and low groove
flying won the admiration of all present. He won five
races and placed third in two others against planes of
much higher power.

A highly interesting race was seen in the multi-
engine event when Ford test pilot Leroy Manning flew
his Wasp-engined Ford trimotor around the course
like a pursuit plane to win at 144.2 mph. W. J. Flem-
ing came in second in a trimotor Bach Air Yacht at
137.4 mph, while an outclassed Sikorsky amphibian,
powered by two Wasps, took a leisurely third at a
little over 100 mph.

Gladys O'Donnell had won the Women's Class
"A" Pacific Derby by flying from Long Beach, Calif.,
to Chicago in 15 hrs. 13 min. flying time, in her
special Wright J-6-7 Shell taperwing Waco, and she
made the fastest speed for women in the closed-course
events, flying superbly to win the women's free-for-all
race at 149.9 mph.

THOMPSON TROPHY

On the tenth and last day of the races, seven
planes lined up for the fastest event of the race meet,
the first unlimited free-for-all contest for the now
world-famous Thompson Trophy.

Jimmy Haizlip was to fly the Shell Oil Company's Travel-Air "Mystery" ship, and Frank Hawks
entered his famous Texaco-13 Travel-Air "Mystery,"
in which he had, on August 13, crossed the United
States from Los Angeles to New York City in 12 hrs.
25 min. 3 sec., averaging 215 mph including three
gas stops. Both ships were practically identical to the
1929 "Mystery."

Paul Adams was to fly a Travel-Air Speedwing,
a biplane with a cowled J-6-9 of 300 hp, and barnstorming Errett Williams entered a 4-cyl. Cirrus-
engined Wedell-Williams. Ben Howard was on the
starting line with his *Pete*, powered by a 4-cyl. 90-hp
Wright Gypsy engine, and was not conceded a
chance.

Marine Capt. Arthur Page was to fly the only
military entry, a Navy modified Curtiss Hawk XF6C-
6. The Hawk was almost a new design, for it was now
a parasol monoplane fitted with a 700-hp Conqueror
engine cooled by wing radiators, and the landing gear
was single-strut type with long graceful wheel pants.
(Page had, on May 31, at Anacostia, D. C., won the
11th and last Curtiss Marine Trophy Race for stock
Navy seaplanes, flying a D-12 engined Curtiss Hawk
at 164.1 mph, a record for the event.) Page's Thompson racer was the largest entry but was also the most
powerful, and so it was expected to win the race.

The seventh and last entry was a Laird Solution
biplane that had been built in 31 days. Its wings had

been bolted on at 3:30 that afternoon for a ten-minute
test hop before it was flown from designer-builder
Matty Laird's Chicago factory to be raced by its test
pilot, Charles "Speed" Holman. The Solution was almost a replica of the famous Curtiss racers with the
exception of its blunt nose — it wore a "waffle iron"
air-cooled 9-cyl. Wasp Jr. engine of 470 hp.

Matty Laird had been building, for the past five
years, the fastest two- and three-seat biplanes in the
United States, selling them to wealthy sportsmen
pilots and airlines for carrying mail. This was his
first purely racing ship.

Capt. Page was first off in his special Hawk
racer. Frank Hawks followed him into the air, and at
10-sec. intervals came Howard, Haizlip, Errett Williams, Holman, and Adams. The race was for a distance of 100 miles, 20 times around a 5-mile triangular course.

Page's superior speed was apparent from the
first. He was flying wide and had almost completed
the first lap before the last ship took off. Each throb of
his engine drew him ahead of the others. The race
had gone three laps when Hawks flew by with a faulty
engine. He wisely swept away to the right and left
the race.

By this time Page had lapped the field, and it
became a match between Speed Holman and Jimmy
Haizlip for second place, with Holman in the faster
ship and Haizlip doing the better flying. Howard was
buzzing closely around the pylons in fourth place. At
the eighth lap Errett Williams dropped out with a
faulty engine.

Page, trailing a wisp of smoke, flew high and
wide around the home pylon on his 17th lap and, to
the horror of the packed grandstands, never recovered
from his turn. The Hawk flew into the ground at a
steep angle, hitting nose down and sending a cloud of
dust 50 feet into the air. Page had gradually been
overcome by deadly carbon monoxide fumes from the
engine but had turned off his ignition before crashing.
He died the next day.

Speed Holman gradually moved up to first place
in his Laird Solution and won the race with an average of 201.9 mph. (Page had averaged 219 mph in
the Air Services' fastest craft since the 1925 Curtiss
racers.) Jimmy Haizlip came in second in his Travel-
Air "Mystery" at 199.8 mph, Ben Howard breezed
in third, and Paul Adams, who had started last, finished fourth and last in his slower Travel-Air biplane.

In winning the first Thompson Trophy Race,
Speed Holman had set a new closed-course record for
a commercial plane and pilot. It was the fastest U. S.
landplane race since the faster 1925 Pulitzer race.

◆   ◆   ◆

James Wedell and his new Wedell-Williams took 2nd place in the 1931 Thompson. Racer was painted red with white trim, wore revolver gun insignia on fuselage side, just ahead of racing number, with the words "Hot as a .44 and twice as fast." Wing panels on this and later Wedell-Williams big-bore racers were only 3" thick, about the same as a barn door.
(Dustin W. Carter)

1931 – National Air Races

The National Air Races at Cleveland, August 29 to September 7, began the second decade of this American aviation classic. Spurred by larger cash prizes, more specialized racing craft were appearing. Gone were the days when cleaned up conventional aircraft could win race after race. Racing craft, designed, built, and carefully groomed for each race, were necessary to assure victory. Racing aircraft of the early 30's could outperform our military fighting planes and were as rugged in construction.

The National Air Races were more important than ever before in the development of flight. The Thompson Trophy free-for-all led the way, and this year a new award, the Vincent Bendix Trophy, appeared. The two trophies complemented each other, for the Bendix was to be an annual cross-country high-speed free-for-all. The race, open to both men and women pilots, was to be flown between two cities on opposite sides of the continent. Special prizes went to any pilot setting a new transcontinental record.

BENDIX TROPHY

Four aircraft were ready for this first Bendix race, two Lockheed Orion six-passenger cabin planes flown by Harold S. Johnson and Beeler Bevins, a Lockheed Altair piloted by Ira Eaker, and James H. Doolittle in a new Laird biplane with fixed landing gear. All three Lockheed craft were low-wing monoplanes with retractable landing gears.

The starter's flag dropped at United Airport, Burbank, Calif., at 5:35 A.M. (E.S.T.), September 4, and Jimmy Doolittle was first off. In a scant 400 feet his tiny new Laird Super-Solution biplane, powered by a souped-up P & W Wasp Jr. engine, was off the ground. Hurdling the mountains, streaking over the Mojave Desert, Jimmy landed at Albuquerque, N. M.,

for fuel. Another stop was made at Kansas City, then a dash across the midwest prairies to land in a splash of mud at Cleveland. After refueling, Doolittle continued on to New York, landing at Newark Airport in 11 hrs. 16 min. 10 sec. elapsed time for the 2,450 miles. His average speed to Cleveland had been 223 mph, and his coast-to-coast average was 217 mph, clipping one hour and eight minutes off Frank Hawk's former record. He then took off, headed west, and landed at Cleveland to claim the Bendix Trophy and prizes — a little over one hour later.

In general design Doolittle's plane remained the same as the original Solution of 1930, but its fuselage and landing gear were more streamlined, wheel pants were added, and the engine was stepped up to deliver 535 hp at 2,400 rpm. The ship's empty weight was 207 lbs. greater because of its complete cross-country and blind-flying instruments.

Of the 29 closed events at Cleveland, most were limited as to engine cubic inch displacement. There was but one military race, the National Guard Race for the Douglas Trophy, won by Capt. J. K. Gill, flying a P & W Hornet-engined O-38 biplane at 143.2 mph.

U.S.M.C. Lt. Sandy Sanderson showed up at the races and again made the headlines by colliding in mid-air, while in formation, with a Lt. Brice. Both pilots parachuted safely from their Sea Hawks!

THOMPSON TROPHY

Highlight of the closed-course races was the second annual Thompson Trophy free-for-all. The race was around a 10-lap 100-mile course and eight air-cooled engined planes lined up for the event. Doolittle entered his Laird Super-Solution, and Red Dale Jackson was to fly last year's winning Laird Solution, now

Jimmy Doolittle poses with his new and factory fresh 1931 Laird Super Solution. Although first test flown by Doolittle in this configuration the wire braced interplane struts were replaced by single I struts before the Bendix race. Fuselage and vertical tail surfaces were painted a medium green, horizontal tail and wings were bright yellow. Pants were white. Bird insignia on fuselage sides with the words "Skyways Inc.," caused ship to be nicknamed "Skyways Buzzard" by some.
(Warren M. Bodie)

Super Solution as it looked when Doolittle flew it to victory in the Bendix, wheel pants now painted the same green as fuselage. He also had the Thompson Trophy race apparently sewed up in his little biplane before the overworked engine gave out. Jimmy had pushed the engine wide open nearly every minute of his coast-to-coast record-breaking flight and back to Cleveland. As usual, he was flying the Thompson wide open also. Jimmy Wedell and his red and white Wedell-Williams racer is seen in the background.
(Warren M. Bodie)

Doolittle (left) led the Thompson until a piston broke on the second lap, forcing him out on the seventh lap. He won the 1931 Bendix in the Laird Super-Solution, averaging 223 mph. Bayles moves into first place with his Gee Bee (middle plane), and Wedell's racer follows. Bayles pulled ahead to win easily with an average speed of 236.2 mph.

Another view of model Z Gee Bee, taken at Cleveland. Dollar cameras of this era had no filters and stock black and white film showed yellow as quite dark, as seen here. Many buffs consider this little ship the nicest proportioned Gee Bee built. (Kinert)

After building nine Gee Bee 2-seater biplanes the Granville brothers built nine single-seat monoplane Sportsters with various engines of 110-125 hp. This ship, NC46V, wore a Warner Scarab 110 hp engine. All Gee Bee Sportsters eventually raced. Note repaired wing tip. (Charles G. Mandrake)

Lowell Bayles standing by large size NACA cowl which housed newly installed 700 hp Wasp Sr. engine for attempt at world's land plane speed record. Fatal crash of Model Z at 300 mph was possibly due to loose gas cap which shattered canopy and injured Bayles.

Granville Brothers built two model Y Super Sportsters, 2-seaters with two cockpits. They were 20% larger than the Sportsters and could wear engines of 250 to 450 hp. This ship, NR11049, 450 Wasp C, was flown to 4th place in 1931 Thompson by designer Robert Hall. (Kinert)

First world famous Granville Brothers Gee Bee racer was this model Z, as it appeared on rollout from Springfield, Mass. factory August 22, 1931. It was painted black and yellow with a thin brown separation stripe. Decorations on engine cowl were gold. The Z was powered by the same 535 hp P&W Wasp Jr. that had flown the Laird Solution to victory in the 1930 Thompson and the engine was on loan to Granvilles. (Warren M. Bodie)

Robert Hall, chief designer of the famous Gee Bee racers, after winning General Tire Trophy race at an easy 189.545 mph. Note gap in landing gear legs now fabric covered. Top speed of the model Z was 270 mph, landing speed 80 mph. Craft had been built to enter both the Bendix and Thompson, tanks held 103 gallons of fuel for a 1000 mile range. Lowell Bayles flew the Z at 267.342 mph average to win 3 km Shell Speed Dashes, did 286 mph on one pass. (U. S. Air Force)

Doolittle's Super Solution wore striped wheel pants for a short time. Number 400 on fuselage side was painted Shell yellow, denoted sponsor's product. Top speed of this Solution was 250 plus mph at best altitude, making it one of the fastest bi-landplanes ever built. (Robert S. Hirsh)

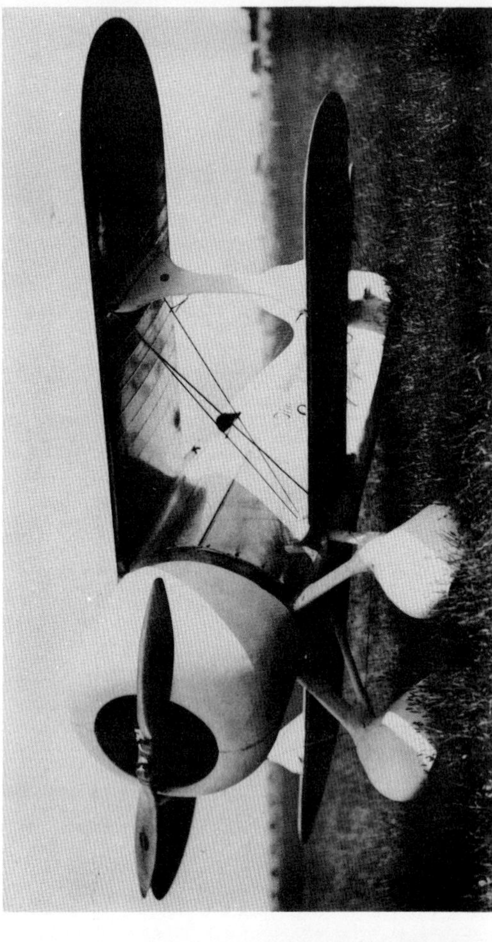

Thompson winner of 1930 appeared again in 1931 Thompson, cleaned up and carrying more horsepower. Dale "Red" Jackson bent the prop in clipping a tree top, still finished 3rd. 11 mph faster than 1930. Wings and horizontal surfaces were still gold, balance of ship was lavender. (Robert S. Hirsh)

John Livingston clipped his Monocoupe wing down to 20 feet from 32, tried several wheel pant and engine cowling combinations, finally achieved 149.466 in one 1931 race with 145 hp Warner engine. John was a top money winner from 1929 through the early 30's with his Monocoupe NR501W. (Dustin W. Carter)

Two beautiful monoplane sister ships, designed by Keith Rider and built under his supervision, raced in the 1931 Nationals. San Francisco I above, Menasco 6 engined, did 185.097 in winning one race, finished 2nd in another when engine went sour. Flown by Ray Moore. (Dustin W. Carter)

cleaned up and powered by a 525-hp J-6-9 Wright. James Wedell entered his new Wedell-Williams racer fitted with a 535-hp Wasp Jr., and Lowell Bayles was to fly a new black and yellow Granville Gee Bee Model Z, also Wasp Jr. powered. Bob Hall, designer of the now famous Gee Bee airplanes, entered a two-seater version of the Model Y Granville Gee Bee Super Sportster now fitted with a Wasp-C 450-hp engine in place of its 215-hp Lycoming engine. Ira Eaker lined up with his Lockheed Altair, Bill Ong entered a J-6-9 330-hp Laird Speedwing, and Ben Howard again entered his little *Pete.*

The starter's flag dropped, and the eight pilots took off and flew straight ahead to the scattering pylon a mile away. First around the pylon and back into the racecourse was Doolittle in his Laird, and he held the lead during the first lap at 209 mph. Unfortunately, the times were taken from the starter's flag, and no allowance was made for the time lost in the standing start or for the distance of about two miles to the scattering pylon and back. Lowell Bayles, in his Gee-Bee, was two miles behind Doolittle, and at wide intervals behind him came Wedell, Jackson, Hall, Eaker, Howard, and Ong in that order. Dale Jackson clipped a tree top and bent his metal propeller which slowed his Laird considerably, but he held on to fourth.

On the second lap Doolittle's engine began trailing smoke and the Laird slowed down — a piston had broken. Bayles quickly moved into first place. Doolittle was forced to land on the seventh lap, and Bayles won the Thompson at a new high of 236.2 mph, the other ships finishing in the order mentioned above.

Three of the planes in the race were biplanes (last Thompson appearance), and five of the eight wore fixed landing gears. All the airplanes but one were constructed nearly alike: fabric-covered fuselages built up of metal tubing and wood stringers, and fabric-covered wings built up of wooden spars and ribs. The Lockheed Altair was all wood, plywood covered, and then covered with doped fabric.

Bayles had flown five laps at over 240 mph, so eight years later an air-cooled monoplane racer had flown nearly as fast as the sleek water-cooled biplane Curtiss racers of 1923, with about equal horsepower. In winning the 1923 Pulitzer at 243.7 mph, Al Williams had dived several thousand feet to flash over the starting line, and the course he flew was 31 miles around as against this year's ten miles.

Later, in quest of the world's landplane speed record, Lowell Bayles was killed in his Gee Bee racer when aileron flutter set up in his 300-mph dive start from 1,200 feet. England and Italy had learned of flutter (wind vibration) in their Schneider plane testing and had corrected for it, but this country was finding it anew as our aircraft speeds rose.

Ray Moore flew this little San Francisco II with a 4-cylinder Menasco engine to win event No. 3, 400 cu. in., in race at 156.546 mph. Both Rider racers had metal fuselages and vertical tail fins. Finish was exceedingly smooth and polished. Landing gear was hand retracted and wheel-well top cover can be seen protruding at wing root. Some of wheel remained exposed when retracted, for roll out in case gear did not let down. (Warren M. Bodie)

1931 – Schneider Trophy Race

England won permanent possession of the Schneider Trophy at Lee on Solent, England, September 13, without a contest.

Great Britain had spent months of hazardous preparation and had built two new Supermarine S-6B racing planes for the great race, only to have France drop out when she found her three new racers hopelessly outclassed. Bad weather and the loss of pilots and machines forced Italy out at the last minute. Rain, a heavy fog, and rough water on the scheduled day postponed the race, but the following day was perfect for speed flying.

Tens of thousands viewed the speed-fest from vantage points on the Solent, and Lady Houston, who had made the British entry possible with the donation of $485,000, viewed the event from her flag-bedecked yacht.

Flight Lt. J. H. Boothman took his Supermarine (Rolls-Royce) S-6B off the water at Calshot in a wall of spray and in a few seconds was darting over Ryde Pier on the first of seven laps around the 31.07-mile triangular course. To those on the ground directly beneath the path of the plane, its passing was marked by a rumbling roar that seemed to shake the very earth and set the spectators' nerves tingling. To those who saw it from a distance, the sharp prop tip slap and engine exhaust roar was trailing the machine by more than a mile, so fast was it flying. The first two laps were the fastest, and Boothman averaged 342.9 mph. When he crossed the finish line and shot his plane skyward in exuberance, his average for the 217.5-mile course was 340.1 mph, a new all-time race record for either land- or seaplane.

Boothman brought his ship in at Calshot, making the hazardous alighting at its normal 124 mph. He had won permanent possession of the Schneider Trophy for Great Britain and had closed the greatest era of air-race history.

The two new S-6B planes were built in less than seven months and were improved versions of the 1929 S-6 planes. Externally the planes were the same as the 1929 S-6 planes excepting the floats, which were now longer. The Rolls-Royce V-12 engine delivered 2,350 hp at 3,200 rpms, and the propeller was geared slower. Water-cooling radiators covered every possible inch of the upper and lower wing surfaces and the upper surface of the floats. The S-6B weighed 745 lbs. more than the S-6, and the wing loading was increased to an unheard of 41.3 lbs. per sq. ft.

The souped-up Rolls-Royce *Buzzard* engine used in the S-6B could not last more than 40 to 90 minutes but the lessons learned later resulted in the dependable Merlin engine of World War II.

The famous Supermarine Spitfire that did so much to save England from invasion was a direct descendant of the S-6B, both having been designed by Supermarine's R. J. Mitchell, and its design features can be seen in the Messerschmitt 109 (German engineers snooped at every Schneider race) and the later North American P-51 Mustang, which was designed by a former engineer from Willy Messerschmitt's plant.

The world's straightaway record for 3-km (1.86 miles), the ultra in speed courses, was always closely allied with the Schneider race, although not a part of it. Squadron Leader A. H. Orlebar had set a new world speed record of 357.7 mph on Sept. 12, 1929, following the 1929 Schneider contest, and it remained only for England to raise this with its new S-6B's.

Lt. Stainforth attacked the record following Boothman's flight and shot over the short course six times to average 379.1 mph and reach 388.6 mph on his fastest lap, a new achievement for man in the air.

Later in the week another specially built Rolls-Royce V-12 engine, burning a mixture of refined gasoline, alcohol, and ethyl, and developing more than 2,600 hp, was installed in the Supermarine, and Lt. Stainforth took off into a gusty sky on September 29, in an attempt to break his own world record and raise the speed to a height which would challenge the genius of other nations for several years. He dived four times across the starting line at better than seven miles a minute, 100 feet above the surface of the water, and electric timing cameras proved his speed at a record 407 mph average, with his fastest lap flown at 409.5 mph!

The 1931 winning Supermarine S-6B, because of its large engine dimensions in relation to fuselage size, was not as pretty in streamline as earlier Supermarine racers. Also the pontoons were quite large in proportion to the fuselage, made necessary because of the S-6B's 6086 lbs. Wings of the S-6B were of conventional two-spar construction. The entire wing, with exception of ailerons and rounded wing tips, were covered with smooth sheet aluminum radiators which screwed directly to the ribs and formed the flying surfaces. (Supermarine)

S-6B fuselage, except radiators along the sides and bottom, rudder fin and lower portion of pontoons was painted Royal blue. Motor banks, wings, elevators, radiators on fuselage, struts and upper half of pontoons was silver. Numbers on rudder and fuselage were black outlined in white. Tail stripes were red, white and blue—red stripe at rudder post. The S-6B, race No. 7, which set the 1931 world's speed record reposes today in the South Bank Exhibition Hall, England. (Supermarine)

Fuselage of the S-6B was an aluminum monocoque structure, aluminum covered. Rudder fin and most of the fairing behind the pilot's head formed the oil tank and was built of tinned steel. The corrugated oil radiators on fuselage sides were shallow channels of tinned steel attached to the fuselage sides. A similar radiator ran under the fuselage belly. Fuselage radiators took oil from the engine to the tail fin and belly radiator returned it. (Supermarine)

Savoia tried to ready their S-65 for the 1931 Schneider but there were too many mechanical problems to overcome. Craft was quite fast, proving that its unique design with two V-12 engines in tandem was basically sound. Propellers turned in opposite directions to each other to counteract torque. All the water-cooling radiators were carried in the wing, thus leaving the floats unmarred in contour. (Peter M. Bowers)

Wing load is in lbs. per sq. ft. throughout

YEAR	COURSE and PLACE		PILOT	NATION	RACE NO.	AIRCRAFT	ENGINE	HP	SPAN	LENGTH	EMPTY	GROSS	WING LOAD	AV. SPEED	REMARKS
1913	Monaco	1	Prevost	France	19	Deperdussin	Gnome 14 cyl. twin	160	44′3″		2095	2646	8.8	45.75	*Av. 60 mph—reflew marker.*
	28 laps—174 mi.		Weymann	U.S.	6	Nieuport	row, all entries	160	39′7″	28′7″	1323	1874	7.27		*Out 5th lap. Av. 68.8 mph.*
1914	Monaco	1	C. H. Pixton	England	3	Sopwith Tabloid	Gnome 9 cyl. rotary.	100	24′7″		992	1433	5.7	86.75	
	28 Laps—174 mi.	2	Burri	Switzerland	7	F.B.A.	both entries	100			1323	1874	9.2	62	
1920	Venice, Italy	1	Lt. Luigi Bologna	Italy	7	Savoia S-12	Ansaldo V-12	500	36′5″			4784	20.62	107.2	*Only contestant—bad weather.*
	10 laps—222 mi.														
1921	Venice, Italy	1	Lt. Briganti	Italy		Macchi M-7	Isotta V-12	250	32′8″		1720	2382	9.4	117.859	*Only ship of 3 to finish.*
	10 laps—222 mi.		Lt. Zanetti	Italy		Macchi M-19	Fiat V-12	720	51′7″		5489	6150			*Forced out, fire. Did 141 mph.*
1922	Naples, Italy	1	Capt. H. C. Baird	England		Supermarine Sea Lion III	Napier Lion V-12	450	31′10″	27′6″	2381	3163	9	145.7	
	13 laps—230.3 mi.	2	Passaleva	Italy		Savoia S-51	Itala (Hispano) V-12	300	32′9″	26′1″	1716	2376	9.2	143.5	*Fastest entry—prop vibration.*
		3	Zanetti	Italy		Macchi M-17	Isotta V-12	250						133	
		4	Corniglio	Italy		Macchi M-7	Isotta V-12	250						90.6	
		1	Lt. D. Rittenhouse	U.S.	4	Curtiss R-3 Navy	Curtiss D-12 V-12	465	22′8″	25′	2119	2747	16.35	177.38	*1 lap 188.17 mph, seaplane record.*
1923	Cowes, England	2	Lt. R. Irvine	U.S.	8	Curtiss R-3 Navy	Curtiss D-12 V-12	465	22′8″	25′	2119	2747	16.35	173.46	*Sister ship to winner.*
	5 laps—214 mi.	3	Capt. H. C. Baird	England	7	Supermarine Sea Lion III	Napier Lion V-12	575	32′	27′6″	2403	3240	9.24	157.17	*Reworked 1922 Sea Lion II.*
			M. Hurel	France	10	CAMS 38	Hispano-Suiza V-12	360	28′2″	25′5″	1675	3200	10.2		*Out 2nd lap. 1st lap 130.4 mph.*
			Lt. Frank Wead	U.S.		Navy Wright NW-2	Wright T-3 V-12	700	28′	28′5″		4447	16.7		*Damaged floats—crashed in trial.*
		1	Lt. James Doolittle	U.S.	3	Army Curtiss R3C-2	Curtiss V-1400	619	22′	20′2″		2738	19.04	232.573	*Set 4 records. 3 km 245.713 mph.*
1925	Baltimore, Md.	2	Capt. Hubert Broad	England	5	Gloster III	Napier Lion VII	700	20′		2028	2650	18	199.169	*Fastest lap 201.536 mph.*
	7 laps—217.49 mi.	3	G. de Briganti	Italy	7	Macchi M-33	Curtiss D-12	435	32′	27′4″	2073	2777	17	168.444	*Fastest lap 173.858 mph.*
			Lt. George Cuddihy	U.S.	2	Navy Curtiss R3C-2	Curtiss V-1400	619	22′	20′2″		2738	19.04		*Out 7th lap.*
			Lt. Ralph Ofstie	U.S.	6	Navy Curtiss R3C-2	Curtiss V-1400	619	22′	20′2″		2738	19.04		*Out 7th lap.*
			Capt. H. C. Baird	England		Supermarine S-4	Napier Lion VII D	675	30′6″	27′	2425	3150	23.1		*Crashed in trials. 226.6 mph.*
		1	Maj. de Bernardi	Italy	5	Macchi M-39	Fiat A.S. II V-12	800	30′4″	22′1″	2760	3263	22.52	246.496	*1 lap 248.520 mph.*
1926	Hampton Roads, Va.	2	Lt. Christian Schilt	U.S.	6	Curtiss R3C-2	Curtiss V-1400	619	22′	20′2″	2050	2738	19.04	231.363	*1 lap 233.164 mph. Same as 1925.*
	7 laps—217.49 mi.	3	Lt. Bacula	Italy		Macchi M-39	Fiat A.S. II V-12	800	30′4″	22′1″	2760	3263	22.52	218.006	*Sister ship to winner.*
		4	Lt. T. Tomlinson	U.S.		Curtiss F6C-1 Navy	Curtiss D-12	435						136.953	
			Lt. Geo. Cuddihy	U.S.	4	Curtiss R3C-4 Navy	Curtiss V-1570	700	22′	20′					*Out 7th lap. 1 lap 242.16 mph.*
		1	Flt. Lt. S. N. Webster	England	6	Supermarine S-5	Napier Lion VII G	875	26′9″		2536	3197	27.85	281.65	*Record 319.5 mph Nov. 4, 1928.*
1927	Venice, Italy	2	Flt. Lt. O. F. Worsley	England	4	Supermarine S-5	Napier Lion VII D	875	26′9″		2602	3043	26.62	273.07	
	7 laps—217.49 mi.		Capt. Guazzetti	Italy	7	Macchi M-52	Fiat A.S. III V-12	1030	28′10″			3439.2	27.99		*Out 6th lap. Record 318.4 mph March, 1928.*
			Flt. Lt. S. M. Kinkead	England	1	Gloster IV B	Napier VII G	875	22′8″	26′4″	2415	3085	22.19		*Out 4th lap. 1 lap 277.14 mph.*
			Maj. de Bernardi	Italy	5	Macchi M-52	Fiat A.S. III V-12	1030	29′5″			3160	23.9		*Out 2nd lap.*

Year	Place	Pos.	Pilot	Country	No.	Aircraft	Engine	HP	Span	Length		Wt.		Speed	Notes
1929	Cowes, England	1	Flt. Off. Waghorn	England	2	Supermarine S-6	Rolls-Royce R V-12	1920	30'	28'8"	4471	5250	36.2	328.63	*Full wt. 5771 lbs. Wing load 39.8.*
	7 laps—217.49 mi.	2	Qtrmstr. T. Dal Molin	Italy		Macchi M-52R	Fiat A.S. III V-12	1030	25'9"			3263	29.69	284.20	*1927 model. One lap 287.78.*
		3	Flt. Lt. d'Arcy Greig	England		Supermarine S-5	Napier Lion VII G	875	26'9"		2536	3197	27.85	282.11	*World record 1928.*
			Flt. Off. R. Atcherly	England	4	Supermarine S-6	Rolls-Royce R V-12	1920	30'	28 8"	4471	5250	36.2		*Cut pylon. Rec. 100 km 331.75, 50 km 332.49.*
			Lt. Remo Cadringher	Italy	7	Macchi M-67	Isotta-Fraschini V-18	1400	29'6"			4740	32.8		*Out 2nd lap. 1st lap 283.88.*
			Monti	Italy	10	Macchi M-67	Isotta-Fraschini V-18	1400	29'6"			4740	32.8		*Out 2nd lap. 1st lap 301.47.*
1931	Lee on Solent, England	1	Lt. J. H. Boothman	England		Supermarine S-6B	Rolls-Royce *Buzzard* V-12	2350	30	28'10"	4590	6086	41.3	340.1	*Record 406.997 mph Sept. 29, 1931, by Lt. Stainforth in a S-68. The engine developed more than 2600 hp.*
	7 laps—217.49 mi.														

(See Vol. I for 1924-25 Pulitzer Race Results.)

NATIONAL AIR RACES – 1926-1929

Year	Place	Pos.	Pilot	No.	Aircraft	Engine	HP	Span	Length		Wt.		Speed	Notes
		1	Lt. George Cuddihy		Boeing FB-3	Packard 2A-1500, V-12	600	32'	23'	2502	3043	12.57	180.495	*New standard shipboard fighter.*
1926	10 laps—120 mi.	2	Lt. L. G. Elliott		Curtiss Hawk P-2	Curtiss V-1400, V-12	500	31'6"	22'10"	2728	3255	13	178.609	*P-1 with larger engine.*
	Kansas City Rotary	3	Capt. Ross Hoyt		Curtiss Hawk P-2	Curtiss V-1400, V-12	500	31'6"	22'10"	2728	3255	13	170.909	
	Club Trophy	4	Lt. C. C. Nutt		Curtiss Hawk P-2	Curtiss V-1400, V-12	500	31'6"	22'10"	2728	3255	13	170.759	
	(Military)	5	Lt. H. T. McCormick		Curtiss Hawk P-2	Curtiss V-1400, V-12	500	31'6"	22'10"	2728	3255	13	169.588	
	Philadelphia,	6	Lt. H. D. Barner		Boeing FB-3	Packard 2A-1500, V-12	600	32'	23'	2502	3043	12.57	163.574	
	Pennsylvania	7	Lt. L. H. Sanderson, USMC		Boeing FB-3	Packard 2A-1500, V-12	600	32'	23'	2502	3043	12.57	163.364	
		8	Lt. A. B. Ballard		Curtiss Hawk P-1	Curtiss D-12, V-12	435	31'6"	22'6"	2041	2841	11.36	159.255	
			Lt. W. McKiernan		Curtiss Hawk P-1	Curtiss D-12, V-12	435	31'6"	22'6"	2041	2841	11.36	176.186	*Disqualified for cutting pylon.*
		1	Lt. Batten	3	Curtiss Hawk XP-6A	Curtiss V-1570-1, V-12	700	30'	23'7"	2350	3048	12	201.239	*Normal engine 600 hp.*
		2	Lt. A. J. Lyon	14	Curtiss Hawk XP-6	Curtiss V-1570-1, V-12	700	31'	22'7"	2109	3011	11.5	189.608	*Normal engine 600 hp.*
		3	Lt. Thomas Jeter	23	Boeing FB-5	Packard 2A-1500, V-12	600	32'	23'7"	2065	3189	13.1	176.940	*Production model of FB-3.*
		4	Lt. H. E. Regan	21	Boeing FB-5	Packard 2A-1500, V-12	600	32'	23'2"	2065	3189	13.1	175.937	
1927	10 laps—120 mi.	5	Lt. Gerald Bogan	22	Boeing FB-5	Packard 2A-1500, V-12	600	32'	23'2"	2065	3189	13.1	172.872	
	Spokane Spokesman-	6	Lt. C. H. Beverly	6	Boeing PW-9C	Curtiss D-12D, V-12	440	32'	23'5"	1935	3039	11.2	169.731	
	Review Trophy,	7	Lt. F. C. Rogers	18	Curtiss Hawk F6C-4	P & W Wasp (a)	435	31'6"	22'	1840	2555	10.22	161.559	
	Spokane, Washington	8	Lt. W. L. Cornelius	11	Curtiss Hawk P-1B	Curtiss D-12	435	31'6"	22'6"	2041	2841	11.36	161.502	
		9	Lt. I. A. Woodring	2	Curtiss Hawk P-1B	Curtiss D-12	435	31'6"	22'6"	2041	2841	11.36	159.184	
			Lt. L. C. Mallory	1	Curtiss Hawk P-1B	Curtiss D-12	435	31'6"	22'6"	2041	2841	11.36		*Ruled out, cut pylon.*

YEAR	COURSE AND PLACE		PILOT	RACE NO.	AIRCRAFT	ENGINE and CU. IN. DISPLACEMENT	HP	SPAN	LENGTH	EMPTY	GROSS	WING LOAD	AV. SPEED	REMARKS
1928	6 laps—60 mi.	1	Lt. Thomas Jeter		Boeing XF4B-1	P & W Wasp R-1340-7	450	30'	20'7"	1664	2557	10.6	172.26	Lapped all entries.
	Military free-for-all—	2	Lt. Edgar Cruise		Boeing F2B-1	P & W Wasp R-1340-3	450	30'1"	23'	1900	2690	11.15	159.86	
	Event 12,	3	Lt. Harrigan		Boeing F2B-1	P & W Wasp R-1340-3	450	30'1"	23'	1900	2690	11.15	151.6	
	Los Angeles, Calif.	4	Lt. Burroughs		Boeing F2B-1	P & W Wasp R-1340-3	450	30'1"	23'	1900	2690	11.15	150.3	
		5	Lt. Crommelin		Boeing F2B-1	P & W Wasp R-1340-3	450	30'1"	23'	1900	2690	11.15	149.8	
		6	Lt. Williamson		Boeing F2B-1	P & W Wasp R-1340-3	450	30'1"	23'	1900	2690	11.15	146	A 7th entry, Lt. Treadwell out 2nd lap.
1929	5 laps—50 miles	1	Douglas Davis	31	Travel-Air "R" "Mystery"	Wright J-6-9 R-975	400	29'2"	20'2"	1475	1940	15.5	194.9	1 lap 208.69 mph. License No. R614K.
	Event 28	2	Lt. R. G. Breene, AC	80	Curtiss Hawk P-3A	P & W Wasp R-1340-3	450	31'6"	22'5"	2180	2788	10.6	186.84	
	free-for-all,	3	Roscoe Turner		Lockheed Vega	P & W Wasp C-1344	450	41'	27'6"	2595	4500	16.35	163.84	High wing monoplane.
	Cleveland, Ohio	4	Comdr. J. J. Clark, USN		Curtiss Hawk F6C-6	Curtiss D-12, V-1145	435	31'7"	22'10"	2280	2902	11	153.38	Prestone radiators in fuselage sides.
		5	H. S. Myhres		Simplex	Wright J-6-9	300	34'4"	22'	1467	2094	13.3	152.15	Low-mono.
		6	I. M. Conaughey		Travel-Air	Wright J-6-9	300	31'	23'6"	1780	2821	11.41	145.2	Biplane.
		7	C. D. Bowyer		Cessna Cabin	Comet 7 cyl. radial	165	40'6"	23'8"	1375	1885	8.4		Out 2nd lap.

THOMPSON TROPHY RACE 1930—1931

YEAR	COURSE AND PLACE		PILOT	RACE NO.	LICENSE NO.	AIRCRAFT	ENGINE and CU. IN. DISPLACEMENT	HP	SPAN	LENGTH	EMPTY	GROSS	WING LOAD	AV. SPEED	REMARKS
		1	Charles Holman	77	NR10538	Laird Solution	P&W Wasp Jr., 985	470	21'	19'6"	1380	1895	16.9	201.91	
1930	20 laps—100 miles	2	James Haizlip	26	NR482N	Travel-Air "R" "Mystery"	Wright J-6-9, R-975	400	29'2"	20'2"	1500	1965	15.6	199.8	
	Chicago, Illinois	3	Ben Howard	37	NR2Y	Howard Pete	Wright Gypsy, 318	90	20'1"	17'9"	669	900	14.28	162.8	
		4	Paul Adams	81	449W	Travel-Air Speedwing	Wright J-6-9, 975	300	31'	23'6"	1784	2825	11.44	142.64	
		1	Lowell Bayles	4	NR77V	Gee-Bee Super Sportster	P&W Wasp Jr., 985	535	23'6"	15'1"	1400	2280	30.2	236.239	
1931	10 laps—100 miles	2	James Wedell	44	NR278V	Wedell-Williams 44	P&W Wasp Jr., 985	535	26'2"	21'3"	1500	2206	17	227.992	
	Cleveland, Ohio	3	Dale Jackson	77	NR10538	Laird Solution	Wright J-6-9, R-1750	525	21'	19'6"	1385	1900	17	211.183	Last year's winner reworked.
		4	Robert Hall	54	NR11049	Gee-Bee 'Y'	P&W Wasp-C, 1344	450	30'	21'	1500	2000	14.5	201.250	Hall is Gee-Bee designer.
		5	Ira Eaker			Lockheed Altair	P&W Wasp S1D1, 1340	550	42'9'	28'11"	3550	4409	15	196.832	Full tank wing load 19.72.
		6	Ben Howard	37	NR2Y	Howard Pete	Wright Gypsy, 318	90	20'1"	17'9"	669	900	14.28	163.573	
		7	William Ong			Laird Speedwing	Wright J-6-9, R-975	330	28'	22'9"	1992	3010	15.3	153.049	

BENDIX TROPHY RACE 1931

YEAR	COURSE AND PLACE		PILOT	RACE NO.	LICENSE NO.	AIRCRAFT	ENGINE AND DISPLACEMENT	HP	TIME	AV. SPEED	REMARKS
		1	James Doolittle	400	NR12048	Laird Super-Solution	P&W Wasp Jr., R-985	535	9:10:21*	223.038	*Doolittle continued on to Newark, N.J., set west-east record (2450 miles)
1931	2043 miles	2	Harold S. Johnson			Lockheed Orion	P&W Wasp SC, R-1344	450	10:14:22	198.816	
	Burbank, Calif., to	3	Beeler Blevins			Lockheed Orion	P&W Wasp SC, R-1344	450	10:49:33	188.992	11:16:10 216.958
	Cleveland	4	Ira Eaker			Lockheed Altair	P&W Wasp S1D1, 1340	550	10:59:45	186.070	

Index

RACING PLANES
and air races
A Complete History
NR2100
by REED KINERT
VOLUME III
REFERENCE
SERIES No. 1

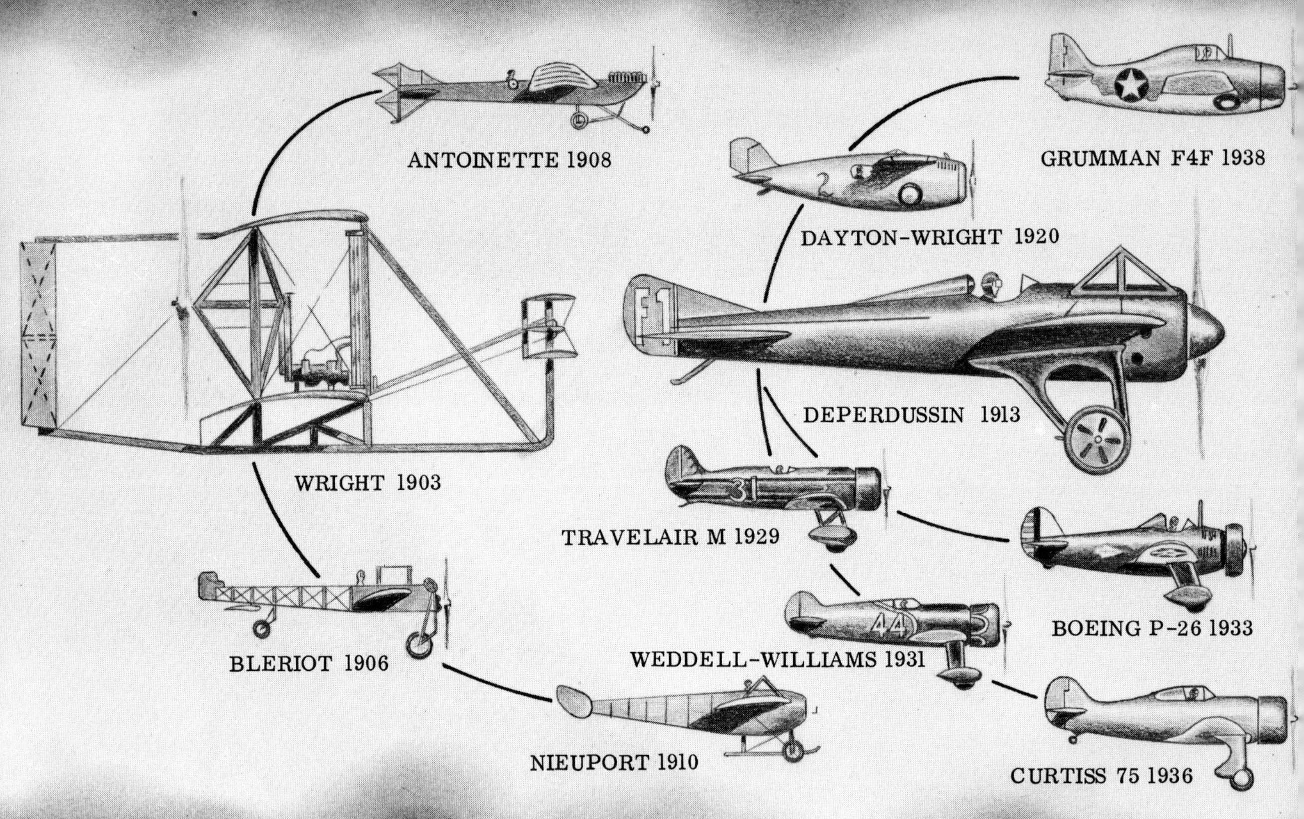

"Instead of the tardy conveyance of ships and chariots, man might use the swifter migration of wings, the fields of air are open to knowledge and only ignorance and idleness need crawl upon the ground."

—Rasselas, DR. SAMUEL JOHNSON, 1759

Written and Illustrated by Reed Kinert

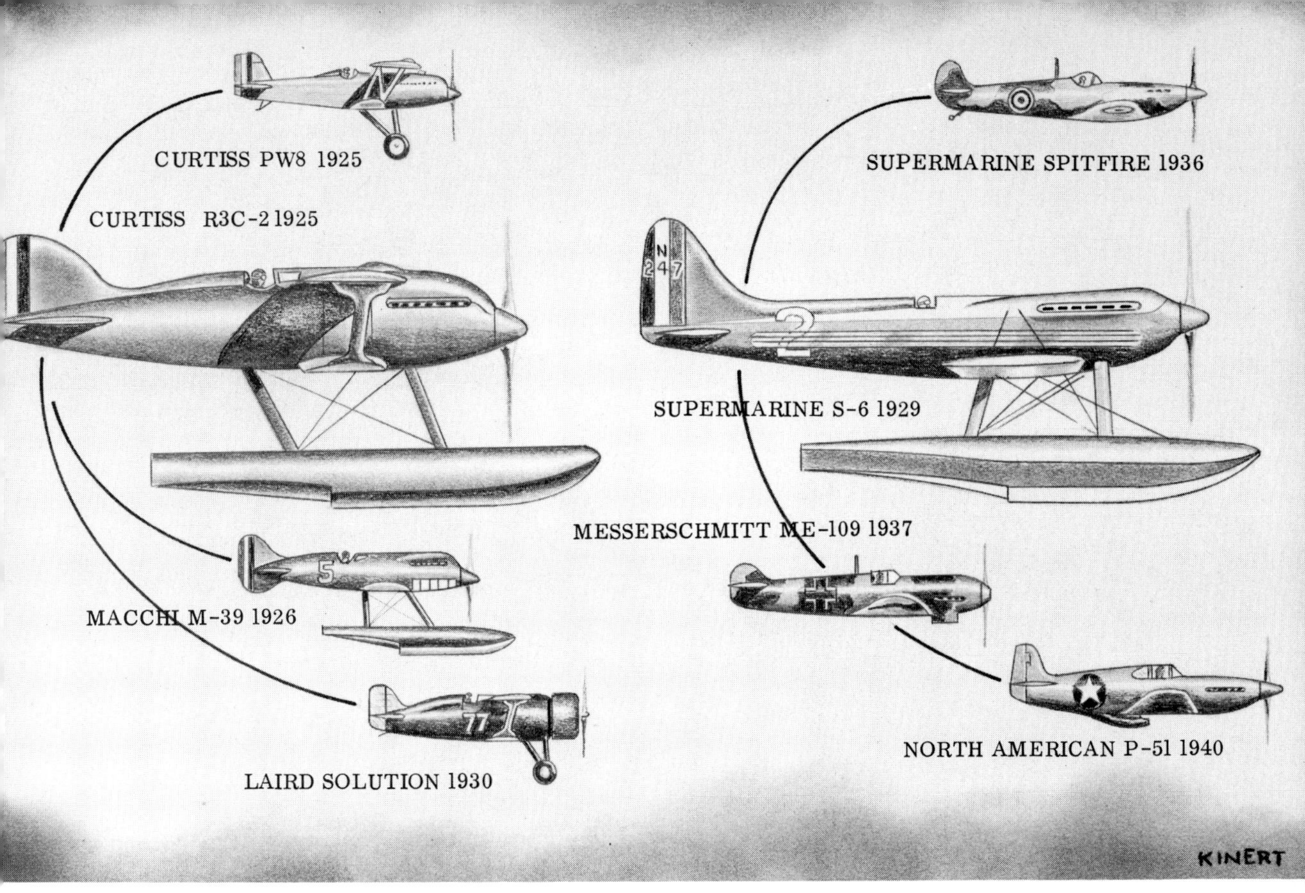

RACING PLANES

and air races

A Complete History

VOLUME III
1932-1939

AERO PUBLISHERS, INC.

Fallbrook, California

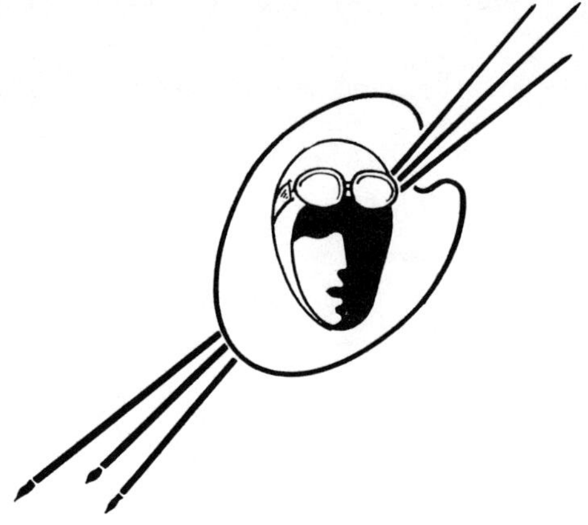

DEDICATION

To the designers, builders, and pilots of racing aircraft, for their contribution to the science of flight.
and
To my patient wife Eleanor who typed the text three times!

FIRST EDITION

SECOND PRINTING – REVISED – 1969

LIBRARY OF CONGRESS CATALOG CARD NUMBER
67-16455

PRINTED IN THE UNITED STATES OF AMERICA

Table of Contents

List of Illustrations

List of Three-Views

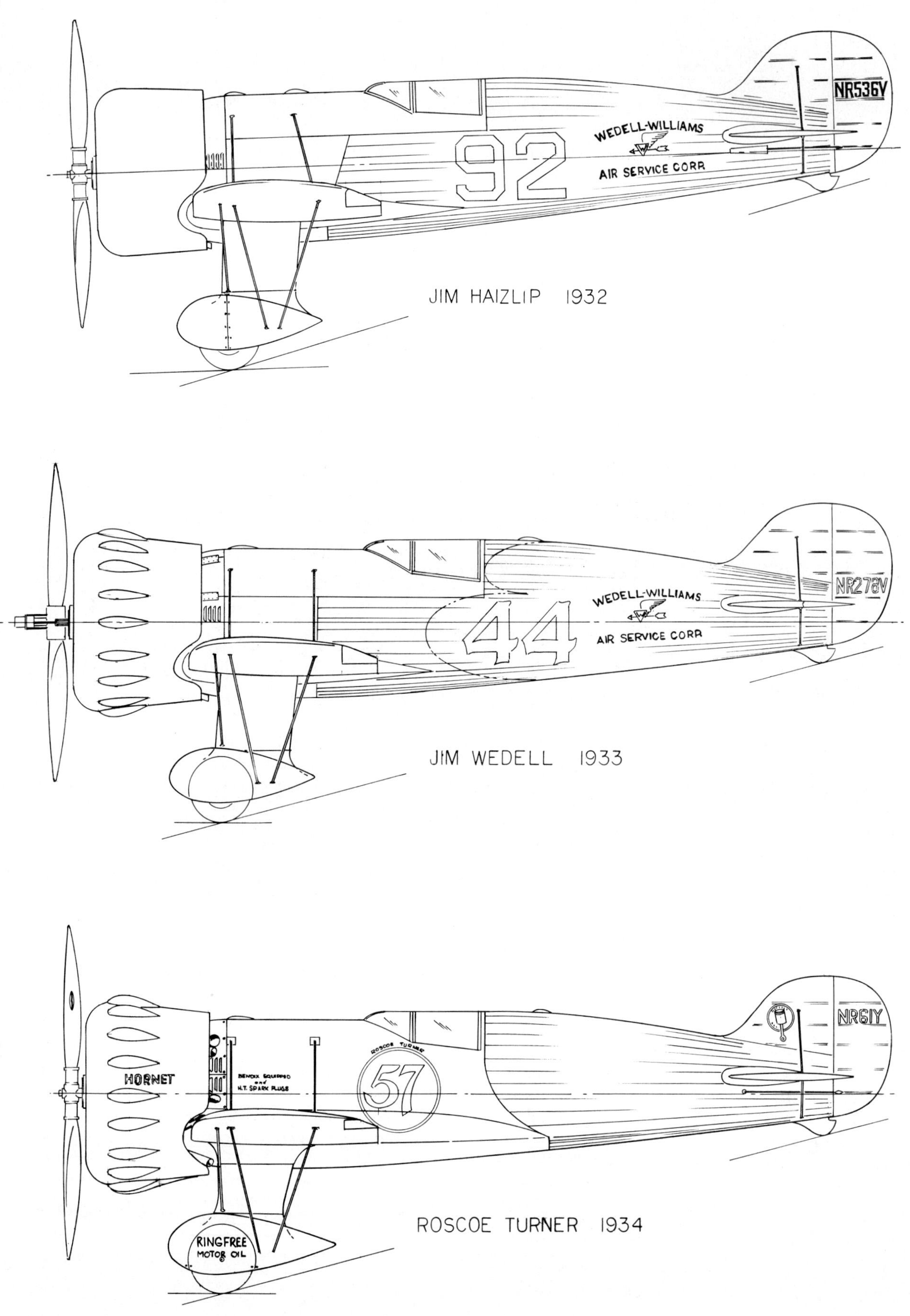

JIM HAIZLIP   1932

JIM WEDELL   1933

ROSCOE TURNER 1934

Special Taperwing Waco built for Lloyd and Gladys O'Donnell, seen at the 1930 Nationals in the colors of its sponsor, Shell Oil yellow and red. Race No. 7, license NC21M. Gladys won the 1930 Women's Pacific Derby and, through 1930-32, Gladys and Lloyd won five races in and above the 800 cu/in class. Best pylon speed was 152.05 mph. Lower wing panels were smoothly faired into the fuselage with fabric, small wheels with pants were fitted and engine was a 9-cyl 300 hp Wright 240.   *(Kinert)*

1932 – National Air Races

The 1932 National Air Races held at Cleveland, August 27 to September 5, had better competition than ever before, and more special ships built for racing.

There were seven cross-country derbies including the Bendix, 21 closed-course races, and two speed dashes. But interest was concentrated on the nine free-for-all races, seven of them limited to engines of various displacements, the remaining two being unlimited, one for men (Thompson) and one for women (Aerol Trophy Race).

For the lower horsepower races Ben Howard had built two larger versions of his *Pete*. Named *Mike* and *Ike*, the planes, powered by newly developed 160-hp Menasco 6-cyl. in-line inverted and air-cooled engines, were indeed alike in appearance, but *Ike* wore two pairs of small tandem landing wheels, while *Mike* wore the regular two wheels. *Pete, Mike,* and *Ike* took three first places, three second, one fourth, two fifth and one seventh place.

Steve Wittman, the now famous designer-pilot from Oshkosh, Wis., flew his new and home-made Cirrus 115-hp *Chief Oshkosh* racer into one first, one fourth, one sixth, and one seventh place.

BENDIX TROPHY

Monday morning, August 29, four wire-braced and fixed-gear low-wing monoplanes took off from Burbank, Calif., to race against time for the Bendix Trophy. Three of the planes were Wedell-Williams racers and the fourth was a new R-2 Gee-Bee Super-Sportster (No. 7) modeled from last year's Thompson winner. All four planes were powered by 550-hp

First of the two most popular Gee Bee racers was this R-1 Super Sportster, which Russell Boardman flew on a throttled back 240 mph test hop August 13, 1932. Craft flew only once with this "bobtail" rudder as Boardman, above, quickly discovered a lack of directional stability. Two feet of vertical fin was then added, offset several degrees to combat engine torque, and the rudder size was increased. Before Boardman could race No. 11 he spun in with a Warner Gee Bee Sportster and was injured.
(Dustin W. Carter)

Boardman, running engine up before first test hop, bought controlling interest in the Springfield Air Race Association (S.A.R.A.) so he could pilot No. 11 in the 1932 Thompson. He test-hopped the craft from Springfield Airport, where the Granville Brothers factory was located, landed at Bowes-Agawam Airport, just across the Connecticut River. Robert Hall was chief designer of the R-1 and R-2 Gee Bee's, left the company before either ship was completed. Zantford Granville then supervised construction. His four brothers assisted.
(Charles G. Mandrake)

Lee Gelbach and Gee Bee R-2, just prior to 1932 Bendix start. Work on this second Super Sportster had been about ten days behind R-1, so additional fin and rudder area was added before it left the factory. R-2 was built to fly in the Bendix race and Lee Gelbach was chosen to pilot the craft. On a test hop, Lee had one of the flying wires snap when it turned flat side to the wind, but control was not affected. (Dustin W. Carter)

Gee Bee R-1 after test hop with added fin and enlarged rudder, which are seen here unpainted in their clear dope under-coats. Gee Bee aircraft were noted for their sleek finish. Many coats of hand-rubbed dope paint were applied, then waxed to a mirror-like gloss. Wing panels were built up of spruce spars, plywood ribs (spaced five inches apart) and the wing then covered with plywood. Tail surfaces were constructed the same. Newly developed Hamilton Standard controllable-pitch propeller greatly aided performance of the R-1 and R-2. (Pratt & Whitney)

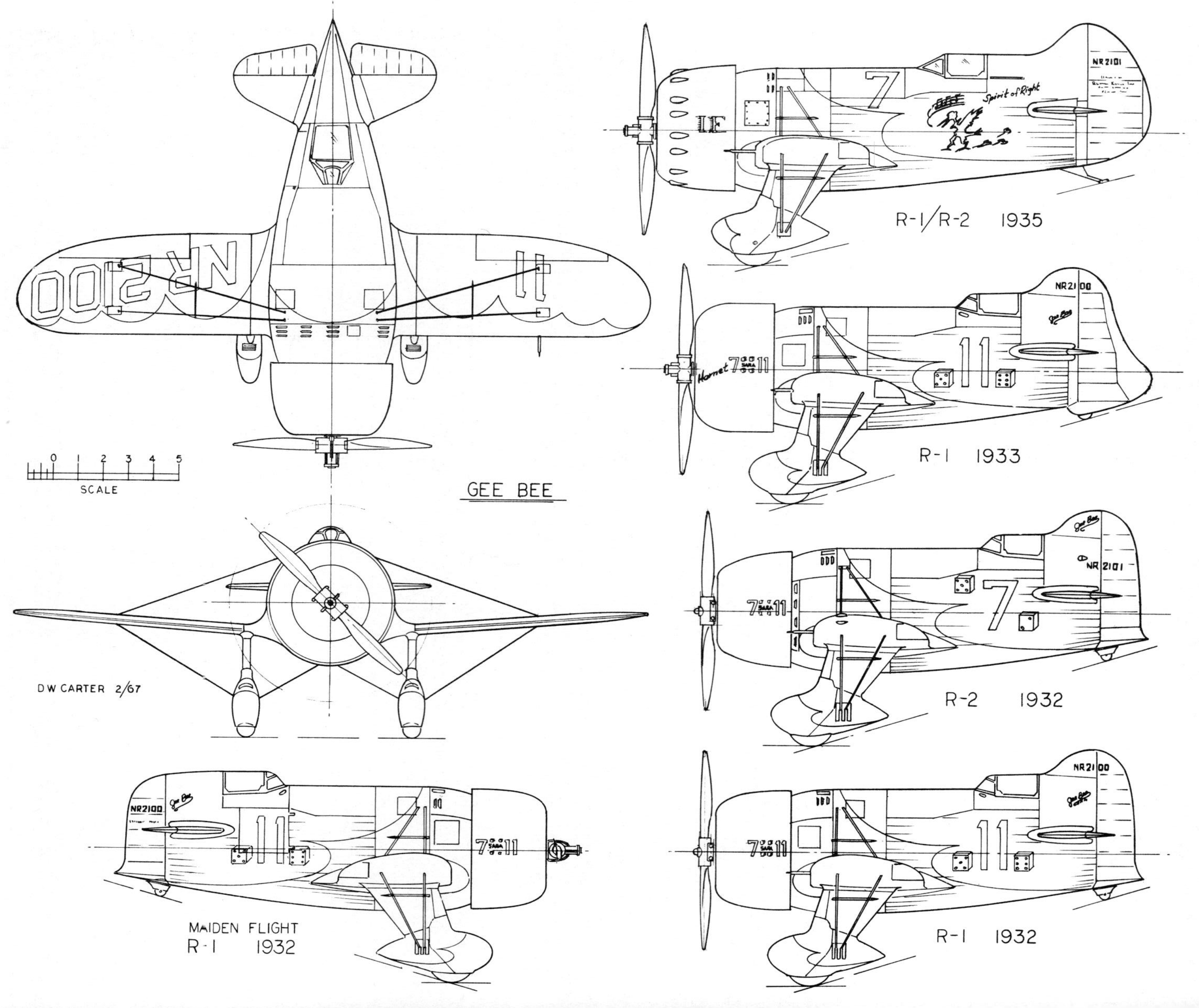
GEE BEE
SCALE
0 1 2 3 4 5
D W CARTER 2/67
MAIDEN FLIGHT
R-1 1932
R-1/R-2 1935
R-1 1933
R-2 1932
R-1 1932

Cockpit access to R-2 is seen here, with padded hatch cover lying on cockpit floor. Cover could be quickly popped out in case of emergency. Seen at 1932 Nationals, the R-2 wore a 550 hp Wasp engine as compared to the 800 hp Wasp of the R-1, so engine cowl was smaller in diameter at the front than on its sister ship. R-1 had a 160 gallon gas tank while the R-2 carried 302 gallons in two tanks for its Bendix try. *(Kinert)*

Wind tunnel tests proved teardrop design to be best for their 300 mph design speed so both No. 7 and 11 were built with the widest part of the fuselage located at 34% of its length, being 61 inches in diameter. Rudder was about one foot thick at its hinge line and was actually a movable end of the fuselage. Fuselage, built up of steel tubing and wood stringers, then fabric covered, was cavernous inside, with only gas and oil tanks taking up space. *(Warren M. Bodie)*

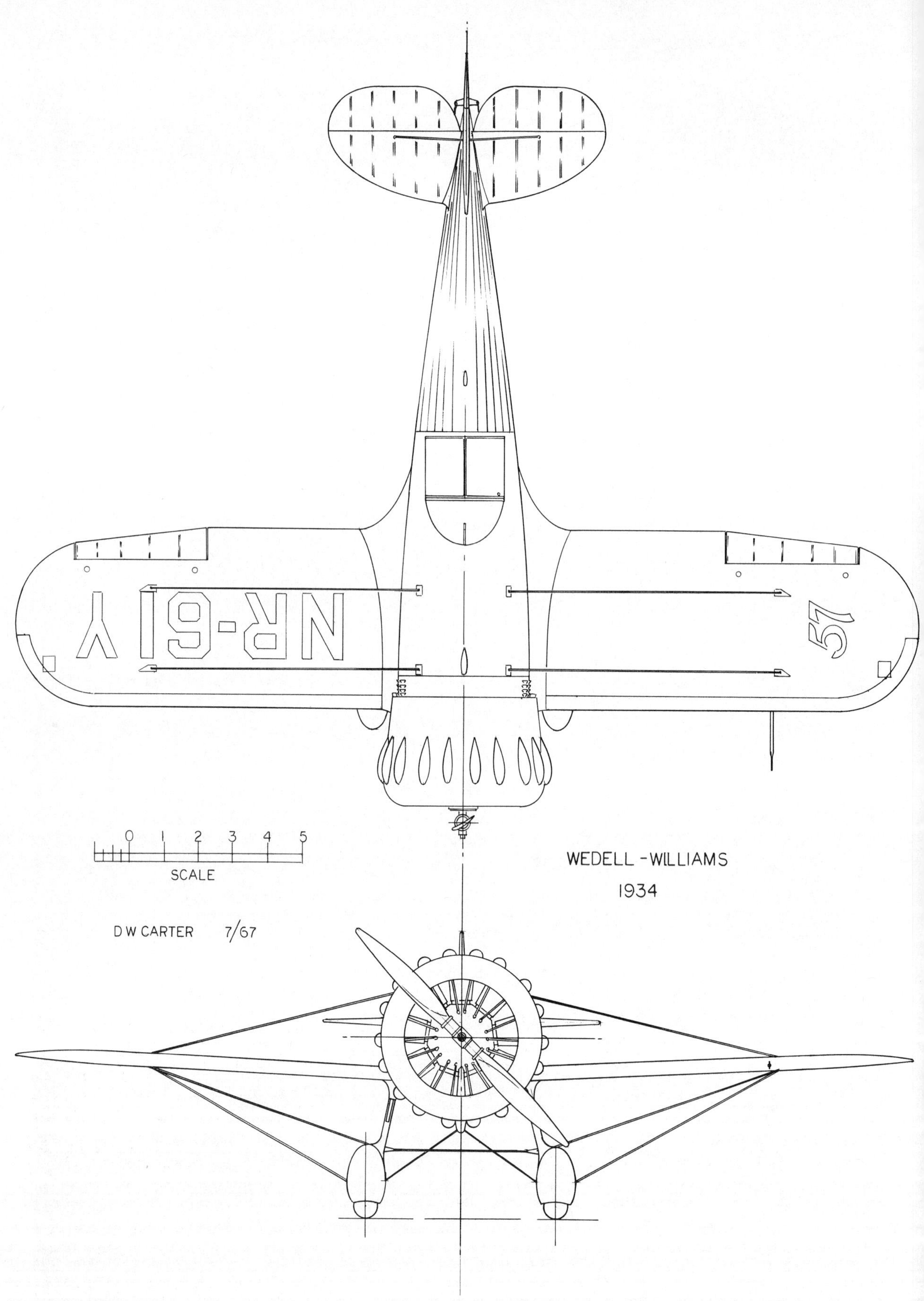

NR-61Y
57
SCALE
0 1 2 3 4 5
D W CARTER   7/67
WEDELL -WILLIAMS
1934

Wedell-Williams in which James G. Haislip won the 1932 Bendix and flew to 4th in the Thompson despite a failing engine. Racer had originally been built in 1930 as a two place sport plane powered by a Wright 225 HP J6-7 and had a 30 foot span. Errett Williams took two 2nd and one 4th place at the 1930 Nationals and dropped out of the Thompson on the eighth lap with engine trouble. Engine was 550 hp Wasp Jr. for 1932 and wing was chopped to 26 feet. (U.S. Air Force)

James Robert Wedell in cockpit of his red and black Miss Patterson which he flew to 2nd place in both the Bendix and Thompson races of 1932. He averaged 242.496 mph in the Thompson, just 10 mph slower than winner Doolittle who had 250 more horsepower. Wedell built this aircraft in 1930 and powered it with a Hisso engine, did 210 mph. In 1931 he cut the length and wingspan down, changed to the larger P&W Wasp Jr. engine which it still wore for 1932. (U.S. Air Force)

Dale Jackson's sharp little 1931 Laird Solution which was sponsored by the Sweet Kiss Toothpaste Company, as seen here. It wore its original gold wings in 1931 Thompson; fuselage, tail and landing gear were lavender.
(Dustin W. Carter)

Menasco-engined Alden Brown racer first appeared at 1932 Nationals. Mud in wheel pants caused Roy Minor to nose over, damaging prop and cowl so did not race. At 1933 Nationals in Gilmore Oil colors, above, Lee Schoenhair had supercharger trouble, copped one 4th place.
(Dustin W. Carter)

Cessna CR-1 Miss Wanda was built in 1932, wore a 125 Warner and sported a retractable landing gear. Roy Liggett, above, took one 2nd and three 3rd places at 1932 Nationals, with best pylon speed 176.519 mph.
(Dustin W. Carter)

Steve Wittman's famous Chief Oshkosh wore a larger Cirrus Hermes engine of 115 hp for 1932 Nationals. Steve won a class race over Howard's Pete, finished 2, 4, 6, and 7 in other events in and above his horsepower class. Later in 1932 Steve won the Glenn Curtiss Trophy in Miami at 166.9 mph.
(Kinert)

Affable Colonel Roscoe Turner and his new Wedell-Williams in which he placed 3rd in 1932 Bendix and Thompson. Sponsor's red lettering on yellow tan background barely left space for race No. on fuselage and knife-edged wing tip. Turner did 266.674 mph over 3 km Shell Speed dash course at the Nationals, placing behind Doolittle and Wedell. Millionaire Harry P. Williams and James Wedell formed the Wedell-Williams Air Service which built the famous barndoor-winged racers.
(Kinert)

Here is the 1930 Thompson-winning Laird Solution looking better than ever. After Dale Jackson raced the craft in 1931 it was acquired by Arthur Knapp who installed a close fitting engine cowl with rocker arm bumps, cleaned up the landing gear struts and added slightly longer wheel pants. Solution was now white overall. After modifications Knapp flew the ship and found it too hot for him to handle, used up entire airport to land and never flew it again so ship missed the 1932 Nationals.
(Charles G. Mandrake)

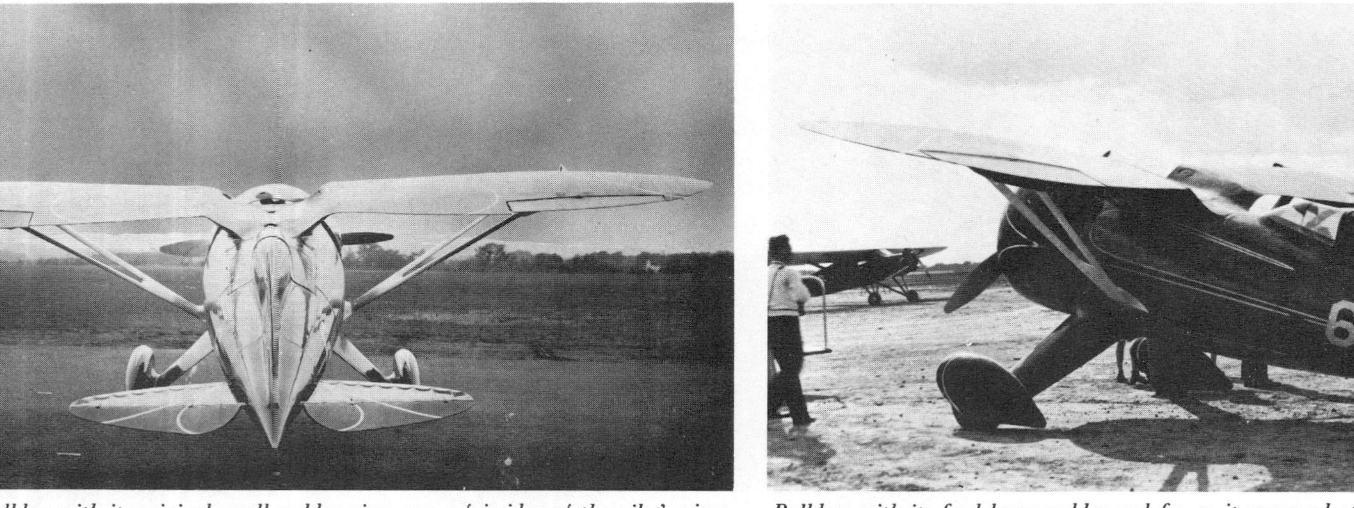

Direct rear of Bulldog with its original small rudder gives one a fair idea of the pilot's view from cockpit. Gull wing should have been inherently stable, and certainly appears to be so from this view. Ribs of fabric covered elevators and their stabilizer are plainly visible.
(Pratt & Whitney)

Bulldog, with its final large rudder and fin, as it appeared at the 1932 Nationals. New larger rudder fin was built up of wood, then metal covered. The fuselage was plywood. Wing was built up of wood spars and ribs, fabric covered.
(Dustin W. Carter)

OX-5-engined racer built by Walter Carr of Saginaw, Michigan appeared at 1932 Nationals and proved that ingenuity does not always pay. Other pilots always protested when Walter showed up to race his homely racer against their stock models in OX-5 class races, so craft seldom raced.
(Stephen J. Hudek)

In 1933 Walter Carr re-worked his Carr Special to wear a Warner 125 engine, which he flew in experimental class races, with limited success. Walter certainly deserved an "A" for effort for his home-built poor man's Gee Bee-like craft.
(Robert F. Pauley)

Superbly proportioned Hall Bulldog as it first rolled from its hangar-factory at Bowles Airport. First flight, on the same day Russell Boardman crashed a Gee Bee Sportster, proved rudder and fin was too small. Large engine cowl blanked off and disturbed the airflow to rudder, and gull portion of wing proved quite de-stabilizing. Note unique cowl indents for exhaust stacks. Bulldog was designed by Robert Hall and built by the Springfield Aircraft Company for Russell Thaw, who was sponsored by Mrs. Marion Guggenheim.   *(Pratt & Whitney)*

Rudder was widened and a triangular-shaped rudder fin, seen here unpainted and clear doped, was fitted to the Bulldog in an effort to improve its flight characteristics. Bulldog's fin was modified three times and the rudder four times before Hall was satisfied. Bob Hall, above, Russell Thaw and famous test pilot Jimmy Collins all flew the Bulldog, trying to ready it in time for the 1932 Bendix. Collins once thrilled a crowd of onlookers with a daring acrobatic show.   *(Ronald W. Harrison)*

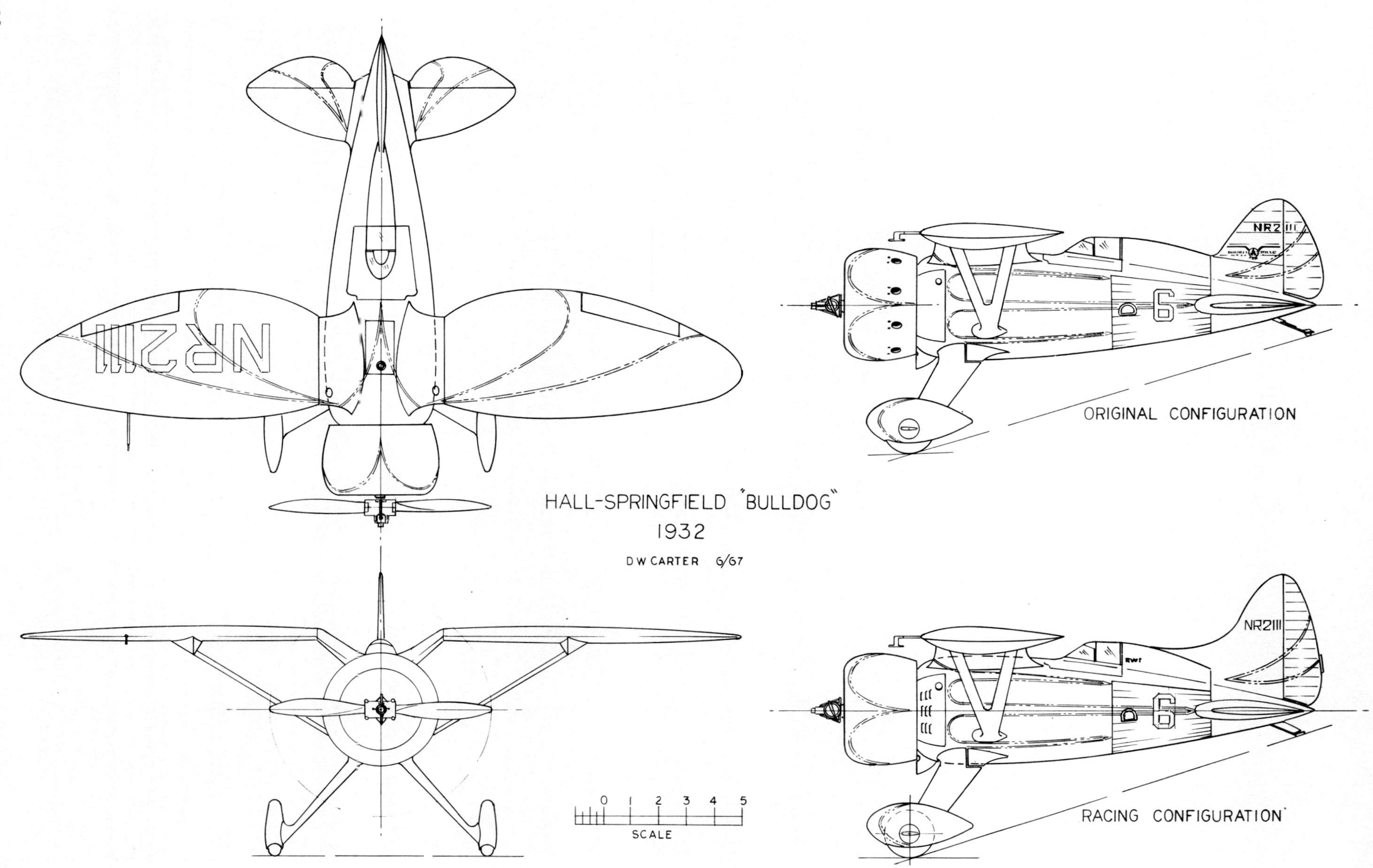

NR2111
ORIGINAL CONFIGURATION
6
NR2111
RACING CONFIGURATION
6
HALL-SPRINGFIELD "BULLDOG"
1932
D W CARTER 6/67
0 1 2 3 4 5
SCALE

Bulldog was quite docile with its new large rudder and fin. On its first take-off with the original small rudder and fin, the ship started to roll left just ten feet off the ground. Hall cut the motor and was barely able to lift wing enough to clear the ground, only blew a tire in the abrupt landing. Bulldog was painted red with black trim, the trim separated by white stripes. Wing struts and race No. 6 were also white.   *(Charles G. Mandrake)*

Only hours after the Bulldog was delivered Russell Thaw backed out of flying the craft in either the Bendix or Thompson; and Hall, above, was unable to get permission from owner Mrs. Guggenheim in time to enter the Bendix. At Jimmie Doolittle's suggestion, the engine exhaust stacks were made to discharge under the engine cowl, in hopes of gaining additional speed, and the cowl indents were covered with doped fabric, as seen here. Bulldog proved to be slower than ever!   *(U.S. Air Force)*

Exquisite little Bulldog never did overcome its engine troubles, which were mainly located in the carburetor. Engine ran closest to normal in the 1932 Shell Speed Dashes where Bob Hall managed to finish 6th at a fairly respectable 243.7 mph on the 3 km course. Engine always sounded as if it were starved and it was quite irregular in beat throughout the Thompson race also. Bulldog is seen here with a new smooth engine cowling which was installed after the 1932 Nationals but craft never raced again.   *(Ronald W. Harrison)*

The Bulldog flew a few times after the 1932 Nationals; then the engine and instruments were removed and the plane sat around the airport until it was vandalized and rotted away. Various people took the cowling, cockpit hatch, headrest, etc., a lamentable fate for such a beautiful aircraft. Robert Hall later went to work for the Grumman Aircraft Corporation where he could put his particular talents into the design of warplanes.   *(Charles G. Mandrake)*

Unique Cicada was designed by Robert Hall and built by the Springfield Aircraft Inc. for Frank Lynch, a wealthy sportsman pilot who, accompanied by his wife, planned to fly the craft around the world. Its fuselage was mainly green with brown patterns edged with yellow stripes, while the tail surfaces were cream with green veins. The wing wore all the same colors to resemble the Cicada insect wings. An eye was painted on each side of the engine cowl.

(Paramount Studios)

Cicada was raced by Bob Hall at Niagara Falls June 26, 1932, where he finished a slow 4th behind Russell Boardman in the Gee Bee Y, who won the race at 199.55 mph. Frank Lynch planned to enter the 1932 Bendix with his Cicada but scratched because of engine trouble. Craft was fitted with another Wasp Jr. engine and Frank flew it to Cleveland along with Bob Hall in the Bulldog. Engine troubles persisted and the Cicada sat out the races. *(Ronald W. Harrison)*

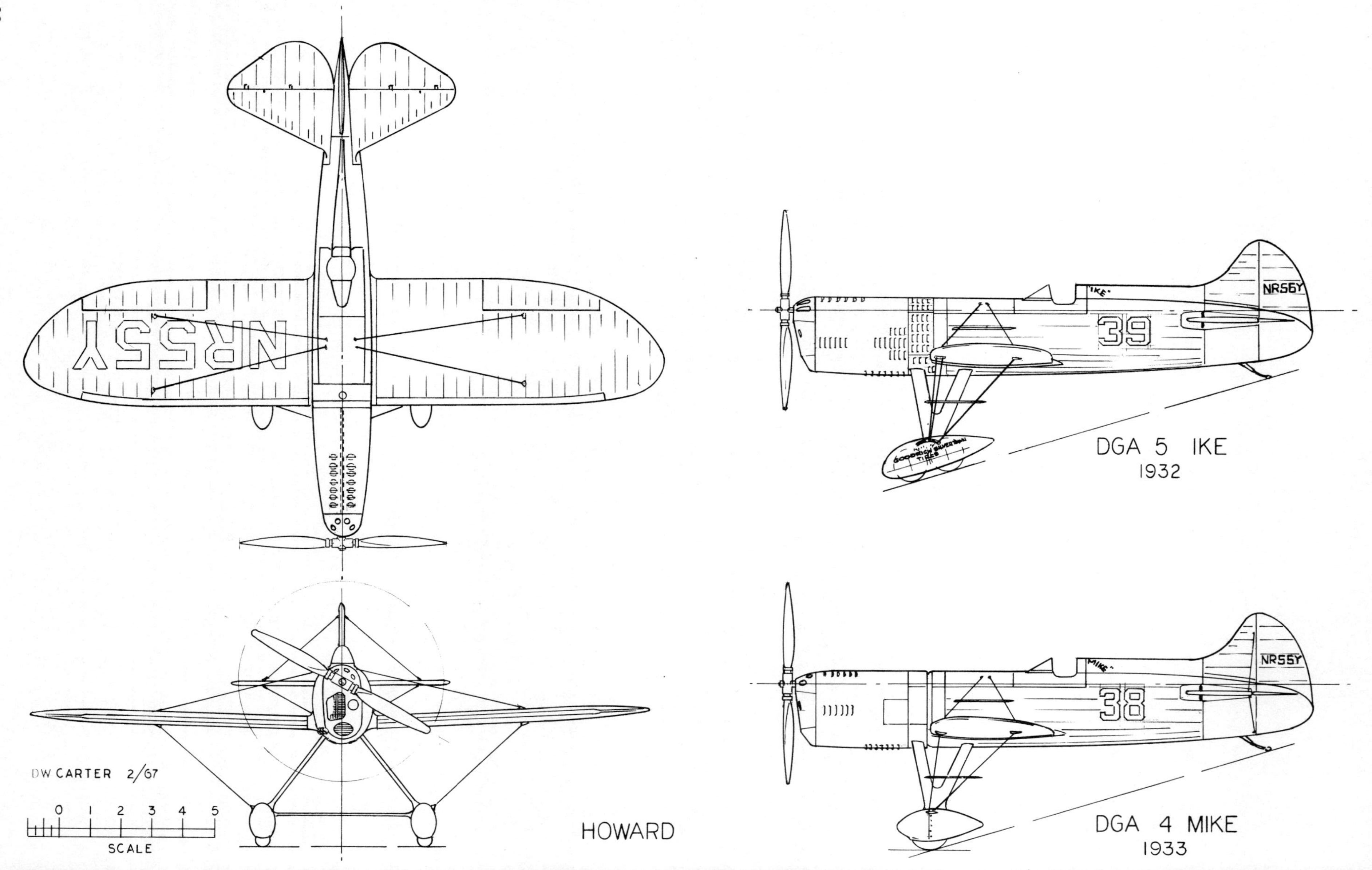

NR56Y
"IKE"
39
DGA 5 IKE
1932
NR55Y
"MIKE"
38
DGA 4 MIKE
1933
DW CARTER 2/67
0 1 2 3 4 5
SCALE
HOWARD

Ben Howard appeared at the 1932 Nationals with his two new look-alikes, Mike and Ike. Mike, DGA-4, license NR55Y, race No. 38, wore a wire-braced landing gear which relied on its Goodrich tires for absorbing shock. Mike was flown to two 2nd, one 4th and two 5th places in class races by William Ong. Fuselages of both craft were built up of steel tubing and wood stringers and the wings of spruce spars and ribs, the whole aircraft then covered with doped fabric.
(Dustin W. Carter)

Ike, DGA-5, license NR56Y, race No. 39, wore unique tandem wheels, which Ben admitted were just for show. Wheels did carry rubber shock cord between them which acted as shock absorbers. This wheel arrangement made it necessary to place a thin spreader bar between the two sets of wheels. Ike was a bit lighter than Mike and its engine was set up to accept higher octane fuel. Ike did 197.073 mph in one pylon race and turned 213.855 mph in the Shell Speed Dashes.
(Peter M. Bowers)

Gee Bee Model D, license NC11043, powered by a Menasco C-4 125 hp engine, was flown in two Derby races at 1932 Nationals by William Rausch, finished 7th and 9th. Single-seat Model D was not built as a racer, was strictly a sports plane. (Charles G. Mandrake)

With Boardman laid up, Z. D. Granville phoned Jimmy Doolittle and asked if he would fly No. 11 at the Nationals. Doolittle arrived at Springfield August 28, minutely inspected the ship, shook hands with Zantford, climbed in and, much to everyone's surprise, flew on to Cleveland! (Dustin W. Carter)

Although the engine cowls of both Gee Bee 7 and 11 were secured by turnbuckles at nine reinforced points, a slight forward pull persisted, as seen on No. 11 above, with paint scraped off engine cowl by propeller. Cowlings were then further secured. (Dustin W. Carter)

Open cockpit of the Cicada seated two people staggered side-by-side. Shortly after the 1932 Nationals Frank Lynch clipped a corner of the hangar top at Bowles-Agawam Airport on take-off, crashed and burned. (Dustin W. Carter)

Jimmy Doolittle had his 1931 Bendix-winning Laird Super Solution highly modified for 1932. It wore new thinner wings, the rudder and fin were modified, and the fuselage was made much deeper to raise the pilot and new semi-bubble canopy for better vision. Cockpit sides were transparent for better visibility. Ship also wore a new and more shallow engine cowl as compared with the one used on the craft in 1931. Solution was painted in her sponsor's Shell yellow and red.
(Truman T. Weaver)

Landing gear of the Solution was made to retract vertically upwards and the wheels turned to the nearly horizontal position as the gear legs retracted, thus making the wheel undersides flush with the fuselage bottom. Unfortunately, on the first test on August 23, 1932, the gear failed to come down properly after retraction. Jimmy tried everything, including acrobatics, to get the gear down but finally had to belly in. Solution was damaged too badly for repair in time for the Nationals.
(William F. Yeager)

Wasp Jr. 9-cyl. air-cooled engines. Jimmy Haizlip flashed by the judges stand at Cleveland 8 hrs. 19 min. 45 sec. later to win the Bendix in his new Wedell-Williams, setting a record speed to Cleveland that held for five years. Jimmy Wedell, in his racer of last year, finished second, Roscoe Turner, also flying a new Wedell-Williams, was third, and Lee Gehlbach was fourth and last in his Gee-Bee.

Haizlip, without landing at Cleveland, flew on to Floyd Bennett Field, New York, cutting 57 minutes off Major Doolittle's record set last year. Haizlip's time coast-to-coast was 10 hrs. 19 min. He had averaged 245 mph to Cleveland including gas stops, and his transcontinental speed was 238.2 mph.

Then, on Sunday, September 4, the Aerol Trophy Race for women was flown. There were four starters: Mae Haizlip in her husband's Wedell-Williams; Mrs. Gladys O'Donnell in Ben Howard's *Mike*, which she had never flown; Florence Klingensmith in John Livingston's clipped-wing Monocoupe; and Betty Lund, wife of Waco test pilot Freddy Lund, in Art Davis' taperwing Waco. The planes were flagged off into the face of an impending storm which broke during the second lap, and the women plowed on through a pouring rain when they couldn't tell one pylon from another, or even the airport from the two northern pylons. The rain struck like bird-shot in the faces of the three women flying open planes, but by some miracle they all stayed on the course. The gals were flagged down at the end of the fifth lap, and their speeds averaged at that stage, but Florence and Betty didn't see the flag and continued for the full eight laps of the 10-mile course.

Gladys O'Donnell flew *Mike* wide open and won the race at 185.5 mph, while Mae Haizlip, who had throttled her powerful Wedell back after turning one lap at 212.8 mph, came in second at 183.1 mph. Klingensmith flew her cabin Monocoupe at full throttle to take third at 174 mph, and Betty Lund, throttled well back, was fourth and last at 101 mph. The race had been a demonstration of nerve and flying ability that would have done credit to seasoned men pilots.

In the Shell Speed Dashes for men, Jimmy Doolittle, flying a new Gee-Bee R-1, flashed four times over the 3-km course to average 294.4 mph and set a new world's record for landplanes. Lt. Al Williams had, in 1923, attained 266.6 mph, and the following year this record had been broken by Warrant Officer Bonnett of France, when he piloted a Ferbois monoplane at 278.5 mph.

Doolittle's R-1 Gee-Bee Super Sportster (No. 11) was a more powerful sister ship of the R-2 that had placed fourth in the Bendix. Powered by a

P & W Wasp Sr. engine, which developed 800 hp at 2,350 rpm, the plane was very short and chubby.

THOMPSON TROPHY

The Thompson Trophy Race (10-mile course-10 laps) was flown on Monday afternoon, September 5, the grand finale of a 10-day thrill-packed race meet. Eight monoplanes lined up for the race-horse start: Doolittle and Gehlbach in their barrel-like Gee-Bee's; Wedell, Turner, and Haizlip in their Wasp Jr. engined Wedell-Williams; Bob Hall, designer of the Gee-Bee planes, with his beautiful new high-gull-wing racer powered by a 550-hp Wasp Jr. engine; and Bill Ong was ready with Howard's *Ike*. Ray Moore sat ready in a new Menasco-engined low-wing *San Francisco I* designed and built by Keith Rider. It was the only entry fitted with a retractable landing gear, the first seen on a pure racer since 1924. It also featured a metal fuselage. Controllable pitch propellers appeared for the first time and were fitted on the two Gee-Bee's and the Hall racer. None of the planes were fitted with wing flaps.

When the starter's flag dropped, the efficiency of the controllable metal prop was seen at once, for the Gee-Bee's and the Hall racer pulled into the air quickly, although Ong's snappy little Howard was right alongside. Soon after the scattering pylon had been turned, the superior horsepower of Doolittle's No. 11 Gee-Bee began building up a commanding lead, and the real race was among the three Wedell-Williams planes for the next three places. Hall's engine started cutting out after the first lap and he dropped back to sixth place.

Doolittle's Gee-Bee trailed black smoke, but it got no worse as he built up his lead. The sleek Keith Rider dropped out on the second lap with engine trouble. Wedell, flying a smoother race than Turner, moved into second place, while Haizlip's engine faltered some causing him to fall back to fourth behind Turner. Gehlbach, in Gee-Bee No. 7, held steadily on to fifth place, while Hall, his engine still cutting out, stayed in sixth place well ahead of Ong, who was in seventh and last place with his outclassed but well-flown Howard.

Strung out in the order above, the seasoned pilots finished the race. Doolittle breezed over the finish line averaging a new high of 252.7 mph, while Wedell finished at 242.5 mph.

For the third straight year the closed-course speeds had increased, and Doolittle, whose winning speed was to hold for four years, had at last bettered the highest speed of the Pulitzer races, set in 1925 at 249 mph by Lt. Cyrus Bettis. The monoplane racer had taken over U. S. competition completely.

◆   ◆   ◆

Jimmy Wedell set a new landplane speed record of 305 mph, Sept. 4, 1933. He had won the 1933 Thompson Trophy Race with an average speed of 238 mph.

1933 – National Air Races

The 1933 National Air Races, held at Los Angeles, were shortened to four days, July 1 to 4, and were restricted to free-for-all races by purely racing-type planes of different cubic inch engined groups. Elimination of derbies and races for NC licensed aircraft did much to speed up the program. The Nationals presented in four days all the major speed and acrobatic events that were formerly spread over a 10-day program.

High points on the daily program were Maj. Ernst Udet, German war ace, and his three dead-stick loops from less than 1,000 feet; Lt. Tito Falconi, of Italy, and his graceful inverted flying; Speed Manning and his delayed-opening parachute jump from more than 12,000 feet; and the Hollywood Trio, Frank Clark, Paul Mantz, and Jack Rand, who went through the book in acrobatic formation, flying their red-white-and-blue Travel-Air biplanes.

BENDIX TROPHY

The only major speed record to fall this year was the east to west transcontinental mark. Roscoe Turner, flying his Wedell-Williams racer fitted with a new P & W 900-hp Hornet, lowered the New York-Los Angeles time to 11 hrs. 30 min. in winning the Bendix Trophy July 1, his third try in the cross-country races. His average speed, including gas stops at Columbus, Indianapolis, Wichita, and Albuquerque, was 214.8 mph. Jimmy Wedell, in his last year's Wasp Jr. engined Wedell-Williams, was a close second and the only other contestant to finish, averaging 209.2 mph.

Russell Boardman, Russell Thaw, and Lee Gehlbach were all forced out in the vicinity of Indianapolis. Boardman, flying last year's No. 11 Gee-Bee, was critically injured when he encountered a sudden cross-wind after a too-quick take-off, and his heavy gasoline-loaded Gee-Bee did a half-roll into the Indianapolis runway. Thaw groundlooped Gee-Bee No.

7, now fitted with flaps and a 750-hp Wasp Sr. engine, damaging a wing, and Gehlbach ran Haizlip's Wedell-Williams of last year's Bendix through a fence when forced down by an air-locked fuel system. Boardman, who in 1931 had made a spectacular non-stop flight from New York to Istanbul, Turkey, in a Bellanca monoplane, died July 3 of his injuries. Amelia Earhart, the seventh and last entry of the Bendix, dropped out at Wichita because the Wasp engine in her Lockheed Vega was running hot. Earhart and Gehlbach later flew their repaired ships on to Los Angeles.

The spectators on any one day could see all the special little racers. Races were scheduled daily for planes powered by engines of 375 and 550 cu. in. displacement, and on Sunday and Monday, July 2 and 3, there was a race for 1,000 cu. in. engines. George Hague, flying a little 4-cyl. Menasco-powered Keith Rider R-2 *Bumble Bee*, and Roy Minor, in Howard's *Mike*, were the most consistent winners of the entire races, though it was their first appearance in the Nationals. Hague flew and placed in the money in every race from the daily 375 cu. in. events up to the unlimited Thompson. The *Bumble Bee* and a 6-cyl. Menasco sister ship, the year-old *San Francisco I*, were the only two racers at Los Angeles fitted with retractable landing gears and metal fuselages. Their wings were plywood. The *Bumble Bee* flew its fastest race in the Thompson as did Howard's *Mike*. Minor won the 550 cu. in. sweepstakes, and Steve Wittman of Oshkosh won the 350 cu. in. sweepstakes, flying his little 4-cyl. Cirrus-engined *Chief Oshkosh* at 159.8 mph in one race.

There were 12 closed-course races and two speed dashes. The Aerol Trophy Race, five laps of a 10-mile course, was the only race for women this year. Mae Haizlip cruised her Wasp Jr. Wedell-Williams into first place at only 168 mph; Marty Bowman, flying

Ike had tandem wheels replaced with normal two wheels for 1933, was flown in American Air Races at Chicago by Harold Neumann. Later in 1933 Roy Minor flew Ike in the International Air Races, took four 1st and one 3rd place, did 215.15 mph in one event.   (Dustin W. Carter)

Keith Rider R-2 (San Francisco II) arrived at 1933 Nationals re-named Bumble Bee, wore a new engine cowl and race number. George Hague picked up one 1st, two 2nd, two 3rd and five 4th places, including the Thompson Race, did 210.12 mph in Shell Speed Dashes.   (Dustin W. Carter)

Steve Wittman's Chief Oshkosh wore smaller wheels at 1933 Nationals, also wore its more familiar 111 race number. Steve took two 2nd and two 3rd places in the 375 cubic inch events, which gave him first place in the standings.   (Kinert)

This Gee Bee Y, one of two built, originally wore a 250 hp Lycoming, was reworked into single-seater with 450 hp Wright by Art Knapp and Bob Hall. Florence Klingensmith won 1933 Women's Free-For-All at Chicago with 189.04 mph, later crashed Model Y fatally.   (Dustin W. Carter)

Gee Bee Super Sportster No. 11 was fitted with a longer "stinger" rudder in 1933, also wore a big P&W Hornet engine with larger NACA cowling. Tail wheel was modified to fair with the new rudder, and tankage was increased for the Bendix. Super Sportsters were variously nicknamed "Bumble Bee's," "Flying Barrel's" and "Silo's" because of their out-sized fuselages. Russell Boardman, above, crashed on his too-quick take-off at Indianapolis July 2, 1933 after a gas stop in the Bendix, died the next day. (Dustin W. Carter)

Gee Bee R-2 Super Sportster No. 7 was also fitted with a longer rudder for 1933, the trailing edge slightly different in contour than that of its sister ship. Engine and cowling from No. 11 was fitted and a new larger wing with flaps was installed. The left landing gear of No. 7 failed during take-off at Indianapolis, and Russell Thaw flying in the 1933 Bendix race planned to go on after minor repairs, but dropped out after seeing Boardman crash. Late in 1933, James Haislip demolished this plane while landing at Springfield Airport, escaped with a cut. (Charles G. Mandrake)

In 1933 Eldon Cessna redesignated the CR-1, rebuilt it as the CR-2 racer. A more powerful 145 hp Warner engine was installed. CR-2 was suspended for above photo and the background touched out on negative. Wing span was 18.5 feet, length 17 feet. *(Dustin W. Carter)*

At the 1933 Miami Air races Roy Liggett and the little CR-2 won the Col. Green Race (500 cubic inches) and placed second in the Unlimited Free-For-All. Roy's best pylon speed was 194.46 mph. Note unusual full-span ailerons. *(Dustin W. Carter)*

In furthering the science, D. W. Tomlinson, above, of the famous Navy Three Seahawk stunt team fame, climbed this Northrop Gamma Experimental Overweather Laboratory aircraft to 20,000 plus feet, flew non-stop from Los Angeles to New York in 11 hours 30 minutes in 1933, set a new record. *(Trans World Airlines)*

First of the Lawrence W. Brown-designed racers appeared at 1933 Nationals, was named Miles and Atwood Special for its builders. Menasco 185 hp engine brought pilot Lee S. Miles two 1st, two 3rd, one 4th and two 5th places. Pylon best was 170.14 mph and dash 210.64 mph. *(Dustin W. Carter)*

Famous Arthur Chester Special was built in 1932, first raced at the 1933 Los Angeles Nationals. Art took one 1st and four 4th places in 375 cubic inch events, averaged 154.365 in his best race. Art ironed out many of the bugs in his little green and cream ship and, later in the year, copped four 1st, two 2nd and two 3rd places in and above his engine class, at the Chicago Air Races. Best speed was now 190.95 mph. (Dustin W. Carter)

James Wedell and his famous 44 in which he set a new World's landplane speed record over a 3 km course at Chicago September 4, 1933, averaged 305.3 mph. Wedell was outstanding both as a pilot and designer-builder of racing craft. He made his climb to fame the hard way, having lost an eye in an earlier motorcycle accident. Jimmy began his aviation career by purchasing two old Thomas-Morse single-seat Scouts and rebuilding them, took one hour of instruction, then soloed a Scout! (Charles G. Mandrake)

Jamieson all-plywood racer had a hand-cranked retractable landing gear that reminded one of the 1922 Bee Line racers, while the nose radiator was almost a ringer to that used on the Loening R-4's, also of 1922. Jamieson had not yet made wheel fairing covers. (Kinert)

On a fast taxi test over the small sod airport near Richmond, Virginia, Jamieson hit a small obstruction which bounced his ship into the air and he had to go on around. Rudder control seemed adequate as Jamieson flew the racer several times with no rudder change. (Charles G. Mandrake)

Redhead was designed and built by Gordon Israel, who helped in the design and building of Ben Howard's stable of fine racers. Redhead was powered by a Menasco 544 cubic inch six-cylinder in-line engine whose supercharger gave trouble. (Dustin W. Carter)

Pert little Redhead wore a unique inverted gull wing, seen in this view. Wing was built up of wood spars and ribs, then covered with plywood. Small balloon tires acted as shock absorbers. Fuselage was built of welded steel tubing and wood stringers, fabric covered. (Dustin W. Carter)

Redhead was plagued by engine troubles most of its career, sat out several races. Gordon did take two 3rd and one 5th place at 1933 Nationals, best pylon speed 173.198 mph. Engine purred smoothly for Shell Speed Dashes and Redhead did 221.746 mph for 3rd place. Later in year Gordon took a 2nd and 3rd place at Chicago Air Races, turned one 197.73 average. Israel worked with Grumman from WWII to 1953, has been with Lear Jet ever since. (Dustin W. Carter)

Wm. L. Jamieson, an air mail pilot for Eastern Air Lines, designed and built this Curtiss D-12 435 hp engined racer in 1933, planned to fly in the Nationals. Working on the racer in daytime and flying the mail at night allowed little time for sleep. On a clear night June 5, 1933, Jamieson flew his Pitcairn Mailwing into a Carolina County mountain side and died. His widow advertised the racer for sale in the Aero Digest magazine but craft never raced. (Peter M. Bowers)

Cessna CR-2 was modified for the 1933 Chicago Air Races, wore a smaller engine cowl with rocker arm bumps and a longer headrest, became CR-2A. In a speed dash Roy Liggett crashed when the engine cowl tore loose and ripped the left wing off at 200+ mph. (Dustin W. Carter)

Cessna CR-3 was built for John Livingston after the CR-2A bested his Monocoupe in several races. Shoulder wing craft was the fastest Cessna racer built, wore the Warner 145 hp engine from John's Monocoupe. Wingspan was 18.5 feet, length 17 feet. (Cessna)

Livingston took first place in every race he flew his little Cessna, averaged 204.54 in one event at Chicago Air Races, then established a new World's Speed Record for 500 cubic inch engines, averaging 237.35 mph, beating Ben Howard's Ike record of 1932. (Dustin W. Carter)

Cessna CR-3 first flew June 11, 1933. On August 1, less than two months and several first places later, Livingston was unable to get the gear down for a Columbus, Ohio landing, bailed out north of the airport and the tiny racer dived straight into the ground. (Cessna)

Fantastic Macchi-Castoldi M.C. 72 seaplane was flown to World's Speed Record of 440.7 mph June 2, 1933. Twin engines set in tandem turning contra-rotating propellers eliminated torque, main bugaboo of twin float racers. Craft first flew June 1931, did 373 mph. Thirty-five flights were made, then the engines were overhauled for record assault. Wing was all metal, its flat tubular water radiators smoothly enclosed in wing. Nose of fuselage was formed by oil tank, its outside wall exposed to airstream.　　　　　　*(Charles G. Mandrake)*

Fuselage of unique Mario Castoldi-designed M.C.72 was metal to cockpit, with rear portion wood monocoque bolted to front tubular portion by four bolts. Each pontoon had three smooth radiators built into its outside surface; the forward one a water radiator and center and rear radiators for oil cooling. Float struts were streamlined by smooth water radiators. For summer flying another radiator was added under fuselage from cockpit rear to tail. Empty weight was 5510 lbs., gross 6667, wing loading 41.4 lbs/sq. ft.　　　　　　*(Charles G. Mandrake)*

Granville's model Y Gee-Bee was second; Gladys O'Donnell did the best her Waco taperwing biplane would allow and finished third at 134; while H. Sumner, flying a Travel-Air biplane, finished fourth and last.

The fastest speeds of the race meet were made in the Shell Speed Dashes over a 3-km course on July 3. The three Wedell-Williams racers of last year, two wearing Wasp Jr. engines, turned in the fastest speeds but did not set any records. Diving from about 1,200 feet, then flying low over the course four times, Roscoe Turner, Jimmy Wedell, and Lee Gehlbach made 280.2, 278.9, and 251.9 mph respectively.

THOMPSON TROPHY

The line-up for the Thompson Trophy Race, July 4, looked like a refly of last year's race, for five of the six planes entered had flown in the previous Thompson. The three Wedell-Williams lined up with pilots Turner, Gehlbach, and Wedell, while Roy Minor sat ready in *Mike*. Z. D. Granville, builder of the famous Gee-Bee planes, was to fly his Wasp Jr. engined Gee-Bee model Y, and Hague, the sixth entry, was in the Keith Rider *Bumble Bee*.

Bunched at the starter's flag in a race-horse start, the six ships went aloft. Turner climbed his powerful ship to 200 feet, twisted around the scattering marker, and came back onto the four-cornered course with a slight lead. Turner roared around the home pylon and into the second lap about 500 feet ahead of Wedell's whirling propeller. Gehlbach was well behind in third place but well ahead of Minor in *Mike*, who was fourth. Then Wedell dashed by and on to his third lap without Turner showing up. Flying so fast in the hazy sky, the pilots were having trouble seeing the pylons, and Turner cut a pylon on lap one and doubled back on his second lap to circle the marker again.

By that time Wedell was a mile ahead, flying full throttle to what seemed a sure victory. But Turner's superior power took only one more trip around the 10-mile aerial saucer to catch his rival, then lengthen his lead to a mile at the 60-mile race finish.

Roscoe, however, was disqualified for not reflying the skipped pylon at the time he cut it, and his protest that he would have risked collision with another racer to have done so was of no avail.

And so Jimmy Wedell was announced as the winner of the Thompson Trophy at 238 mph, while Lee Gehlbach was second at 224.9 mph, and Roy Minor moved into third place money in *Mike* at 199.9 mph. Hague flew the *Bumble Bee* into fourth place, while Granville and his Gee-Bee Y finished fifth and last. Turner had averaged 241 mph in his fourth try in six years at winning a major closed-course race.

Jimmy Wedell later fitted his No. 44 racer with the same 800-hp Wasp Sr. engine that Doolittle used in winning the 1932 Thompson and, on Sept. 4, 1933, at Chicago, flew four times over a 3-km course to average 305.3 mph and set a new landplane world record. Earlier in the year on June 2, Italian pilot Warrant Officer Francesco Agello had flown a Macchi-Castoldi M.C. 72 seaplane four times over 3 km on Lake Garda to average a breath-taking 440 mph. This speed, made official at 440.7 in 1934, was not exceeded for six years and then by a landplane. The Italian ship holds the seaplane record to this day.

Agello's plane was one of several Macchi-Castoldi low-wing monoplanes with which the Italian Air Force High-Speed Flight had been experimenting at Lake Garda for several years. The two Fiat V-12 engines were set in tandem, the rear engine's drive shaft resting between the V banks of the forward engine, and each engine operated independently, with their propellers revolving in opposite directions. The engines turned 3,200 rpm and delivered a total of 3,000 hp.

The tandem-engined Macchi-Castoldi 72 which on June 2, 1933, pushed the world's speed record to a then fantastic 440 mph.

Keith Rider BUMBLE BEE, *former* SAN FRANCISCO II

1934 – National Air Races

Racing aircraft design has always been directly dependent on the types of engines available. In the late 20's and through most of the 30's, the military claimed most of the available liquid-cooled engines. Further, these engines were considered too heavy and the cooling problems too complex, making them impractical for racing purposes.

This left civilian race designers with only two logical choices: either use a big radial "waffle iron" air-cooled engine and depend on its higher horsepower for winning; or design around a lower-priced in-line air-cooled engine of smaller dimensions and horsepower, depending on streamlining alone to win. There were a few good foreign engines of high cost available, but U. S. manufacturers often furnished their engines gratis or sold them at cost to race-plane builders for the advertising value. Some designers were even forced to buy used engines, for it must be remembered that the United States was still in the depths of its worst depression, and money was hard to come by. Thus it was that oil companies and other large concerns helped U. S. aviation progress in the development of racing craft through the 30's, either by ordering aircraft direct or by sponsorship of those already built.

Racing-plane designs and speeds improved steadily during this period, contributing in many ways to commercial and military aircraft designs of the future. The Air Corps, finally swinging to monoplanes as a direct result of racing progress, was at this period flying its new Boeing P-26 pursuits, copied from the earlier Travel-Air "Mystery."

Commemorating a quarter-century of air racing and aviation development, the 1934 Nationals, held in Cleveland, August 31 to September 3, were complete sell-outs on Sunday, Monday, and Labor Day, with thousands paying for standing room only and other thousands turned away.

Best show act was the U. S. Army trio, the "Men on the Flying Trapeze," Capt. Claire Chennault, and Lts. J. H. Williamson and Haywood Hansell, who flew their Boeing P-12D's through one of the finest close-formation acrobatic variations ever witnessed. Next best act was Milo Burcham, world's greatest acrobat as proven in International competition in Europe. Milo flew a Boeing 100 (P-12A) through low, precise, and beautiful inverted air work that held the crowd spellbound.

BENDIX TROPHY

Hampered by headwinds, only two of the six pilots that managed to leave Burbank before dawn on August 31, in the Bendix race, crossed the finish line ahead of the 6:00 P.M. deadline. Douglas Davis, winner of the 1929 free-for-all at Cleveland, flew Jimmy Wedell's Thompson-winning Wedell-Williams of last year from Los Angeles to Cleveland at an average speed of 216.2 mph including gas stops, to win the race. J. A. Worthen was second, flying a new Wedell-Williams 45 with retractable gear at an average speed of 203.2 mph.

Out of the Bendix start because of fuel leaks, Roscoe Turner, on September 2, flew his Wedell-Williams from Los Angeles to New York through turbulent winds and rain to break his own record by 2 min. 39 sec., averaging over 244 mph including four gas stops for his new 1,000-hp supercharged Hornet.

Almost all of the ships at Cleveland this year were old racers with increased horsepower. The time-worn practice of clipping wing area was very much in evidence. Steve Wittman's *Chief Oshkosh* had been clipped from 78 sq. ft. wing area down to 42 sq. ft. Steve had encountered wing tip flutter and simply chopped off wing span until the flutter stopped! Howard's clean little *Mike* and *Ike* were there, but the cleanest fixed-gear plane at the races was a new Brown racer, *Miss Los Angeles.* Similar in design to *Mike* and *Ike,* the Brown ship wore a Menasco engine souped up to 300 hp. Flying the Brown racer, Roy Minor took the Shell Qualification Trials for 550 cu. in. engines at 243.1 mph.

The fastest speed of the race meet was turned in during the unlimited Shell Qualification Trials by Doug Davis when he flew Wedell's old 44 over the 3-km course four times, to average a new high of

Keith Rider and associates built this all metal unpainted R-3 mainly for the London to Melbourne McRobertson Race. Not ready for the foreign race, pilot James Granger entered the 1934 Bendix. Extra long propeller dug in on take-off, craft nosed over, killing Granger. (Dustin W. Carter)

Brown B-2 Miss Los Angeles at the Menasco engine factory ready to go a-racing. Another Brown built racer, the B-1 Brown Special, also appeared in 1934. It looked very much like the B-2 but was smaller and wore a 185 hp Menasco without provision for a spinner. (Menasco)

Steve Wittman shows off new 1934 wing panels on Chief Oshkosh racer. Span was only 16 feet. Steve picked up two 3rds, two 4ths and two 5ths at Nationals, best speed 186.60 mph. The Chief was two years old but just beginning a fabulous career. (Dustin W. Carter)

Homely and tiny Tilbury-Fundy Flash flew the air race circuit in 30's. Flown by Art Carnahan, Flash won the 115 cubic inch event at 1933 Chicago Air Races, did 114.92 mph with its little 45 hp Church engine. (Dustin W. Carter)

Lawrence Brown designed and built the B-2 for 1934 Nationals, where it enjoyed its best year. The scarlet red beauty looked very much like Ben Howard's *Mike and Ike* except for the large spinner which graced its nose. After turning 243.14 mph for a first in the 550 cu. in. Shell Speed Dashes and a fifth in Unlimited Dashes, Roy Minor nosed over No. 33 while landing. Repairs were made and *Miss Los Angeles* took a third place, then finished 2nd in Thompson. Best pylon speed was 213.25 mph. *(Robert C. Morrison)*

Marion McKeen purchased No. 33 in 1935, raced it "as is" until 1938 when a new plywood and full cantilever wing with retractable gear was fitted. Gear failed to extend after qualifying runs and landing damage kept it out of races. Craft turned 230.465 mph in 1936 Nationals for fifth in the Thompson. Then, with original wing refitted for the 1939 Nationals, Lee Williams stalled at the scattering pylon in the Greve Race start and crashed to his death. *Miss Los Angeles* was demolished. *(Dustin W. Carter)*

Wedell-Williams Model 45, license NR62Y, was the last racer designed by Jimmy Wedell and wore a full cantilever wing with retractable landing gear. Power was the Wasp Sr. out of racer No. 44. Paint job was red with black cowl and gear covers. Number 45 first raced in February 1934 at the American Air Races, New Orleans. There were still many bugs to work out but Jimmy did manage 264.703 mph in one race. Wasp Sr. and Wasp Jr. engines were interchangeable with ship No. 44.   (Wm. F. Yeager)

John Worthen flew No. 45 to second place at 203.13 mph in the 1934 Bendix, could have won the race easily had he not overshot Cleveland then retraced back to the finish line. In the Shell Speed Dashes Worthen turned 292.14 mph with Wasp Jr. engine he used in the Bendix. Borrowing the larger Wasp Sr. engine from Wedell's No. 44, Worthen then did 302.36 mph over the Shell 3 km course. Number 45 was later donated to Louisiana State University.   (Dustin W. Carter)

Roscoe Turner installed a big 1000 hp P&W Hornet engine for 1934, the most power carried by a racer until that time. Turner failed to start in Bendix because of fuel leaks, then won the Thompson Trophy race after Doug Davis fatally crashed his leading Wedell-Williams 44. Roscoe's craft took 2nd in Shell Dashes at 295.47 mph, wore race number 57 for his new sponsor, the H. J. Heinz Co. and their 57 varieties of food. Gold paint job remained unchanged.

(Dustin W. Carter)

Wedell-Williams 92 appeared in 1934 unchanged in outward appearance. Fuel tank troubles kept Lee Miles out of the Bendix but he later flew ship to Cleveland for Nationals. Walter Wedell, brother of James, flew 92 to 2nd place in 1000 cu. in. event at 219.49 mph, then John Worthen tooled the ship to 4th place and 248.91 mph in Shell Speed Dashes—took 3rd place in Thompson with 208.37 mph. Jimmy Haislip poses with No. 92 at 1932 Nationals, above. *(Dustin W. Carter)*

Geared Conqueror engine seems lost in fuselage designed for a big radial air-cooled engine. Gamma was stock except for Conqueror—and extra range tanks for the McRobertson Derby. All metal Gamma was quite large overall, had a wingspan of 47 feet 9.5 inches.

(Peter M. Bowers)

Jackie Cochran's Conqueror-engined Northrop 2-G Gamma was factory rebuilt after its Texas crash, wore a new P&W Twin Row Wasp Jr. engine of 700 hp and a three-bladed prop. In 1935 Bendix Jackie encountered a violent line squall over Arizona and returned to Burbank.

(Peter M. Bowers)

Granville, Miller & DeLackner Model R6H GED, an obvious descendant of the 1932 Gee Bee racers, was originally built for entry in the late 1934 McRobertson Race. It finished out of the money in 1934 Bendix when Pilot Lee Gehlback had time-consuming loose cowl problems.

(Robert C. Morrison)

In 1934 Wiley Post rigged his famous Winnie Mae with a belly skid, dropped his landing gear at Glendale for an assault on the Transcontinental record. Engine trouble forced him down at Purdue University where Wiley stall-landed and damaged Winnie. Craft resides in Smithsonian Institution.

(Lockheed)

Curtiss Conqueror-powered 2-G Gamma was the only Northrop single engined aircraft to ever wear a liquid-cooled engine. Conqueror SVG-1570F-4 V-type geared engine delivered 705 hp at 2,450 rpm at 7,000 feet. Prestone-cooled engine made the Gamma a rare bird indeed. Built for Jackie Cochran to fly in the 1934 London-Melbourne race, the beautifully streamlined ship was wrecked before the race by its delivery pilot in a Texas crash landing when the supercharger failed.   *(Peter M. Bowers)*

Cleanly cowled Conqueror engine improved cruise and top speed performance of the 2-G Gamma over its stock Wright Cyclone radial-engined counterpart but Conqueror was never as dependable as the newer air-cooled types. Gamma models had originally been designed and built by Jack Northrop as a one place mail plane but proved to be so fast and efficient that most of those built were purchased for cross-country record breaking! License NC13761 was later changed to NX-13761. Flush type riveting was not yet employed.   *(Warren M. Bodie)*

Miles and Atwood Special was cleaned up for 1934. Uncowled wheels were replaced by smaller panted wheels and the struts faired into the pants. Engine cowling fitted tighter and a spinner cleaned up the nose. In February 1934 Lee Miles and the green painted Special won three firsts in 375 cu. in. events at Pan American Races, New Orleans, was forced out of five events. At the 1934 Nationals Lee took six 1st, one 3rd and a 4th, did 206.241 mph on pylons and 233.44 mph in Shell Dashes.

(Dustin W. Carter)

As a new wing had been installed on Gee Bee R-2 for 1933, the Granville's had the 1932 wing intact. They rebuilt the wrecked fuselage of R-1, installed the 1932 wing. Fuselage was lengthened two feet and a more conventional rudder was fitted. Tail wheel was replaced with skid to improve ground control. A big P&W Hornet engine was installed and the craft was named "Intestinal Fortitude." In testing R-1, R-2 hybrid No. 7 for 1934 Nationals, Roy Minor ran into a ditch, eliminating the racer.

(Warren M. Bodie)

306.2 mph. Jimmy Wedell, former record holder, had been killed in a dual training crash.

THOMPSON TROPHY

Of the eight racers that had qualified for the Thompson free-for-all on September 3, only the Brown racer, *Miss Los Angeles,* to be flown by Roy Minor, was new. Lee Miles, who had earlier in the meet won the first Greve Trophy Race (restricted to 550 cu. in. engines or less) at 206.2 mph, was to fly his year-old Miles & Atwood Brown Special; Art Chester, who had not flown in last year's Nationals, entered his year-old *Jeep;* airline pilot Roger Don Rae was sitting in the Keith Rider *San Francisco 1;* and Harold Neumann was to fly *Ike.* All were powered by 4- or 6-cyl. Menasco engines of 200–300 hp.

Roscoe Turner, J. Worthen, and Doug Davis were lined up in their old Wedell-Williams racers. Davis had installed Wedell's 800-hp Wasp Sr. for the speed trials and race; Worthen's engine was the ship's original Wasp Jr.; while Turner's new P & W Hornet delivered 1,000 hp.

Doug Davis, soon after rounding the scattering pylon in the race-horse start, began building up a nice lead on the 4-pylon, 8⅓-mile course, flying a low groove race and taking the pylons very close. Roscoe Turner, in the fastest ship, was flying his usual high and wide pylon turn race. He was in second place, well ahead of the other six closely bunched and excellently flown planes, by virtue of superior horsepower alone. Soon the clean streamlining of the Brown racer asserted itself, as expert Roy Minor grooved it into a fairly comfortable third in the 100-mile race.

Lee Miles, who trailed in the race from the start, was forced out with engine trouble and landed safely. Eastern Airline pilot Doug Davis had gracefully flown his Wedell into a commanding lead, when on the eighth lap Death flagged him down. He had just cut inside a pylon about three miles behind the grandstand when he suddenly swerved to the left as if to circle back around the pylon. His plane, traveling about 250 mph, high-speed stalled out of control, twisted crazily, and plunged its nose into the ground.

No advancement of any science has been made without loss; and in man's conquest of the air, in his striving for speed and yet more speed, losses were inevitable.

Roscoe Turner, experiencing no trouble at his safer height, flew on to win his first Thompson Trophy in three tries at 248.1 mph. Roy Minor, who had been flying more than a lap behind Turner, zipped over the finish line well ahead of the other four racers, averaging 214.9 mph.

BEN ODELL HOWARD

Ben Howard's victory smile after he and his racers had made a clean sweep of the Bendix, Greve, and Thompson Trophies in 1935.

BEN HOWARD *was born in Palestine, Tex., Feb. 9, 1904. At the age of 18 he purchased an OX-5 Standard biplane for $175, $10 down and $10 a week. With no flight instructors available, Ben simply climbed in the Standard and taught himself to fly. Soon after, however, he spun into the ground, completely demolishing the ship. Undaunted, Ben climbed into another plane, this time with an instructor, and quickly learned the finer points of flying. Holder of Commercial Pilot License No. 1083, Ben worked as a flight instructor and did cotton dusting from 1923 to 1928. Then he flew for several airlines, finally settling down with United Air Lines, and by 1936 had become United's chief engineering pilot. In 1936 Ben formed the Howard Aircraft Company in Chicago. He built fast 5-place cabin planes modeled after his famous MR. MULLIGAN racer and remained as president of the company until 1940.*

Ben showed up at the 1930 National Air Races with the smallest racer (PETE) ever built for its 90 horsepower and, after taking several races in and above his horsepower class, finished a surprising third in the free-for-all Thompson Trophy contest with a superb exhibition of close pylon flying. With the prize money earned by PETE in 1930-31, Ben built two larger, more powerful racers, MIKE and IKE, and the immediate success of these ships in turn financed the building of his sleek MR. MULLIGAN of 1935. Ben was restrained from pylon racing in 1932 by United Air Lines, but carefully groomed his race planes and coached their pilots to many victories.

In 1940 Ben became supervisor of the Douglas Aircraft Company flight-test department and assistant to Donald Douglas. In 1947 he went to Convair at San Diego as consultant and board member and remained there until 1950. Following a brief sojourn as general manager of the Aircraft Division of Fairchild in Hagerstown, Md., in 1950, Ben and his wife Maxine returned to southern California — their adopted homeland — where Ben's keen analytical technology is again in action for Convair.

Unlucky We Will Jr. *was built and flown in 1930 Cirrus Derby by James Wedell, finished 7th. Landing gear was skirted then. In 1932 wing was clipped 8 feet and the fuselage 4 feet, gear cleaned up with pants. Menasco engine was fitted in 1933. Craft looked its best in 1935 as Dave Elmendorf, above, placed 7th in Greve, did 175.106 mph in one heat. (Dustin W. Carter)*

1935 — National Air Races

With two or three exceptions, the main events of the 1935 Nationals, held at Cleveland, August 30 to September 2, were contested by old race planes, and there was hardly a challenge to the achievements of past. Only eight of the 18 racers that figured in the prize money did over 200 mph and few went far beyond this mark.

BENDIX TROPHY

Eight planes took off from Burbank early on August 31 in the fifth annual cross-country dash, but Earl Ortman was forced out, and Cecil Allen crashed fatally shortly after take-off. Ben Howard and his copilot, Gordon Israel, flying their jointly built 4-place cabin plane, *Mr. Mulligan*, took off with an overload of fuel, climbed to 26,000 feet, and using oxygen for the first time in a Bendix, cruised nonstop into Kansas City for fuel. Then on their take-off they climbed over poor weather, inadvertently leaving their flaps in take-off position until nearing Cleveland, where they landed through rain and a heavy overcast to win the trophy at 238.7 mph. Roscoe Turner, who had to refuel three times along the route, finished a heartbreaking 23.5 seconds later in his old Wedell racer, while Russell Thaw, flying a Wright Cyclone engined Northrop Gamma, was third. Roy Hunt finished fourth in a Wasp Lockheed Orion, while Amelia Earhart was fifth and last in her Wasp Vega.

In the small plane races at Cleveland, Art Chester flew his *Jeep* 200.6 mph in the fastest 375 cu. in. race, and Harold Neumann won the second annual Greve Trophy for 550 cu. in. engines, flying Howard's *Mike* at 212.7 mph.

THOMPSON TROPHY

Seven planes took off on the afternoon of September 2 in the National's climaxing 150-mile Thompson Trophy Race, and again this year, Roscoe Turner, with his superior horsepower, began easing ahead of the field after the race-horse start. He was taking the pylons at 240 mph with his 1,000-hp Hornet-engined Wedell. Leading the field by half a lap and with only 20 miles to go, Turner's engine began belching a tremendous black trail of oil smoke, and Roscoe, nearly blinded and asphyxiated, pulled up at once to a safe altitude, cut his engine, and quickly determining that his golden ship was not afire, made a safe dead-stick landing on the airport turf.

Harold Neumann, who had been flying *Mr. Mulligan* in second position, assumed the lead and flew on to win the Thompson at a slow 220.2 mph. Ben Howard's planes, in sweeping the Bendix, Greve, and Thompson races, caused this year's Nationals to be referred to as the Benny Howard National Air Races! Steve Wittman, flying a beautiful groove race, finished a close second at 218.7 mph though troubled with an overheated engine. His new racer, built closely to an old Curtiss D-12 435-hp engine, was the first liquid-cooled U. S. racing plane since 1930.

Roger Don Rae, in the 3-year-old Keith Rider I, finished third, while fourth place went to Joe Jacobson, flying 3-year-old *Mike*. Fifth place went to Lee Miles, piloting the first and only amphibian to ever race in the Thompson, a golden-hued 715-hp Wright Cyclone engined Seversky, and he averaged 193.6 mph! Sixth and last place went to Marion McKeen, who, with a faulty engine, averaged only 188.9 mph in his little Brown racer.

Mr. Mulligan, the only cabin plane to win the Thompson, was very clean in design. Powered by a super-charged Wasp and capable of 830 hp, only 485 hp was used in winning the race.

Wittman's new D-12 racer *Bonzo* was the most unique of all the new ships this year. Converted from water coolant to Prestone, the radiator was set directly in front of the engine.

Roscoe Turner's Wedell-Williams 57 at Burbank Airport, California, scene of the 1935 Bendix start, with Sierra Madre mountains forming background. Roscoe was delayed at Kansas City fuel stop, finished a heartbreaking 23.5 seconds behind Bendix winner Ben Howard and his Mr. Mulligan! Then, leading the Thompson, his big Hornet engine throbbing out a 240 mph beat, the Hornet began pouring a huge trail of jet black smoke. Roscoe pulled up, then made a bobbling-cork-type deadstick landing on the airport. (Dustin W. Carter)

Cecil Allen and the ill-fated Gee Bee 7-11 hybrid appeared at Burbank for the 1935 Bendix. Cecil had scraped and scrounged the money to purchase No. 7, had just enough money left to fill the gas tanks for race start. Allen and Jackie Cochran waited until 3 a.m. to take off in Bendix, the other six having left just after midnight. Fog had rolled in when Allen began his take-off run, the Gee Bee became airborne, then crashed, demolishing the aircraft and killing Allen. (Dustin W. Carter)

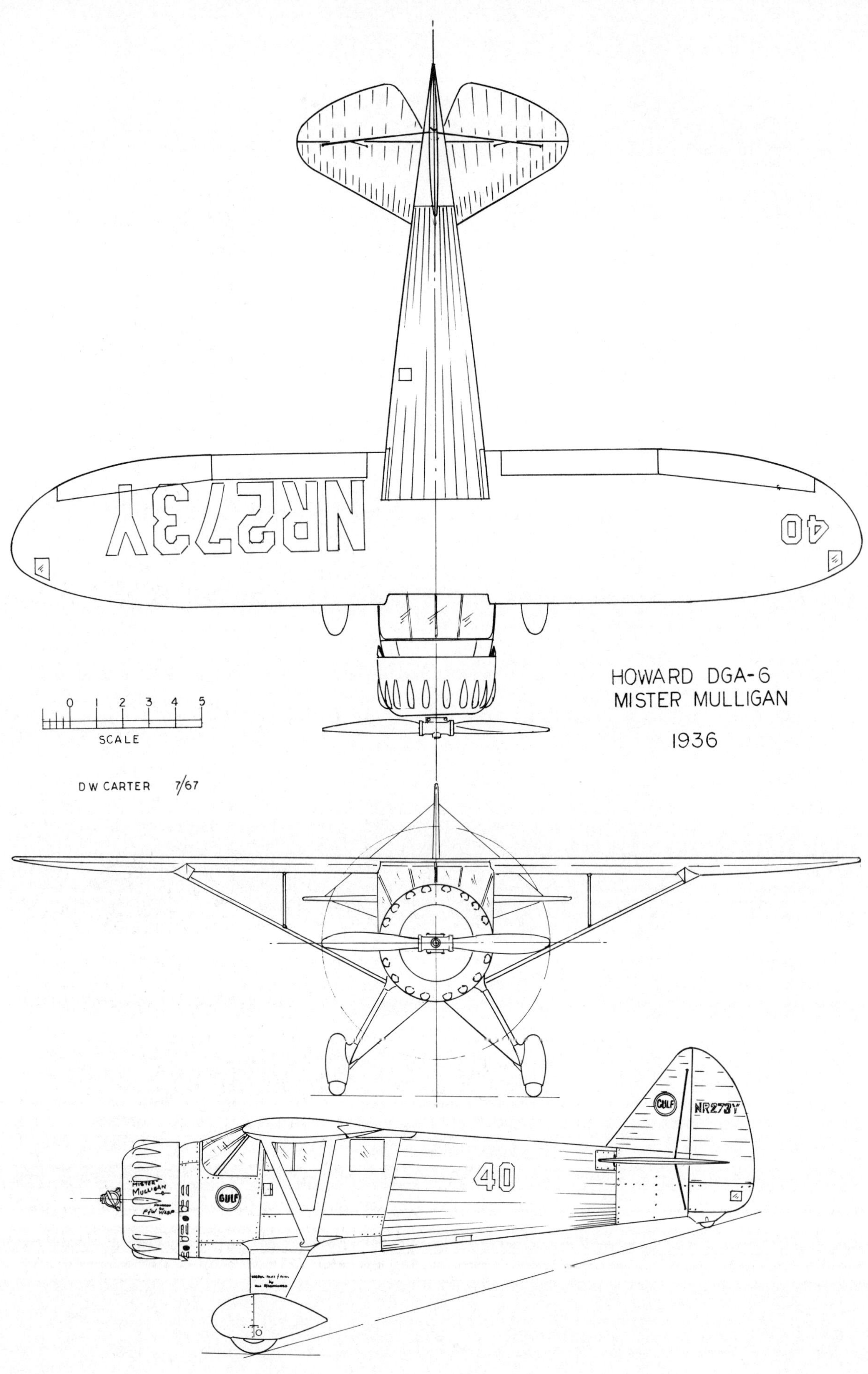

NR273Y
40
HOWARD DGA-6
MISTER MULLIGAN
1936
0 1 2 3 4 5
SCALE
D W CARTER   7/67
GULF
NR273Y
40
MISTER MULLIGAN
P&W WASP

Winner of the two main events of the 1935 National Air Races at Cleveland, Mr. Mulligan (DGA6) was a four-place high wing monoplane—and looked like a King-size Monocoupe. Fuselage was made of welded steel tubing fabric covered. Wing panels were built with solid spruce spars, built-up ribs covered with doped fabric. 92 octane fuel was used in Bendix take-off, 87 for cruise and 100 octane was used by Harold Neumann to win the Thompson Trophy race.

(Peter M. Bowers)

At take-off for start in the Bendix Mr. Mulligan carried a load of 2700 lbs., giving it a gross weight of 5300 lbs., increasing wing loading to more than 39 lbs./sq./ft. Take-off run was only 1500 ft. using but 550 hp of the 830 hp available. Mr. Mulligan was quite a remarkable aircraft. At sea level it had a speed of 251 mph using 550 hp and 287 mph utilizing its full 830 hp. Using 550 hp at 11,000 ft. its speed was 292 mph.

(Peter M. Bowers)

Seversky SEV-3 amphibian which finished fifth in 1935 Thompson with 193.6 mph average. Top level speed was 220 mph at sea level and 260 mph at 11,000 ft. Major De Seversky later installed a 1000 hp Wright Cyclone engine, set a 3 km World's record 230.4 mph for amphibians.

Mr. Mulligan stirs up dust as Ben Howard warms engine for test hop at St. Louis. Ben's wife Maxine "Mike" stands beyond cowl nose attired in capri's of the day, sailor pants. Mr. Mulligan had a climb rate of 4450 ft./min. using all its 830 hp. (Peter M. Bowers)

Although the Keith Rider R-3 was test flown in 1934 unpainted, the fuselage was painted black with race No. 9 on its flanks when James Granger nosed over in 1934 and was killed before the ship could race. Damage was minor and ship was repaired for 1935. (Dustin W. Carter)

Keith Rider R-3 wore the Gilmore Oil Company colors in 1935 and cockpit was enclosed for the Bendix. Earl Ortman became lost between Albuquerque and Amarillo in the Bendix, then discovered cowling damage at Kansas City fuel stop, withdrew from race. (Dustin W. Carter)

Roscoe Turner poses with his sleek gold Wedell-Williams just before 1935 Bendix. No. 57 had already picked up a first (1933), second (1934), and third (1932) in Bendix races, a first (1934) and a third (1932) in Thompson races. After 57 broke in half sparing Roscoe in 1936 the ship was rebuilt for 1937. Joe Mackey, its new pilot, was forced out of both Bendix and Thompson races. Mackey and 57 finished 5th and 6th in 1938-39 Thompson. Famous racer now resides in Thompson Museum, Cleveland. (Col. Roscoe Turner)

In 1934 Steve Wittman built his now famous Bonzo as closely to a second-hand Curtiss D-12 engine as was possible. Problems were not worked out in 1934 so Steve showed up at the 1935 Nationals ready to go, as above. The small Prestone radiator proved inadequate to cool the D-12's 435 horses and engine ran quite hot in the Thompson but Steve managed a close second place by flying a beautiful groove race. Note tiny aileron. Bonzo had hand-operated flaps. (Peter M. Bowers)

"Filaloola" bird insignia seen on Cecil Allen's hybird 7-11 and other Gee Bee's was lifted from a comic strip. Allen was too poor to fill gas tank until Bendix take-off so might have encountered stick forces he could not over-ride.   (Charles G. Mandrake)

Cecil Allen modified No. 7 extensively for 1935. A new wing was built which the Granville brothers objected to, said it was unsuited to the design. Note increased dihedral. New wheel pants were also fitted. New paint scheme eliminatetd scalloped design on wing.
(Warren M. Bodie)

Northrop Gamma owned by Bernarr McFadden, fanatic health faddist owner of Liberty magazine, was flown to 3rd place in 1935 Bendix by Russell Thaw. Engine was a 775 Wright Cyclone, standard installation on Gamma models. Color was natural aluminum, waxed and polished.   (Robert C. Morrison)

Amelia Earhart dropped out of 1933 Bendix, finished 5th and last in 1935 Bendix with same famous Lockheed Vega "Record Breaker." Achievements were lettered on fin. N. Y. Los Angeles 14 hours, Honolulu Oakland 18 Hrs., Los Angeles Mexico City 12 Hrs., Mexico City New York 14 Hrs.   (Lockheed)

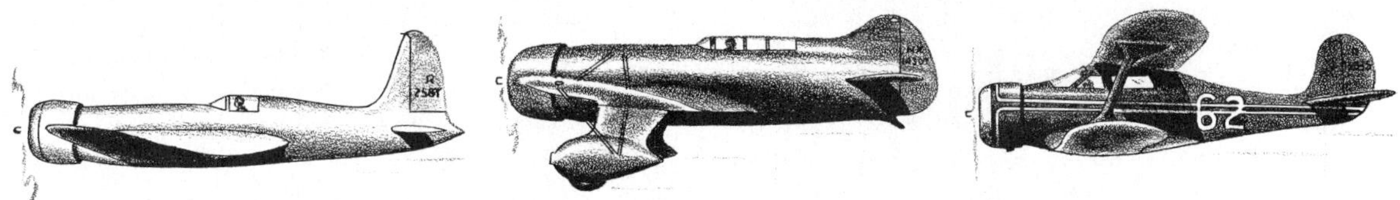

Just after last year's Nationals, Howard Hughes set a new landplane record of 352.4 mph with his special H-1 (left). Lee Miles was forced out of the Thompson in the ill-fated big Granville Q.E.D. (center). Louise Thaden cruised her Beechcraft (right) to victory in the 1936 Bendix race, averaging 165.3 for a new women's east-west record.

1936 – National Air Races

The 1936 National Air Races, held at Los Angeles, September 4 to 7, were especially rich in new racers of novel design. The Bendix Trophy Race, while not turning in any impressive speeds, was marked by a varied assortment of aircraft types. Roscoe Turner, flying east for the Bendix start, made a forced landing on rough ground near Gallup, N. M., and his old Wedell racer broke in two. Roscoe, however, walked away with nothing worse than scratches.

BENDIX TROPHY

Eight planes left Floyd Bennett Field, N. Y., in the dawn of September 4, to race for the coveted Bendix Trophy. Joe Jacobson climbed his Northrop Gamma high into the sky and set out to fly coast-to-coast nonstop, only to have his ship explode near Stafford, Kan., and blow him out of the cockpit. He parachuted safely and turned up at Los Angeles in time to race. Ben Howard and his wife Maxine, in *Mr. Mulligan,* crash-landed 40 miles north of Crownpoint, N. M., when their propeller broke. Caught in the twisted wreckage with injured legs, they were trapped three hours before superstitious Indians could be prevailed upon to go for help. Lee Miles dropped out but landed his big Granville Q.E.D. safely. Louise Thaden, with Blanche Noyes as copilot, cruised their Wright 450-hp Beechcraft at only 68% of its power to win at an all-time slow speed of 165.3 mph. Even so, she broke the women's east-west record held by Laura Ingalls, who flew her Wasp 550-hp Lockheed Orion into second place with 157.5 mph.

Wm. Gulick upheld the male species somewhat by flying his single-engined 10-passenger Wright Cyclone engined Vultee into a close third. Engine trouble again held Amelia Earhart to fifth and last place in her new twin-engined Lockheed Electra. Amelia later disappeared in the Southwest Pacific with this craft.

In-line air-cooled engines took most of the closed-course race money this year, and full-cantilever mono-planes with retractable landing gears held complete dominance.

The only new racer to appear in the daily Shell (three days) 375 cu. in. races was a Folkerts Special, and flown by veteran Harold Neumann, it won all three races, once averaging 231.3 mph.

Art Chester had trimmed down his now famous *Jeep* and finished a close second to the Folkerts in each race, once doing 230.5 mph. Steve Wittman had installed a Menasco 4 in his *Chief Oshkosh* and showed higher speed, but he misjudged a forced landing in his second race and landed atop one of the Army's new low-wing A-17 Northrop Attack planes. Surprisingly, Steve was not hurt, nor his plane badly damaged!

Not since the 1912 Bennett Cup races had a purely racing foreign landplane appeared in the United States, but this year, Michel Detroyat of France showed up with a Renault-engined Caudron C-460. Its 6-cyl. inverted air-cooled engine delivered 340 hp at 3,200 rpm, and his racer, a beautiful job of streamlining, was a low-midwing fitted with a skin type oil radiator, wing flaps, and a fully retractable landing gear. With this aircraft M. Delmotte of France had, in December, 1934, set a new world's landplane speed record of 314.2 mph.

GREVE TROPHY

Detroyat, flying the only racer fitted with a variable pitch prop, was first off and, after building up a commanding lead, throttled well back to win the race easily at 247.3 mph. Harold Neumann was second at 225.9 mph, with his Folkerts again tailed closely by Art Chester in his *Jeep*, who finished third at 224.7 mph.

Rudy Kling, who had decided to save his fire for the Thompson Trophy Race, finished fourth at 218.3 in his Rider I, renamed *Suzy.* Kling later stated, "I was flying well under top speed and sweeping a little

Steve Wittman made many changes on Chief Oshosh for 1936. Menasco four-cylinder engine replaced Cirrus, landing gear was leaf type with spring-steel struts and a new wing of only 13 foot span was fitted! Forced landing crash onto a Northrop A-17 eliminated Chief from races.
(Peter M. Bowers)

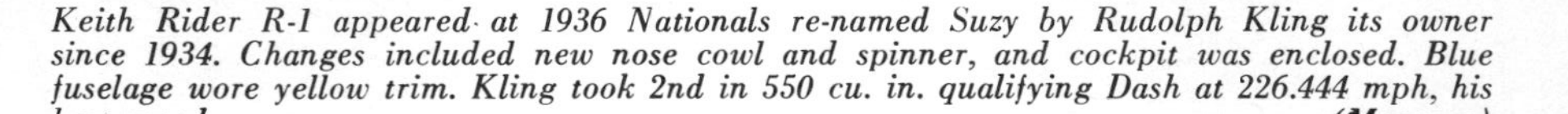

Unlucky Granville Q. E. D. entered its only Thompson race in 1936, its pilot Lee Miles hoping the big 750 hp Hornet would place it in the money. Quite large for the Thompson the Q. E. D. averaged well over 200 mph until forced out in 11th lap with engine trouble. (Dustin W. Carter)

At the 1936 National Air Races the Chester Special appeared under a new name, The Jeep, taken from a character in the famous Popeye comic strip. Paint job was changed to a cream with green trim. All Angles had been carefully filleted, no matter how small. (Dustin W. Carter)

Keith Rider R-1 appeared at 1936 Nationals re-named Suzy by Rudolph Kling its owner since 1934. Changes included new nose cowl and spinner, and cockpit was enclosed. Blue fuselage wore yellow trim. Kling took 2nd in 550 cu. in. qualifying Dash at 226.444 mph, his best speed.
(Menasco)

*French Caudron C-460 was the only racer to ever sweep both the Greve and Thompson races. Craft also won the Quali-
fying Speed Dashes, at 273.773 mph. Pilot Michel Detroyat could easily have won the Shell Cup race for 550 cu. in.
engines but graciously stayed out. Interesting feature was its Ratier propeller. Before each race air was pumped into
spinner, causing the blades to go into low pitch. On take-off a valve slowly let air out of spinner, allowing prop pitch
to increase!*　　*(Thompson Products)*

*Extremely sleek French Caudron was built up entirely of wood, covered first with plywood then fabric doped, waxed
and highly polished. Color was dark blue with white stripe and lettering. Landing gear was fully retractable into wing
wells. A metal covering on each wheel and strut closed the aperture when wheels fully retracted. American pilots put
up such a beef that France had sent a government subsidized aircraft and pilot to compete against them that France
never came back—and no other nation ever tried!*　　　　　　　　　　　　　　　　　　　　　　　　*(U. S. Air Force)*

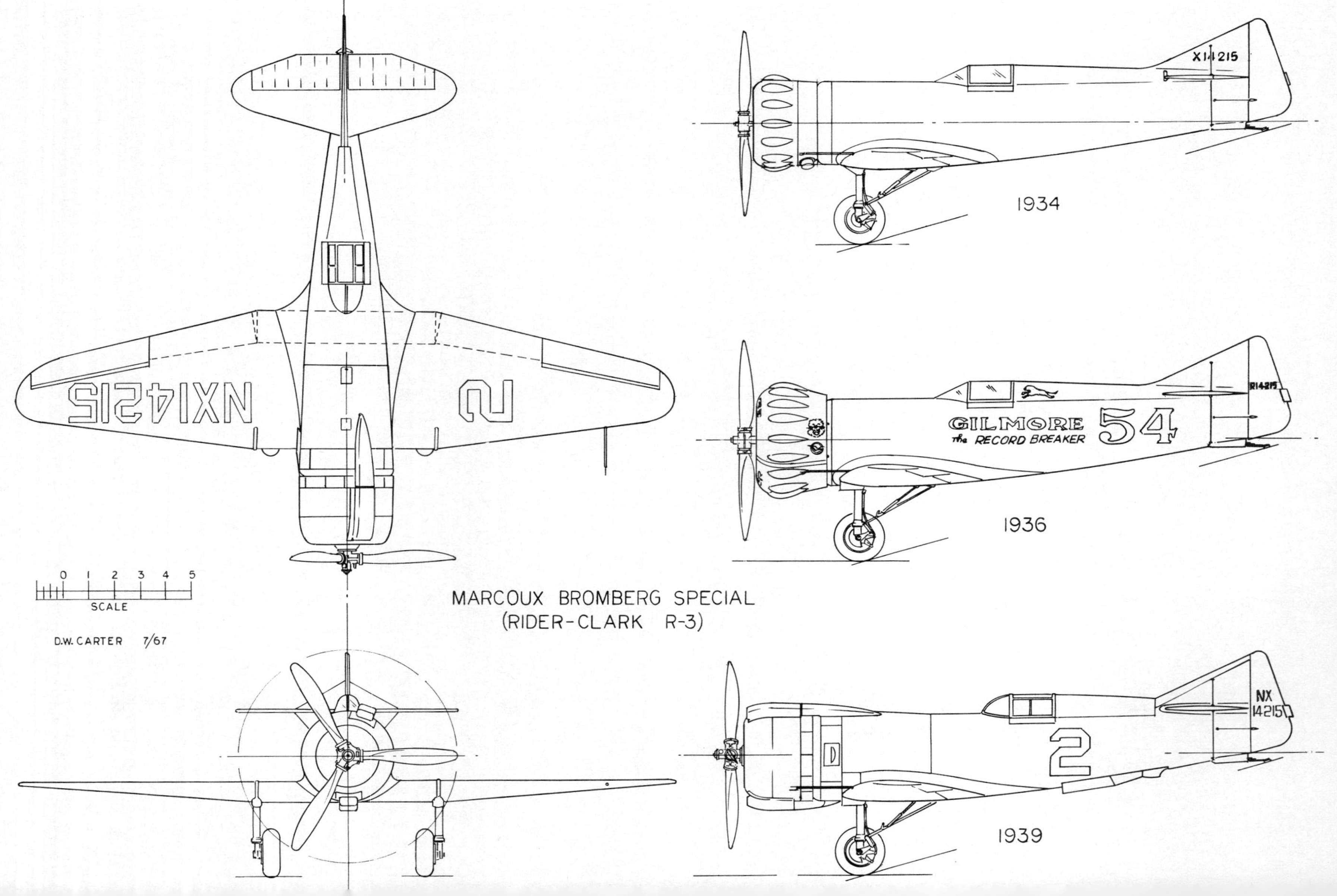

X14215
1934
R14215
GILMORE 54
The RECORD BREAKER
1936
NX
14215
2
1939
NX14215
2
0 1 2 3 4 5
SCALE
D.W. CARTER 7/67
MARCOUX BROMBERG SPECIAL
(RIDER-CLARK R-3)

In 1936 Earl Ortman and Keith Rider R-3 showed up at the Nationals with most of its bugs ironed out. Big waffle-iron Wasp engine and poorly designed engine cowl with its almost flat front was no match for the much lesser powered but clean-nosed Caudron so Earl had to settle for 2nd in Thompson. Coloring was familiar Gilmore cream with red lettering edged in gold. Fuselage of all-metal R-3 was built with protruding rivets while wings were flush riveted.
(Robert C. Morrison)

During 1936 Earl Ortman set several speed records with the R-3. One of these was the Three Flags Record, Canada to Mexico, 5 hours, 27 minutes, 48 seconds. The R-3 in its 1936 configuration was not the cleanest of racers. In addition to big awkward cowl and protruding fuselage rivets the rudder control horns were built externally and a brace wire ran around tail surfaces, lending drag. Wheel wells were never covered on retractable landing gear throughout the R-3's career.
(Robert C. Morrison)

Howard Hughes H-1, built in 1935, was one of the cleanest radial air cooled engined aircraft ever built—and proved to be the world's fastest. Special wing of only 25 ft. span was used to set 3 km speed record of 352.4 mph. (Peter M. Bowers)

New and bright yellow Keith Rider R-4 first raced in 1936 Nationals. Roger Don Rae won 550 cu. in. Shell Dashes at 225.544 mph, was 3rd in Thompson at 236.559 mph and 6th and last in Greve race with 212.325 mph. (Robert C. Morrison)

Clayton Folkerts designed and built his new midwing racer Toots for the 1936 Nationals. Flown expertly by Harold Neumann, Toots compiled an impressive record of wins. It took three firsts, two seconds (including Greve) and was fourth in the Thompson. Best speed, 231.344 mph. (Dustin W. Carter)

Harry Crosby designed the fuselage so shallow on his new all metal racer that he practically sat on the floor. Ship was test hopped by Harry just one week before 1936 Nationals and three landing mishaps left no time to install fairing that covered landing gear when retracted. (Robert C. Morrison)

Folkerts Special, Toots, was slightly larger than other racers of its class, had a long graceful fuselage with cantilever wing and tail surfaces. Fastest in her class Toots had a fully enclosed retractable landing gear and sported large wing flaps. Entire fuselage was built of steel tubing, fabric covered, and wing was of wood construction, plywood, covered. Neumann flew his racer close to the ground, pulling up a bit for pylon turns then back to the deck to use boundary layer of air to best advantage.
(Dustin W. Carter)

There was no time to fit a spinner to nose of Crosby CR-3 for the races and a temporary windshield with no enclosure was hastily fitted. Prop pitch was probably the highest of any racer present, as seen here, giving it a very slow take-off, so craft did its best in the longer Thompson Trophy race. Racer was thoroughly wind-tunnel tested before it was built and was fitted with split trailing edge flaps. Note rags stuffed in exhaust pipes to keep dust and moisture out.
(Dustin W. Carter)

Perfectionist Art Chester had his Jeep traveling faster each year but throughout his racing career Art, a superb pilot, almost always saw the winner's tail. At 1936 Nationals the beautifully proportioned little Jeep took three 2nd places in 375 cu. in. races and finished 3rd in the Greve Trophy race. At Miami races, Art did take two 1st and one 2nd place. Best pylon speed was 230.479 mph. Jeep turned out at about 255 mph in straight flight.   (Warren M. Bodie)

Mechanic running up Wright engine of stock C17R Beechcraft which Louise Thaden and co-pilot Blanche Noyes cruised to victory in 1936 Bendix. Louise was as surprised as everyone else that she had won the race, having expected to only place in the event. Normal cruise speed was 202 mph at 10,000 ft. Empty weight 2225 lbs, gross 3900 lbs. 98 gallons of fuel gave a 700 mile cruising range. Landing speed, with flaps, was 50 mph, service ceiling 22,000 ft. Climb rate was 1400 ft. per min.   (Beech)

Howell Miller, former Granville Chief Designer, along with Mark Granville and most of the former Granville workers, formed the Hawks Aircraft Company to build Time Flies for Frank Hawks in 1936. Sponsor was the Gruen Watch Company. Permission was obtained to use a military P&W Twin Wasp R-1830BG engine of 1,150 hp. Rate of climb was figured at 7,000 feet a minute, cruising speed 340 mph and top 375 mph. 230 gallons of fuel gave cruising range of 1700 miles. Wingspan was 31 feet, length 22 feet. (Peter M. Bowers)

Time Flies had a retractable skylight atop cockpit which acted as a windscreen for take-offs and landings. Skylight was flush with fuselage top in flight. Seat raised and lowered with skylight. During a test flight a fur-lined mitten jammed the landing gear so Hawks couldn't lower the wheels. Belly landing washed out the gear. Soon repaired Hawks made a rough landing at dusk, cracked a wing spar and did other damage so Time Flies was left in a hangar to gather dust. (Peter M. Bowers)

Delgado Maid was designed by Byron A. Armstrong, Chief Airplane ground school instructor at Delgado Trades School and the craft was built for the 1936 Nationals by students of the school. Originally fitted with a Curtiss D-12 engine it later wore a Conqueror engine. A Prestone filled coolant radiator was made to form with the engine bottom cowling, the only cooling surface on the Maid. Wingspan was 22 feet 9 inches, length 22 feet. Ship was extremely sensitive on the controls and was purportedly clocked at 420 mph.   *(Dustin W. Carter)*

Delgado Maid was dogged by cooling problems, paint blistering off the engine cowl and one test pilot even blistering his feet on the rudder pedals! Eighteen flights were made with the all-plywood racer when Arthur J. Davis had the engine blow up and throw him out just after unfastening his seat belt. Davis parachuted safely, saw the Delgado Maid dive straight into the ground and bury itself to the rudder post. License number was NR65Y and race number 6 had been applied to sides.   *(Robert S. Hirsch)*

wide on the turns when something shot by above and inside me just as I was rounding the home pylon on the fourth lap. It was Detroyat going by me as though I was tied and cutting in close to the pylon much in the same style Don Rae uses. I wondered what would happen if I swept out just as he swept in. Hayseed salad with French dressing!"

Joe Jacobson, in *Mike*, finished fifth, while Roger Don Rae was sixth at 212.3 mph in a new Keith Rider, and Marion McKeen was seventh and last in his *Miss Los Angeles*. All but the French ship were powered by Menasco engines.

Lee Miles had dropped out safely with his M & A Special. After the race, Jacobson nosed *Mike* over on landing. Don Rae came in and shot safely between overturned *Mike* and the home pylon, then Kling, heading for the same slot, tried to avoid a truck and people and plowed through an auto. There was not much left of *Suzy* or the auto — neither Kling nor Jacobson were injured!

THOMPSON TROPHY

Again Detroyat was first off in the race-horse start and first back onto the 15-lap 150-mile course. He did 301 mph on his second lap in building up a nice lead, and then eased back to win the Thompson at a new high of 264.3 mph. Earl Ortman, flying a new all-metal P & W Wasp Jr. powered Keith Rider, was second at 248 mph, while Don Rae finished third at 236.6 mph in his new Menasco Rider.

Harold Neumann averaged 233.1 mph with his Folkerts to take fourth, and Marion McKeen did 230.5 mph in his Brown B-2 *Miss Los Angeles* for fifth place. Harry Crosby, in a new and sleek but unfinished all-metal Menasco-engined racer of his own design, was sixth and last.

Lee Miles, flying Jacqueline Cochran's huge Granville Q.E.D. that had been built for the fouled-up 1934 MacRobertson London-Australia Race, did quite well in the Thompson until the plane's Hornet engine acted up, forcing him to land.

Detroyat's victory in both the Thompson and Greve stimulated racing-plane development here; it had been a long, long time since France had won a major race.

At Santa Ana, Calif., on Sept. 13, 1935, millionaire sportsman-pilot Howard Hughes, flying a specially built plane powered by a 1,000-hp twin-row Wasp Jr. engine, averaged 352.4 mph on a 3-km course to better Delmotte's speed and set a new landplane record. His ship, only 25 feet in wing span, had not shown up at the Nationals — America missed it!

SYLVESTER (STEVE) J. WITTMAN

Steve Wittman, at the 1938 National Air Races.

STEVE WITTMAN, *born in Byron, Wis., Apr. 5, 1904, and graduated from Fond du Lac, Wis., high school, is best known for his ability to design, build, and fly to perfection extremely simple and fast aircraft for their horsepower. It is unfortunate, in this day of complex aircraft, that Steve's talents for simplification have been overlooked by large manufacturers of military planes.*

Steve learned to fly at Fond du Lac in 1924 and, as most pilots of those times, built up his flying by barnstorming. He also flew as test pilot for the Pheasant Aircraft Company and later the Dayton Aircraft Company. Since 1931 he has managed the Winnebago County airport at Oshkosh, and also operates a flying service and flight school there.

Steve began his racing career in 1926, entering racing events at air shows. He showed up at the 1931 Nationals with his first home-built racer, CHIEF OSHKOSH, which is credited with the first use of a "Laminar Flow" wing curve — ten years before the N.A.C.A. announced the revolutionary curve. Steve later installed a Menasco 4 engine in this ship and in 1937 flew it over a 100-km course at De-
troit to set a world's record (still standing) for its class of 238 mph.

Steve entered the big time in 1935. Having purchased a used V-12 engine of 435 hp, he built history's smallest racer for its power. Plagued by coolant troubles and plain hard luck, Steve flew his little BONZO in four Thompson races but could never quite win, although in 1939 BONZO did 325 mph on the straightaway pulling only 485 horsepower.

Since the first Goodyear Trophy Race in 1947 and the first Continental Engine Trophy Race in 1948, Steve and his protégé Bill Brennand have taken so many first and second places in these events that one loses count. Steve's friends want him to quit racing, he claims he is too old to change his habits.

Steve's closest call came in January, 1950, when he and Brennand were flying their ships home from Miami, Fla., after taking first and second place in a race there. While flying over Tennessee, Steve's gas tank was pierced with a bullet fired by a witless mountaineer, and Steve, nearly overcome by fumes, was barely able to choose a field in the densely wooded area and glide to a landing before passing out.

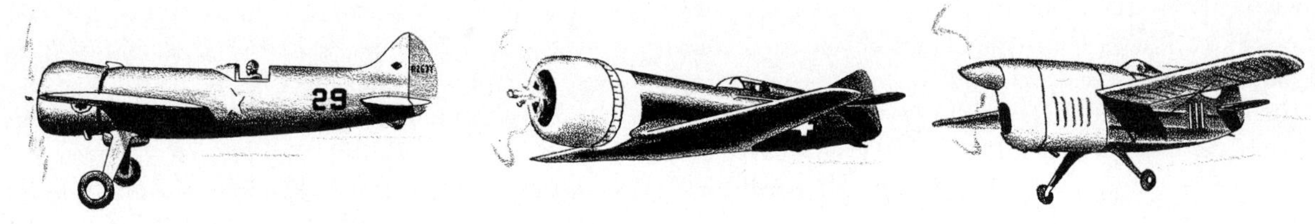

Roscoe Turner's new Brown racer (left). Earl Ortman's Keith Rider (center) was painted black and yellow this year. Steve Wittman's CHIEF OSHKOSH *(right) wore his newly patented spring-steel landing gear.*

1937 – National Air Races

The 1937 National Air Races got underway at Cleveland, September 3, opening a four-day demonstration of aerial progress and development. There was a powerful display of Army, Navy, and Marine squadrons. From Maxwell Field, Ala., came the Army's "Three Skylarks," Capt. McAllister and Lts. Aring and Hughes, who flew their P-12E's through intricate acrobatics as if glued together.

BENDIX TROPHY

Eight planes took off before dawn Friday, September 3, from Burbank in the Bendix Trophy Race. Perlick crashed his Beechcraft on take-off but was uninjured, and Joe Mackey, flying Turner's old 57, was forced out at St. Louis by oil trouble.

Sportsman-pilot Frank Fuller (Fuller Paint), flying his new all-metal Seversky P-35 pursuit, refueled at Kansas City, and at 2:49 P.M. his silver ship, powered by a 14-cyl. twin-row Wasp 1,000-hp engine, dived over the finish line at Cleveland to win the Bendix at a record 258.2 mph, breaking Haizlip's 1932 record by nearly 26 minutes. Without landing, Fuller flew on to Floyd Bennett Field to break Turner's 1934 speed record and set a Bendix record of 9 hrs. 35 min.

Earl Ortman, almost overcome by heat and fumes, managed to finish second in his 700-hp Twin Wasp Jr. Keith Rider, averaging 224.8 mph. Jacqueline Cochran was third in a 450-hp Beechcraft, while Frank Sinclair, Seversky test pilot, was fourth in a P-35 Seversky. Milo Burcham finished a hair-line fifth in a Lockheed Electra powered by two 400-hp Wasp Jr. engines. Eiler Sundorph, flying his Sundorph metal cabin plane powered by a 9-cyl. 285-hp Jacobs, was a slow sixth and last at 166.2 mph but was faster than last year's winner!

There were 11 closed-course races at Cleveland this year, and Steve Wittman, using his two racers, won four, finished second in one, and fifth in another.

There was one fatality at Cleveland, and aviation lost another fine pilot when lanky Lee Miles, practicing the day before the races, lost a wing of his 4-year-old souped-up Miles-Atwood racer while rounding a pylon.

GREVE TROPHY

Five Menaco-engined racers took off into a high wind full of "bumps" for the Greve, Sunday afternoon, September 5. For the first half of the race (10-lap 100-mile course) it was a hammer-and-tongs affair between Wittman's *Chief Oshkosh*, Don Rae in last year's Folkerts, and Rudy Kling, who was flying a new Folkerts named *Jupiter*. Then Wittman and Kling moved out ahead, the inverted 4- and 6-cyl. in-line engines of all the racers bleating a song of rhythmic power as they tilted their exhausts at the pylons. At the finish bare fractions separated Kling, who won the Greve with 232.3 mph, and Wittman with 232 mph. C. H. Gotch, flying a Schoenfeldt-modified Rider, eased by Don Rae (224.2 mph), to take third place with 231.6 mph, while Marion McKeen finished fifth and last in *Miss Los Angeles*.

THOMPSON TROPHY

Nine racers took off in the Thompson Trophy Race, Labor Day, September 6. Frank Sinclair and Ray Moore flew their stripped-down Seversky P-35 pursuits; C. H. Gotch was in the Schoenfeldt-Rider, which had placed third in last year's Thompson; while Rudy Kling entered his new Folkerts, powered, as was the Rider, with a Menasco 6, which Kling turned 3,300 rpm to derive a little over 400 hp.

Roscoe Turner, who had flown into Cleveland the day before, flew his Lawrence Brown built racer that had been revamped by Matty Laird, powered by a 1,000-hp Twin Wasp. Earl Ortman was in his Wasp Jr. Keith Rider, and Steve Wittman was flying his

Earl Ortman readies his Keith Rider R-3 for the 1937 Bendix. The Racer, renamed Marcoux-Bromberg Special for its new owners, wore a Twin Row Wasp Jr. engine in place of its former Wasp Sr. R-3 now wore a new cockpit enclosure (removed above) and a smooth NACA cowl with cowl flaps. Ship was painted a high gloss black over all except its natural aluminum nose. Race and license lettering was white. Ortman was out horse-powered in the Bendix, finished second. *(Peter M. Bowers)*

R-3 was the only 1937 Thompson racer equipped with a radio receiver for its pilot, Earl Ortman. On the advice of his ground crew, with Ben O. Howard on the mike, Ortman had throttled well back in the race when Rudy Kling dived over the finish line purportedly to take first place. Ben Howard and his crew protested that Ortman had already lapped Kling but to no avail. There were a lot of spectators who also thought Ortman had won the race. *(Peter M. Bowers)*

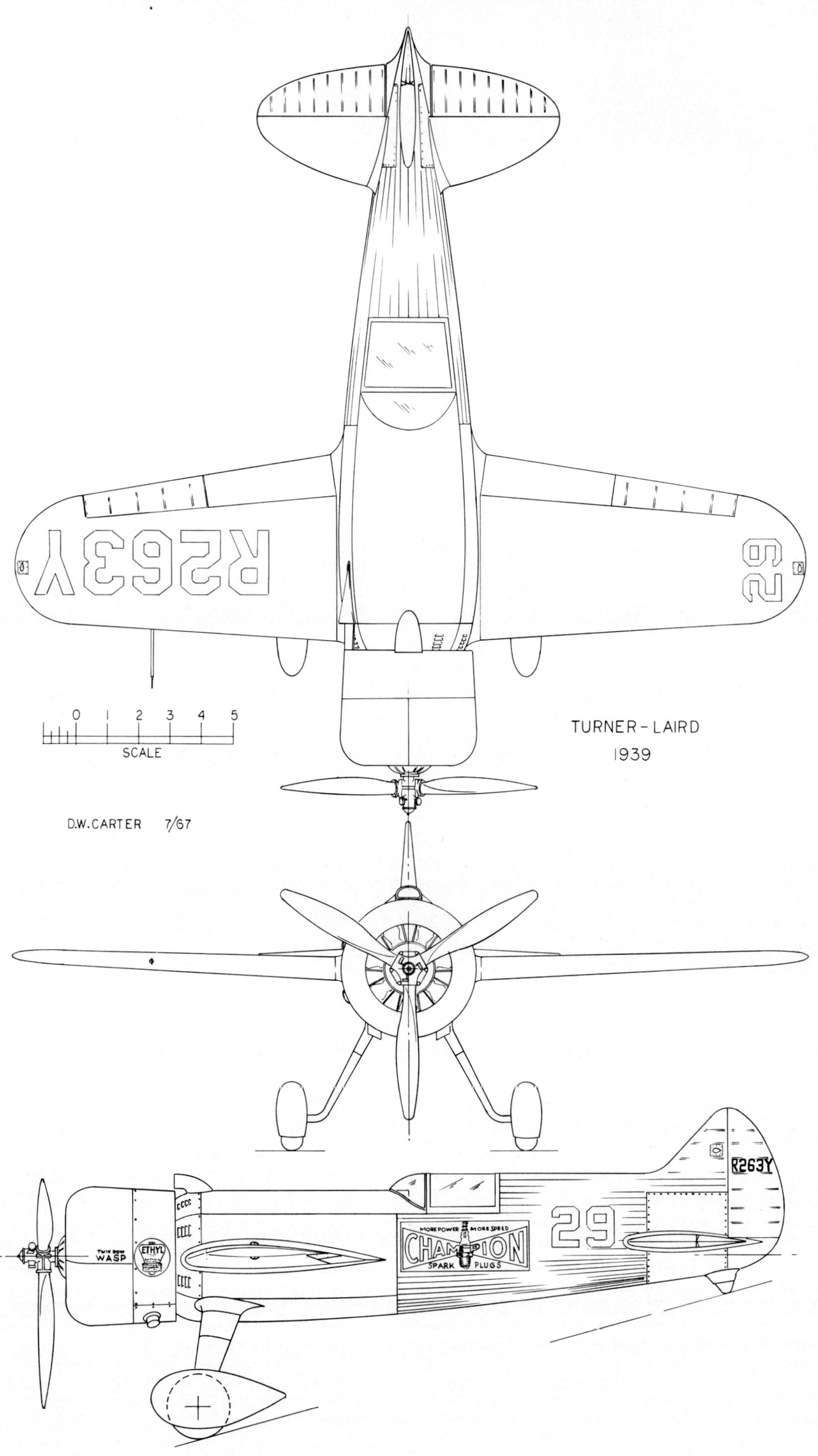

R263Y
29
TURNER-LAIRD
1939
SCALE
0 1 2 3 4 5
D.W.CARTER 7/67
R263Y
29
TWIN ROW WASP
ETHYL
MORE POWER MORE SPEED
CHAMPION
SPARK PLUGS

Frank W. Fuller Jr. and his Bendix winning Seversky SEV-S2. This aircraft, except for markings, was identical to the Seversky P-35 pursuit planes being supplied to the U. S. Air Corps at this period. P-35 had a wing span of 36 feet, length 25 feet 4 inches. 1,000 hp P&W Twin Row Wasp engine delivered a top speed of 300 mph at 10,000 feet. Service ceiling was 29,685 feet, rate of climb 3174.6 ft. per min. Cruising range, with 200 gallons of fuel, was 1,200 miles.
(Dustin W. Carter)

Turner-Laird Meteor design was sketched by Colonel Roscoe Turner, engineered by Howard Barlow and built by the Lawrence Brown Aircraft Company, in California. Completed in mid-1936, Roscoe decided the Meteor was too heavy for its 22 foot wing of narrow chord, shipped the aircraft to Matty Laird in Chicago. A new wing of 25 foot span was fitted and other changes made. Welding accident kept Roscoe out of 1937 Bendix and he barely made the Thompson, having to repair a hail-stone damaged wing.
(Dustin W. Carter)

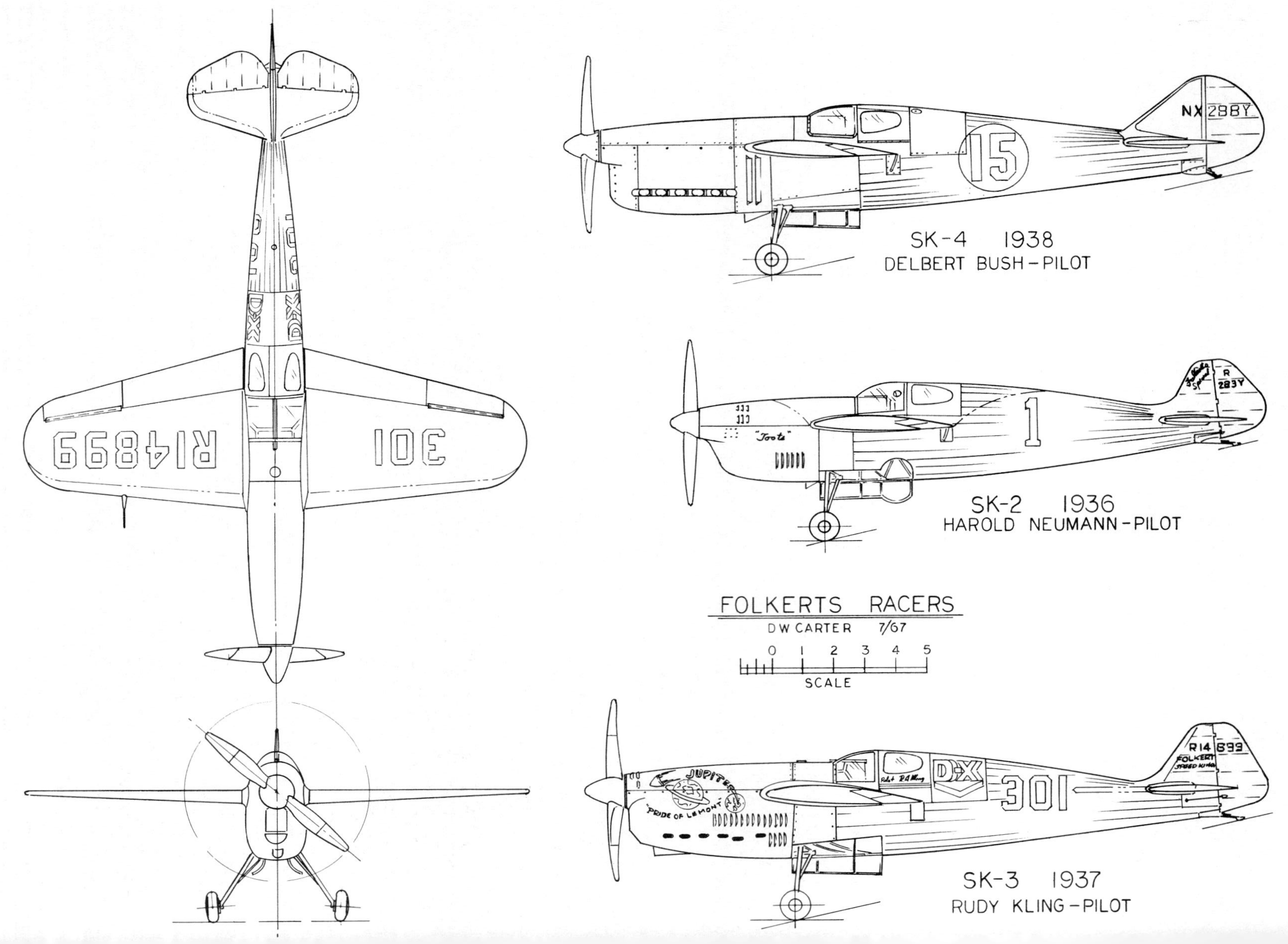

NX 288Y
SK-4   1938
DELBERT BUSH-PILOT
R 283Y
SK-2   1936
HAROLD NEUMANN-PILOT
FOLKERTS   RACERS
D W CARTER   7/67
0 1 2 3 4 5
SCALE
R14 699
FOLKERTS SPEED KING
JUPITER
"PRIDE OF LEMONT"
DX
301
SK-3   1937
RUDY KLING-PILOT
R14899
301
DX

Beautifully proportioned SK-3 Pride of Lemont was designed and built by Clayton Folkerts on order for Rudy A. Kling of Lemont, Illinois. Kling barely beat out Steve Wittman and his smaller Chief Oshkosh to win the 1937 Greve Trophy and then, as so often was the case in Thompson races, won that event almost by default. Every inch a racer in appearance the SK-3 wore an especially built wooden propeller of extremely high pitch. Color scheme was cream with red trim.
(Robert C. Morrison)

The rhythmatic throb of a Menasco engine in full flight was a symphony of sound and a joy to the ear. C6S engine in the Pride had a normal rating of 250 hp at 2250 rpm but Kling pulled over 400 hp at 3300 rpm to make the ship faster than all other Menasco engined racers before it. Retractable landing gear operated by an ingenious linkage system, the pilot raising or lowering the gear with a simple push or pull lever.
(Warren M. Bodie)

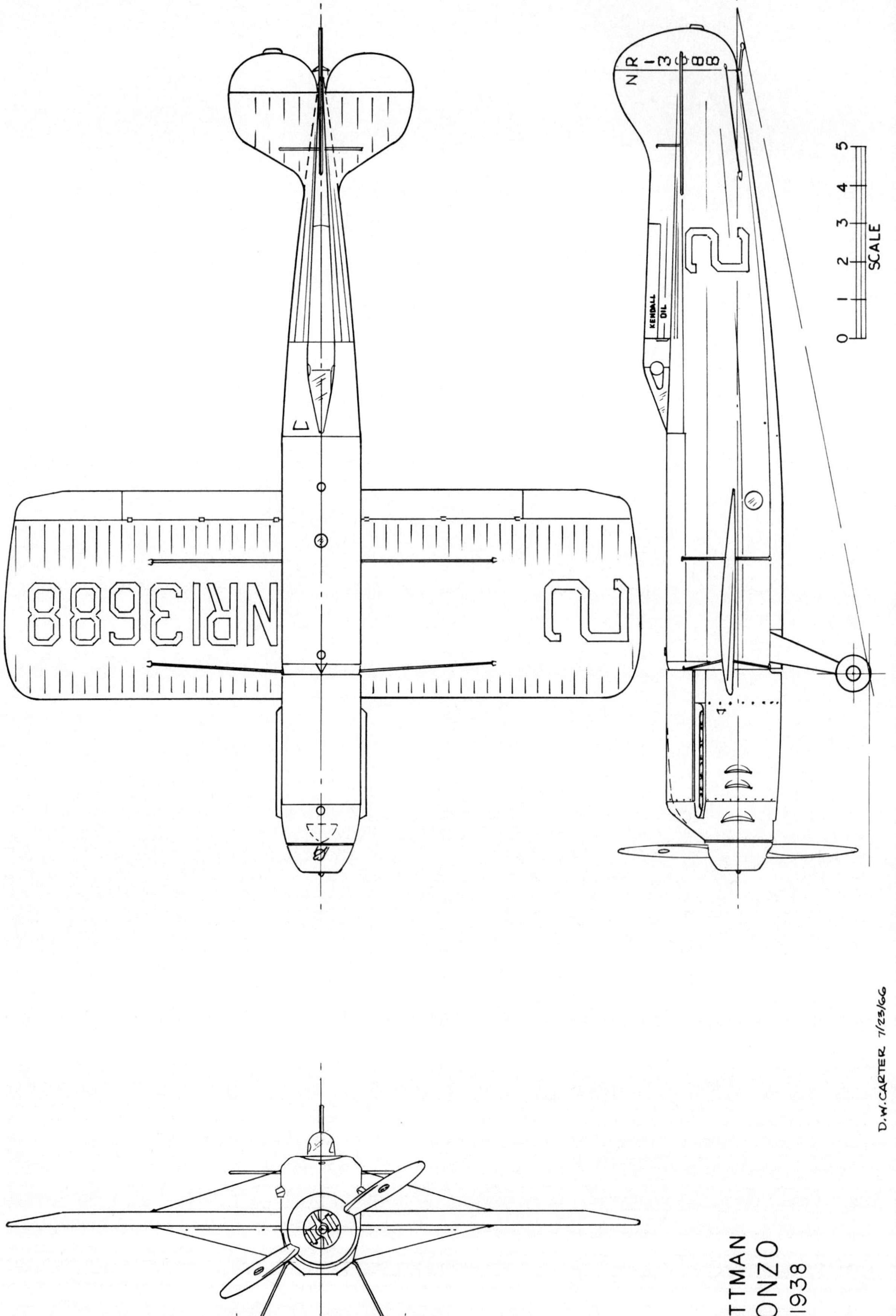

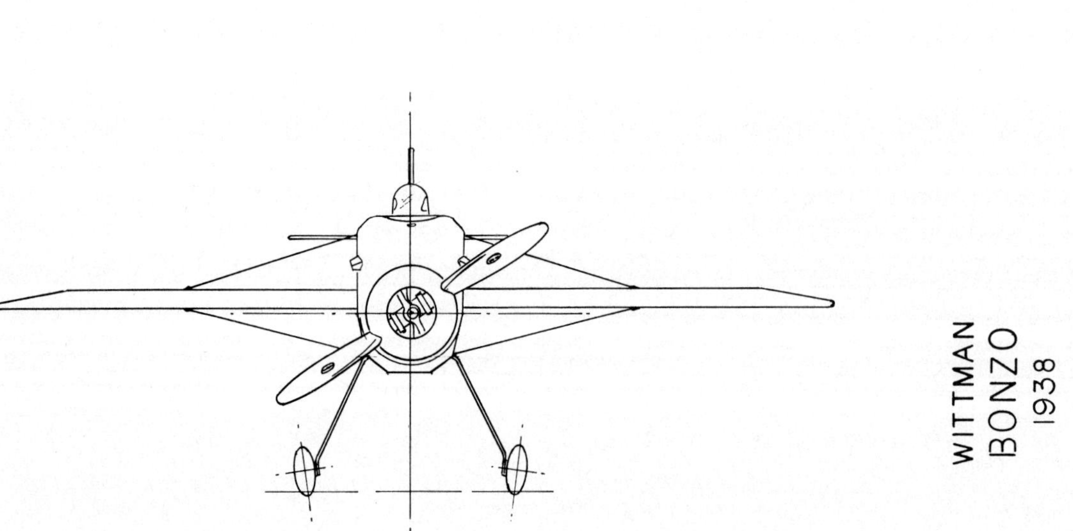

NR-3688
KENDALL OIL
2
NR13688
2
SCALE
0 1 2 3 4 5
D.W. CARTER 7/25/66
WITTMAN
BONZO
1938

It was quite a shock to come upon this extremely simple little Wittman Bonzo racer as it waited, along with the other contenders, for the Thompson race to be run later that day. Date was September 6, 1937. One of the most unique aircraft ever built, Bonzo's Prestone radiator was now set directly back of the propeller center and a blower fan just forward of the radiator pulled cooling air through an opening in the propeller spinner. Bonzo was all red except for aluminum engine cowl. (James Tenety, Jr.)

Bonzo wore a simple Wittman designed spring-steel landing gear for 1937, to which was fitted small doughnut tail wheels. Steve patented the landing gear and receives royalties from Cessna, who use the gear on their clean sports planes. A unique feature of Bonzo was its two-tunnel center section, into which the extra long wing panel spars slid, the flying and landing wires thus keeping the wings on! Only small mishaps prevented Bonzo from winning the Thompson Trophy three times—by a country mile. (Peter M. Bowers)

Seversky SEV-S2 Executive model flown to 4th place in 1937 Bendix and Thompson by Frank Sinclair was identical to Frank Fuller's SEV-S2 flown to 6th in Thompson by Ray Moore. Ships wore light metallic blue paint, flew a beautiful groove Thompson. Superchargers would not allow full throttle. *(Dustin W. Carter)*

1937 Folkerts SK-3 Jupiter had shortest wing of any Thompson winner and its 16 ft. 8 in. wing was shorter than all but a few Thompson contenders. Kling and SK-3 crashed out of prop wash in a 1938 Miami race as he attempted to pass underneath. *(Dustin W. Carter)*

Delgado Flash, another school effort designed by Byron Armstrong, came to Cleveland in 1937 hastily built. Cowling and wheel skirts were roughly bumped out and no spinner was fitted. Clarence McArthur had 544 cu. in. Menasco act up, flagged down 3rd in a qualifying heat. *(Dustin W. Carter)*

Roger Don Rae appeared at 1938 Nationals with a new Folkerts SK-4 which was similar to the successful SK-3 Jupiter, even to engine. Race numbered 15, the little ship developed wing flutter, reappeared at 1939 Nationals but Delbert Bush fatally crashed in qualifying run. *(Dustin W. Carter)*

On January 17, 1937 Howard Hughes flew his superb H-1 from Los Angeles to New York non-stop in 7 hours, 28 minutes, 10 seconds, to set a new transcontinental record, averaged 332 mph. Howard had perfected his cross-country technique by taking off on the afternoon of January 13, 1936 at Burbank in a Cyclone-engined Northrop Gamma with 700 gallons of fuel, flew non-stop into Newark at one o'clock the next morning with a new record of 9 hours, 26 minutes and 10 seconds. *(Hughes)*

The H-1 was designed according to Hughes' own ideas by Richard Palmer of later Vultee design fame, and D. E. Odekirk was in charge of shopwork, directing a crew of Hughes men. About 18 months were required to complete the H-1 and its two sets of wings, during which strict secrecy was maintained. H-1 was the first aircraft to have a flush-riveted metal fuselage, and first with flush (butt) joints between the skin sheets, thus being first with a smooth all-metal fuselage. *(Hughes)*

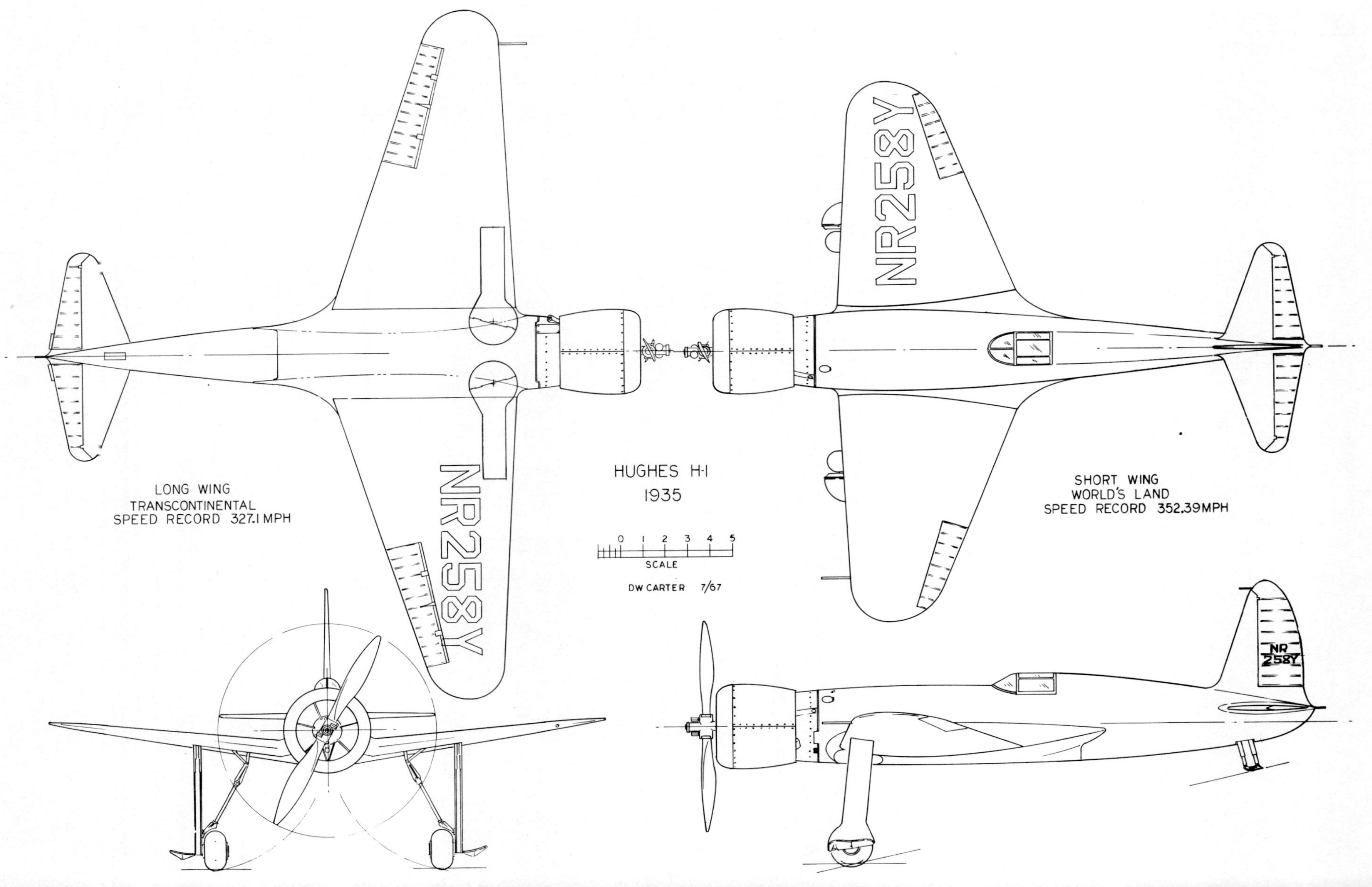

NR258Y
LONG WING
TRANSCONTINENTAL
SPEED RECORD 327.1MPH
HUGHES H-I
1935
0 1 2 3 4 5
SCALE
DW CARTER 7/67
NR258Y
SHORT WING
WORLD'S LAND
SPEED RECORD 352.39MPH
NR 258Y

Short-wing version of the Hughes H-1 as compared with long-wing configuration below. Hughes had planned to fly the short wing in Thompson Trophy race, long wing in Bendix. Certain race pilots cried when it was learned that Hughes planned to enter 1936 Nationals so Howard withdrew. He could have won the Thompson easily, set World's landplane 3 km speed record of 352.388 mph at Santa Ana September 13, 1935. 25 foot speed wing had an area of only 140 square feet.   *(Charles G. Mandrake)*

Stressed skin wings, both long and short versions, were built up of both wood and metal. Plywood skin was covered with balloon cloth doped with a hand-rubbed blue finish. Wing flaps on speed wing were hand-operated to save weight and long wing was the first to have power-driven retractable landing gear. Howard Hughes was an exacting but superb pilot—and had money to do as he liked. It is to his credit that he did so much to further aviation.   *(Hughes)*

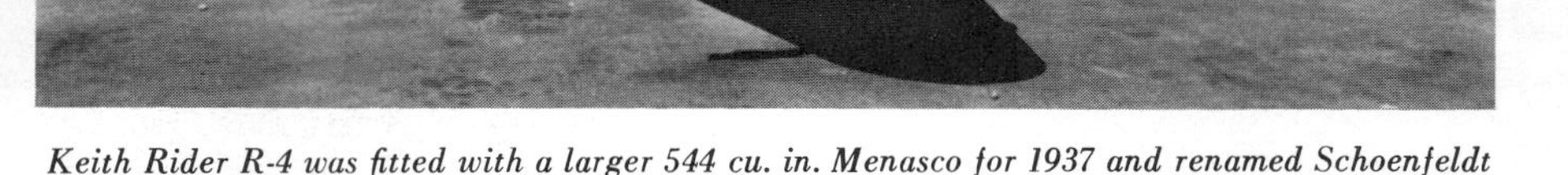

Earl Ortman flew his Keith Rider R-3 15.703 mph faster in his 1937 Thompson Qualifying Race than Rudy Kling flew his Folkerts to win the Greve Trophy Race, and 24.871 mph faster than Kling had flown his Greve Qualifying Race.   (Dustin W. Carter)

Keith Rider R-4 was fitted with a larger 544 cu. in. Menasco for 1937 and renamed Schoenfeldt Firecracker by its new owner. Gus Gotch won feature race at St. Louis with 251.6 mph, took 3rd in Greve at Cleveland, 7th in Thompson.   (Dustin W. Carter)

Interesting Sundorph cabin plane which Eiler Sundorph finished 6th and last in 1937 Bendix at 166.2 mph. Fuselage was all metal and wing was built up of wood, fabric covered. Exceptionally clean ship developed wing flutter, apparently never flew again.   (Dustin W. Carter)

Little red Folkerts SK-1 (Speed King), was built for 1930 Cirrus Derby, raced nearly every year under new owners, ended up at 1937 Nationals as above, named Matilda. Ship did 142 mph at 1930 Nationals, with best speed of 187.65 mph with Harold Neumann at 1935 Nationals.   (Warren M. Bodie)

H-1 was the most aerodynamically clean radial-engined aircraft built to its date, was the first to have jet thrust exhaust and the first with a bell-shaped engine cowling. As Hughes did not need a sponsor the H-1 was devoid of all markings except for license number on wing and rudder. Fuselage was natural aluminum finish, highly waxed and polished. All movable control surfaces were built up of wood and metal, fabric covered. Hydraulic shock-strutted tail skid was retractable in flight. (Hughes)

Hughes H-1 was the first aircraft with wing leading edge air duct intakes. Landing gear wore quite small Airwheel doughnut tires and gear had an exceptionally wide track of 10 feet. Ever since its record-breaking flights Mr. Hughes has kept the H-1 in a corner of his Culver City factory where the humidity and temperature is maintained at a constant even temperature in deference to the wood in the aircraft's construction! (Hughes)

little D-12 engined *Bonzo*, which had not flown in last year's races because of fire damage. Joe Mackey piloted Turner's famous old Wedell 57, and Marion McKeen was in his little Brown B-2.

When the signal mortar boomed, all nine stub-winged racers bounded across the Cleveland airport. Steve Wittman was first off the ground and was around the scattering pylon before some of the ships got off. *Bonzo's* cooling troubles had been corrected, and the old D-12 engine was now delivering 485 hp. By the end of the first lap it was Wittman first by a widening margin, Turner and Ortman battling for second, and Kling holding fourth. Lap after lap the tall designer-pilot from Oshkosh, flying below the pylon tops in his home-built winged orange crate, appeared to be on an invisible greased track as he moved over half a lap beyond the Turner-Ortman duel for second. For 17 laps Wittman was far out in front, with the coveted trophy seemingly in the bag. Then, after rounding the home pylon for the 18th lap, he pulled up high above the course and dropped slowly back. His propeller tip had struck a bird, and the bent prop vibrated an oil line loose, spraying oil on his windshield and obscuring his vision dangerously.

Turner, flying smoothly, took the lead. Ortman was close behind and Kling tailed them doggedly.

Turner increased his lead, and as he roared into the last lap it seemed to be his race by a safe margin. Then, with the race in his pocket, he was blinded by the late afternoon sun on the westward leg and returned to make sure of the pylon. Ortman, the only radio-directed entry, swung into first and on the advice of his ground crew throttled back some. Kling was behind and above him, Turner back in the race in third, Sinclair grooving at fourth, and Wittman hanging on to fifth. Coming around the last pylon, Ortman led Kling slightly. Then on the home stretch, Kling dived his ship to get every ounce of speed and crossed the finish line 25 feet ahead of Ortman to win the race at 256.91 mph. Ortman finished second at 256.86, Turner third, and Frank Sinclair fourth. Steve Wittman, in the fastest ship of the races (he qualified at 276.5 mph), had to be content with fifth place at 250.1 mph, while Ray Moore was sixth, and Gotch finished in seventh and last. McKeen had dropped out on the 13th lap and Mackey on the 17th. The race had been full of excitement, and Kling's fire-ball finish was a fitting climax to the Thompson classic and to the National Air Races.

Here is the 1930 Thompson winning Laird model LC-DW Solution dolled up with a red and white scalloped fuselage! Ownership and paint scheme changed several times during the years and craft underwent several airframe modifications and engine changes, with parts also used from Jimmy Doolittle's 1931 Bendix winning Laird Super Solution, namely the wheel pants. It appeared at various air shows and finally as a sport plane, was found gathering dust in the corner of a Carolina hangar. (Charles G. Mandrake)

Keith Rider R-6 named 8 Ball was the last Rider designed racer, and the only all wooden one. Menasco 6-cylinder engine of 489 cu. in. powered the pale blue 8 Ball, racing number 18, license NX96Y. Joe Jacobson found the racer justly named at 1938 Nationals, was able to place 3rd in the Greve at 218.278 mph and 6th and last in Thompson, averaged 214.57 mph before being flagged down. (Dustin W. Carter)

1938 — National Air Races

Outstanding new records in the Greve and Thompson Trophy races were highlights of the Nationals, September 3–5, at Cleveland. Only three race events were held, with prize money doubled to encourage race-plane development.

Harold Johnson again looped, rolled, and spun a 6-ton Ford trimotor. Tex Rankin did beautiful acrobatics with pink smoke pouring from his Menasco Great Lakes biplane. "Kokomo Mike" Murphy gave two amazing exhibitions—he took off from and landed on the turf with a twin-pontoon seaplane Cub, and he also landed on and took off from a moving auto with a wheeled Cub! An Army squadron of Seversky P-35's and a Marine Squadron of new Cyclone F3F-4 Grummans, our last fighter biplane, performed daily.

BENDIX TROPHY

Ten Bendix racers left Burbank, Calif., in the pre-dawn, Saturday, September 3, with stormy weather reported from Winslow clear into St. Louis. Jacqueline Cochran, in her modified P-35 Seversky 1,200-hp Twin Wasp pursuit, flew on top at 16,000 to 22,000 feet nonstop into Cleveland to win with 249.8 mph, 16 minutes slower than Fuller's record of 1937. After a 15 minute gas stop, she continued to Bendix, N. J., averaging 242.1 mph to set a new women's west-east record. Frank Fuller, in his Seversky P-35, second into Cleveland, averaged 238.6 mph for the 2,043 miles, including a gas stop at Wichita.

Paul Mantz took third place at 206.6 mph with his 750-hp Wright Cyclone powered Lockheed Orion. An encounter with a bird at 14,000 feet had slowed him, and he landed with a hole in the leading edge of his wing and the bird wedged in the trailing edge. Max Constant was fourth in elapsed time to Cleveland in a Wasp Jr. Beechcraft; Ross Hadley was fifth in an identical Beechcraft; and Charles La Jatte was sixth and last with his Wasp Jr. Spartan Executive, four others having dropped out with mechanical trouble.

GREVE TROPHY

The Greve Trophy Race, flown on Sunday, September 4, over a 30-lap 300-mile course, was a hot dingdong contest between Tony LeVier in his 1936 Keith Rider *Firecracker* and Art Chester in his new sleek *Goon*. Leading the other four contestants by a wide margin, Tony and Art exchanged the lead several times and lapped the other four planes. Then on lap 15, Chester, his windshield oily, cut No. 2 pylon and recircled, giving LeVier a lead of almost half a lap. Thinking that Chester was out, LeVier throttled back, while Chester pushed his throttle to the firewall and, in the next three laps, closed the gap. On the 18th lap Chester was clocked at 278.3 mph. Near the end of lap 19 LeVier spotted Chester again on his tail and also opened up, turning his 20th lap at 269.6 mph to win the Greve with an average of 250.9 mph —besting the 1936 record.

Art Chester finished second just seconds (250.4 mph) behind LeVier, while Joe Jacobson, in a new Keith Rider all-plywood *Eight Ball*, was a slow third at 218.3 mph. Earl Ortman finished fourth, averaging 192.5 mph, in his Marcoux-Bromberg *Jackrabbit*, a reworked 1936 sister ship to LeVier's Rider.

George Dory, a newcomer, flying a Bushey-Mc-Grew Special (the old 4-cyl. Menasco-engined Rider *Bumble Bee*), had motor failure in his 12th lap. He landed down through the trees onto a dead-end street and crashed into trees at the street's end. Though severely injured, he survived. Harry Crosby, flying his new Crosby CR-4, the only all-metal plane in the Greve, lost his exhaust manifold early in the race and landed safely after his 14th lap with his ship afire. Then Tony LeVier, after winning, landed in a rough spot and cracked up. He was unhurt but out of the next day's Thompson. The planes, except for the *Bumble Bee*, were powered by Menasco 6-cyl. engines, which delivered up to 400 hp, but were designed for far less hp delivery, accounting for the repeated engine failures characteristic of the Greve races.

THOMPSON TROPHY

Monday's main attraction and highlight of the

Only visible change in Bonzo for 1938 was additional louver on engine cowl side and race No. 2 instead of 6. Steve had tinkered with the engine, took 3rd in Thompson at 259.187 mph, 9 mph faster than last year, despite throttling back because of Prestone obscured windshield (Dustin W. Carter)

Red and white Cyclone engined Lockheed Orion which Paul Mantz flew to 3rd place in the 1938 Bendix at a respectable 206.579 mph despite a hole in the wing leading edge, result of a mid-air collision with a bird at 14,000 ft.! (Dustin W. Carter)

Russell Chambers' beautiful Chambermaid, powered by a Menasco BS4, had a span of only 13 feet 8 inches, was 17 feet 3 inches long. Interesting feature was spring-leaf retractable landing gear. Chambers cracked up in landing after qualifying run at 1938 Nationals, died from injuries. (Dustin W. Carter)

Old Wedell-Williams 92 had been nosed over by Art Davis on the way to 1937 Bendix start, appeared for 1938 Bendix looking real sharp in all white paint job and a constant speed propeller. Lee Gehlback was forced out of Bendix race. (Dustin W. Carter)

Art Chester designed and built his sleek cream colored Goon for 1938 Nationals, took a close 2nd in Greve handicapped by oil on his windshield from French Ratier propeller. Prop started throwing oil in Thompson race also, forcing Chester out. Fuselage was built up of steel tubing with metal covering to rear of cockpit for easy access, had wood stringers and fabric covering aft. Full cantilever wing and horizontal stabilizer was built of spruce, covered with plywood, then fabric.   *(Peter M. Bowers)*

Art Chester also raced the Goon in 1939 Nationals. The propeller oil leaks had been sealed off and the engine further hopped up. Art set a new Greve record in winning at 263.39 mph after other four racers had dropped out. Art held third place in the 1939 Thompson for 17 laps, averaged 264 mph, then dropped out when his engine tired. Landing gear retracted manually. The wheels retracted into the fuselage, actuating the doors which smoothly enclosed the gear.   *(Peter M. Bowers)*

Tiny 90 hp Pobjoy engined "Flaggship," 3rd and last racer designed and built by C. Claude Flagg. Built in 1937 it appeared at 1938 Nationals with new 13 foot tapered wing (above), crashed on take-off before it could prove itself. (Kinert)

Tony LeVier, in cockpit, took two 1st and one 3rd place at International Air Races at Oakland in 1938 with Keith Rider R-4. Best pylon speed, 260.89 mph. Tony then won 1938 Greve, landed downwind and wiped Firecracker out of Thompson start. (Lockheed)

Jacqueline Cochran's new 1938 Bendix winning Seversky had flush retracting landing gear, was stripped version of Seversky XP-41 pursuit. Ship was all-metal except for fabric covered moveable controls. Sign over race No. 13 asked "Please keep hands off" as Seversky was highly waxed. (Dustin W. Carter)

Twin Wasp SBG#177 engine in Roscoe Turner's Meteor for 1938 was rated 900 hp at 2450 rpm at 6500 feet with 1000 hp at 2600 rpm for take-off (41.3 inches manifold pressure). Turner flew entire Thompson at 2600 rpm with 47 inches manifold pressure! (Pesco Products)

Pearson-Williams 1938 Mr. Smoothie wore an 825 hp Curtiss Conqueror V-12 Prestone cooled engine, was capable of 375-385 mph. Wingspan was 24 feet, length 26 feet. During test flights in Cleveland a hard landing by Leland Williams bent up retractable landing gear so they fixed it in down position, filled openings with sheet metal. Then, as Mr. Smoothie was being towed past grandstands a wheel came off, damaging the axle and scratching ship from the Thompson race. Someone had forgotten a cotter pin! (Burton Kemp)

Orange Mr. Smoothie was one of the cleanest and best designed racers ever built. Blower fan in back of propeller apparently supplied sufficient cooling air for radiator which fitted snugly to front of engine. No funds were available to race Mr. Smoothie in 1939. Harry Crosby bought it and was making it into a fake Messerschmitt 109 for the movies during the war. When Harry was killed the beautiful racer faded away. (Dustin W. Carter)

Marcoux-Bromberg (Keith Rider R-3) at 1938 Golden Gate International Air Races. Earl Ortman barely beat Roscoe Turner with 265.539 mph. New air scoop was fitted atop engine cowl, fuselage yellow with race No. 4, wing still black. R-3 was all yellow for 1938 Nationals, race No. 3.
(Warren M. Bodie)

Keith Rider R-5 for 1938 sported black fuselage, yellow wing and horizontal stabilizer. New owners Marcoux and Bromberg named R-5 the Jackrabbit and race No. was 22. Earl Ortman was flagged down in Greve with a slow 192.503 mph average for 18 laps, awarded 4th place.
(Dustin W. Carter)

Addition of a greenhouse canopy did much to change appearance of Military HM-1 and fuselage was now black, wing and horizontal stabilizer chrome yellow. Two-place tandem craft had a top speed of 365 mph, cruised 320 mph and climb rate of 6000 feet per minute.
(Ronald W. Harrison)

Delgado Flash was beautifully cleaned up for 1938 with new smooth engine cowl, spinner and pants. On June 26, 1938 Clarence McArthur set a new 100 km closed circuit record of 227.027 mph for single-seat planes with engine displacement between 397-549 cubic inches.
(Dustin W. Carter)

Charles Babb purchased the Granville Q.E.D., overhauled it for the 1938 Bendix. George Armistead encountered rain and sleet over Kingman, Arizona, had the carburetor ice up then lost oil pressure. Oil temperature rose alarmingly and a lost radio knob did nothing to aid his plight so George called it a day, landed at Winslow. Later a loose rag was sucked into the carburetor on a Bolling Field take-off over the Potomac River and new owner Francisco Sarabia of Mexico drowned. Q.E.D. was junked. (Dustin W. Carter)

Damaged Hawks HM-1 was purchased and returned to Springfield where Howell Miller and new Military Aircraft Corporation modified it into a military fighter hopeful. HM-1 was entered in 1938 Thompson and flown by Leigh Wade. Racing jets installed on Pratt and Whitney Twin Row Wasp to keep engine cool gulped so much fuel that Wade had to reduce throttle to finish race. Later in 1938 Earl Ortman tore the Military HM-1 apart in violent acrobatics and bailed out. (Ronald W. Harrison)

races was the 300-mile Thompson Trophy Race, with a field of eight starters. To spread out prize money and encourage racer development, no aircraft could compete this year in both the Bendix and Thompson races. For the first time, Bendix planes could not enter.

Earl Ortman, in his familiar old Marcoux-Bromberg (Keith Rider), led Roscoe Turner around the course for the first five laps, then his 900-hp souped-up P & W Twin Wasp Jr. engine, pushed beyond take-off limits, began trailing blue-black smoke. Turner slipped into the lead with his Laird-Brown L-RT, powered by a 1,100-hp Twin Wasp, and Ortman hung on. Both were well ahead of the field.

Hard luck Harry Crosby, after a poor start and after cutting No. 2 pylon in laps one and two, dropped out on his tenth lap, almost overcome by gas fumes. At the 27th lap, Turner still led and Ortman was right on his tail, with Turner flying wide to avoid cutting pylons and Ortman taking the pylons closer. Art Chester, after flying a beautiful race, had been forced to land his *Goon* after the 20th lap. His French Ratier prop was throwing oil. Then in the 27th lap, Ortman's engine completely ruptured a leaking oil line, and he pulled up to 1,500 feet. Turner crossed the finish line well ahead to set a new record, averaging 283.4 mph from a standing start and hitting 293 mph on his fastest lap.

Although lapped by Turner in the final seconds of the 30-lap race, Ortman managed to take a clean second place at 269.7 mph and landed with a bone-dry oil tank.

Steve Wittman, in his Curtiss D-12 *Bonzo*, did 259.2 mph to take third, although handicapped by a leaking radiator that sprayed Prestone on the windshield through most of the race, while Leigh Wade, in his Twin Wasp powered Military Aircraft HM-1 pursuit, developed from Frank Hawks' *Time Flies*, edged into fourth place near the finish line after battling throughout the race with Joe Mackey, who finished fifth in Turner's old Hornet Wedell-Williams. Joe Jacobson, in his faltering *Eight Ball*, was flagged down after the 27th lap and credited with sixth and last.

Roscoe Turner, resplendent in his powder-blue uniform, became the only two-time Thompson winner, and it was Earl Ortman's third consecutive second place in the Thompson!

ROSCOE TURNER

Roscoe Turner's victory smile, after winning his third Thompson Trophy in 1939.

Roscoe Turner, *born in a small clapboard cabin near Corinth, Miss., Sept. 29, 1895, learned, along with his four brothers, to plow and work his father's farm at a very early age. He worked on any mechanical object in sight, especially automobiles, and soon became a speed lover and a stickler for mechanical perfection, attributes which were to later gain him fame.*

It was only natural that Roscoe tried, in 1917, to enlist in the Aviation Section of the Signal Corps, but was turned down for lack of college training. When the United States went to war he enlisted in the Ambulance Corps, then transferred to aviation at the earliest moment and soon learned to fly. He reached the front just as the Armistice was signed and, in 1919, was honorably discharged as a first lieutenant.

Buying half interest in a war surplus Curtiss JN4D Jenny, Roscoe barnstormed, did exhibition acrobatics, and later flew as stunt man for the movies. His stunts included transfer from Jenny wings to automobiles and trains and return, where one slip meant sudden death.

Holder of Commercial Pilot License No. 388, Roscoe was ever resplendent in a powder-blue uniform, complete to a black-visored cap, black boots, and Sam Browne belt, set off by a waxed and spiked mustache, all of which became his trademark. When he was barnstorming, this showmanship had the customers lined up for rides. In 1929 Roscoe began breaking speed records. In fact he did so well in the following ten years that he earned the title of "Mr. Aviation."

Roscoe had pylon trouble in most of his closed-course racing. Three times he had the Thompson Trophy all but won and had to refly cut pylons. In only one instance did he regain the lead and go on to win. He could take either victory or defeat in his stride. In almost every race Roscoe managed to have the fastest aircraft, and so he flew the course high and wide, where pylons are most easily cut, shunning the close-pylon rat race below that was engaged in by pilots who were short of horsepower and were making every inch count.

Roscoe wisely retired from racing in 1939 while on top (the only three-time winner of the coveted Thompson Trophy, 1934, 1938, 1939) and settled down to the business of owning and operating the Turner Aeronautical Corporation at the Indianapolis Muncipal Airport.

1939 – National Air Races

The 1939 National Air Races, held at Cleveland, September 2–5, vied for attention with a declared European war. Again there were three races. There were no new racing planes, but the old ones had been reworked to perfection.

BENDIX TROPHY

Frank Fuller took off from Burbank early September 2, climbed his Seversky P-35 up through a fast-forming fog bank, and flew uneventfully on to Cleveland, averaging 282.1 mph for a new Bendix record. He then raced on to Bendix, N. J., setting a new Burbank-to-Bendix record of 273.1 mph. Art Bussy was second in elapsed time to Cleveland, averaging 244.5 mph in the Bellanca trimotor racer that had dropped out of last year's Bendix races because of engine trouble. This ship had been built for a later-cancelled trans-Atlantic flight. Paul Mantz again finished third in his Lockheed Orion.

GREVE TROPHY

The 200-mile 20-lap Greve Trophy Race, held Sunday, September 3, was flown for the last time and was the most hectic. Five California pilots in Menasco-engined racers lined up for the starter's flag, and George Byars, in the Keith Rider *Eight Ball*, didn't even start because of engine trouble. Then newcomer Lee Williams, in the little Brown *Miss Los Angeles*, stalled on the scattering-pylon turn with a faltering engine and tumble-crashed fatally.

Art Chester, in his beautiful *Goon*, crossed the starting line well in the lead, due to his controllable pitch prop, the only one in the race. Tony LeVier, flying the Rider-built Schoenfeldt *Firecracker*, had engine trouble from the start but managed to pull up and pass Chester on the sixth lap, holding the lead until forced out after 11 laps by magneto trouble. He flew one lap at 285.6 mph!

Harry Crosby, unable to retract the landing gear of his CR-4, was flagged down after averaging only 165 mph for 13 laps. Art Chester, virtually alone in the race from halfway point, decided to go for a new record and did so, winning the trophy with a new high of 263.4 mph.

THOMPSON TROPHY

The Thompson Trophy Race, rained out on Labor Day, was held over to make the Nationals a four-day event.

Seven planes took off in the 300-mile 30-lap race, and Tony LeVier pushed his *Firecracker* into the lead at the fifth lap, followed by Art Chester's *Goon* and Earl Ortman's Marcoux-Bromberg. Roscoe Turner was fourth after a slow take-off in his Turner-Laird, but cut a pylon on the second lap and recircled to trail the field. LeVier held the lead until the ninth lap, when Roscoe Turner's superior horsepower pulled him into the lead, which he increased steadily, going on to win the trophy at 282.5 mph, while LeVier finished second at 272.5 mph. Art Chester had engine trouble on the 18th lap and was forced to drop out of third place and the race. Earl Ortman took over third and finished in that position.

Harry Crosby finished fourth, while Steve Wittman, penalized an entire lap for cutting the crowded scattering pylon, finished fifth at 241.4 mph in *Bonzo* despite burning his exhaust valves severely in a wide-open attempt to make up for his lost lap. Joe Mackey, flying his last race, finished sixth and last in Turner's famous golden Wedell-Williams 57 at 232.9 mph. The old ship was tired — it had flown a bit faster than this when it was new seven years previous, and with a lot less horsepower!

Roscoe Turner, having won the Thompson Trophy for the third time, announced that he was retiring, and today you can find the jovial gentleman, racer and all, at the Indianapolis Airport, where he operates a flying school.

And so ended another great era of air racing, cut short by World War II. During the 1920–25 race era, commercial aircraft had copied the innovations introduced in military racers, then, after the 1926–29 racing "doldrums," the military designers copied unabashedly from the back-yard-built craft. The Curtiss Hawk model 75, a monoplane built in 1936 and exported to France early in the war, had the exact profile of the earlier Wedell-Williams. Later fitted with retractable gear, the Hawk became the Army P-36, and when fitted with an Allison V-12 engine it became the famous P-40. Designer Keith Rider's racers of 1932 featured a retractable landing gear that left enough of the wheels protruding to allow a safe emergency landing. Seversky copied this idea into his P-35 pursuit; Boeing used it on their early 247-D airliners and on the B-17; and Douglas featured it on the famous DC-3.

During the 30's, a racing period in which the use of air-cooled engines predominated, speeds did not increase greatly, but the full-cantilever monoplane was perfected. Faster wing curves, dependable retractable landing gears, better fuels and lubricants, as well as countless engine improvements, owe their heritage directly to the racing craft of the 30's.

Special built racing shell built by Germany and designated a Messerschmitt Bf 109R so world would believe it to be a stock fighter. On April 26, 1939 Fritz Wendell set piston-engined landplane speed record of 469.220 mph which still held in 1967.   (Warren M. Bodie)

Paul Mantz cleaned his Lockheed Orion up further for the 1939 Bendix, fitted a special NACA engine cowl with rocker box bumps. Paul finished a respectable third in Bendix with 234.875 mph in the all-wood ship.   (Robert C. Morrison)

Tri-motored Bellanca 28-92 was flown in 1933 Bendix by Frank Cordova but was forced out with engine troubles. Ship had originally been built for Captain Alex Pappana of Poland for a proposed trans-Atlantic flight to his home country.   (Charles G. Mandrake)

Bellanca tri-motor was again entered in 1939 Bendix, finished second with pilot Art Bussy at 244.486 mph. Ship had a 420 hp inverted V-12 Ranger on the nose and Menasco 200 hp inverted 6 engines outboard. All three engines were hand cranked.   (Dustin W. Crater)

Jovial Colonel Roscoe Turner closed the wonderful Golden Era of American air racing in 1939 with his usual flair, cut a pylon which he had to refly, in the famed Thompson Race, then barrelled his powerful Meteor from last place to win the coveted Trophy for the third time. In 1938 and 1939 the grueling Thompson course was only 10 miles around for 30 laps, too short for the big boys to really do their best, so Roscoe showed special ability in winning the hard way.

(Colonel Roscoe Turner)

Frank Fuller Jr. won the demanding Bendix race in 1939 for the 2nd time in his Seversky SEV-S2, averaged a fast 282.098 mph into Cleveland, scene of the Nationals, and broke his 1937 record. After flashing over the finish line at the home pylon he pulled up, continued on to Bendix, N. J. to again set a coast-to-coast record speed for the annual event. Seversky was still metallic blue, highly waxed and polished and paint was, of course, a Fuller product!

(Dustin W. Carter)

Harry Crosby appeared at 1939 Nationals with his new CR-4 which he had designed and helped build at Aero Industries Technical Institute, a trades school in Los Angeles. One of the cleanest aircraft ever built, the CR-4 was powered by a Menasco Super Buccaneer inverted engine which normally delivered 290 hp at 2400 rpm but which was hopped up faster for racing to give 350 plus horsepower. Wingspan was only 16 feet on this little gem which never did get to fully prove itself. (Warren M. Bodie)

Hard Luck Harry Crosby qualified his CR-4 at 263 mph. He was unable to fully retract his landing gear in the Greve race, was flagged down after 13 laps and awarded 3rd and last place, having averaged only 164.874 mph. Harry then finished 4th in the Thompson despite a sour engine. This excellent designer-pilot later lost his life in a war plane test flight. (Robert C. Morrison)

Wittman Bonzo was painted all red for 1939 Thompson. Propeller spinner had been removed so radiator was now visible. Steve had devised a ram-air carburetor system to pack more fuel into rear cylinders of his Curtiss D-12 engine, in an effort to keep them cool. Front valves then ran so lean they burned up in the race. This and a re-flown cut pylon cost him a chance to win. Bonzo, later clocked at 325 mph, reposes in EAA Museum, Hales Corner, Wisconsin. (Kinert)

Extremely sleek and beautifully proportioned Heston Type 5 racer was built expressly for World Speed Record attempts. On first flight June 12, 1940 from Heston it was damaged in forced landing due to inadequate elevator controls. No further work was carried out due to the War and a sister ship never completed. Big 24-cylinder H type sleeve-valved liquid-cooled Napier Sabre VA engine delivered 2310 hp at 3850 rpm at sea level. Racer was expected to do at least 480 mph. Wingspan was 32 feet. *(Napier)*

THOMPSON TROPHY RACE 1930—1939

YEAR	COURSE AND PLACE		PILOT	RACE NO.	LICENSE NO.	AIRCRAFT	ENGINE and CU. IN. DISPLACEMENT	HP	SPAN	LENGTH	EMPTY	GROSS	WING LOAD	AV. SPEED	REMARKS
1930	20 laps—100 miles	1	Charles Holman	77	NR10538	Laird Solution	P&W Wasp Jr., 985	470	21'	19'6"	1380	1895	16.9	201.91	
		2	James Haizlip		NR482N	Travel-Air "R" "Mystery"	Wright J-6-9, R-975	400	29'2"	20'2"	1500	1965	15.6	199.8	
	Chicago, Illinois	3	Ben Howard	37	NR2Y	Howard *Pete*	Wright Gypsy, 318	90	20'1"	17'9"	669	900	14.28	162.8	
		4	Paul Adams		449W	Travel-Air Speedwing	Wright J-6-9, 975	300	31'	23'6"	1784	2825	11.44	142.64	
1931	10 laps—100 miles	1	Lowell Bayles	4	NR77V	Gee-Bee Super Sportster	P&W Wasp Jr., 985	535	23'6"	15'1"	1400	2280	30.2	236.239	
		2	James Wedell	44	NR278V	Wedell-Williams 44	P&W Wasp Jr., 985	535	26'2"	21'3"	1500	2206	17	227.992	
	Cleveland, Ohio	3	Dale Jackson	77	NR10538	Laird Solution	Wright J-6-9, R-1750	525	21'	19'6"	1385	1900	17	211.183	*Last year's winner reworked.*
		4	Robert Hall	54	NR11049	Gee-Bee 'Y'	P&W Wasp-C, 1344	450	30'	21'	1500	2000	14.5	201.250	*Hall is Gee-Bee designer.*
		5	Ira Eaker			Lockheed Altair	P&W Wasp S1D1, 1340	550	42'9"	28'11"	3550	4409	15	196.832	*Full tank wing load 19.72.*
		6	Ben Howard	37	NR2Y	Howard *Pete*	Wright Gypsy, 318	90	20'1"	17'9"	669	900	14.28	163.573	
		7	William Ong			Laird Speedwing	Wright J-6-9, R-975	330	28'	22'9"	1992	3010	15.3	153.049	
1932	10 laps—100 miles	1	James Doolittle	11	NR2100	Gee-Bee Sr. Sportster R-1	P&W Wasp Sr., 1344	800	25'	17'9"	1840	2415	24.15	252.686	*Full tank wing load 30.75.*
		2	James Wedell	44	NR278V	Wedell-Williams	P&W Wasp Jr., 985	550	26'2"	21'3"	1500	2206	17	242.496	
	Cleveland, Ohio	3	Roscoe Turner	121	NR61Y	Wedell-Williams	P&W Wasp Jr., 985	550	26'2"	21'3"	1500	2206	17	233.042	
		4	James Haizlip	92	NR536V	Wedell-Williams	P&W Wasp Jr., 985	550	26'2"	21'3"	1500	2206	17	231.304	*Full tank wing load 20.54.*
		5	Lee Gelbach	7	NR2101	Gee-Bee Sr. Sportster R-2	P&W Wasp Jr., 985	550	25'	17'9"	1796	2371	23.71	222.098	*Full tank wing load 38.83.*
		6	Robert Hall	6	NR211	Springfield Hall *Bulldog*	P&W Wasp Jr., 985	550	26'	19'			39.6	215.570	
		7	William Ong	39	NR56Y	Howard DGA-5 *Ike*	Menasco 6, 489	160	20'1"	17'	822	1100	15.94	191.073	
1933	6 laps—60 miles	1	James Wedell	44	NR278V	Wedell-Williams	P&W Wasp Jr., 985	550	26'2"	21'3"	1510	2216	17	237.952	*Record 305.33 Sept. 4, 1933.*
		2	Lee Gehlbach	92	NR536V	Wedell-Williams	P&W Wasp Jr., 985	550	26'2"	21'3"	1510	2216	17	224.947	
		3	Roy Minor	38	NR55Y	Howard *Mike*	Menasco 6, 489	225	20'1"	17'	920	1200	17.39	199.870	*Spl. Supercharger.*
	Los Angeles, Calif.	4	George Hague	1	NR52Y	Rider R-2 *Bumble Bee*	Menasco 4, 363	125	17'	19'	800	1100	15.5	183.206	*Original* San Francisco II.
		5	Z. D. Granville	154	R11049	Gee-Bee Model "Y"	P&W Wasp Jr., 985	550	30'	21'	1500	2000	14.5	173.079	*Engine faulty.*
1934	12 laps—100 miles	1	Roscoe Turner	57	NR61Y	Wedell-Williams	P&W Hornet, 1690	1000	26'2"	21'3"	1800	2506	19.27	248.129	*75 gal. of fuel, 8 gal. of oil.*
		2	Roy Minor	33	NR255Y	Brown *Miss Los Angeles*	Menasco C-6S, 544	300	19'3"	19'10"	882	1299	21.65	214.929	*Wing flaps B-2.*
	Cleveland, Ohio	3	J. A. Worthen	92	NR536V	Wedell-Williams	P&W Wasp Jr., 985	550	26'2"	21'3"	1510	2680	21	208.376	
		4	Harold Neumann	39	NR56Y	Howard DGA-5 *Ike*	Menasco B-6, 489	225	20'1"	17'	827	1105	16	207.064	
		5	Roger Don Rae	131	NR51Y	Keith Rider R-1	Menasco C-6, 544	250	16'6"	19'	900	1200	17.4	205.358	
		6	Art Chester	15	NR12930	Chester *Jeep*	Menasco C-4S, 363	225	16'8"	15'	765	1150	24	191.597	
1935	15 laps—150 miles	1	Harold Neumann	40	NR273Y	Howard *Mr. Mulligan*	P&W Wasp, 1344	830	31'8"	25'1"	2600	4210	30.7	220.194	*DGA-6 qualified 247 mph.*
		2	Steve Wittman	4	R13688	Wittman *Bonzo*	Curtiss D-12, 1145	435	17'6"	20'	1650	2470	26.55	218.686	*Wing flaps. Cooling faulty.*
	Cleveland, Ohio	3	Roger Don Rae	131	NR51Y	Rider R-1	Menasco C-6S, 544	250	16'6"	19'	900	1200	17.4	213.942	
		4	Joseph Jacobson	38	NR55Y	Howard DGA-4 *Mike*	Menasco B-6, 489	225	20'1"	17'	827	1105	16	209.103	
		5	Lee Miles		X2106	Seversky SEV-3	Wright Cyclone, R-1820	715	36'	28'	4035	5500	25	193.594	*Amphibian record 230 mph.*
		6	Marion McKeen	33	R255Y	Brown *Miss Los Angeles*	Menasco C-6S, 544	250	19'3"	19'10"	882	1299	21.65	188.859	*B-2*

YEAR	COURSE AND PLACE		PILOT	RACE NO.	LICENSE NO.	AIRCRAFT	ENGINE AND DISPLACEMENT	HP						AV. SPEED	REMARKS
1936	15 laps—150 miles	1	Michel Detroyat	100	C4606909	Caudron C-460	Renault Bengali, 588	380	22'1"	23'4"	1298	2090	27.8	264.261	*Engine change for Thompson.*
	Los Angeles, Calif.	2	Earl Ortman	54	NR14215	Rider R-3	P&W Wasp Jr., 1344	750	25'	22'	1800	2970	23.8	248.042	*All metal—1st Thompson try.*
		3	Roger Don Rae	70	R261Y	Rider R-4	Menasco B-6S, 489	250	18'	18'	925	1325	19.25	236.559	*New—all plywood.*
		4	Harold Neumann	1	NR283Y	Folkerts *Toots*	Menasco C-4S, 363	225	16'	21'	700	1000	20	233.074	*New—steel tubing, plywood fabric.*
		5	Marion McKeen	33	NR255Y	Brown *Miss Los Angeles*	Menasco C-6S, 544	300	19'3"	19'10"	887	1305	21.66	230.465	*B-2*
		6	Harry Crosby	52	R260Y	Crosby	Menasco C-6S, 544	300						226.075	*New—all metal.*
1937	20 laps—200 miles	1	Rudy Kling	301	R14899	Folkerts KF-1 *Jupiter*	Menasco C-6S4, 544	400	16'8"	21'	841	1385	27.5	256.910	*New*
	Cleveland, Ohio	2	Earl Ortman	4	R14215	Marcoux-Bromberg	P&W Twin Wasp Jr., 1535	800	25'	22'	2400	3470	27.7	256.858	*Keith Rider R-3.*
		3	Roscoe Turner	29	R263Y	Laird-Turner L-RT	P&W Tw. Wasp Sr., 1830	1000	25'	23'4"	3300	4923	51.8	253.802	*Brown built—Laird reworked.*
		4	Frank Sinclair	63	R18Y	Seversky SEV-S2	P&W Tw. Wasp Sr., 1830	1000	36'	25'6"	3852	6390	29	252.360	*"Executive" model of P-35.*
		5	Steve Wittman	6	R13688	Wittman *Bonzo*	Curtiss D-12, 1145	485	17'6"	20'	1650	2470	26.55	250.108	*Qualified 275.6 mph, 5 laps.*
		6	Ray Moore	23	R70Y	Seversky SEV-S2	P&W Tw. Wasp Sr. 1830	1000	36'	25'6"	3852	6390	29	238.411	*"Executive" model of P-35.*
		7	C. H. Gotch	70	R261Y	Schoenfeldt *Firecracker*	Menasco C-6S4, 544	330	18'	18'	925	1325	19.25	217.810	*Keith Rider R-4.*
1938	30 laps—300 miles	1	Roscoe Turner	29	R263Y	Laird-Turner L-RT	P&W Tw. Wasp Sr. 1830	1100	25'	23'4"	3310	4933	51.81	283.419	*1 lap 293 mph. Name—Meteor.*
	Cleveland, Ohio	2	Earl Ortman	3	NR14215	Marcoux-Bromberg	P&W Tw. Wasp Jr. 1535	900	25'	22'	2400	3470	27.7	269.718	*Rider R-3.*
		3	Steve Wittman	2	NR13688	Wittman *Bonzo*	Curtiss D-12, 1145	485	17'6"	20'	1650	2470	26.55	259.187	
		4	Leigh Wade	41	NX2491	Military Aircraft HM-1	P&W Tw. Wasp Sr. 1830	900	31'	23'6"	4028	6000	37.5	249.842	
		5	Joe Mackey	25	NX61Y	Wedell-Williams	P&W Hornet, 1690	1000	26'2"	21'3"	1800	2506	19.27	249.628	
		6	Joe Jacobson	18	NX96Y	Rider R-6 *Eight Ball*	Menasco C-6S4, 544	400	20'5"	19'	1400	1800	24	214.570	*Out 27th lap.*
1939	30 laps—300 miles	1	Roscoe Turner	29	NX263Y	Laird-Turner L-RT	P&W Tw. Wasp Sr. 1830	1000	25'	23'4"	3310	4933	51.81	282.536	
	Cleveland, Ohio	2	Tony LeVier	70	NX261Y	Schoenfeldt *Firecracker*	Menasco C-6S4, 544	350	18'	18'	925	1325	19.25	272.538	*Rider R-4.*
		3	Earl Ortman	3	NX14215	Marcoux-Bromberg	P&W Tw. Wasp Jr. 1535	850	25'	22'	2405	3475	27.71	254.435	*Rider R-3.*
		4	Harry Crosby	52	NX92Y	Crosby CR-4	Menasco C-6S4, 544	400	16'	21'6"	1540	1940	30.3	244.522	
		5	Steve Wittmann	4	NX13688	Wittman *Bonzo*	Curtiss D-12, 1145	485	17'6"	20'	1650	2470	26.55	241.361	
		6	Joe Mackey	25	NR61Y	Wedell-Williams	P&W Hornet, 1690	1000	26'2"	21'3"	1805	2511	19.28	232.926	

BENDIX TROPHY RACE   1931—1939

YEAR	COURSE AND PLACE		PILOT	RACE NO.	LICENSE NO.	AIRCRAFT	ENGINE AND DISPLACEMENT	HP	TIME	AV. SPEED	REMARKS
1931	2043 miles	1	James Doolittle	400	NR12048	Laird Super-Solution	P&W Wasp Jr., R-985	535	9:10:21*	223.038	*Doolittle continued on to Newark, N.J., set*
	Burbank, Calif., to	2	Harold S. Johnson			Lockheed Orion	P&W Wasp SC, R-1344	450	10:14:22	198.816	*west-east record (2450 miles)*
	Cleveland	3	Beeler Blevins			Lockheed Orion	P&W Wasp SC, R-1344	450	10:49:33	188.992	11:16:10 216.958
		4	Ira Eaker			Lockheed Altair	P&W Wasp S1D1, 1340	550	10:59:45	186.070	

Year / Route		Pilot	No.	Reg.	Aircraft	Engine	H.P.	Time	M.P.H.	Notes
1932 2043 miles	1	James Haizlip	92	NR536V	Wedell-Williams	P&W Wasp Jr., R-985	550	8:19:45*	245	*Haizlip continued to Floyd Bennett Field,
Burbank, Calif., to	2	James Wedell	44	NR278V	Wedell-Williams	P&W Wasp Jr., R-985	550	8:47:31	232	N.Y., set west-east record (2450 miles)
Cleveland	3	Roscoe Turner	121	NR61Y	Wedell-Williams	P&W Wasp Jr., R-985	550	9:02:25	226	10:19:00 238.153
	4	Lee Gehlbach	7	NX2101	Granville Gee-Bee	P&W Wasp Jr., R-985	550	9:41:35		
1933 2050 miles	1	Roscoe Turner	2	NR61Y	Wedell-Williams	P&W Wasp Sr., R-1344	900	11:30:00*	214.78	*New east-west record.
New York City to	2	James Wedell	44	NR238Y	Wedell-Williams	P&W Wasp Jr., R-985	550	11:58:18	209.23	
Los Angeles		Russell Boardman	11		Granville Gee-Bee R-1	P&W Wasp Sr., R-1344	800			Fatal crash, Indianapolis.
		Russell Thaw	7		Granville Gee-Bee R-2	Wasp Sr., R-1340	750			Ground loop near Indianapolis.
1934 2043 miles	1	Douglas Davis	44	NR278V	Wedell-Williams	P&W Wasp Jr., R-985	550	9:26:41	216.237	
Burbank, Calif., to	2	John Worthen	92	NR536V	Wedell-Williams	P&W Wasp Jr., R-985	550	10:03:00	203.213	
Cleveland		Lee Gehlbach	77	NX14307	Granville R-6H Q.E.D.	P&W Hornet, R-1690	800			Finished after 6:00 P.M.
					Wedell-Williams		1000	10:02:51	244.880	Roscoe Turner set a new coast-to-coast record one day after this race.
1935 2043 miles	1	Ben Howard	40	NR273Y	Howard Mr. Mulligan	P&W Wasp, R-1344	830	8:33:16.3	238.704	
Burbank, Calif.,	2	Roscoe Turner	57	NR61Y	Wedell-Williams	P&W Hornet, R-1690	1000	8:33:39.8	238.522	
to Cleveland	3	Russell Thaw			Northrop Gamma	Wright Cyclone, R-1820	775	10:06:45	201.928	
	4	Roy Hunt			Lockheed Orion	P&W Wasp S1D1, R-1340	550	11:41-03	174.766	
1936 2450 miles	1	Louise Thaden	62	NR15835	Beechcraft C-17R	Wright, R-975E-3	420	14:55:01	165.346	
New York City to	2	Laura Ingalls			Lockheed Orion 9D	P&W Wasp S1D1, R-1340	550	15:39:38	157.466	
Los Angeles	3	William Bulick			Vultee V1A	Wright Cyclone, SR-1820	735	15:45:25	156.492	
	4	George Pomeroy			Douglas DC-2	Wright Cyclone (two)	735	16:16:51	151.467	
1937 2043 miles	1	Frank Fuller, Jr.	23	R70Y	Seversky SEV-S2	P&W Twin Wasp	1000	7:54:26*	258.242	*Frank Fuller continued on to Bendix, N.J.,
Burbank, Calif., to	2	Earl Ortman	4	R14215	Marcoux-Bromberg	P&W Twin Wasp Jr.	700	9:49:21	224.833	to set a new west-east record.
Cleveland	3	Jacqueline Cochran	13	R18562	Beechcraft D-17W	P&W Wasp Jr.	450	10:29:08	194.740	9:35:00 255
	4	Frank Sinclair	63	R18Y	Seversky P-35	P&W Twin Wasp	1000	11:02:33	184.920	
1938 2043 miles	1	Jacqueline Cochran	13	NX1384	Seversky SEV-S2	P&W Twin Wasp	1200	8:10:31*	249.744	*Jackie Cochran continued to Bendix, N.J., to
Burbank, Calif., to	2	Frank Fuller, Jr.	77	R70Y	Seversky SEV-S2	P&W Twin Wasp	1200	8:33:29	238.604	set a new women's west-east record.
Cleveland	3	Paul Mantz	23	NR12222	Lockheed Orion	Wright Cyclone	750	9:36:25	206.579	10:07:10 242.088
	4	Max Constant	31	R18562	Beechcraft D-17S	P&W Wasp Jr.	450	10:14:39	199.330	
1939 2043 miles	1	Frank Fuller, Jr.	77	NX70Y	Seversky SEV-S2	P&W Twin Wasp	1000	7:14:19*	282.098	*Frank Fuller continued on to Bendix, N.J., to
Burbank, Calif., to	2	Arthur Bussy	99	NX2433	Bellanca 28-92	Ranger & 2 Menasco	870	8:21:08	244.486	set a new Bendix coast-to-coast record.
Cleveland	3	Paul Mantz	23	NR12222	Lockheed Orion	Wright Cyclone	750	8:41:38	234.875	8:58:08 273.140
	4	Max Constant	31	NX18562	Beechcraft D-17W	P&W Wasp Jr.	450	8:49:33	231.366	

GREVE TROPHY RACE 1934—1939

YEAR	COURSE and PLACE		PILOT	RACE NO.	LICENSE NO.	AIRCRAFT	ENGINE	THRUST LBS.	AV. SPEED	REMARKS
1934	Cleveland, Ohio	4	Roy Minor	33	NR255Y	Brown *Miss Los Angeles*	Menasco C-65	544	213.257	*4th place on points.*
	Note: Race flown in	3	Harold Neumann	39	NR56Y	Howard Dga-5 *Ike*	Menasco B-6	489	211.553	*3rd place on points.*
	3 heats, each plane	2	Roger Don Rae	131	NR51Y	Rider R-1 *San Francisco I*	Menasco C-6	544	211.003	*Tied for 2nd place on points.*
	awarded points. Next	1	Lee Miles	6	NR225Y	Miles & Atwood Special	Menasco C-4	363	206.241	*Greve trophy winner on points.*
	column shows point	2	Art Chester	15	NR12930	Chester *Jeep*	Menasco C-4	363	203.382	*Tied for 2nd place on points.*
	winners.									
1935	Cleveland, Ohio	1	Harold Neumann	38	NR55Y	Howard DGA-4 *Mike*	Menasco B-6	489	212.716	*1st place on points.*
	Note: Race flown in	2	Roger Don Rae	131	NR51Y	Rider R-1	Menasco C-6S	544	210.126	*2nd place on points.*
	3 heats, each plane	5	Marion McKeen	33	NR255Y	Brown *Miss Los Angeles*	Menasco C-6S	544	206.425	*5th place on points.*
	awarded points. Next	3	Art Chester	15	NR12930	Chester *Jeep*	Menasco C-4	363	199.078	*3rd place on points.*
	column shows point	6	Lee Miles	1	NR225Y	Miles & Atwood Special (Brown)	Menasco C-4	363	189.603	*6th place on points.*
	winners.									
		4	Steve Wittman	111	R12047	Wittman *Chief Oshkosh*	Cirrus	349	189.384	*4th place on points.*
		7	David Elmendorf	22	NR60Y	Wedell-Williams	Menasco B-6S	489	175.106	*7th place on points.*
1936	Cleveland, Ohio	1	Michel Detroyat	100	C4606909	Caudron C-460	Renault Bengali	488	247.3	*World landplane record, Dec., 1934, 314.2 mph.*
	One race. All entries race-horse start.	2	Harold Neumann	1	R283Y	Folkerts *Toots*	Menasco C-4S	363	225.858	
		3	Art Chester	3	NR12930	Chester *Jeep*	Menasco C-4	363	224.682	
		4	Rudy Kling	131	NR51Y	Keith Rider I *Suzy*	Menasco C-6S	544	218.331	
1937	Cleveland, Ohio	1	Rudy Kling	301	R14899	Folkerts KF-1 *Jupiter*	Menasco C-6S4	544	232.272	
	One race. Race-horse	2	Steve Wittman	111	R14855	Wittman *Chief Oshkosh*	Menasco C-4S	363	231.990	
	start.	3	C. H. Gotch	70	R261Y	Schoenfeldt-Rider R-4	Menasco B-6S	544	231.593	
	10 laps—100 miles	4	Roger Don Rae	15	NX288Y	Folkerts Special	Menasco C-4S	363	224.197	
1938	Cleveland, Ohio	1	Tony LeVier	70	NX261Y	Schoenfeldt-Rider R-4	Menasco C-S4	544	250.886	
	One race. Race-horse	2	Art Chester	5	NX93Y	Chester *Goon*	Menasco C-S4	544	250.416	*18th lap 278.3 mph.*
	start.	3	Joe Jacobson	8	NX96Y	Rider R-6 *Eight Ball*	Menasco C-S4	544	218.278	
	30 laps—300 miles	4	Earl Ortman	22	NX264Y	Marcoux-Bromberg Rider R-5	Menasco B-6S	489	192.503	*Flagged down 18th lap.*
		1	Art Chester	5	NX93Y	Chester *Goon*	Menasco C-6S4	544	263.390	
1939	Cleveland, Ohio		Tony LeVier	70	NX261Y	Schoenfeldt *Firecracker*	Menasco C-6S4	544		*Rider R-4 out 11th lap.*
	20 laps—200 miles		Harry Crosby	52	NX92Y	Crosby CR-4	Menasco C-6S4	544		*Out 13th lap.*
			Lee Williams	33	NX255Y	Brown *Miss Los Angeles*	Menasco C-6S	544		*B-2. Crashed at scattering pylon.*

Index

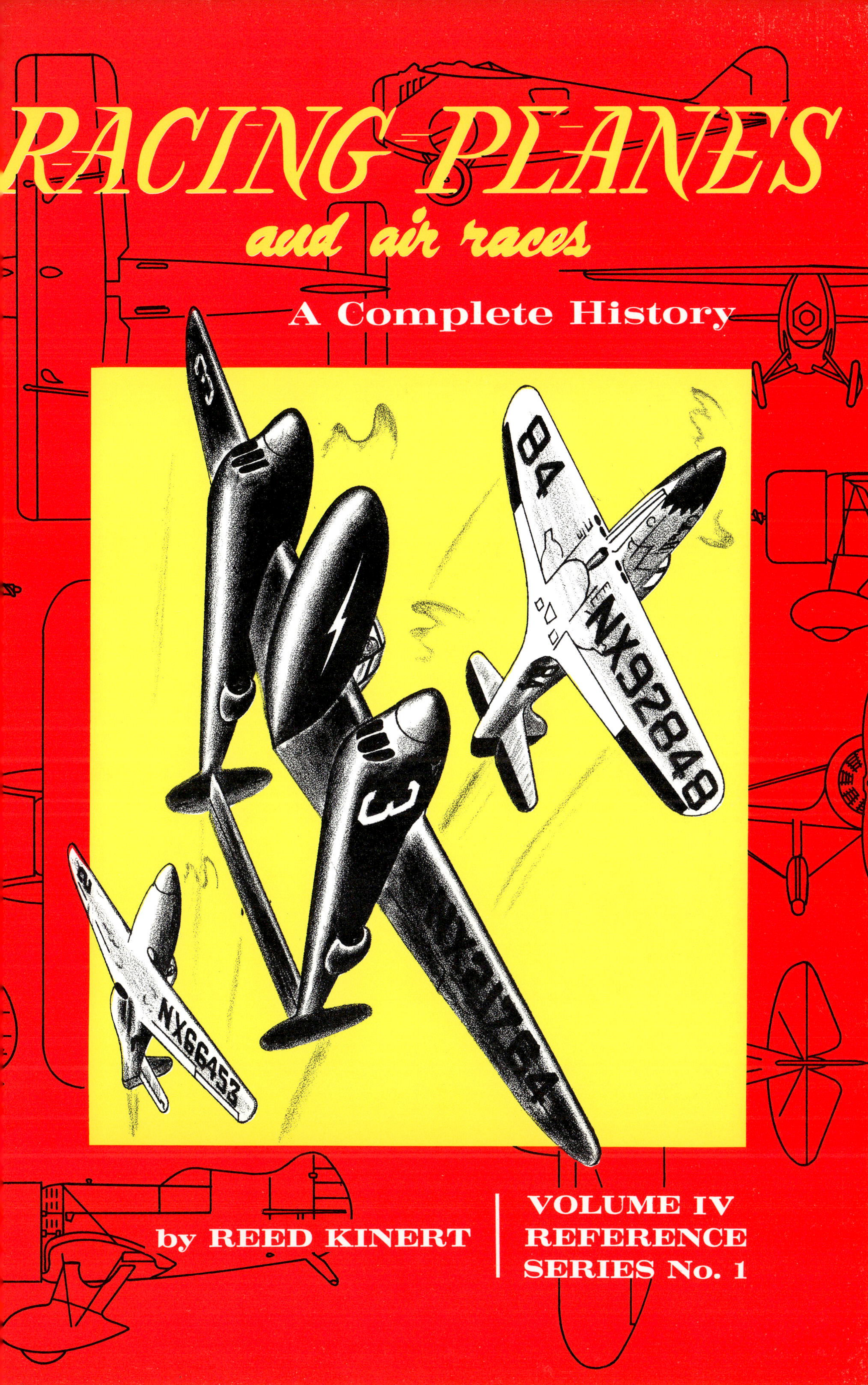

RACING PLANES
and air races
A Complete History
VOLUME IV
REFERENCE
SERIES No. 1
by REED KINERT

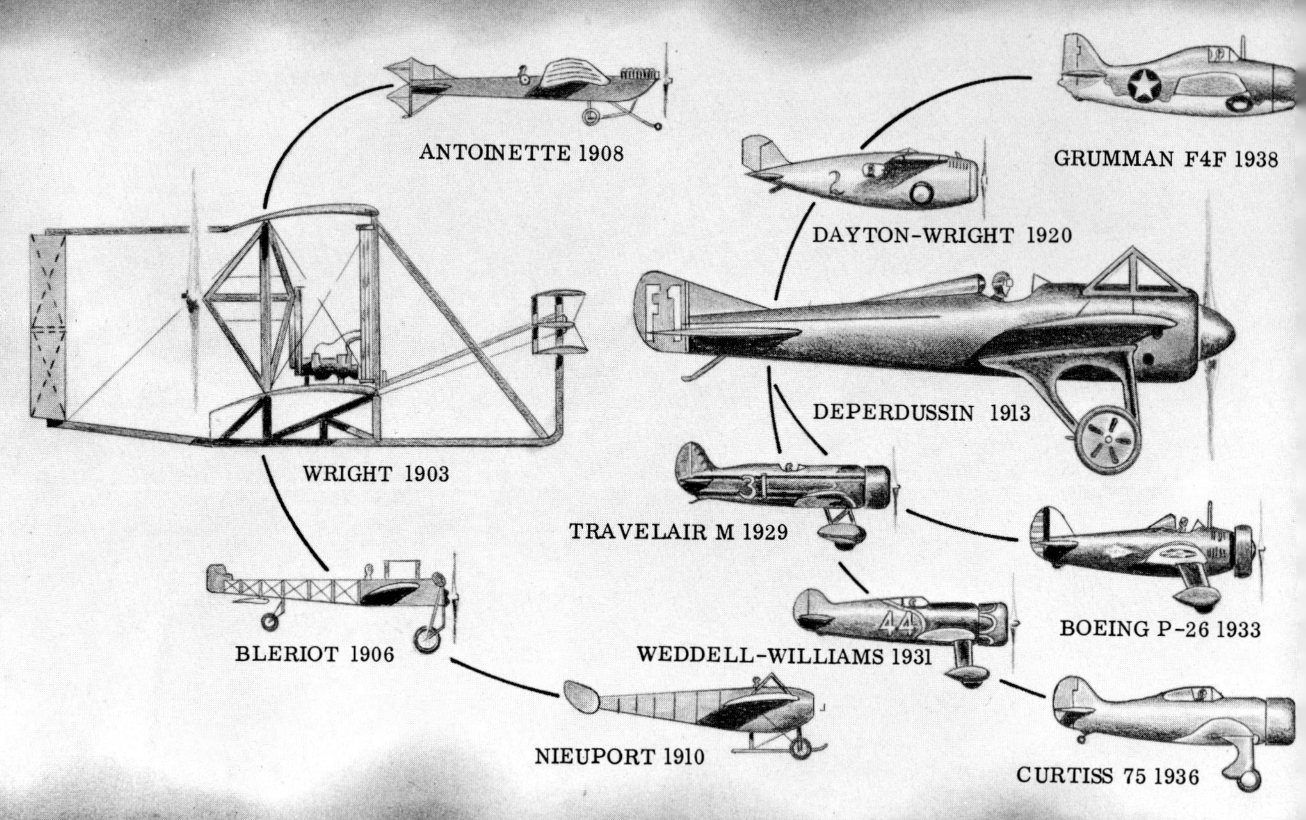

"Instead of the tardy conveyance of ships and chariots, man might use the swifter migration of wings, the fields of air are open to knowledge and only ignorance and idleness need crawl upon the ground."

—Rasselas, DR. SAMUEL JOHNSON, *1759*

Written and Illustrated by Reed Kinert

Scale & 3-View Drawings
by Dustin W. Carter

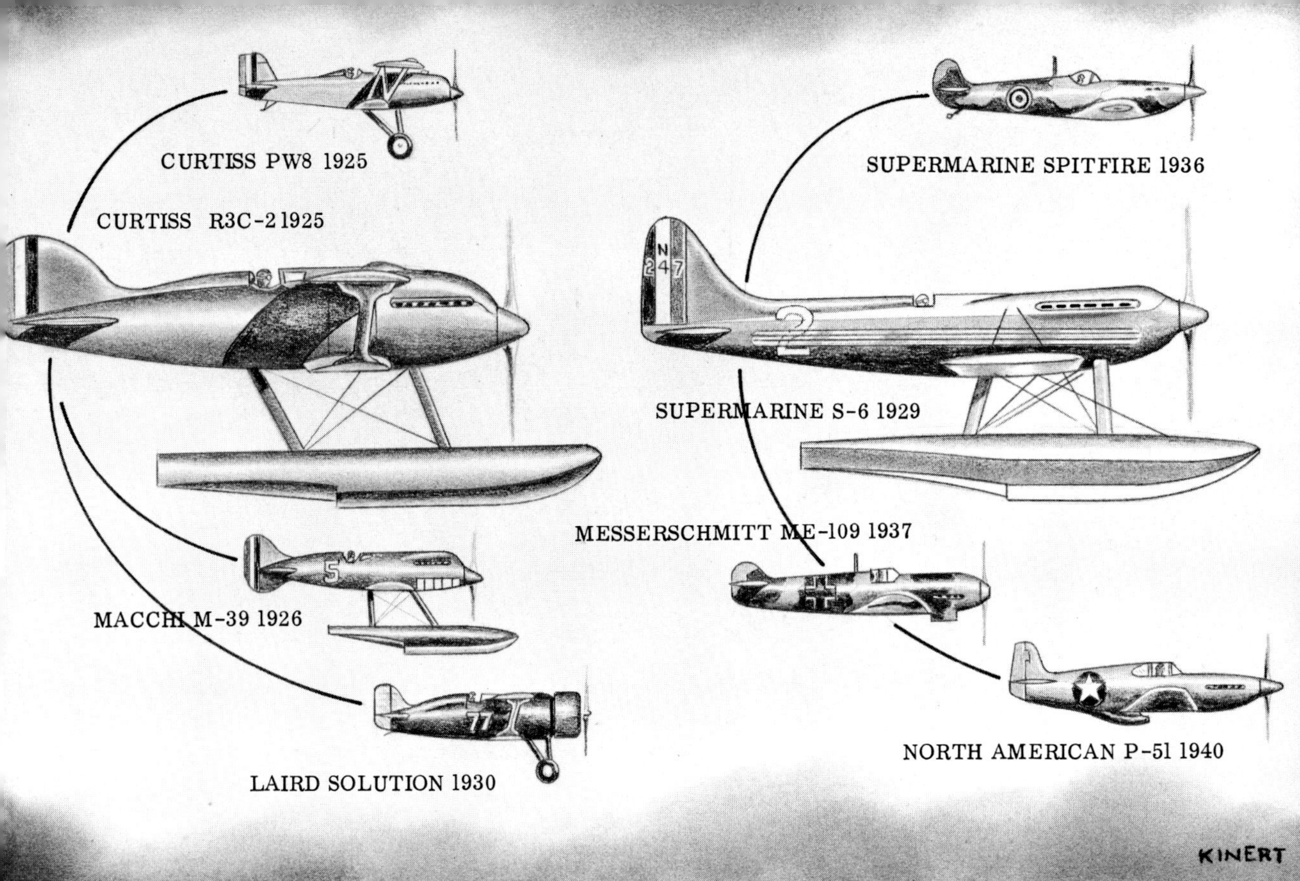

RACING PLANES
and air races

A Complete History

VOLUME IV
1946–1967

AERO PUBLISHERS, INC.

Fallbrook, California

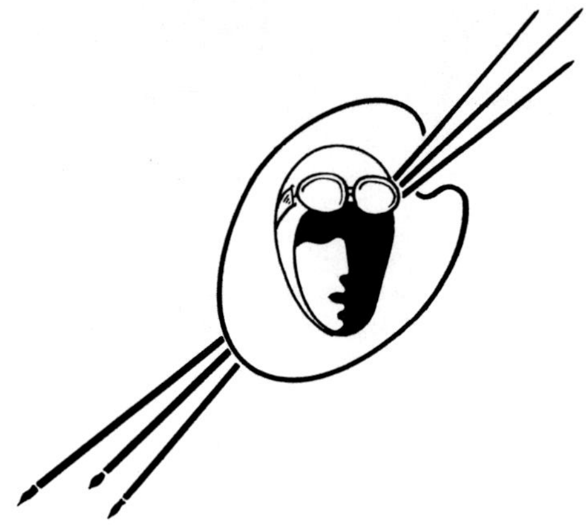

FIRST EDITION

SECOND PRINTING - REVISED - 1969

LIBRARY OF CONGRESS CATALOG CARD NUMBER

67-16455

Table of Contents

List of Illustrations

List of Three-Views

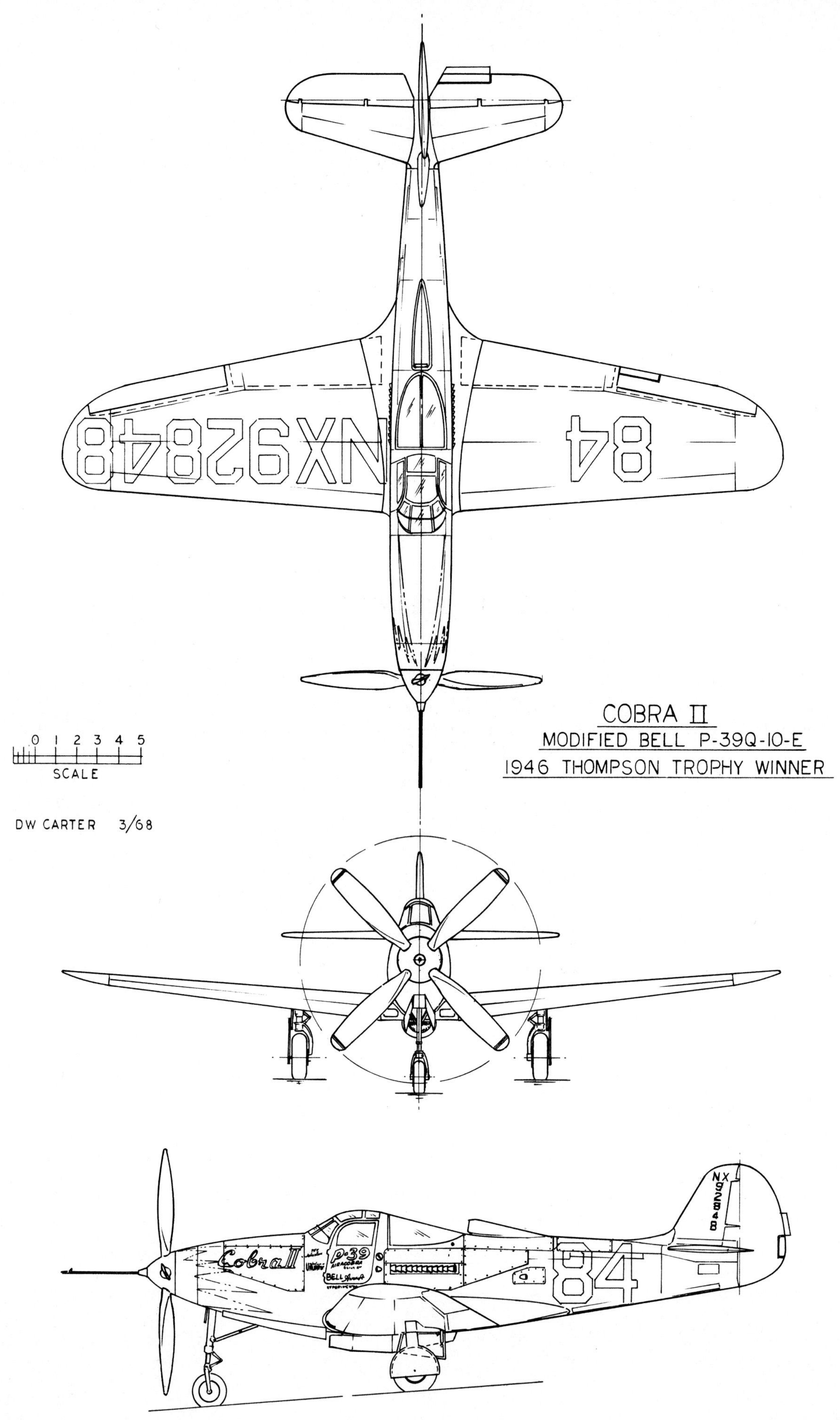

NX92848
84
COBRA II
MODIFIED BELL P-39Q-10-E
1946 THOMPSON TROPHY WINNER
0 1 2 3 4 5
SCALE
DW CARTER 3/68
Cobra II
P-39
AIRACOBRA
BELL Aircraft

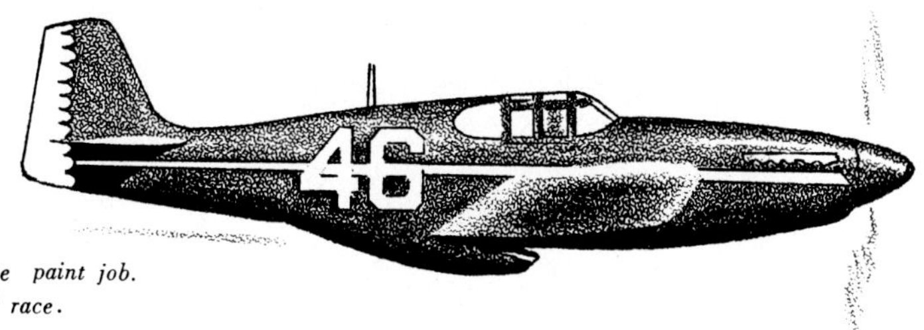

Paul Mantz' P-51C had a mirror-smooth red-and-white paint job. He averaged 435.5 mph in winning the 1946 Bendix "R" race.

1946 – National Air Races

The first post-World War II National Air Races, held at Cleveland, August 30 to September 2, was a war surplus affair. Fighter planes stripped down by their pilot-owners, and the engines souped up to win-or-bust. Military races were resumed after 16 years, and war-developed jet planes, giant kerosene-burning blowtorches in the form of Lockheed P-80 Shooting Stars, were flown.

BENDIX "R" TROPHY

Twenty-two revamped all-metal war planes took off Friday, August 30, from Metropolitan Airport, Van Nuys, Calif., in a nonstop attempt to win the coveted Bendix Trophy. Paul Mantz, veteran stunt pilot, flew his P-51 Mustang at 33,000 feet all the way into Cleveland in only 4 hrs. 42 min. to finally win a Bendix race, averaging 435.5 mph! This was Paul's fourth try, having flown to fifth place with Amelia Earhart in 1935 and taking third in 1938 and '39. He was nearly forced out this year when his landing gear fairing doors closed before the wheels retracted, but a tight loop tripped the gear in properly. Second place went to Mustang-pilot Jacqueline Cochran, 1938 Bendix winner and wartime commander of the Wasps.

BENDIX JET TROPHY

Fast as it was, Mantz's speed was eclipsed in the new jet division of the Bendix by Army Col. Leon Gray, who pushed an FP-80A Shooting Star into Cleveland in 4 hrs. 8 min., to beat three other P-80A starters, with an average speed of 494.8 mph including a fuel stop. Two entries landed in Kansas with engine trouble.

The fastest speed of the air meet was turned in by Lt. W. J. Reilly, when he dived a P-80A from 6,000 feet twice, flying low over a measured mile for an average of 578.4 mph to win the Weatherhead Jet Speed Dash Trophy. Hampered by low clouds and a cross-wind, Reilly was short of the world's record held by an English Gloster Meteor jet, 616 mph.

There was a race for planes unable to qualify for the Thompson Trophy, the Sohio Trophy, won by P-51 pilot Dale Fulton over six other entries at 352.8

mph, and a women's race, the Halle Trophy for AT-6 Texan Trainers won by Marg Hurlbert over four other ladies at 200.6 mph. But again the Thompson Trophy races, one for conventional piston engines and a new jet division, were the main events.

This year all pilots wore crash helmets, their aircraft were fitted with shoulder straps to prevent the pilots from lunging forward in a crash, and the pilots of the big planes wore tight-fitting G suits, which filled up with air around their arms and legs when high load turns were made, helping to prevent the pilots from "blacking out." Also, most of the pilots used oxygen masks to prevent their becoming asphyxiated from leaking gasoline or exhaust fumes.

THOMPSON JET TROPHY

Early Labor Day afternoon, September 2, six G-suited Air Force P-80 pilots took off in the usual bumpy air of Cleveland to fly the world's first closed-course jet-plane race. Maj. Gus Lundquist, 26, set a new closed-course record, averaging 515.9 mph, and flew one lap at 549 mph to win the race, pushed all the way by Maj. Robin Olds, 24, who clipped one lap off at 533.3 mph and finished less than three seconds behind to average 514.7 mph.

Maj. Lundquist stated, "I started off badly in this first jet closed-course race in aviation history, but managed to catch up and take the lead at the second pylon (3-pylon 30-mile course). These P-80's really burn fuel fast at low altitude, and I held back some to conserve fuel. I poured it on only once, when I saw Olds closing in, and indicated well over 550 mph. It was very rough. I bounced pretty hard, but my crash helmet kept me from being injured.

"I had some trouble with the pylons. They're awfully hard to see at high speeds. Yesterday in practice I missed the home pylon twice. The fuel problem was ticklish. I started with 470 gallons, good enough for an hour and a quarter at 35,000 feet, but burned it all in the 17-minute 180-mile race."

THOMPSON "R" TROPHY

Briefed, as usual, before the Thompson "R" Race, starter Earl Steinhower cautioned the pilots,

William Eddy, race No. 31, NX66851, gets flag from official starter Larry Therkelson at Metropolitan Airport, Van Nuys, for 1946 Bendix take-off in his P-51D Mustang City of San Diego. Eddy finished 4th with 404.080 mph. Dustin W. Carter

Douglas A-26C Caribbean Queen was flown non-stop into Cleveland 1946 at 367.889 mph average by Don Husted to take 6th place. Ship was stock except for nose modification and long range tanks installed in bomb bay. Dustin W. Carter

Bell P-63F Kingcobra No. 21, NX1719, flown to 10th place in 1946 Thompson by H. L. Pemberton, was the only F series P-63 built, serial 43-11719. Fin and rudder were much taller for better control and was quite pointed. Fin extension was added by Bell. Warren M. Bodie

Ill-fated red and yellow Bell P-39C NX92847 Cobra I which Jack Wollams crashed fatally into Lake Ontario on test hop. After wreckage was inspected it was determined fuselage had broken aft of engine so Cobra II was beefed up with longeron stiffeners. Stephen J. Hudek

P-51C Mustang No. 46, NX1202 flown non-stop by Paul Mantz to win 1946 Bendix. Photo taken at Cleveland in 1947 after Mantz had again won Bendix. Ultra sleek red and white paint scheme was the same both years. Paul wrapped gas filler hose with dry ice to condense fuel just before races, was thus able to fast cruise all the way in long Bendix flights.
Warren M. Bodie

Jacqueline Cochran's green P-51C Mustang was handicapped by external long-range tanks but finished an easy 2nd in 1946 Bendix. No. 13, NX28388 had "Wanted, a strong coequal Air Force" lettered under exaust stacks.
Warren M. Bodie

Natural finish Bell P-63C-5 Kingcobra No. 30, NX63231, was flown to 7th place in 1946 Bendix by Charles Tucker. 38 foot wing was clipped to 30 feet and Lockheed P-80 wingtip tanks were fitted. Photo taken at Cleveland just after Bendix. Both of Tucker's Kingcobras were modified under supervision of Caltech Aero instructor Stan Corssin.
Warren M. Bodie

Goodyear-built Vought FG-1D Corsair flown by Thomas Call in 1946 Bendix, finished 15th. No. 90, NX63382 was stock, wore big long-range tank under fuselage, as seen here. Aircraft was all white with black markings, was highly polished. FG-1D was not the fastest Corsair built. P&W R-2800-8 delivered 2000 hp and 417 mph at altitude. Wingspan was 41 feet, same as all Corsairs.
Bodie/Carter

P-39C Bell Airacobra and Tex Johnson after winning 1946 Thompson Trophy. Cobra II and sister ship Cobra I were the first WWII ex-fighter aircraft to wear highly modified engines. Allison V-1710 single-stage V-12 delivered 2000 hp and 400+ mph at sea level. Climb was an exceptional 6000 ft/per/min. Empty weight was pared to 5578 lbs. and gross, with 240 U.S. gal. of fuel, was 7886 lbs. In race horse start Johnson was in the air wheels up before others left ground!
Warren M. Bodie

Fire-truck red Lockheed P-38L-5 Lightning with which owner Tony LeVier took 2nd in 1946 Thompson. Superchargers were removed and their wells faired over, and stabilizer tips were removed. Allison V-1710 engines delivered 1700 hp at 3200 rpm at sea level. Two additional gas tanks were installed for the 300 mile full throttle grind. Just before race time Tony and his crew used hundreds of yards of cellophane tape on his craft to seal up all openings, including flaps.
Warren M. Bodie

George Welch, North American test pilot, took off in his P-51D Mustang right alongside Tony LeVier's P-38 in 1946 Thompson, back of Tex Johnson's Cobra II. Pulled up and out of race 2nd lap trailing white smoke from overworked engine.   Dustin W. Carter

Cook Cleland flew this FG-1D Corsair into 6th place in 1946 Thompson, the only race in which this aircraft, N69900, flew. Corsairs earned nickname "bent wing" because of inverted gull wing which allowed shorter landing gear legs.   Warren M. Bodie

Lockheed P-80A in which Lt. Wm. J. Reilly won 1964 Weatherhead Speed Dash at 578.360 mph in quest of world's speed record which he failed to break in cross wind. Craft wore 94th Pursuit Squadron hat in ring insignia.   Warren M. Bodie

This P-80A Shooting Star, flown by Capt. J. E. Sullivan, finished last in Weatherhead Dashes and flown by Major R. O. Chilstrom, dropped out of "J" Thompson 3rd lap with mechanical problems. Craft was assigned to Flight Test Division, Wright Field.   Warren M. Bodie

Col. Leon Gray dropped wing tanks of his Lockheed FP-80A into the Mississippi River, went on into Cleveland to win 1946 "J" Bendix Trophy at 494.799 mph. Shooting Stars were about the most sleekly streamlined jet fighters ever built. Newly developed grey lacquer finish was applied, baked and then waxed and buffed for extremely slick finish. This Shooting Star was photo-recon version, had cameras removed from nose for race.

Warren M. Bodie

Lockheed P-80A-1 Shooting Star with which Major Gus Lundquist won 1946 "J" Thompson Trophy at 515.853 mph. Ship was assigned to Flight Test Division, Wright Field, where it was groomed for racing. When the P-80's rolled off the assembly line they were the world's fastest. Allison J-33 engine delivered only 4600 lbs. of thrust. The airplane was extremely maneuverable, with good stall characteristics. Hard to get into a spin, the P-80 recovered in one-fourth to one-half turn.

Warren M. Bodie

Highly polished white and red Bell P-63C Kingcobra, flown by Charles Tucker in 1946 Thompson, had 6½ feet of each wing tip chopped off, bringing span down to a fantastic 25 feet, the shortest wing ever flown in post-war unlimited races! At a pre-race gathering of the pilots a three pylon racecourse was considered. Chuck said he couldn't hold altitude with this ship for more than a 90 degree turn so a four pylon course was chosen.

Warren M. Bodie

"Five minutes before 4 P.M. a red flag will go up. One minute before four a white flag will go up. It will come down exactly at four. It's up to you to be ready."

Race referee Art Chester warned, "Don't start revving up your engines when the white flag first goes up. I know how hard it is not to do that but you've got to conserve gas. Remember, the 10- to 15-mph NW cross-wind will drift you toward the first pylon. Watch the man on the left; give him clearance; don't crowd him at the pylon. Those of you who get off ahead, be sure you are plenty far ahead before cutting in. Rules on passing are that you must fly 150 feet to the right or 50 feet above, which, in my opinion, is too damn close. Pass underneath only if the man you are passing is flying high."

All through air-racing history the pilots were plagued by prop wash from the aircraft in front of them on the racecourse. The propellers created a swirling vortex, and the aircraft itself tore the air into a burbling turmoil that could have flipped a close-following ship into an uncontrollable high-speed roll. In these post World War II races, the pilots, because of the higher speeds attained and the more powerful engines, had to be more respectful of vortex than any pilots had before them.

First off in a field of 12 in the race-horse start, Bell test pilot Alvin "Tex" Johnston, flying a stripped-down P-39 Bell Airacobra fitted with a more powerful Allison engine, was pushed closely by George Welch in his P-51 Mustang, until Welch was forced out in the second lap. Newcomer Tex slowly but steadily forged ahead of the field to win at 373.9 mph, topping Roscoe Turner's 1938 record by 90 mph!

Lockheed test pilot Tony LeVier, not conceded a chance, grooved his P-38 in for second place, nearly 4 mph slower. Another veteran race pilot, Earl Ortman, finished third in a P-51 Mustang, and for the fifth time saw another pilot win the coveted Thompson Trophy. LeVier's P-38 was stock in appearance except for removal of the horizontal stabilizer tips.

To Tex Johnston went the honor of finally breaking the closed-course record (for conventional engines) set by England's Supermarine S-6 seaplane 15 years previous, but it took a landplane to do it!

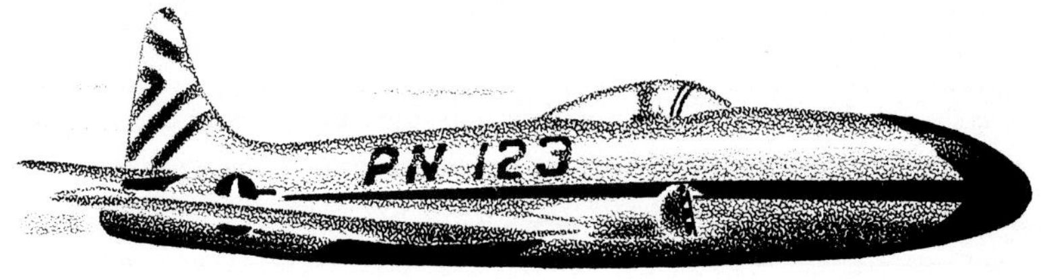

Major Lundquist dropped his P-80A wing tanks into the Mississippi River and flew on to win the 1946 Thompson "J" Trophy, averaging 515.9 mph.

Jim Ruble's fast Bendix P-38 had a cut-down canopy. It lost a wing tank on take-off, then caught fire over Arizona. Ruble bailed out.

1947 – National Air Races

Some 3,500 private planes were flown into Cleveland for the races, August 30 to September 1, and over 2,500 of these were parked on the airport — the largest aggregation of private planes in the world.

BENDIX "R" TROPHY

Twelve ex-warplanes, loaded to the gills with fuel, took off from Van Nuys, Calif., Saturday, August 30, in the all nonstop Bendix "R" Race. Jim Ruble, flying an early model P-38, cleaned up and fitted with larger engines, swerved dangerously on take-off when his right wing tip tank dropped off. Then while clipping over 500 mph 33,000 feet above the Arizona desert, his left engine caught fire. Concluding that it wasn't his day, he bailed out and landed safely. Paul Mantz again made the best speed into Cleveland, and despite a rainstorm that cancelled all other race events for the day, set a new reciprocating engine record speed of 460.4 mph in his red P-51 Mustang. Joe DeBona, in another P-51, finished a heartbreaking 78 seconds later.

BENDIX JET TROPHY

Col. Leon Gray again won the Bendix Jet Race and in the same ship, at a speed of 507.3 mph. He was the only P-80 pilot of four to finish, one dropping out in Kansas, the other two landing at Dayton because of a storm.

Ruth Johnson won the second annual Halle Trophy Race for women at a 223.4 mph clip. All the entries were AT-6 Texan planes.

A new event was the Kendall Oil Trophy Race for P-51's, won handily by Steve Beville at 384.6 mph.

The Tinnerman Trophy Race for P-63's was also new, and won by Hubert Knight Jr. at 352.1 mph.

The Sohio Trophy Race, limited this year to P-38's, was taken easily by Tony LeVier at 360.9 mph. Tony and Steve Wittman (third in the Tinnerman) were the only pre-war race pilots competing.

The first Allison Jet Trophy Race — a 500-mile cross-country sprint for P-80's, from Cleveland to Indianapolis and return—was won by Capt. Dick Burnor over five other ships with a speed 494.3 mph.

Goodyear put up a 3-year trophy limited to 190 cu. in. engined midget planes with fixed props and landing gears and an empty weight of 500 lbs. Thirteen little ships showed up. Three were pre-war, and all wore Continental 4-cyl. opposed engines, which were turned far above their normal rpm to deliver up to 125 hp. Elimination heats were flown. The midget races were highly interesting for they flew low over a 4-pylon 15-lap 2.2-mile course within easy sight of all. William Brennand, 108 lb. protege of Steve Wittman, won the close race, flying Steve's revamped *Chief Oshkosh* fitted with new wings and renamed *Buster*, with an average speed of 165.9 mph.

THOMPSON JET TROPHY

Flown over a shorter course, the winning speed of the Thompson Jet Race fell below last year's record when Lt. Col. Bob Petit flew in from last place to best five other P-80A's and win at 500.7 mph, handicapped by a bird-bloodstained windshield. Rivets were popped and skin buckled and torn in the high-speed rough-air flight.

THOMPSON "R" TROPHY

The Thompson Jet Race had been flown in early afternoon, Labor Day, and then came the climax of

Edmund Lunken's P-51 Buttonpuss, NX61151, in early hours before 1947 Bendix start. Ed made fuel stops, finished 3rd at 408.723 mph. Tail of Douglas B-26 entry is seen over top of fuselage.
Kinert

Bruce Gimbel poised for take-off in 1947 Bendix in Jackie Cochran's P-51B. Although huge external wing tanks held sufficient fuel for non-stop flight to Cleveland their drag held Bruce to 4th place. Wording under exhaust stacks now read "Air Power is Peace Power."
Dustin W. Carter

Jim Ruble warming engines just before topping tanks for 1947 Bendix start. Light green P-38 had larger engines installed for race and low capacity radiators caused Allisons to overheat with resulting fire and bailout over Arizona. Huge cockpit canopy was cut down.
Charles G. Mandrake

Frank Witton's Goodyear FG-1, unchanged for 1947 except for race number, was the only Corsair to ever fly in Bendix races. Witton picked up $500 for 7th place, last money award for the event. Fuel stops were necessary despite huge external fuel tank.
Warren M. Bodie

Paul Mantz taking his famous wet-wing No. 46 off for 1947 Bendix at Metropolitan Airport. Paul obtained factory drawings, made exact wing templates then spray painted low areas to make wing perfectly smooth, wet sanded, waxed and polished entire red aircraft to mirror gloss. Paul flew Bendix races at 20 to 30,000 feet, depending on winds aloft. Reliable reports say he flew his hopped up Rolls Royce Merlin wide open, pulled 105 inches of mercury!

Kinert

Joe DeBona making his 1947 Bendix start at Metro Airport, Van Nuys. Joe fitted his black and white P-51D Mustang Magic Town No. 90, with wet-wings after noting success of Mantz in 1946, also flew wide open non-stop at high altitudes. Finished race with 458.203 mph average, just over 2 mph behind Mantz. Mustangs took first six places in 1947 Bendix, always dominated race. Their take-offs were surprisingly short despite heavy fuel loads.

Kinert

Reynold's Little Bombshell, stock Lockheed F-5G flown by Bill Lear Jr., finished 14th in 1946 and 8th in 1947 Bendix. Aircraft was used by Bill and his father in developing their aircraft radio equipment.
Kinert

Douglas A-26 Invader taking off for 1947 Bendix. No. 91, NX67807, was flown by diminutive Dianna Cyrus and was fitted with bomb-bay tanks for non-stop flight. Would have finished in the money but Dianna got lost, landed in Michigan, missed Cleveland deadline.
Kinert

Stock Bell P-63C flown by Joe Kinkella in 1947 Bendix dropped out of race at Pueblo, Colorado with engine trouble. Kingcobra was one of the few of its type to fly in Bendix. Aircraft was in natural finish.
Kinert

Republic P-47M Thunderbolt NX4477N was the only craft of its type to enter Bendix. Bill Odum, celebrated long distance record setter, was to fly in 1947 Bendix but leak in jettisonable wing fuel tank prevented start.
Kinert

Jim Ruble flew the most highly modified Lockheed P-38 Lightning in Bendix history. Early series craft was fitted with late series Allison engines to take advantage of clean low-profile engine nacelles. P-80 Shooting Star jettisonable wing-tip fuel tanks were fitted and canopy cut down. Gun firing buttons on control wheel were hooked up to release tip tanks when empty and Ruble inadvertently hit button just after becoming airborne on Bendix start, releasing starboard tank. Ship swerved dangerously with heavy non-stop fuel load. Lockheed

Listed as a P-63A this clipped-wing Bell Kingcobra wore a reworked high fin and rudder to resemble P-63F. Ship was 9th in 1946 Thompson, piloted by Howard Lilly, race No. 64. Flown by William Bour, ship was 6th in 1947 Thompson and 5th in Tinnerman. Then, in 1948 this same aircraft, painted black and flown by Robert Euker, won the Sohio Trophy race and dropped out in 9th lap of Thompson! Ship wore race No. 55 in 1947 and 48.
Warren M. Bodie

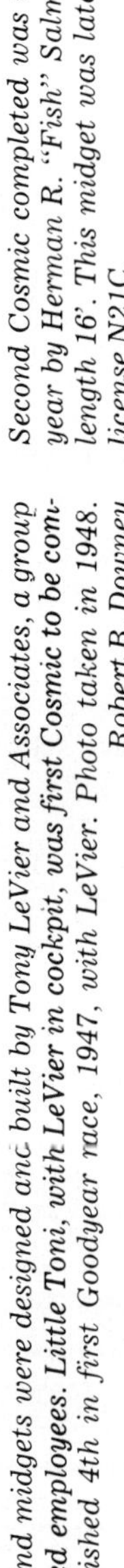

Second Cosmic completed was named Cosmic Wind, flown to 3rd place in 1947 Goodyear by Herman R. "Fish" Salmon, Lockheed test pilot. Wingspan of Cosmics was 18', length 16'. This midget was later named Minnow, race number changed to No. 4 and license N21C.
Warren M. Bodie

Loose Siem, built for 1947 Goodyear by Warren Siem, used windshield brace as cabane strut for landing wires. Warren took 5th place in 1947 Goodyear finals. Cockpit was so cramped that Warren, although diminutive in stature, had to fly in stocking feet!
Dustin W. Carter

Cosmic Wind midgets were designed and built by Tony LeVier and Associates, a group of Lockheed employees. Little Toni, with LeVier in cockpit, was first Cosmic to be completed, finished 4th in first Goodyear race, 1947, with LeVier. Photo taken in 1948.
Robert B. Downey

Brown B-1 was built for Ralph Bushey who raced and crashed ship in 1934. Partially restored wreckage was bought from Tony LeVier by Bill Robinson and rebuilt for 1947 Goodyear, placed 6th. Canary yellow craft was unaltered in appearance except for engine and cowling.
Dustin W. Carter

Fabulous red and yellow Buster, designed and built by Steve Wittman with parts from his Chief Oshkosh of 1931-39 fame, was flown to victory in 1947 Goodyear by 105 lb. jockey-size William Brennand, whom Steve had taught to fly. Extremely simple fabric covered Buster wore spring-steel landing gear developed and patented by Steve. Buster weighed just over 500 lbs. empty so ship usually got off and around scatter pylon first, finished in or near top money every race. Craft now reposes in Smithsonian Institution.   Dustin W. Carter

Beautiful butterfly-tailed green and white Swee' Pea, designed and built by Art Chester, had engine completely cowled over, relied on four brace vanes inside spinner to draw in and blow air over engine from hole in spinner nose. Cockpit was only 19" wide at shoulder level, wingspan 18'6", length 15'7". Swee' Pea, flown by Paul Penrose, finished a close 2nd in 1947 Goodyear. Butterfly tail of plywood midget did not respond quickly in turbulant air.   Warren M. Bodie

Chubby, short-coupled Flightways Special No. 70, NX18219, was flown to 2nd place in 1947 Goodyear consolation race by Charles W. Bing. Wire braced fabric covered craft had 19' wingspan, 14'6'' length.
Dustin W. Carter

Here is Ben Howard's 1930 Pete, reworked to accept Continental engine by owner-pilot Ray Baker. Enclosed cockpit was much larger than original open cockpit version. Pete was quite heavy after re-work, was eliminated in early heat races, 1947 Goodyear.
Dustin W. Carter

Unique mid-wing The Whistler, designed and built by Harold Angell and Gerald Francis, flown by Bob Chonoski, was eliminated in 1947 Goodyear heat races. Span 17'6'', length 15'8''. Craft was later extensively modified.
Dustin W. Carter

Hornet midget No. 71, NX68379, designed and built by Arnold Hanes and his brothers in LA. Former Retz R-10 aircraft supplied many parts. Nicely proportioned craft featured vertical landing gear legs that fitted to wing spars. Eliminated in 1947 heat races.
Dustin W. Carter

Pftttt, NX67894, designed and built by Rod Nimmo, a Lockheed engineer, was flown to last place in 1947 Goodyear consolation race by Mike Argander, who aided in construction. Span 19'6", length 16', empty weight 535 lbs. Parts were later used in Sorensen Deerfly.
Dustin W. Carter

Hurricane, No. 85, NX1223, was built by Marge Hurlburt, Anna Logan and Mildred Caldwell, proving the ladies could built airplanes as well as fly them. Ship was eliminated in 1947 Goodyear heat races, which was restricted to male pilots, as usual.
Dustin W. Carter

Homely midget Chester Special was rebuilt from Art Chester's pre-WWII beautiful Jeep by William F. Falck who won 1947 Goodyear consolation at 141.615. Race No. 89, N12930. Falck gained valuable design and racing experience in ship for later success with famous Rivets.
Dustin W. Carter

Beautiful fiber-glassed Californian, built by Ed Allenbaugh, No. 95, NX67893, was handicapped by uncowled engine. Dwight Dempster piloted ship to 3rd place in 1947 Goodyear consolation at 137.253 mph. Span 18', length 14'11".
Dustin W. Carter

North American AT-6 No. 75, NX6377 with which Ruth Johnson won 1947 Halle Trophy race, 223.602 mph. Windshield was stock, rear canopy removed and cockpit faired over. Note three-bladed prop for hopped-up P&W R-1340 engine. Warren M. Bodie

North American SNJ-2 flown to 3rd place in 1947 Halle Trophy race by Edna Whyte at 210.789 mph was stock except for unique canopy which had a raised plastic blister over rear cockpit for pilot. Wing and tail clipping was forbidden in Halle. Warren M. Bodie

NAA XAT-6E, No. 61, which Margaret McGrath qualified in 1st for 1947 Halle at 223.325 mph. Ranger V-770-9 delivered 575 hp and 240 mph top, acted up during race, forcing Margaret out. Only one XAT-6E, AT-6D with engine change, was factory built. Warren M. Bodie

Highly modified red, white and blue AT-6, No. 49, which pretty Dori Marland safely crash-landed on last lap of 1947 Halle. Windshield and front cockpit was stock, rear canopy reworked. Newly installed Ranger engine never did act right, qualified 202.399 mph. Warren M. Bodie

Blue and white Goodyear built Vought F2G-1 Corsair in which Cook Cleland won 1947 Thompson at 396.131 mph after qualifying fastest with 401.787 mph. Cook said he had to win race as he had mortgaged himself to the gills in purchasing and modifying three F2G-1's for racing, won $19,500 dollars with No. 74. 28-cylinder four-row air-cooled radial R-4360-4 Pratt & Whitney Major engine normally delivered 3,650 hp, emergency rating with water injection, giving the F2G-1 450 mph at 16,000 ft.   *Warren M. Bodie*

Cook Cleland-owned F2G-1 in which Richard Becker finished 2nd in 1947 Thompson, won $8,100 dollars. Cook flew this aircraft in 1948 Thompson, turned one 410.366 mph lap, was forced out 5th lap with engine trouble. In 1949 Cook flew same craft to win Thompson. Third Cleland-owned F2G-1 crashed fatally with Tony Janazzo while turning pylon 2. Torque stick forces from big four-bladed propellers on F2G's was tremendous in turns, required both hands on stick to overcome them.   *Dustin W. Carter*

Cobra II was unchanged outwardly for 1947 except for new race No. 11 and new pilot's name, Jay Deming, replacing that of Tex Johnston on doors. Allison V-1710-135 engine had special pistons to allow high manifold pressure with "exotic" fuels without detonation, took 3rd in Thompson.
Warren M. Bodie

Clipped wing Bell P-63, No. 72, NX6394. Raymond Eiche had engine quit at 390 mph after passing pylon 2 at 200 ft. on qualifying run. Eiche pulled up to 1,000 ft., jettisoned door and bailed out, was bruised by tail but landed safely.
Warren M. Bodie

Ronald G. Puckett took this F2G-1 Corsair off in 1947 Thompson after other racers had completed 1st lap. Official failed to give him adequate start warning. Ron had gained 4th place when engine forced him out. Finished 2nd in 1949 Thompson with same aircraft.
Warren M. Bodie

Elaborately painted red and white P-38J flown by Charles Walling Jr. of Houston, Texas in 1947 events at Cleveland had needlenose to gain a few extra mph. Normally exposed turbo-supercharger wells atop twin booms were completely covered.
Warren M. Bodie

Highly modified P-38J Lightning had well designed air-intake scoops built atop engine nacelles, wing tips and outboard stabilizers were clipped. No. 14, NX25Y, named Sky Ranger, was flown to 2nd place in Sohio Trophy Race for P-38's at 351.785 mph. Its pilot, Charles Walling Jr., above, later dropped out of the Thompson race on 2nd lap with engine trouble, landed safely. Warren M. Bodie

Lockheed P-38L, N61121, flown by John Thompson to 4th place at slow 328-739 mph in 1947 Sohio Race, also had wing tips and outboard stabilizers clipped and its nose more streamlined. Flame, caused by engine backfire on engine start, barely seen above wing leading edge root at right engine nacelle, started at supercharger well, was quickly put out with no damage. Warren M. Bodie

XP-60E Connie II, No. 80, was highly modified by Curtiss for James DeSanto who sold his flying school to purchase craft. Wing was clipped 10'2" down to 31'2" and P&W R-2800 engine hopped up to deliver 2440 hp and 90 inches of mercury with water injection. Just before 1947 qualifications DeSanto had tail surfaces fail on test hop and bailed out. In 1946 DeSanto had spark plugs foul on port engine of his stock Lockheed F-5D Connie I, took 6th in Sohio.
Richard Kolthoff

Only Curtiss P-40Q Hawk built, from which Joe Ziegler bailed out and broke a leg as engine failed just after passing pylon 4 in 14th lap of Thompson. Ziegler qualified 13th and too slow for Thompson, took off anyway! Wing of beautiful Hawk tore off top of a boxcar on NYC siding, then struck ground between cars and exploded, ripping up several tracks. Wingspan 35'4". Allison V-1710-121 engine delivered 1425 hp and 422 mph at altitude.
Warren M. Bodie

the air meet, the Thompson "R" Race. The fastest, wildest, and most destructive Thompson Trophy Race in its 12-year history, it was the most spectacular air race ever staged. Thirteen planes lined up for the 20-lap 300-mile race although only 12 had qualified. It was to be a race of horsepower, as exemplified by the big "waffle iron" air-cooled Corsairs, against the streamlined V-12 engined racers. The race was scarcely under way when Jack Hardwick's Merlin engine conked out as he passed the home pylon in the racehorse start. He belly-landed but tore a wing off, escaping from his burning P-51 with only a bruised elbow. P-38 pilot Charles Walling was next to drop out, landing his faltering plane during the second lap. Jay Demming led for the first lap of the race in the 1946-winning P-39Q, but Dick Becker, flying a Corsair, took over the lead on the second lap. Then after the fourth lap, Cook Cleland shaved paint off the home pylon with his Corsair to grab the lead.

Just after pushing by Deming to take third place in the sixth lap, Paul Penrose' P-51 engine quit cold and he landed on the airport.

Lady Luck turned her head away for an instant in the seventh lap, and Tony Jannazo flew into the ground near pylon 2 at 400 mph, he and his F2G-1 Corsair exploding to bits. Then Woody Edmundson's P-51 Merlin engine exploded as he rounded pylon 3 in lap 11. He attempted to land but crashed, and was taken bloody and dazed from the burning wreckage and whisked to a hospital, where he recuperated. This left 8 of the 13 starters, but the race was not over. Joe Ziegler (who hadn't even qualified for the race — he just took off in the confusion at the start) pulled up just after the 13th lap and bailed out of his dead-engined P-40Q. The falling cockpit canopy injured a woman, and Ziegler broke a leg. Meanwhile Ron Puckett, having failed to get the starter's signal, had taken off one lap behind and sped his F2G-1 Corsair past one after another to climb into fourth place, ahead of Tony LeVier. With only one lap to go, his Wasp Major engine failed and he landed intact.

Flying his big F2G-1 Corsair on above wrecked and burning planes, Cook Cleland, who was pulling well over 4,000 hp from his big Wasp Major as against the V-12 engine's 2,000 hp, hit several laps at 404 mph to shake off pursuers. He led the other five surviving racers from the fourth lap and was going away with a 6-mile lead when he crossed the finish line, averaging 396.1 mph to win history's fastest piston-engined race.

COOK CLELAND

Cook Cleland, after winning his second Thompson Trophy in 1949.

COOK CLELAND *was born in Cleveland, Ohio, Dec. 24, 1916. He graduated from Shaw High School (East Cleveland) and the University of Missouri. He then went to work for Thompson Products, Inc., donor of the famous Thompson Trophy. Joining the Navy one month before Pearl Harbor, Cook learned to fly at Pensacola, Fla.*

After serving in the Atlantic and the Mediterranean on the aircraft carrier WASP *as a fighter pilot, he was transferred with the flattop to the Pacific, where he was the first of its pilots to down a Japanese plane.*

When the WASP *went down he swam for four hours before being rescued. Later, when assigned to the aircraft carrier* LEXINGTON, *he was credited with sinking a Jap carrier by dive bombing and with downing three more Jap planes. He won the Navy Cross, the Air Medal with three stars, the Purple Heart, the Navy Commendation, and a Presidential unit citation. Following his combat duty, he served as a Navy test pilot, flew captured German and Japanese planes, and then did experimental work in rocket firing.*

After the war he operated the Euclid Avenue Airport in Willoughby, a suburb of Cleveland. Then Cook became interested in air racing. He purchased and flew a Goodyear-built FG-1D Corsair in the 1946 Thompson, finishing sixth. In late 1946 he put every dime he owned into purchasing and modifying for racing three Vought-designed Goodyear-built F2G-1 Navy fighters, the world's most powerful piston-engined fighters.

Winning the piston-engined division of the Thompson Trophy in 1947 and 1949 (he dropped out because of air scoop trouble in 1948) and setting new speed records both times, Cook became the only pilot other than Roscoe Turner to win the coveted Trophy more than once. His 1949 speed will probably be recorded as history's fastest for closed-course piston-engined racing.

Well liked and affable, Cook was selected Cleveland's "Young Man of the Year," an award presented not only for his flying ability but for his civic work for the youth of Cleveland — his Y.M.C.A. work, hospital drives, and general interest in the community.

Cook returned to active duty Feb. 1, 1951, as a lieutenant commander and Commanding Officer of carrier-based Fighting Squadron 653, somewhere off Korea, where he led his Corsair pilots against the enemy.

Anson Johnson's 1948 Thompson-winning conventional P-51D.

Ed Lunken's Bendix P-51D had a cut-down canopy, finished fourth in the Bendix "R" race.

1948 – National Air Races

The 22nd annual National Air Races, held at Cleveland, September 4–6, saw no records fall in the big engine class and there was no Thompson Jet Race. However, the low-flying, pylon-dusting Goodyear midget racers more than made up the difference, as 24 handmade craft flew through three days of qualifying trials, four preliminary-heat races, two semi-finals, a final, and a consolation race.

The racers, either built up of steel tubing and fabric-covered wooden wings, or all metal in construction, copied almost without exception Steve Wittman's spring-steel landing gear. Bucking tricky cross-winds and rough air, Herman "Fish" Salmon, Lockheed test pilot, won the final race with 169.7 mph in his all-metal *Minnow*. He was closely trailed by Steve Wittman and passed once by Wittman on a pylon turn, but he pulled ahead again on the straightaway. Steve finished second at 168.9 mph in a newly built sister ship to his old *Buster*, while another veteran race pilot, Art Chester, finished a close third in a new self-built *Swee' Pea II*, which was almost identical to his 1947 racer. Chester's ship was fitted with a V "butterfly" tail, and its engine was completely enclosed, cooling air being drawn through a spinner-opening by a blower fan placed in back of the prop. It was known that Art's ship did not handle properly in turns, and to the deep regret of all who knew him, he was killed the following year while turning a pylon during a midget race at San Diego.

BENDIX "R" TROPHY

Only six ex-war planes took off from Long Beach, Calif., to fly through adverse winds in the 12th annual Bendix race. Paul Mantz came in a 3-time winner, flying his light green P-51 over the 2,045 miles at an average speed of 448 mph. The finish of the first three racers was the closest in history, Linton Carney placing second with 446.1 mph, Jacqueline Cochran third with 445.8 mph, while fourth place went to Ed Lunken with 441.6 mph. All flew P-51 Mustangs, Carney piloting Mantz' 1947 Bendix winning red ship, now light green. Jesse Stallings limped into fifth and last place with a dead engine on his twin-engined De Havilland Mosquito, while P-51 pilot Joe DeBona landed out of fuel at Elyria, Ohio, almost within sight of Cleveland. Paul Mantz had guarded against fuel shortage by packing his tanks and the filler hose with Dry Ice, thus condensing the gasoline.

BENDIX JET TROPHY

Six Navy FJ-1 Furys and, unofficially, two California National Guard F-80 Shooting Stars took off from Long Beach in the Bendix Jet Race. Ens. F. E. Brown was credited with first place in his Fury at 489.5 mph, though the Cleveland airport tower clocked F-80 pilot Maj. Bob DeHaven in one minute faster. The Secretary of Defense had forbidden competition between the services. Seven of the jets made Cleveland. One Fury, short of kerosene, landed at Tiffin, Ohio. Fury pilot Lt. Comdr. Bob Elder landed on the Cleveland airport completely out of fuel — unable to taxi over the finish line!

The Tinnerman Trophy Race, Saturday, September 4, was restricted to 2,850 cu. in. engines to keep the big 28-cyl. Wasp Major engined Corsairs out. Bruce Raymond finished first over five starters,

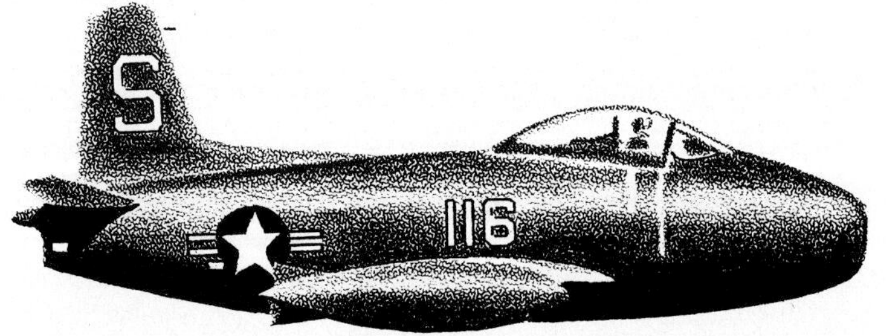

Ens. Brown's 1948 Bendix "J" winning FJ-1 Fury jet fighter.

Oilman Glenn McCarthy sponsored Paul Mantz' three North American P-51's in 1948 Bendix Trophy. Ships were light green with darker green markings. Spinner, prop, all surface tips, license number and shamrock was darker green than other markings. Mantz won 1948 Bendix in this ship at 383.767 mph, a slower race than 1947 because of adverse winds. Tom Mayson flew this aircraft to 6th place in 1947 Bendix wearing race No. 60. Mantz had re-worked wings to carry fuel for non-stop flight. *Warren M. Bodie*

Buttonpuss, NAA P-51D, had the most modified canopy to appear on a Mustang. Vision would probably be too restricted for pylon racing. Ed Lunken finished 4th in 1948 Bendix, flying non-stop with wet-wing fuel supply. He had taken 3rd in 1947 with same, making fuel stops. Wearing McCarthy colors and red, white and blue spinner Buttonpuss' name is seen under exhaust stacks, was named Texan on fuselage sides for Bendix race. *Warren M. Bodie*

Linton Carney flew this Mantz-owned P-51C to close 2nd place in 1948 Bendix at 446.112 mph. Named Houstonian, this is same wet-wing ship in which Mantz won 1946 Bendix. Race number 60 worn for 1947 was confusing switch of numbers.　　Warren M. Bodie

Red and white single-seat all-wood DeHaviland Mosquito, flown in 1948 Bendix by Jess F. Stallings, limped into Cleveland on one engine in non-stop attempt. WWII English fighter wore Rolls Royce Merlin engines and was sponsored by Capitol Airways of Nashville.　　Dustin W. Carter

North American FJ-1 Fury, Fighting Squadron 5 Able No. 116 which Ensign F. E. Brown flew from Long Beach to win 1948 Bendix at 489.526 mph with fuel stops. Factory-fresh craft is seen here sans markings, wore wing tip tanks in race.

North American

Steve Wittman shows 15'4" wingspan of his marvelous yellow and red midget Bonzo which he flew to 2nd place at 168.862 mph in 1948 Goodyear. Note the Wittman developed scimitar-bladed wood prop which would change pitch in flight. Dr. A. L. King Jr.

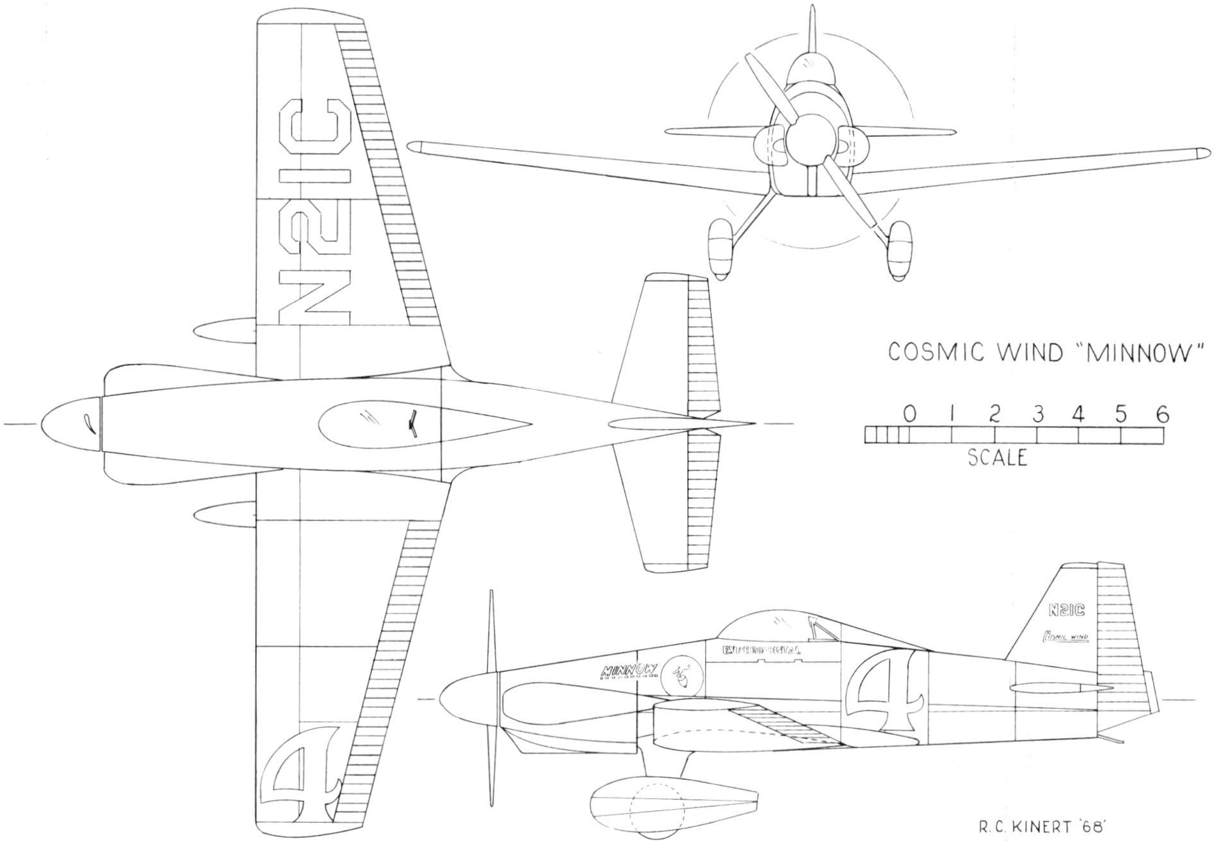

Beautiful, posed in-flight view of Cosmic Wind Minnow No. 4 and Little Toni No. 3 silhouetted against backdrop of oil refinery debris smoke which Los Angeles politicians carefully blame on auto exhaust! John Paul Jones is piloting No. 4, Eddie Custer in No. 3 as they fly over San Fernando valley. Herman "Fish" Salmon took 1st place in 1948 Goodyear with bronze and cream Minnow and Bill F. Robinson finished 5th in red and cream Little Toni. Wingspan of both craft 18', length 16'.

Robert B. Downey

Pitts Pellet is the first of several highly successful midgets designed and built under supervision of Curtis Pitts of Florida who also designed the beautiful Pitts biplanes. Pellet finished 6th in 1948 Goodyear finals, flown by Paul C. Quigley.   Warren M. Bodie

Fuselage of Pellet NX52120 was steel tubing with wood stringers, fabric covered. 17'7" wing was wood and plywood covered. Pellet finished 3rd in January 1949 Continental Motors race with Bob Heisel at Miami, crashed fatally with Bob in San Diego heat race April 24, 1949.
Warren M. Bodie

Bob Downey qualified new Cosmic Wind Ballerina No. 5, N22C, 8th, took 7th in 1948 Goodyear at 161.435 mph. All-metal ship was third Cosmic Wind built, wore green paint with cream trim. Vincent Ast is landing No. 5 after 1949 Newhall race. Robert B. Downey

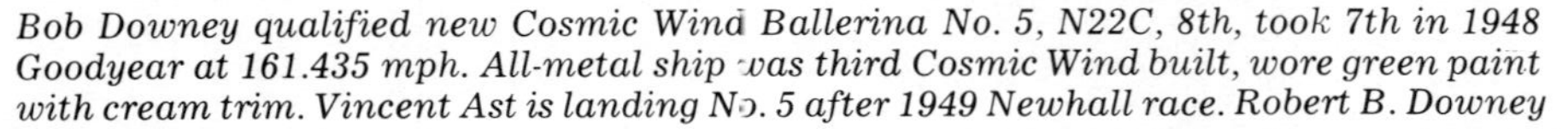

M. L. LeFevers qualified black and white Falcon Special II Lil Rebel 10th in field of 32 midgets to earn start in 1948 Goodyear finals, finished 8th and last after No. 42 and 67 dropped out. Lil Rebel raced for several years.
Warren M. Bodie

Art Chester modified Swee' Pea extensively for 1948, replaced aft fuselage plywood covering with wood stringers and fabric to lessen weight by 50 lbs. Ship still weighed 522 lbs. empty. Chester also deepened fuselage to accept small rudder. But improved ship still did not respond sharply on pylons. Art qualified 1st for 1948 Goodyear at 180 mph, took a close 3rd in finals. Art and Swee' Pea crashed fatally in 2nd heat race at San Diego April 24, 1949.
Warren M. Bodie

Sky Baby was built as sister ship to Swee' Pea by Art Chester for Lynn Kaufold in late 1947. Fabric covered fuselage was extended to 17'6" as against 16' of Swee' Pea in effort to improve flight characteristics. Span was 18'6" against 17'8" of Swee' Pea. Empty weight was a heavy 611 lbs. Sky Baby was eliminated in 1948 Goodyear heats, finished 4th in finals at Newhall May 8, 1949 flown by Bill Broadbeck, above, never made finals again.
Robert B. Downey

All metal P-Shooter was designed and built by David Long, a Piper engineer. Yellow craft, often referred to as a midget Mustang, qualified 7th for 1948 Goodyear, dropped out 9th lap of finals. Ship enjoyed limited success later. Span 18'5", length 16'.
Warren M. Bodie

Beetle Bomb, designed and built by Alvin E. Anderson of Anderson Propeller Company Alvin is seen here after heat race in 1948 Goodyear, did not make finals. Diamond shaped fuselage was clean but thick wing handicapped speed.
Goodyear Co.

Little Toot, Coonley Special designed and built by Harold D. Coonley of Miami, Florida, an EAL flight engineer. Plywood covered Little Toot failed to make finals in 1948 heat races, crashed and was destroyed September 1949.
Robert B. Downey

Mirage, N3154K, built by William Leighnor, qualified for 1948 Goodyear finals in heat races but engine forced pilot Harold Bangerter out of finals start. Red craft appeared in many races later and was flown by various pilots. Span 18'7", length 17'5".
Robert B. Downey

Miss Nashville, Pack Model A NX66311 was the first midget built by Garland Pack and Associates, featured unique wheel streamliners instead of usual pants. Al Bennyworth was eliminated in 1948 Goodyear heat races and ship was later dismantled to built another midget.   Robert B. Downey.

Betty Jo was designed and built by airport owner Luther Johnson of Greenville, S. C. Span 17'4", length 16'4", empty weight 551 lbs. Pilot Charles Barton lost out in 1948 Goodyear heat races. Craft was later aptly named Never Never!   Robert B. Downey

Zipper, No. 59, N5713H, built and raced by Harvey Christiansen failed to survive 1948 Goodyear heat races although clean lines showed great promise. Span 16', length 16'. Note extremely sharp pointed spinner.   Dustin W. Carter

The Whistler was highly reworked for 1948 Goodyear races with sleek new canopy, shortened rudder and single-strut landing gear legs. White and red Whistler, flown by Robert Chonoski, qualified at a disappointing 149.068 mph, 11th place, never made finals.   Goodyear Co.

Connie III, P-51K, was third Nationals try for James DeSanto, had 2½ feet clipped off each wing, first known clip on Mustang. On qualifying run DeSanto tried to pull 100 inches of mercury but #3 Allison engine blew a header tank.   DeSanto/Aaron L. King Jr. in race.

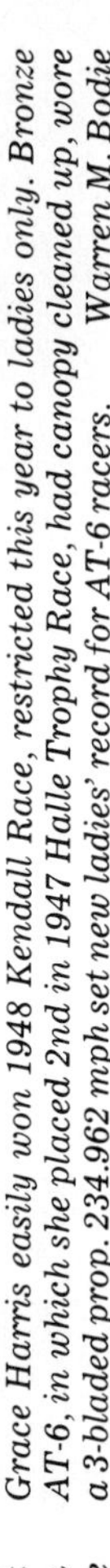

Grace Harris easily won 1948 Kendall Race, restricted this year to ladies only. Bronze AT-6, in which she placed 2nd in 1947 Halle Trophy Race, had canopy cleaned up, wore a 3-bladed prop. 234.962 mph set new ladies' record for AT-6 racers.   Warren M. Bodie

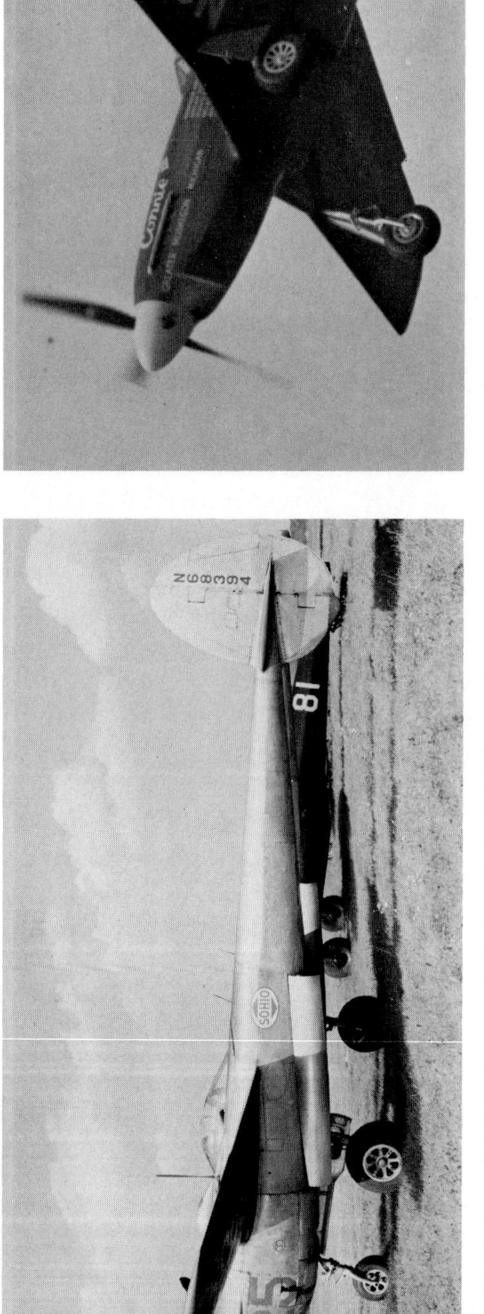

Highly modified late model P-38 flown to 2nd place in 1948 Sohio race by H. S. Gidovlenko. Wings and outboard stabilizers were clipped, superchargers removed and wells faired over, outboard radiator air scoops were removed but ship averaged 317.952 in race.   Warren M. Bodie

Cook Cleland clipped 18" off each wing tip of his F2G-1 Corsair, turned one lap at 410.366 mph in 1948 Thompson, then had air scoop tear loose and was forced out 5th lap. Loose scoop is plainly seen atop engine cowl after race.   Charles G. Mandrake

Dark blue P-51D with yellow markings with which Anson Johnson flew to a surprise 1st place in 1948 Thompson. He just fire-walled the throttle from start to finish and everything held together. Mustang was stock on outside except for paint and high gloss wax job.   *Warren M. Bodie*

Cobra II P-39Q-10 Airacobra wore a V-1710-G6 Allison in 1948, with oversize blower and 4-barrel carburetor. Special fuel and alcohol-water injection allowed manifold pressure of 113 inches of mercury at 3200 rpm and 2850 hp! Oversize glycol cooler was installed and entire exterior was smoothed with fillers and many coats of paint. Chuck Brown set new 418 mph record qualifying, lapped entire field in Thompson with one 413.097 mph lap then dropped out after 19th lap with sick engine, believing he had won race.   *Warren M. Bodie*

flying his P-51D seven laps over a 15-mile course at 362.2 mph. Bob Euker finished a close second at 362.1 mph with a P-63A. The next day he flew over the same course to win the Sohio Trophy, a restricted and handicap event this year, at 320.2 mph. John Saum tied for first but was disqualified for clipping tree tops with his P-38.

The Kendall Trophy Race replaced the previous Halle Trophy for women, and Grace Harris pushed her AT-6 into an easy first at a new high of 235 mph.

Lt. L. Thompson set the second fastest speed of this year's Nationals by winning the Indianapolis-to-Cleveland Allison Jet Trophy Race with an FJ-1 Fury, but top speed honors went to F-86 Sabre jet pilot Maj. Dick Johnson, when he set an unofficial world's record of 669.5 mph in four streaking sweeps over a 3-km course at a level below 300 feet! A faulty timing camera prevented the record from being official.

THOMPSON TROPHY

Although using 145-octane fuel and gallons of water-alcohol in their injection systems in an effort to keep their engines running wide open yet smooth and cool, seven of the ten starters dropped out of the 13th annual Thompson Trophy Race held Labor Day afternoon, September 6, but all landed safely! Dick Becker was forced out on the third lap when an air scoop atop the engine cowl shook loose, and Cook Cleland, Willoughby, Ohio, airport operator and last year's winner, went out in the fourth lap for the same reason. Both were flying Cleland-owned Corsairs. Cleland, former Navy dive bomber pilot credited with sinking a Jap ship during the war, had turned two laps at 410 mph.

Charles Brown, 24-year-old war ace of Indianapolis, who had qualified at a new high of 418 mph flying the 1946 winning Bell Cobra II, led the Thompson for 19 laps of the 20-lap 300-mile race and was going for a new record — he hit one lap at 413.1 mph. But his big Allison engine began cutting out in the 14th, and he was forced to land within seconds of victory.

Anson Johnson, 28-year-old airline pilot, roared to a surprise victory, averaging 383.8 mph in his P-51. He had raced in last year's Kendall Trophy Race in the same ship but was forced out in the fifth lap. This year he was the only Thompson starter not plagued by mechanical trouble!

Bruce Raymond took second place in another P-51, while Wilson Newhall limped in third and last in a P-63 King Cobra.

Johnson was surprised to learn that he had won the relatively slow Thompson, not knowing that Cleland and Brown had dropped out. Nearly $17,000 richer with cash prizes, Johnson recalled that last year in Cleveland he had to borrow $5 to get out of town!

John Saum dropped out 1st lap of Sohio with vapor-locked engines due to unfilled glycol coolant tanks on stock P-38L. For 1948 Saum clipped wings, removed outer stabilizers and radiator air scoops. In Sohio race he tied for 1st but was disqualified for clipping tree on safety lap while laboring over stuck fuel selector valve. Other pilots flew as low in race but Saum's Lightning had marks to prove it! Inboard wings and pilot nacelle painted white, balance of P-38 natural metal.
Charles G. Mandrake

1949 – National Air Races

David Long's PEASHOOTER *had the lines of a P-51, except for its fixed gear.*

The 1949 National Air Races, held at Cleveland, September 3–5, will probably be history's fastest over a short course — with new records set in all major events as speed reached human and mechanical endurance peaks for low-level rough-air pylon flying.

BENDIX "R" TROPHY

The piston-engined Bendix record was the first to fall when Joe DeBona, who led five planes in a racehorse start from Rosamond Dry Lake, Calif., flashed over the Cleveland Airport, 2,008 nonstop miles away, to average 470.1 mph.

Stan Reaver finished 11 minutes later to cop second place, at 450.2 mph, while Herman "Fish" Salmon, Lockheed test pilot, edged in third at 449.2 mph. All three pilots flew P-51C Mustangs, Salmon flying Paul Mantz' famous NX1202. Don Bussart, flying a DeHavilland Mosquito MK-25, had engine trouble five minutes after take-off and limped into Cleveland out of oxygen, with his right prop feathered, to take fourth and last place. Lee Cameron put down his Martin B-26C at North Platte, Neb., to repair a fuel-line, finishing after the deadline, and Vince Perron, in a Republic AT-12, was forced out in Colorado.

BENDIX JET TROPHY

In the Bendix Jet Trophy Race, Maj. Vernon Ford, in an Air Force F-84E Republic Thunderjet fighter, flashed over the California-Cleveland route in only 3 hrs. 45 min. 51 sec. to average a new high of 529.6 mph including a fuel stop. Three other Thunderjet pilots finished closely behind Ford, while a fifth was forced to land at Peoria, Ill., when his engine quit at 20,000 feet.

Little Bill Brennand won the third annual Goodyear Midget Race, flying Wittman's *Buster* to a new high of 177.3 mph. Several of the midgets would do 220 mph on a straightaway with their small 125-hp 4-cyl. engines, so as usual, many builders of commercial and sport planes were on hand to study and take notes on the racers. Wittman developed an S-shaped wood prop, which would twist to low pitch under take-off loads and twist back for more pitch in level flight, enabling him, flying his *Bonzo*, to place third in the Goodyear.

Lt. R. S. Laird, flying a McDonnell F2H-1 Banshee jet, raced 432 miles from the carrier *Midway* in the Atlantic Ocean off New York to beat three team-

On his 3rd Bendix try Joe DeBona won 1949 Bendix in this wet-wing F-6C, photo-recon version of P-51C Mustang. In 1948 Bendix in same craft, DeBona was plagued by headwinds, ran out of fuel almost within sight of Cleveland Airport. Only six aircraft took off from Rosamond, California dry lake in the only race-horse start of Bendix. DeBona set a new record 470.136 mph in his dark blue, yellow trimmed Mustang. Warren M. Bodie

Republic AT-12 Guardsman, No. 61 NX55311, was forced out of 1949 Bendix at Grand Junction, Colorado. Wet-wing AT-12 wore stock 600 hp P&W R-1813-45 engine. Top speed at altitude, 285 mph. Wingspan 41', length 27'8".   Dustin W. Carter

Paul Mantz' P-51C NX1202, flown by Herman Salmon in 1949 Bendix. Mantz won 1946 and '47 Bendix in this same aircraft and Linton Carney took 2nd place in 1948 with it. Craft wore original red and white colors for 1949.   Dustin W. Carter

Wooden Wonder, DeHavilland Mosquito, No. 81 N66313, flown by Donald E. Bussard in 1949 Bendix, again limped into Cleveland with starboard prop feathered after engine failed. Ship had been painted red for 1948, was light yellow for 1949.

Warren M. Bodie

Valley Turtle, Martin B-26C Marauder medium bomber was the only B-26 to fly in Bendix. Pilot Lee H. Cameron carried extra fuel tanks in bomb-bay to fly non-stop in 1949 try but stop for fuel line repairs brought Lee in after deadline.   Warren M. Bodie

Paul Mantz was off on an Asian aerial mapping contract so his 1948 Bendix winning P-51C, restored to original red and white paint, was flown in 1949 Bendix by Stanley Reaver, finished 2nd.   *Dustin W. Carter*

Grace Harris won the 1949 Women's Trophy Race in the same AT-6 aircraft in which she took 1st in 1948. Rules stated standard engines and two-bladed propellers for the first time. William Ong's Aircraft Corporation had improved the canopy since 1948. Grace averaged 216.7 mph in her gold-bronze ship. Six AT-6 aircraft entered Women's race, two dropped out before start because of mechanical problems.   *Peter M. Bowers*

Cosmic Wind Minnow was extensively modified for 1949 Goodyear. Low wing was moved up to mid-section and engine cowl extended to wing. Fabric covering replaced metal fuselage aft of cockpit and new tail was built. Herman Salmon placed 5th in finals with lightened craft.

Kinert

Screaming Meany, No. 40 N1210M, was first of three midgets designed and built by EAL Captain Carl Thomspon, in cockpit. Homely craft had steel prop and landing gear but qualified 24th at slow 126.5 mph in 1949, dropped out of consolation race 8th lap.

Robert B. Downey

Highly interesting midget pusher was built by Lawrence Institute of Technology students. Because of insufficient testing its pilot, Carlton Ambler, used only 70 percent power to qualify at 127.9 mph for 1949 Goodyear, Fabric covered wing had single spar.

Stephen J. Hudek

Crosswind swung pusher to right in heat take-off so pilot Ambler cut engine to prevent fouling other aircraft. He placed 8th in consolation at slow 127.9 mph. One landing wheel would have sufficed but rules called for two!

Dustin W. Carter

Steve Wittman's marvelous midget Buster won 1949 Goodyear races at Cleveland, flown by jockey Bill Brennand at a new high of 177.340 mph. Steve and Bill took four 1st places, two 2nds, two 3rds and five 5th places in Buster, then Bob Porter took one 2nd place and two 3rds in other races before the little veteran racer was retired to Smithsonian Institution after the 1954 Dansville, N.Y. midget races.   Dustin W. Carter

Midgets lined up for start of heat race at Saugus, California, near Newhall, May 8, 1949. Deerfly, No. 39, was plagued with sour engine, did not race in finals. Deerfly was built with parts from 1948 Pftttt No. 39, took 2nd place in 1949 Goodyear finals at Cleveland with Keith Sorenson flying, 176.726 mph. Keith finished 3rd at 1950 Detroit midget races with 184.576 mph.   Lockheed Aircraft Corp.

Dark red Mirage, No. 42, built by William Leighnor, was highly improved for 1949 Good-year races. Sleek cowl completely enclosed engine and bubble canopy replaced awkward windshield. Harry Ragland took 2nd in consolation race at 149.6 mph.　　　Kinert

Homely Thompson-Balbone Special No. 84, N1305V, designed and built by Ralph and Harry Thompson, had distinction of qualifying last at 126.1 mph in field of 25 midgets at Cleveland 1949, also finished last in two heat races, flown by Ralph Thompson.

Robert B. Downey

Clean and well-proportioned Lil' Spook, No. 77 N42M, flown by Steve Beville, above, turned in a disappointing 143.3 mph to qualify 20th in 1949 Goodyear. Steve cut two pylons in a heat race, finished 7th in consolation.　　　Robert B. Downey

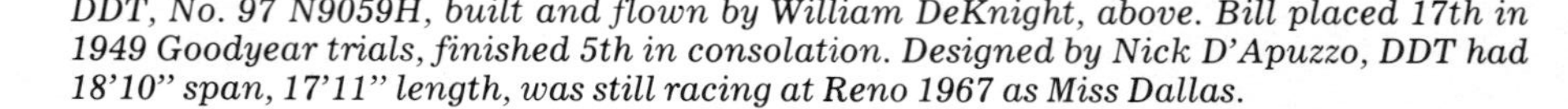

DDT, No. 97 N9059H, built and flown by William DeKnight, above. Bill placed 17th in 1949 Goodyear trials, finished 5th in consolation. Designed by Nick D'Apuzzo, DDT had 18'10" span, 17'11" length, was still racing at Reno 1967 as Miss Dallas.

Robert B. Downey

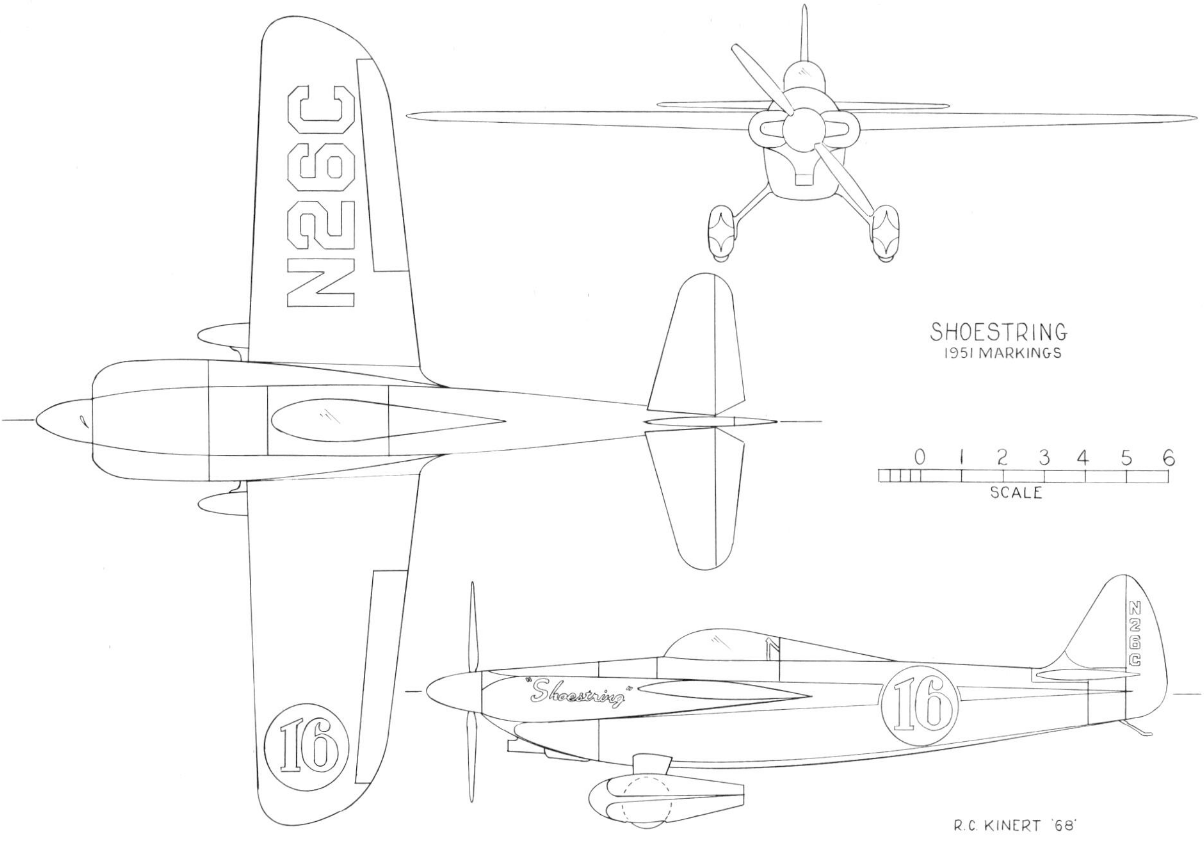

Wonderful little Shoestring, designed by Rod Kreimendahl, built by Carl and Vincent Ast. Chartreuse and red, highly waxed and polished. Bob Downey qualified now famous No. 16 seventh in 1949 Goodyear trials, took 7th in finals. Span 19', length 17'9". Shoestring has had several owners and pilots, always gave a good race. Still racing in 1967, owner-pilot Ray Cote took 3rd in finals at Reno with 200.557 mph. Dustin W. Carter

La Jollita, designed by Bill Statler, had steel tubing fuselage, fabric covering and a plywood wing. Owner James J. Kistler, above, placed 8th in 1949 Goodyear trials, took 9th and last in final event. Has raced often. — *Robert B. Downey*

Al Foss and his beautiful all-metal Jinny at Newhall 1949. Jinny was handicapped early in career by wood prop and strictly stock engine. Foss qualified No. 94 N68732 12th in 1949 Goodyear, was forced out of finals by engine. Span 17'6", length 14'11". — *Robert B. Downey*

Beetle Bomb was vastly improved for 1949 Goodyear. Lt. O. A. Smith took 4th in consolation. New tight cowl, pants and larger spinner were added. Thin 15' tapered wing, with anti-skid strips underneath, replaced thick straight wing. Ship was demolished in 8-12-50 crash. — *Dustin W. Carter*

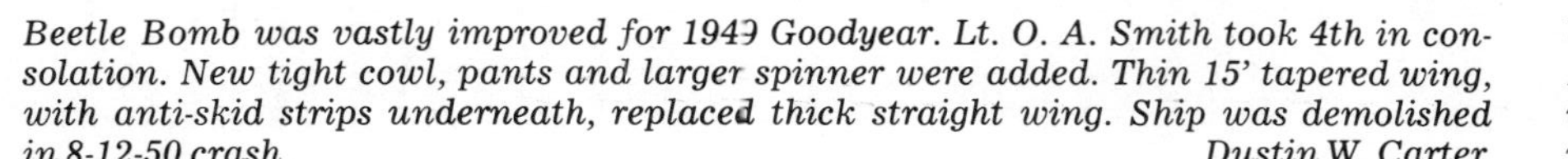

Unique P.A.R. midget pusher, designed by George Owl, built by Parks Alumni Inc. in 1950. 20' fabric covered wing had variable incidence to allow horizontal take-off. Front wheel steerable and brakes applied by pushing stick forward. Never raced, was dismantled. — *Warren M. Bodie*

Fabulous Rivets started its career in 1948 very homely in appearance, took 2nd in Goodyear consolation race at 141.5 mph. Wing was natural metal and fuselage, built up of steel tubing fabric covered, was silver. For 1949 Goodyear, above, builder-pilot Bill Falck had modified canopy, cut down rudder and fin. Pants were added and fuselage was red. Falck committed a rare error of cutting pylon in 1st heat of 1949 Goodyear, won consolation race at 162.6 mph. Span 17'8", length 17'.　　　　　　　　　　　　　　　　　　　　　　　*Warren M. Bodie*

Anson Johnson painted his P-51D Mustang yellow with red markings for 1949 Thompson. Through 1st lap of race his landing gear would only partially retract. After correcting this trouble the exhaust stacks started burning off and Anson noticed his big Rolls Royce engine was throwing off a substantial amount of oil. Oil temperature and pressure gauges checked OK but rather than risk possible loss of his Mustang Anson pulled out of race on lap 9 and landed.　　　　　　　　　　　　　　　　　　　　　　　*Peter M. Bowers*

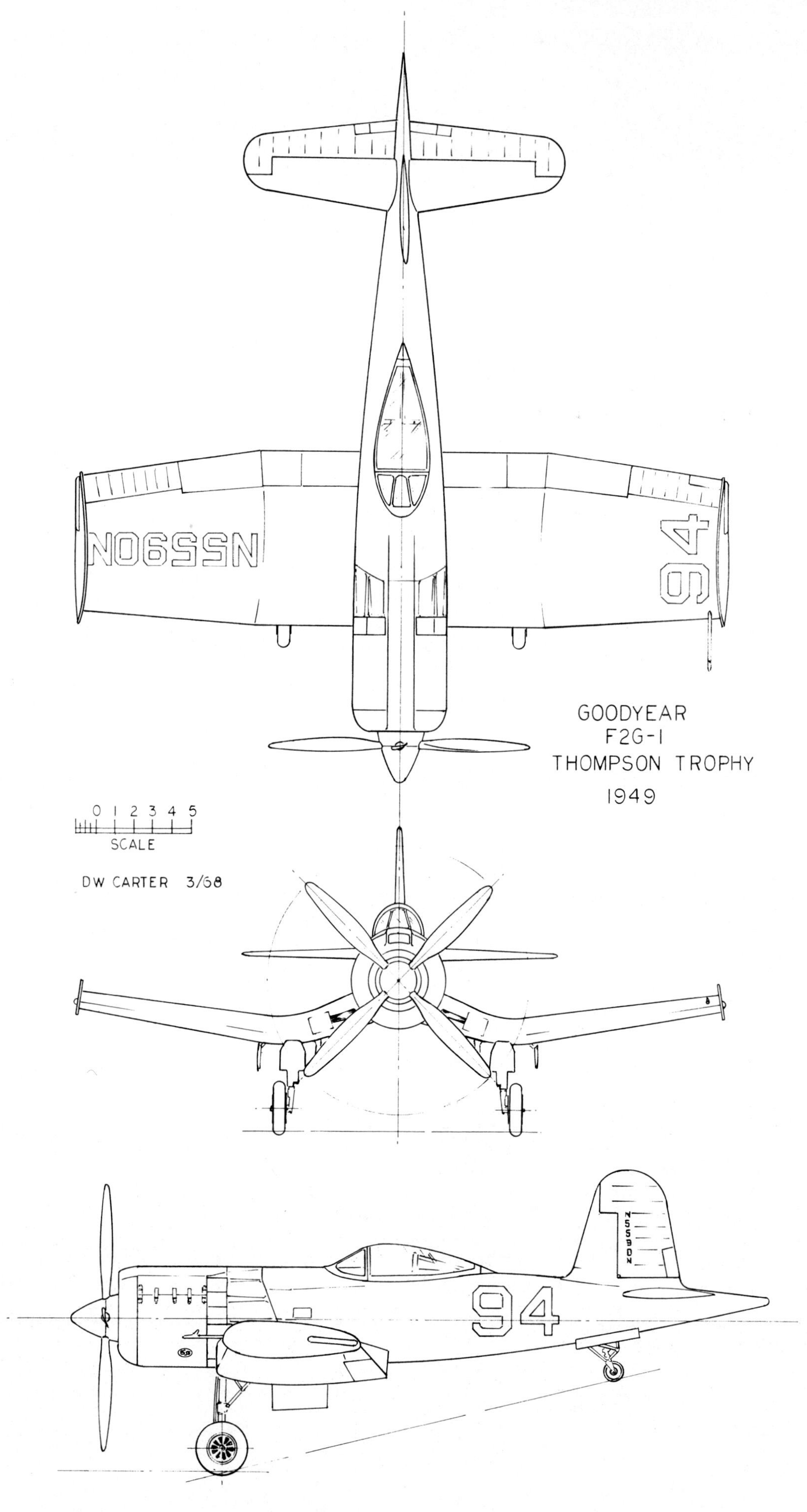

N06SSN
94
GOODYEAR
F2G-1
THOMPSON TROPHY
1949
0 1 2 3 4 5
SCALE
DW CARTER 3/68
N5580X
94

Cook Cleland qualified his F2G-1 white Corsair at 407.211 mph, won 1949 Thompson at a new high after Anson Johnson dropped out and Bill Odum crashed. Cleland figured he could pull 4000+ hp from his 28-cylinder four-row Pratt & Whitney R-4360 Wasp Major engine at 65 in. Hg. at 2800 rpm, with hydrogen peroxide injection, which he did not need in race. Wingtips had been clipped 18" each in 1948 and were cut an additional 29" on both tips for 1949, bringing span down to only 33'2"!　　　　　*Warren M. Bodie*

Wing tip clipping resulted in a greatly reduced roll rate so Cleland fitted end plates onto the tips, the first of their kind. Plates provided an increased aspect ratio, gave the big Corsair good handling with reduced drag of lowered tip losses. All three Corsair pilots wore oxygen masks as it was believed Tony Janazzo could have been overcome by fumes in 1947 Thompson. Pilots were not allowed to use ground control radio to learn standings in 1949 Thompson.　　　　　*Warren M. Bodie*

Estrellita, Art Williams Special N44183, was extremely clean midget, had exhaust thrust augmentation. Kip Mone qualified Estrellita in 2nd place for 1949 Goodyear events with 181.6 mph, took 2nd in finals. Wing span was 19'6", length 16'5". Craft was crash-destroyed 9-4-50.
Dustin W. Carter

Airline pilot Anson Johnson removed oil and glycol radiators and scoop from belly of his P-51D, relocated radiators inside wing. Air intakes were then built into wing leading edge. Radical changes suggested trouble but radiators worked well at high speed.
Charles G. Mandrake

Flying his first race, Benjamin McKillan Jr. took off quickly in 1949 Tinnerman Race, gradually increased lead in F2G-1 Corsair to win at 386.069 mph, turned a 396.6 mph lap. Ben said, after race, "It was rougher than hell up there!"
Kinert

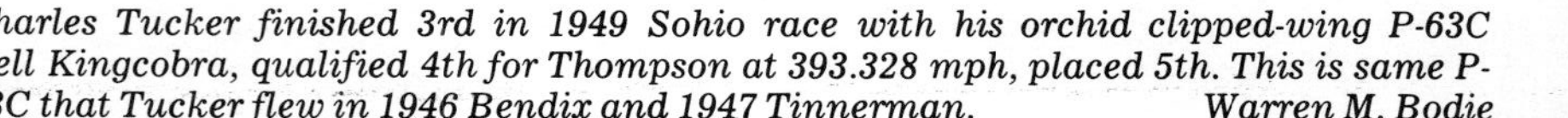

Charles Tucker finished 3rd in 1949 Sohio race with his orchid clipped-wing P-63C Bell Kingcobra, qualified 4th for Thompson at 393.328 mph, placed 5th. This is same P-63C that Tucker flew in 1946 Bendix and 1947 Tinnerman.
Warren M. Bodie

Ben McKillan's red and white F2G-1 Corsair was 1st off in 1949 Thompson, closely followed by Cook Cleland's Corsair. Ben held pole position for Thompson start as he made fastest time on first day of trials, qualified 3rd fastest at 396.280 mph. Ben led for two laps, was overtaken by Cleland and then Ron Pucket's Corsair, finished 3rd. One blade of McKillan's 4-bladed prop was painted white, giving effect of a loafing engine in race.
Warren M. Bodie

Flight Lieut. J. H. G. McArthur, RCAF, qualified his natural-metal finish Supermarine Mk XIV Spitfire at 370.110 mph as alternate starter for Thompson. His Spitfire, No. 80 CF GMZ, a direct descendent of the 1931 Supermarine S-6B racing seaplane, was flown stock in 1949 Tinnerman, placed 3rd. Five-bladed propeller was necessary to absorb power from big V-12 Rolls Royce Griffin 65 which delivered 2,035 hp at 2750 rpm.
Warren M. Bodie

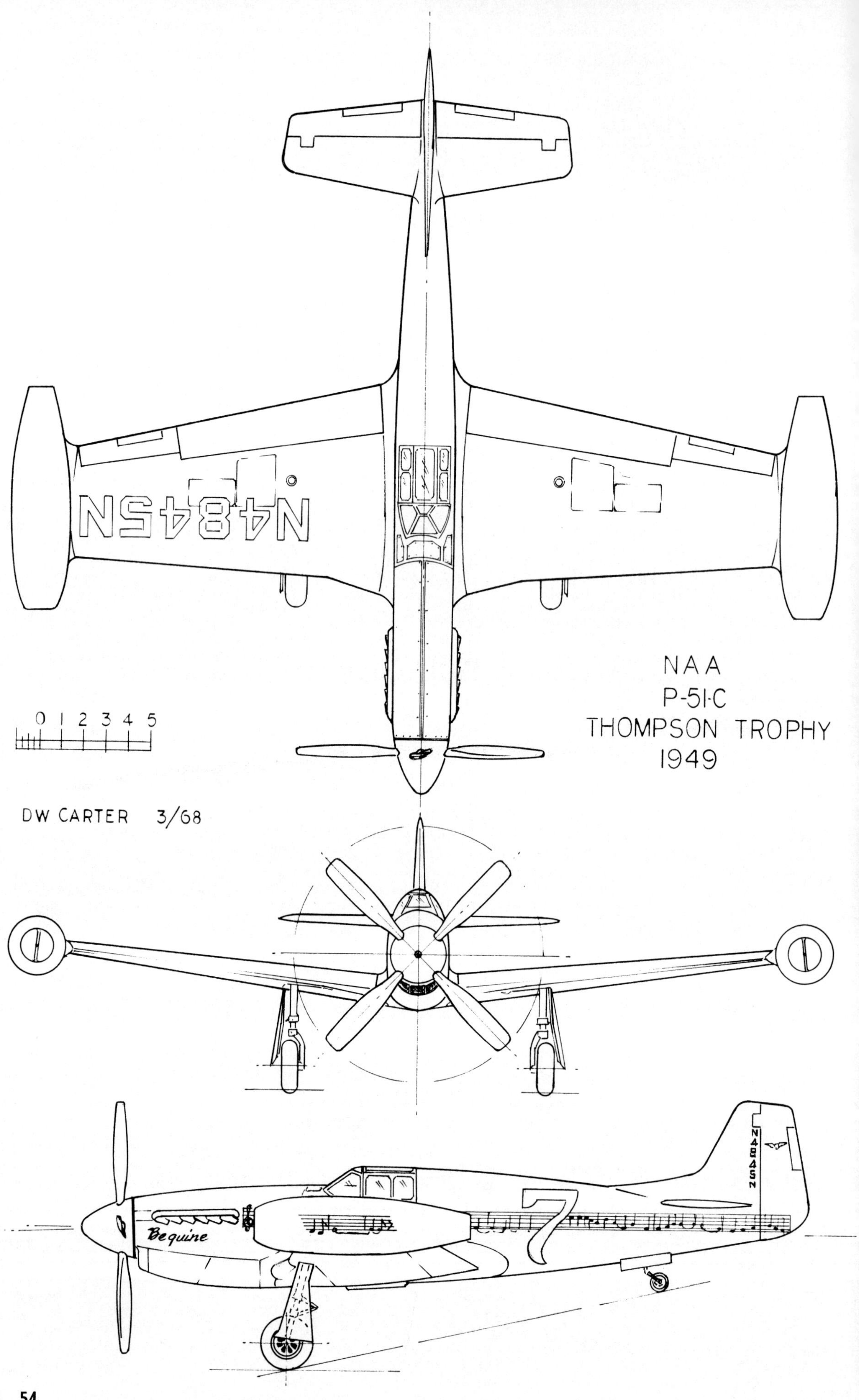

N4845N
NAA
P-51-C
THOMPSON TROPHY
1949
0 1 2 3 4 5
DW CARTER 3/68
N4845N
7
Bequine

Bill Odum's 1949 dark green A-36 (P-51C) Mustang Beguine had belly radiators moved to wing tip nacelles. 20-30 inches of each tip and aileron were clipped to make room for coolant radiator. Combination of radiator relocation, reduced wing area and end-plate effect reduced drag considerably and radiator heat added thrust. Beguine utilized a "one of a kind" extremely thin section Hamilton Standard paddle-bladed propeller especially made for tests at NAA during WWII. Speed increment was about 12 mph.   Dustin W. Carter

NNA engineers worked on Cochran-owned Beguine as outside project. A brand new Merlin engine and accessories were installed and engine reworked to turn 3400 rpm. Bill Odum qualified Beguine at 405.565 mph and engine was not open. Odum flew in 1949 Sohio Race to gain pylon practice, cruised to an easy 1st place. Ship was reportedly the fastest piston-engined aircraft to date and, except for tragic over-control piloting error, Odum would probably have won 1949 Thompson as he was closing fast.   Warren M. Bodie

mates into Cleveland at 549 mph. This speed was soon bested by Lt. Walt Rew, California National Guard pilot, who won the third annual Allison Jet Trophy Race by flying his F-80C from Indianapolis to Cleveland at 594.8 mph.

The Sohio Trophy was won over eight other contestants by Bill Odom at 388.4 mph. Odom, one of the most famous civilian pilots since Lindbergh and Wiley Post by dint of his solo flight around the world in 73 hrs. 5 min. with a Douglas A-26 and a solo nonstop 5,000-mile flight from Hawaii to New Jersey in a Beech Bonanza, held his engine back in the Sohio Race with an eye on the Thompson. Undoubtedly one of the fastest piston-engined planes in the world, the Jackie Cochran owned P-51C flown by Odom in his first pylon race was fitted with wing-tip radiators in place of the regular air scoop. However, clipping off the wing tips and ailerons 25% to make room for the radiators had raised the stick forces to critical values.

The Tinnerman Trophy Race was won by Ben McKillen, who bested six other entries in his F2G-1 Corsair at 386.1 mph.

Grace Harris copped the Kendall Trophy Race again, averaging 216.7 mph in the stock AT-6 event.

THOMPSON JET TROPHY

Three North American F-86A Sabre fighters took off at 3:35, Labor Day afternoon, September 5, to fly the Thompson Jet Trophy Race, 10 laps around a 15-mile circular course. Breaking all closed-course race records, Capt. Bruce Cunningham averaged 586.2 mph from take-off, and Capt. Martin Johansen posted a fastest lap of 635.444 mph in taking second place. Capt. Vern Henderson pulled out after a steep pylon turn broke his seat to the floor and, in a crouching position, brought his jet in for a safe landing.

Since the course was flown in a circle because of the high speeds, it is obvious that nearly 20 actual air miles were flown in covering the 15-mile course. The F-86 was flying at precisely sonic speed (speed of sound) in full view of 80,000 spectators! That both jet jockeys exceeded the craft's placarded critical Mach number of 0.95 (Mach 1 is speed of sound) was evidenced by the extensive and dangerous damage done to Capt. Cunningham's ship. He managed to cross the finish line, zoom into the air, and make a perfect landing near 200 mph, with the outer two-thirds of each elevator shredded away, tips of the horizontal stabilizers "chewed," and the fuselage skin badly wrinkled at the nozzle! Capt. Johansen lost a 10 by 16 inch left-wing inspection door, causing tremendous wing drag, but he too landed safely.

Flying the small racecourse in a steady bank, the F-86 fighters imposed a constant 6–7G's on the pilots, an acceleration once considered maximum even for test pilots. Highly turbulent air gave sharp gust loads of 8–9G's. The race could not have been flown without anti-G suits, which were also worn by the piston Thompson pilots. All Thompson pilots (piston and jet divisions) used oxygen throughout their race, confiding that the oxygen gave them the "lift" necessary to overcome fatigue on the gruelling course.

THOMPSON "R" TROPHY

With three years of post-war racing experience to fall back on, the big piston-engined racers showed up at Cleveland with many startling innovations. Engines were stepped up greatly, all were fitted with fluid injection systems and their gas tanks were filled with 130–170 octane fuel. In addition to Odom's P-51 already noted, Anson Johnson replaced his P-51D Prestone radiator air scoop from under the fuselage into the wings, where the machine guns had been located. Cook Cleland's big Corsair was the most modified of all. He had clipped four feet off each wing tip bringing the span down to 33 feet, and had added wing-tip plates to increase his roll rate and reduce vortex. He had also added a big prop spinner, and the prop itself was sleekly chromium plated to increase performance.

Ten civilian-owned fighters, three Corsairs, six Mustangs, and one Kingcobra took off at 4:40 P.M. in the Thompson "R" Race — eight finished. Ben McKillen's big Corsair was first around the scattering pylon and led the lap, with all planes flying below 200 feet — a split second from the earth. Entering the second lap, it was McKillen leading, Cook Cleland second in his clipped-wing Corsair, then Bill Odom, who had gotten off seventh in the race-horse start, already in third place with his fast P-51C. Then Odom, who should never have been in the race because of insufficient racing practice, over-turned pylon 2, high-speed stalled to the right when he tried to get back onto the course, and flipped over and exploded into a house, killing Odom, a mother, and her 13-month-old boy.

Ben McKillen led through the second lap; then Cleland, flying 386 mph, and Ron Puckett, also in a Corsair, flying 379 mph, pulled by McKillen. Cleland gradually stepped up his speed until on lap five he hit 406.4 mph, though not once using his newly installed hydrogen peroxide injector system, as he slowly forged ahead to win at a new record speed of 397.1 mph, 19 seconds and two miles ahead of Puckett's 393.5 mph. McKillen finished third to make it 1-2-3 for the big Corsair F2G-1's, whose 28-cyl. engines pulled 4,000 + hp and were over twice the cubic inch displacement of the liquid-cooled V-12 engined racers. All three Corsair's were in astonishingly good condition after their fast rough-air race, without oil trails or bent skin, but some control surface fabric had been torn away.

1951 – National Air Races

Held at Detroit, Michigan, August 18 and 19, after having skipped 1950, the 1951 National Air Races were reminiscent of the early 20's races, for once again the military predominated, both in numbers and speed.

One of the most complete public displays of this nation's air power yet shown was a top drawing card. More than 200,000 people jammed highways leading to Detroit's Wayne Major Airport. There were flight demonstrations by the services, and the Navy conducted a climb contest between an F8F Grumman Bearcat prop-driven fighter and an F2H-1 McDonnell Banshee twin-jet fighter. The Bearcat, holder of the world's record for a climb to 10,000 feet from a standing start (less than one minute), lived up to its record. The Banshee did overtake the Bearcat somewhere above 10,000 though, and then quickly climbed to 45,000 feet before leveling off.

BENDIX JET TROPHY

Highlighting the first day was the arrival of the Bendix racers. Seven jet bombers and fighters took off from Muroc Dry Lake, Calif., Saturday morning, and Col. Keith Compton, flying an F-86A Sabre jet, flew the 1919.6 miles to Detroit in only 3 hrs. 27 min. 56 sec., including two 6-minute touch-downs at Denver and Omaha for fuel, and set a new record of 553.8 mph for the event. Second place went to Col. Emmett Davis, who piloted an F-84E Thunderjet nonstop into Detroit, averaging 534.9 mph. Two B-45C Tornado 4-engined jet bombers finished third and fourth, also flying nonstop.

After the race, Col. Compton said that most of his flight had been made at 45,000 feet, and in letting down from Chicago he had exceeded 700 mph in slightly turbulent air — when his ship approached the speed of sound, it had a tendency to "curl up" — go out of control because of shock-wave disturbances. All pilots in the race rationed their fuel closely, and Compton landed with less than 25 gallons of fuel — about three to five minutes flying time!

The new cross-country speed of the Bendix was soon broken, however, when Capt. C. F. Bleese led three other F-86A Sabre pilots into Detroit from Chicago in 21 minutes to win the General Electric Trophy with 670.2 mph, the fastest speed of the Nationals. The four jets flew across the finish line so close together it was first believed they were flying in formation!

The Allison Trophy Race, from Detroit to Indianapolis and back, was flown on Sunday by three F-84E Republic Thunderjets and was won by Lt. William Blaisley, who averaged 580.5 mph — slower by 14 mph than the 1949 record for the 500-mile course.

In a trial run, while preparing for a Sunday assault on the world's speed record over a 100-km (62.14 mile) course, veteran combat pilot Col. Fred Ascani had, on Friday, streaked his F-86E Sabre around the course at a record-breaking 635.411 mph. The old record was 605.2 mph, set by John Douglas Derry of Great Britain in a DeHavilland Sapphire jet, April 12, 1948.

THOMPSON JET TROPHY

Then on Sunday afternoon Col. Ascani took his orange-nosed F-86E off to fly the same course in quest

Red and cream Lil Monster, N1961M, designed and built by Curtis Pitts, began long and successful career by placing 4th in 1950 Continental finals at Miami with Phil Quigley. It next placed 4th in 1951 Continental finals at Detroit with Bill Brennand.
Dustin W. Carter

Metallic blue Mr D, designed and built by Robert Mayer had nice lines but Hank Orlowski could only get 160 mph in qualifying at Detroit 1951. Ship never raced again. Note P-51-type bubble canopy, Wittman gear.
Dustin W. Carter

Little Gem, built and flown by James Miller, first wore license N56231, now N14J. Long and successful career began by cutting pylon in 1949 Goodyear consolation, took 4th in 1950 Detroit consolation. Grey and red ship was heavily damaged in 1951 crash, rebuilt.
Dustin W. Carter

Miss Cosmic Wind, N36C, was 4th and last Cosmic built, 1949. Although incorporating best features of Cosmics 3, 4 and 5, and built like 1949 modified Minnow, Miss Cosmic weighed 602 lbs. empty, was never very successful though still racing in 1967.
Dustin W. Carter

All metal Petit Special No. 18, N5715N, built by George Petit in 1948, appeared at Detroit in 1951, did not race. Deflector plates were added to tips of wire braced straight wing to improve handling but ship was still awkward, and drive shaft gave trouble.
Robert F. Pauley

Dark and light green Mr. Zip, No. 27 N32C, was built in 1951 by Paul Schaupp, had fiberglass fuselage. Pilot Robert Pflieger could wrest but 176 mph from Mr. Zip in 1951 Goodyear heats at Detroit. Photo taken at San Diego races, 1956.
Dustin W. Carter

Beautiful Loving Special No. 64, N351C, designed and built under supervision of Neal Loving, Wayne School of Aeronautics. All wood craft featured inverted gull wing to which landing gear was directly attached. Spinner trouble kept Neal out of 1951 Goodyear.
Robert B. Downey

North American F-86E Sabre in which Col. Fred J. Ascani, USAF, set 100 km (62 mi.) world's closed course speed record of 635. 411 mph at Detroit, August 18, 1950. Sabre was flown stock and machine gun blast tubes were even left untaped.
Warren M. Bodie

Former Foss Jinny appeared at Detroit 1951 considerably modified by pilot Keith Sorenson. Renamed Little Mike, it had a shorter wing, cleaner carburetor air scoop, wore pants and was painted blue and white, with gold stripes. Clean up paid off as Keith took 3rd in Continental finals. Span 17'6", length 14'11", empty weight 535 lbs.
Dustin W. Carter

of the famed Thompson Trophy, which he won with a new Thompson high of 628.7 mph, but he failed to better his Friday speed, due to slightly turbulent air and poor visibility. Ascani was the only Thompson entry. The Air Force had, after the 1949 Jet Thompson, decreed that there would be no more competitive low-level pylon races between their planes. The Air Force and Navy had earlier been barred from competing against each other.

The midget plane race, now sponsored by Continental Motors, was the only civilian race and the only pylon race this year, but John Paul Jones tooled his *Shoestring* racer 15 laps around the 2½-mile course in the finals, to a new record of 197.2 mph. Jones had also won the Continental Trophy at De-

troit's 1950 International Air Fair in the only race held there. Veteran pilot-designer Sylvester "Steve" Wittman breezed in with 192.2 mph to take second place with his *Bonzo*, while Keith Sorenson finished third in revamped *Jinny*, now named *Little Mike*. In qualifying, Jones had made 199.8 mph, a remarkable speed for the tiny 2½-mile rectangular course. Indeed, the fastest midgets would give the old pre-war II Greve racers a battle, though their engines were but two-fifths as large as the Greve jobs!

Three records had been set in the first all-jet entry into the major events, and the Nationals' future seemed assured, with the promise of major Navy participation in the next meet.

The super-sleek SHOESTRING *, winner of the 1951 Continental Trophy finals.*
It was flown by John Paul Jones at an average speed of 197.2 mph.

1964–National Championship Air Races

Air racing was kept alive in the U.S. from 1949 to 1960 by a dedicated group of midget racing plane fanatics, who would not be denied their sport.

Goodyear Tire and Rubber Company sponsored the first midget class races in 1947, specifications for the class being drawn up by the Professional Race Pilots' Association, Art Chester President, at meetings after WWII.

The Continental C-85 engine of 188-cubic-inch displacement, which delivered 85 horsepower at 2600 rpm, was chosen to power the midgets and maximum displacement was set at 190 cu. in. Rigid construction rules were made—fixed landing gear, fixed propeller, exacting visibility factors, 66 square feet minimum wing area and empty weight was to be not less than 500 pounds. Flight tests were also imposed.

Goodyear sponsored the midgets from 1947 through 1949, then passed the ball to Continental Motors for they were the main beneficiaries in the midget boom. Continental sponsored the midgets from 1948 through 1954, then dropped ball for various sponsors to pick up. The Continental C-85 engine had been improved, through the pressures and demands of air racing, to the point where the engine now delivered 115 hp at more than 3200 rpm, with no appreciable weight increase.

Pilot-designer-builders, not to be deterred, continued to build their tiny monoplanes and raced where and when they could for peanuts or dollars, and sometimes more peanuts were promised than produced.

On the tiny midgets raced from the hot, dry air of Saugus, California, through the hot, humid and rough air of the midwest and to the eastern reaches of this broad land—then back to the cool sea air of San Diego.

Many race miles were safely flown by the mighty midgets around their designated 2½-mile aerial saucers in full view of avid spectators. Accidents were few, but at 200 mph, nearly always fatal.

Air racing doldrums set in and no races were flown in 1961 through 1963. Then, in the winter months of 1963-64, a group of racing enthusiasts headed by rancher-pilot Bill Stead of Reno, Nevada, formulated plans for a re-birth of air racing, Cleveland style.

The first major air races in fifteen years took place at Sky Ranch, north of Reno, Nevada, September 12-20, 1964. There was a transcontinental race for unlimited class piston-engined aircraft, pylon races for homebuilt single-seat biplanes, midget monoplanes and an unlimited class race for piston-engined aircraft. There was even a Women's race, flown in Piper Cherokees, won by Irene Leverton at a respectable 143.46 mph clip. To round out the program there was ballooning, aerobatics, soaring and parachuting. The first official U.S. National Aerobatic Championships were held at Reno and winner was Duane Cole, who flew his red and cream clipped-wing Taylorcraft through intricate maneuvers to perfection.

CROSS COUNTRY RACE

Revival of unlimited cross-country racing for piston-engined aircraft, held September 12, drew eight entries and all were North American P-51D Mustangs. The race, Harold's Club Transcontinental Trophy Dash, sponsored by a Reno gambling casino, was won by Wayne Adams, who flew the only wet-wing aircraft in the race, against headwinds from St. Petersburg,

Chocolate brown P-51D wet-wing Mustang in which Air National Guard officer Wayne Adams won 1964 Harold's Club Trophy. Photo taken at Reno after race.
Robert F. Pauley

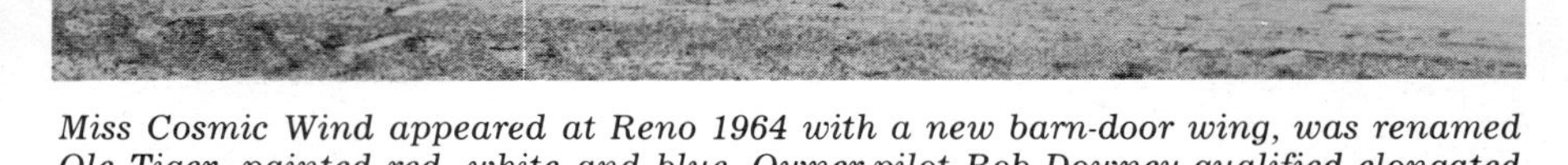

Red and white Miss San Bernardino, No. 31, built 1949 by Jim Kistler as Skeeter, was rebuilt under supervision of pilot-instructor Arthur Scholl, by San Bernardino Valley College students. Art qualified 4th at Reno, 175.193 mph, took 3rd in finals.
Robert F. Pauley

Miss Cosmic Wind appeared at Reno 1964 with a new barn-door wing, was renamed Ole Tiger, painted red, white and blue. Owner-pilot Bob Downey qualified elongated craft at 184.27 mph, placed 4th in finals. Photo is start of 1st heat race. Robert F. Pauley

Cassutt Special I, designed and built by Tom Cassutt in 1954, raced often. Named Jersey Skeeter at one time craft won at Ft. Wayne 1958, was later destroyed in hangar fire, but replicas are available in plan or kit form. Many are racing. Dustin W. Carter

Orange and black Lil' Rascal Quarton-Cassutt was first midget built from purchased plans. Jerry Quarton built ship just in time for 1964 Reno races, took 5th in finals, made history in spectacular mid-air collision with Nick Jones' ship at 1966 Washington Nationals.
Robert F. Pauley

Lockheed test pilot Darryl Greenamyer appeared at Reno 1964 with Grumman F8F-2 Bearcat No. 1 which was stock in appearance except for sealed landing flaps and cut down canopy. Qualified 2nd with 359.51 mph, won heat 1B at 356.58 mph, placed 4th in finals but was disqualified in both cases for failing to land at race site. N1111L was in natural aluminum finish, wore Goldwater elephant on engine cowl sides. Robert F. Pauley

Beautiful fiberglassed white Knight Twister was built by Clyde Parsons from purchased plans first made available in 1929. Clyde has been flying ship for 9 years, doing aerobatics at air shows, holds distinction of winning first biplane class races, Reno 1964. Twisters were ruled out in 1966 with new minimum wing area regulations, 75 sq. ft. and 12 lb./sq./ft. wing loading. Wing area of Twister was about same as midgets, had 15' span. Photo of Clyde at Reno 1965. Charles Rogers/Clyde Parsons

Red trimmed aluminum RCAF surplus P-51D Mustang Phoebe II took 4th place in transcontinental race, was handicapped by drag of external fuel tanks. Pilot Dick Snyder, FAA employee, made two fuel stops. Race No. 45.   *Robert F. Pauley*

Stan Hoke finished 6th in 1964 XC race in his father's Cavalier, modified 2-place P-51D Mustang, lost 2 hours refueling at USAF base when weather prevented planned Albuquerque stop. Red and white ship wore two large pylon tanks under wings.   *Robert F. Pauley*

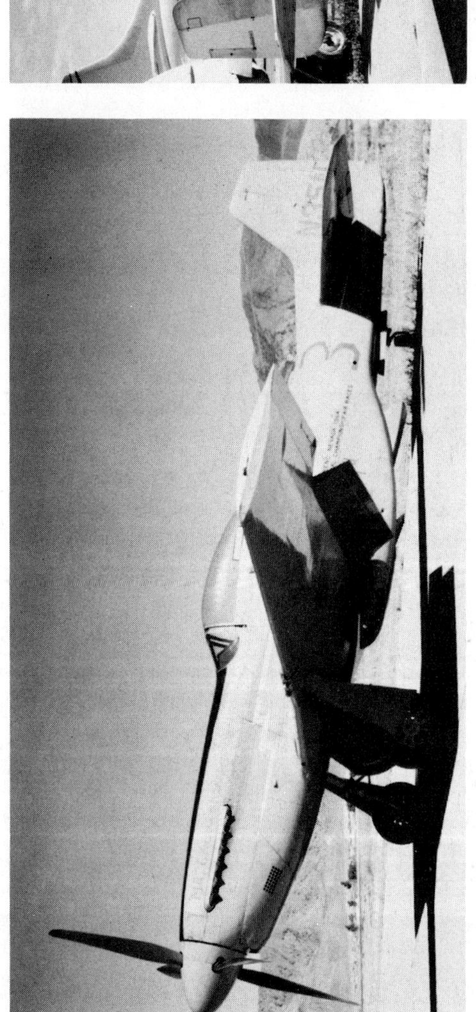

Mr. Choppers, light blue-green NAA P-51D Mustang, purchased as RCAF war surplus. C. E. Crosby Jr. finished 3rd in 1964 Harold's transcontinental race at 296.03 mph despite 3 fuel stops. Qualified at 316.89 mph for closed course event, did not race.   *Robert F. Pauley*

Jack Shaver flew No. 69, a two-place Cavalier, modified P-51D Mustang, to 5th place in 1964 cross-country despite 1½ hr. Oklahoma City delay when starter failed and engine had to be hand-propped. Ship was red and white with black trim.   *Robert F. Pauley*

Seattle Miss, a stock P-51D Mustang, was aluminum with black and yellow trim. Ben Hall of Seattle qualified 5th at Reno 1964 with 344.49 mph, placed 2nd in two heats, 4th in finals and standings with 344.45 mph, indicating full throttle effort.
Robert F. Pauley

E. D. Weiner was forced out of 1964 XC race with his bronze P-51D Mustang by weather, qualified 8th and last for pylon races at 288.40 mph, dropped out of heat 1A with oil-cooler door trouble, took 6th in final with slow 282.72 mph.   Robert F. Pauley

Little Mike, former Foss Jinny, appeared at Reno 1964. Out-classed little all-metal beauty was painted dark blue with white and gold trim. FAA inspector James M. "Mike" Dewey qualified 5th at 172.38 mph, dropped out 1st heat with engine trouble.
Robert F. Pauley

Dark blue, white trimmed stock F8F-2 Grumman Bearcat, No. 10 N7827C. Cmdr. Walter Ohlrich, USN, qualified 4th at Reno 1964 with 351.29 mph, took 2nd in heat 1A at 339.55 mph, 3rd in 2A with 337.41 mph, 5th in finals and standing with 343.43 mph.
Robert F. Pauley

Florida, to Reno with one refueling stop, averaging only 318.88 mph.

Paul Mantz had been the first race pilot to use the then military secret wet-wing principal, wherein the wing itself was sealed to retain fuel. Alexander P. DeSeversky originally thought up the idea and designed it into his aircraft before and during WWII. Several of the aircraft flown in the cross-country later qualified, raced in the unlimited closed course races.

BIPLANE RACES

Ten little single-seat home-built biplanes showed up to race in this event, the first of its kind in many years. Two heats of five planes each were flown, and the fastest five flew in the final event on September 14. Big 220-pound Clyde Parsons squeezed into his beautiful little fiberglassed 620-pound white and gold Knight Twister to take his heat—and the final race in which he averaged 144.57 mph after being slow in the race-horse start. Tom Shannon, in another Knight Twister was not far behind at 143.41 mph. The biplanes flew the same short 2.375-mile racecourse as the midgets did, in full view of the spectactors, ten laps being flown for a total 23.75 miles.

MIDGET RACES

Only six midget racers showed up for the revival of this class race and two of the craft were from the east. Sixty-year-old veteran race pilot Steve Wittman flew his 16-year-old *Bonzo* 1700 miles from his Winnabago County Wisconsin Airport to Reno in one day-nine hours at an average 186 mph, and brought along a suitcase, tool kit and an extra prop as well!

Wittman was first off in the race-horse start finals on September 18, but *Bonzo's* engine was tired after its long cross-country trek and Bob Porter, flying a beautiful race in his very fast *Little Gem*, quickly overtook *Bonzo* and went on to win the 23.75-mile race at 193.44 mph. Bob Downey in his *Cosmic Wind* and Art Scholl's *Miss San Bernardino* put on a battle royal for third place with Art's speed finally taking

over. Jerry Quarton and his new Cassutt racer finished last at 162.86 mph.

UNLIMITED CLOSED COURSE RACE

The dirt runway scratched out of the high desert was too narrow for a race-horse start, so the four preliminary and final unlimited heat races were made from flying starts. Five North American P-51D Mustangs and three Grumman F8F-2 Bearcats qualified for the unlimited races. Except for their colors, all the ex-fighter planes were stock in outward appearance except one, an F8F-2 Bearcat owned and flown by Darryl Greenamyer. The canopy had been cut down considerably and a small headrest added.

Points were awarded for each heat race; so, unfortunately for the race fans, Bob Love in the fastest aircraft of the races, wisely throttled back his hopped-up Mustang to win the final heat at a slow 366.82 mph. Love had cut two pylons in one of the previous heat races, so Mira Slovak who had qualified his white Smirnoff F8F-2 Bearcat at 356.29 mph and who had taken second in the final heat race at 355.52 mph, was awarded first in the unlimited final standings. Bob Love, who had qualified his snow-white Bardahl Special at 395.46 mph and turned 405 mph in one heat race, flew a P-51D Mustang that was practically stock in outward appearance, but his Rolls Royce Merlin engine had been highly modified by Ron Musson and his Bardahl crew. The Merlin now delivered an estimated 3400 hp at 110 inches manifold pressure!

Darryl Greenamyer, who had sealed his landing flaps to further streamline his natural finish Grumman F8F-2, found visibility too poor from his cut-down canopy, plus the critical weight-balance of his Bearcat too tricky to land on the Sky Ranch runway. He chose the wide runways at Reno Municipal Airport for his take-offs and landings, thus was disqualified from the final standings. Over 100,000 people turned out for the nine-day return of major air racing and even grander race meets were to follow.

Famous Little Gem appeared at Reno 1964 painted black and white. Airline pilot Bob Porter qualified 1st at 200.70 mph, won final event. Builder Jim Miller holds 209.56 mph one lap record for midgets. Span 14'1", length 16'8", empty weight 535 lbs.

Robert F. Pauley

1965 was one of the busiest years for air racing in the annals of the sport, with major air races being held near Los Angeles, Reno and Las Vegas; home-built biplane and midget races at St. Petersburg, and midget races at Palm Springs, California. To tell the whole story would fill a volume in itself so one must, as usual, refer to the complete charts in the back of this book.

St. Petersburg International Aviation Exposition

The first air races of 1965 were held at St. Petersburg, March 22-23, and featured the baby biplanes and mighty midget monoplanes. There was bad weather all around St. Pete and it was threatening there—and the Sebring Grand Prix was held nearby, preventing a big turn out. But a good air show was seen by the enthusiasts who did appear. Unlimited piston-engined races were scheduled but persistent poor weather kept all but two racing ex-fighters from getting into St. Petersburg, so Chuck Lyford and Jimmy Leeward flew their P-51D's around the 8-mile course for the spectors to view.

Only five little home-built biplanes made it into St. Pete and Pat Ledford of Homestead, Florida, took both preliminaries and the final heat race, March 28, flying his Pitts 137.7 mph to take the final. Five midget racers made it into St. Petersburg by auto trailer! Fly-in race pilots like Steve Wittman were unable to cut through the thick weather.

Bob Downey in *Little Gem*, now *Ole Tiger*, won both the preliminary heats, while Bill Falck and *Rivets* loafed through the heats with two third places.

The final event of the 190 midgets was probably the greatest race in their history. For all 12 laps, Bob Downey and Bill Falck fought for first place with the lead changing several times. The finish by stop watch was a tie at 200.75 mph, but all judges said Falck's *Rivets* had won by a few feet. Bob Porter in elongated *Miss Cosmic Wind No. 6* and John Martin in *Shoestring* had battled throughout the race for third place with Porter edging *Shoestring* by only .73 mph at 185.98 mph. Roy Berry brought up the rear in *Mr. Zip* at 168.62 mph.

Los Angeles National Air Races

Air races were scheduled for May 29, 30 and 31, 1965, at Fox Field, Lancaster California, but due to high winds and dusty sands blowing over Mojave Desert, the final day's events were postponed until the following Sunday, June 6.

Chief timer for the races was Jimmy Haislip, while Tony LeVier was Chief Judge—both were air racing greats.

BIPLANE RACES

Eleven little homebuilts originally qualified for their class race. Clyde Parsons and his Reno winning Knight Twister set an unofficial record of 152.4 mph in one of the heat races. When the rescheduled biplane race took place June 6, Clyde was off on an aerobatics commitment, three other fast qualifiers declined the long flight back to Lancaster, while aerobating pilot Don Pittman dropped out to save his engine. Total prize money was scarce!

The tiny biplanes, with their lower wing loadings, suffered more than the midgets in the rough, gusty air, so the final race went to Bob Harendeen flying a Pitts Special at only 126.5 mph. He had won a heat race at 139.1 mph earlier. Don Jackson was sixth and last with his Miniplane at a slow 99.6 mph!

MIDGET RACES

Bill Falck, who had won the midget races at St. Petersburg earlier in the year with his little *Rivets* at 200.8 mph, finishing a few feet ahead of Bob Downey and his Miller *Little Gem*, did not appear at Lancaster. This left the field to eight western pilots and Steve Wittman, who again flew *Bonzo* over the plains and mountains from Wisconsin. As only nine midgets appeared at Lancaster, the pilots were asked to fly two-heat races each to fill in the program, making four-heat races, a consolation race in which two slow finalist contenders were allowed to join, and then the final race.

Postponed until June 6 because of weather, the midget finals turned out to be quite a race. Bud Jury and his *Grey Ghost* was first off, but was quickly overtaken on the first lap by Bob Downey, who flew nonchalantly through rough air and prop wash alike. Steve Wittman had fuel problems so, between trying to adjust his mixture control and avoid the traffic, he cut three pylons and was disqualified. Art Scholl, in *Miss San Bernardino* battled Bud Jury for second place and managed to finish about 300 feet ahead of Jury.

Bob Downey and *Little Gem* went on to win handily at 195.0 mph, while Mike Dewey and his beautiful *Little Mike* slipped by Wittman to take fourth, and Bill Stead in his heavy *Cosmic Wind, Miss Reno*, finished fifth. Bob Terrill was last at 153 mph.

UNLIMITED CLOSED COURSE RACE

Eleven brightly painted surplus fighters flew into Fox Field to race in the Unlimited class but a Vought-designed Corsair, an FG-1D, was lost when its pilot, Lynn Winney, crashed fatally while practicing low over

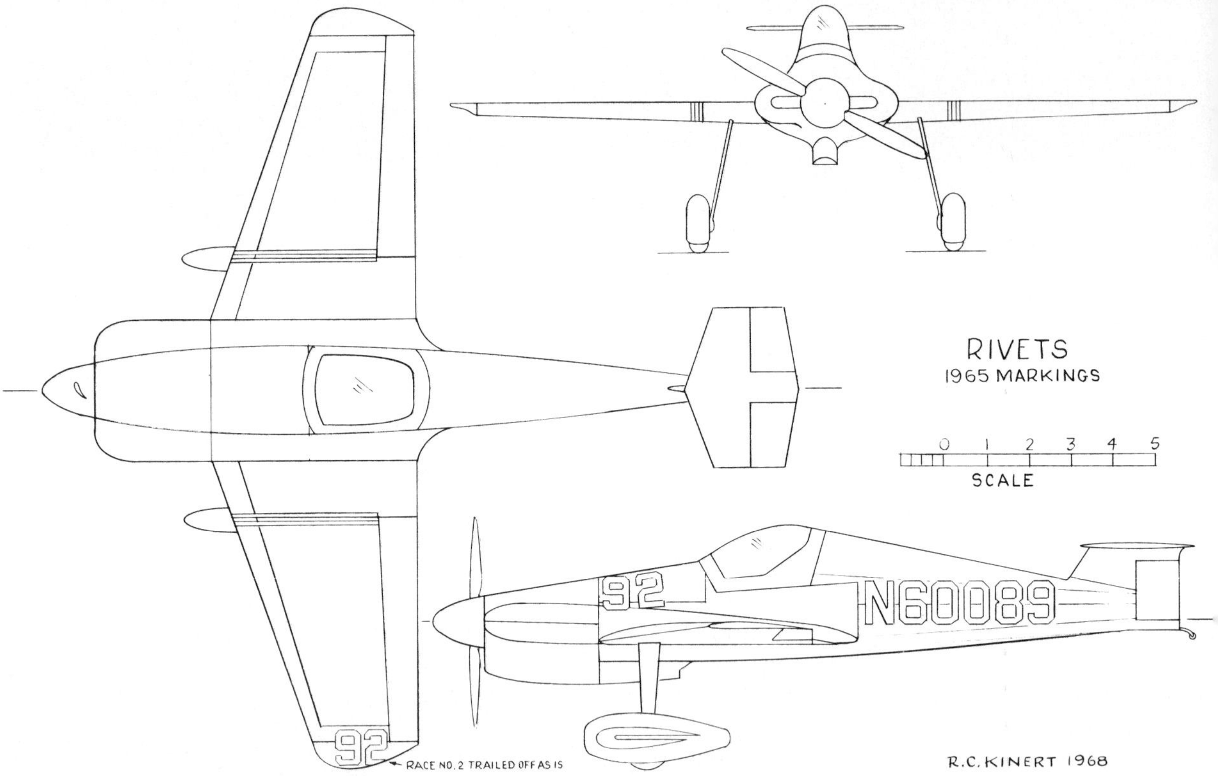

Rivets appeared at Reno in 1965 looking as pert as ever. Unique landing gear legs join at front wing spar, allowing wider tread. Colors, red with yellow trim. Natural aluminum wing. Bill Falck qualified fastest with 205.48 mph, took his two heat races, then finished 2nd in finals as engine wasn't ginning properly.

Sheldon Winer

E. D. Weiner won the 1965 Harolds Club Transcontinental Trophy with this spectacular wet-wing black and white checkerboard P-51D, license N335, which wore same race No. 14 as did his P-51D of previous year, which is confusing. His other P-51D, which was being readied for 1966 closed-course racing, wore license N335J. Weiner qualified No. 14 8th at only 315.44 mph for closed-course races, was eliminated in heat races.   Robert F. Pauley

Darryl Greenamyer, who hangars his F8F-2 Bearcat at Reno, had installed a tiny midget-type canopy, cut the wing down to 28'6" with Hoerner tips and added a prop spinner. Finish was still natural metal. He qualified at 369.70 mph, won final event easily at a throttled-back 375.10 mph. Later in year, at Las Vegas, Greenamyer qualified at a sizzling 423.40 mph to surpass 1948 Cobra II Bell P-39 closed-course record, then dropped out of main event with engine trouble.   Robert F. Pauley

Bob Porter qualified *Deerfly* at Reno 1965 with 203.16 mph behind Falck's *Rivets* then surprised many be beating *Rivets* in finals, repeated at Las Vegas by edging *Rivets* by .2 mph fraction at 202.4 mph.   *Robert F. Pauley*

Miss San Bernardino shows off clean lines at Reno 1965 where aerobatic pilot Art Scholl qualified 5th at 182.93 mph, took 4th in finals. Art then qualified 6th at Vegas with 192.5, took 4th again in final race.   *Sheldon Winer*

Baby Cyclone, built by Jim Wilson in 1959, had vertical deflectors on horizontal stabilizer tips. Jim qualified a disappointing 9th at Reno with 162.45 mph, took 6th and last in consolation. Deflector tips were later removed for eastern racing.   *Robert F. Pauley*

Darryl Greenamyer's Bearcat was being modified for later Reno and Las Vegas races so he raced at Lancaster 1965 with Yippee, a fire-truck red Lockheed P-38L photographic version of Lightning. He qualified 5th at 334.0 mph, took 4th in finals.   *Dustin W. Carter*

the desert floor far from the airport. Five P-51D Mustangs, all of which had raced in the 1965 finals at Reno were there, as was Mira Slovak and his 1964 F8F-2 Bearcat. Darryl Greenamyer's Bearcat was being modified so Darryl flew a bright red Lockheed P-38L Lightning in the unlimited race.

On June 6, after a weeks delay, the seven ex-fighter planes climbed off the desert runway one by one —and Darce Allender quickly pulled out with his P-51D as the plug for his coolant temperature probe had dropped off, giving him a false high temperature reading. A unique start was used this year to send the unlimited's on their way. After take-off the pilots lined themselves up line abreast by radio control, then flew over the starting line a few hundred feet high to take the starters flag.

Mustang pilots Chuck Lyford, Clay Lacy and Ben Hall turned pylon #1 in that order. Lyford was flying the same P-51D with the hopped-up Merlin that Bob Love flew the previous year at Reno. They completed lap one in the same order, with Mira Slovak's Bearcat in fourth, Greenamyers stock engined red Lightning, fifth, and E. D. Weiner in his unique black & white checkered Mustang. Ben Hall, also flying a P-51D with an engine that had been highly modified by the famous Bardahl crew, pulled ahead of P-51 pilot Clay Lacey, who was not flying a stock engine either.

Then, on the sixth lap, Ben Hall suddenly called a "May Day" over his radio, pulled up and headed for the runway. The other pilots lifted up a bit to give him room and Ben just did get onto the runway. A connecting rod bolt had broken, snapping the drive shaft which nearly cut the engine in two.

Chuck Lyford, well in the lead at this point, cut his power back to 90% then to 70% for the last two laps to win the race easily at 390.3 mph. Clay Lacy eased his throttle back a bit on lap 13 while in second place to save his engine and Mira Slovak took this opportunity to slip under Clay. Clay opened his souped-up Packard Merlin to regain second place, finished three seconds ahead of Slovak, who had beaten him at Reno.

Greenamyer and his P-38 grooved the entire race in 4th place while E. D. Weiner in his nearly stock Mustang finished last at 347 mph.

After the races, the contestants and their crews tarried but shortly for they had to get on with readying their steeds for races to be held at Reno in September.

1965 National Championship Air Races

The second annual Reno Air Race, held at Fox Field September 10-12 was a big success this year, with good races in all three divisions—biplane, midget and unlimited. There were excellent aerobatics, hot-air balloon races, a women's stock-plane race—and the USAF Thunderbirds in Super Sabres put on dazzling formation acrobatics. The weather, in contrast to Lancaster earlier in the year, was beautiful as it only can be on the desert.

Nine aircraft took off from St. Petersburg, Florida, September 6th in quest of the second annual Harolds Club Trophy at Reno. All seven finishers were North American P-51D Mustangs and three of these had placed in last year's event. E. D. Weiner flew his checkerboard Mustang in first with one 10 minute stop at Duncan, Oklahoma taking on 400 gallons of fuel. Although stock in appearance, Weiner's Mustang was fitted with a 25 gallon water-Methanol tank behind the pilots' seat for cooling and antidetonation, and the wing had been reworked to a wet-wing for extra fuel. Weiner averaged 348.6 mph to win the Trophy while Clay Lacy finished 2nd and Wayne Adams, who won the race in 1964, finished 3rd at 331.4 mph, over 12 mph above his 1964 winning speed.

Bill Boland topped all nine qualifies in this class with his Mong Sport at 152.80 mph, won his heat race and then the main event at 148.68 mph. Clyde Parsons, last year's winner, qualified his Knight Twister in second place at 148.76 mph, far ahead of the other seven pilots, also took his heat race and then finished just behind Boland in the final on September 12, with 146.06 mph.

Eleven midgets qualified at Reno this year and most of the aircraft were several years old, reworked, repainted and sometimes even renamed!

Bill Falck towed his little Rivets all the way from New York to qualify fastest at 205.48 mph, took his two heat races faster than any other midget; then, in the finals, had his engine go slightly sour to take 2nd place.

Bob Porter qualified second in his old Sorenson Deerfly at 203.16 mph, also took both his heat races, then took the final race on Sunday Sept. 12 at 202.14 mph.

Ten aircraft qualified in the Unlimited class at Reno, seven North American P-51D Mustangs and three Grumman F8F-2 Bearcats. Four of the Mustangs had flown in the cross country race. All aircraft were subjected to two heat races each, in addition to qualifying, so there were not enough healthy engines left to have a consolation race in which the pilots would further burn their engines up—for peanut money.

Darryl Greenamyer qualified his F8F-2 Bearcat

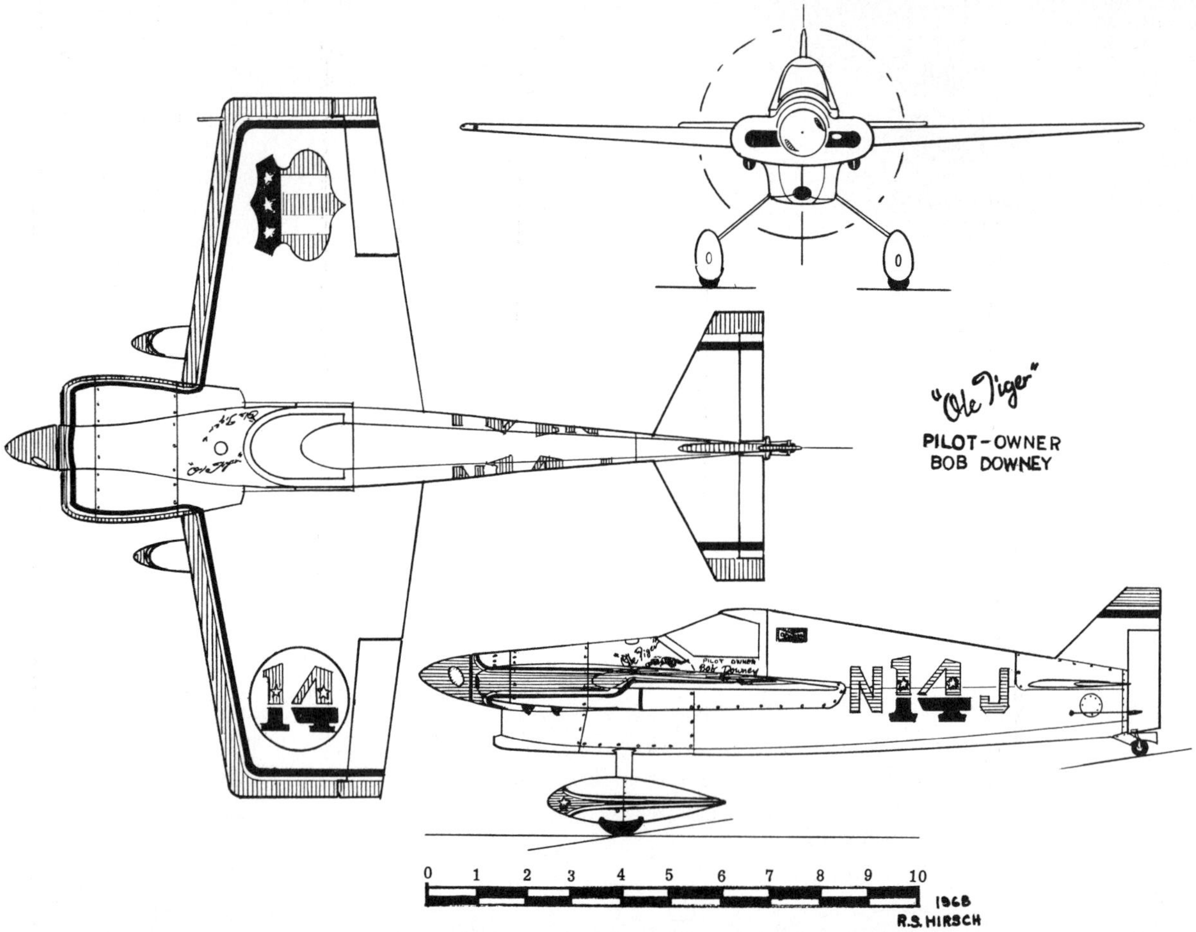

After the 1965 Reno races Bob Downey traded Miss Cosmic Wind, No. 6, and $5,000 to Denny Sherman for 16-year old Miller Little Gem, used his paint store best to repaint it a beautiful red, white and blue, renamed craft Ole Tiger. One of the four fastest midgets built, Ole Tiger's cockpit is so narrow Downey must fly it cross-hand-ed, left hand on right throttle, right hand on the stick!

Downie & Associates

Airline pilot Miraslav Slovak flew into Lancaster 1965 with his white Grumman F8F-2 Bearcat unchanged in outward appearance except for the word Vodka being deleted from under sponsor Smirnoff's name, and his 1965 championship emblem was added to cowl sides. Mira, who had made world headlines by commandeering an airliner to escape his Czech homeland 17 years previous, loafed through qualifications at 296.0 finished 3rd in finals. He later took 4th at Reno, 3rd at Vegas, has not raced since.   Dustin W. Carter

Bardahl Special, at Lancaster 1965, was little changed in outward appearance except for added gold outline stripes around No. 8, and word Bardahl now black with gold outline. Charles Lyford, who had flown No. 8 to 2nd place in 1964 transcon race, took an easy 1st with 391.62 mph. No. 8 always wears the hottest reworked engines ever flown. Note huge oversize propeller necessary to absorb increased power.   Dustin W. Carter

North American P-51D, race No. 13, N630T, ex-RCAF Mustang at Reno 1965 after Dick Kestle finished 4th in Harold's Club Transcontinental Dash. Dick later took 2nd place in St. Petersburg to Palm Springs XC race in highly polished craft.   Robert F. Pauley

Ole Yaller, No. 58, built in 1965 by Bob Greiger from Cassutt plans. Marion Baker qualified 10th at Reno with 159.86 mph, took 3rd in consolation race at 161.67. E. E. Stover qualified Yaller 9th at Vegas with improved 176 mph, then had engine troubles.   Robert F. Pauley

Tom Cat, built in 1964 by Tom Cooney, in cockpit. Tom qualified 11th and last at Reno 1965, placed 5th in consolation with 150.15 mph. He then qualified 11th at Vegas with improved 160.9 mph, took 4th in consolation, 151.9 mph.   Robert F. Pauley

Denight Special DDT, former No. 0, showed up at Reno 1965 all slicked up in new paint and wearing race No. 97, and was renamed Miss Dallas. Roy Berry qualified 8th with 167.29 mph, took 2nd in consolation at 172.78 mph.   Robert F. Pauley

fastest at a slow 369.70 mph, then went on to win the final race, held Sept. 12, with his engine throttled well back to average 375.10 mph. First prize money was only $2,000.00, about enough for an engine overhaul. Roscoe Turner had picked up $18,000 for winning the 1938 Thompson Trophy plus $4,000 additional for setting a new closed course record. And a dollar was a dollar in those days!

P-51 pilots Chuck Lyford and Clay Lacy battled for second place in the Unlimited race, with Lyford finally pulling away with a 368.57 mph average. Mira Slovak ended up by giving Lacy a tussle for 3rd, but had to settle for 4th at 356.00 with his white Bearcat.

Walt Ohlrick finished 5th with his stock Bearcat at 333.22 mph while Lyle Shelton in a stock Mustang brought up the rear at a slow 331.99 mph to close out the successful three-day races.

1965 Las Vegas Inter-National Air Races

Las Vegas' first air races were held at Boulder City Airport, September 23-26 with a well rounded program. Starring the midgets and unlimited racers, the show also featured a home-built biplane exhibition race due to lack of prize money for a real race. There was an assortment of aerobatic flying and a women's stock event, a closed-course race of five laps around the 2½-mile oval won by Judy Wagner in a Beech Bonanza, followed by Irene Leverton in a Bellanca, Pat Arnold and Elaine Loening in Comanche's and Dorothy Julick in a Cessna 182. This was the only race held which could be called an "improvement of the breed" type race for surely, if there are many more to follow,

builders of the slower aircraft are going to begin a clean up program and the fastest will improve their craft to stay ahead also. Claimed performances go for naught on the race course.

MIDGET RACES

Twelve gaily painted sleek little midget monoplanes qualified at Boulder City and famous *Shoestring* returned to the racing fold to stay. John Paul Jones promptly qualified *Shoestring* in first place at 207.9 mph, just .5 mph faster than Bill Falck and *Rivets*. Bob Porter in *Deerfly* and Bob Downey with the Miller *Ole Tiger*, also qualified over 200 mph.

After three heat races and a consolation race, the fastest six midgets climbed a few feet off the desert on Sunday, Sept. 26, in a race-horse start to fly for the City of Las Vegas Trophy. Bob Porter and *Deerfly* got off to a surprising lead for Wittman's *Bonzo*, flown by Paul Booth was not performing well.

Bill Falck and *Rivets* was, as usual last off and Bill climbed to his customary groove high above the other midgets. Porter, taking the pylons low and close continued to widen his gap between second place John Paul Jones and *Shoestring* who was followed by Art Scholl's *Miss San Bernardino*. Bob Downey in *Ole Tiger*, whose engine was not quite right, and Booth in *Bonzo* taking up the rear.

Rivets steadily eased past all but *Deerfly* whom he could not quite catch. *Deerfly* crossed the finish line having averaged 202.4 mph, just .2 mph ahead of *Rivets*. The others finished in the order above in what had been a beautiful display of racing.

UNLIMITED CLOSED COURSE RACE

Darryl Greenamyer qualified his beautiful white Grumman F8F-2 Bearcat at Boulder City with a new

Seattle Miss at Lancaster 1965. Ben Hall qualified colorful P-51D Mustang 3rd at 379. mph proving engine was far from stock, dropped out with engine problems 6th lap of finals. Ben could not ready ship in time for Reno, loafed through Las Vegas qualifications 10th with 328.39 to save engine, then took a throttled-back easy 2nd in Paul Mantz Trophy Race behind Chuck Lyford's hot No. 8 Mustang.
Dustin W. Carter

high of 423.40 mph thus finally surpassing the closed-course lap record of 418.30 mph set by Chuck Brown in 1948 at Cleveland with the Bell Airacobra, *Cobra II*. Chuck Lyford's P51D Mustang, bellowing a throaty roar from its short stacks, turned in a healthy 418.14 mph to also exceed *Cobra II's* speed.

Again the highly tuned and hopped up engine of the unlimited aircraft were subjected to two heat races each and Bob Abrams pulled out of heat 2-A with a blown engine, crashed his P-51D Mustang fatally while turning too tightly into final approach.

Three North American P-51D Mustangs and three Grumman F8F-2 Bearcats took off at Boulder, Sunday Sept. 26, in quest of the Paul Mantz Trophy and from the first it was a duel for first place between Chuck Lyford's Bardahl Mustang and Darryl Greenamyer's Bearcat.

The P-51 and F8F battled neck and neck for six laps with the lead changing frequently, both flying low and taking the pylons close. Just when it seemed the onlookers were to see the closest finish of all time between two of the fastest piston-engined fighters to ever race, Greenamyer on lap seven, began slowing. Lyford eased back his throttle well ahead of Clay Lacy and Ben Hall in their Mustangs, who were fighting it out for third place. Greenamyer finally had to drop out of the race on lap 9 so Lyford's Mustang crossed the finish line to complete his 10 laps at a good 391.62 mph average, followed by Ben Hall and his Mustang at 363.30 mph, Clay Lacy and his Mustang would have finished well up in the standing, but was penalized for cutting two pylons. Mira Slovak took an easy throttled-back 3rd place with his Bearcat while Walt Ohlrick was 4th and last in his Navy blue stock Bearcat at a slow 319.37 mph. With nowhere to go but take last place Walt had throttled well back to save his engine.

1965 International Aeroclassic

This long-handled air meet, held at Palm Springs, California November 11-14 featured all phases of civil aviation with sport, private and business flying being represented. The 190 cubic inch midget races were the only competitive events of the show, but numerous demonstrations of soaring, aerobatics and sky diving were featured. Veteran midget pilot John Paul Jones fittingly closed out the big year of 1965 air racing by qualifying wonderful little *Shoestring* at a new high of 210.28 mph on the 2½-mile course November 10. Jim Miller had set the previous record at Ft. Wayne September 14, 1959 with his Miller *Little Gem* (now *Ole Tiger*) at 209.56 mph. Bill Falck qualified *Rivets* at 203.62 mph, then was disqualified in the final race for cutting a pylon, a rare thing indeed for Falck!

Twelve midgets qualified and three others arrived too late to do so, the largest number of midgets to appear in the west for racing. John Paul Jones took the main event November 14 at 202.17 mph, ahead of Bob Porter and *Deerfly* who turned in 201.35 mph on the 12-lap 2½-mile course. He was followed by Steve Wittman and *Bonzo*, Bob Downey with *Ole Tiger* and Art Scholl who was last in *Miss San Bernardino* at a respectable 190.14 mph. Bill Falck would have finished 3rd with his 191.35 mph but pylon cutting put him in last money.

Clay Lacy's P-51D, ex-RCAF Mustang, at Lancaster 1965. High gloss lavender ship was stock in outward appearance but, like most of the unlimited racers, was fitted with a water-methanol tank for cooling and anti-detonation purposes. The injection system adds some additional power but is most effective in keeping engine from disintregrating at high power settings. Clay had a busy year, took 2nd at Lancaster, 3rd at Reno then cut 2 plyons at Vegas, a rarity for Clay.
Dustin W. Carter

There were major air races at Los Angeles and Reno, plus homebuilt biplane and midget races at St. Petersburg and Washington, D.C. to make 1966 another big year of air racing—and the sport lost the man who had done so much to bring major air racing back. An unsecured linkage bolt came off the elevator push-rod control on Bill Stead's newly acquired Sorenson *Deerfly* on a test hop and Bill crashed fatally into Tampa Bay just before the St. Petersburg races.

St. Petersburg-Clearwater International Aviation Exposition

This air meet, believed to have the longest title ever conceived for such an event, was held at St. Pete the last 3 days of April and the 1st of May, 1966. An attempt was made at St. Petersburg to set three new world speed records in two light plane categories, but faulty timing and camera equipment prevented it.

In the speed runs Bill Falck and *Rivets* was fastest of the meet with 238.695 mph for Class A and Bob Downey with *Ole Tiger* turned 227.129. In the Class C try Don Washburn did 235 mph in an Aero 200.

BIPLANE RACE

Only four homebuilts showed up for the second eastern race of these little beauties, and three of the four were built from plans drawn up by Curtis Pitts of Homestead, Florida. L. J. "Skeeter" Royall, on May 1, took an easy 1st at 148.76 mph while Jack Lowers in his Lowers Special and Bob Abernathy tussled for 2nd, with Lowers finally taking over at 140.68 mph, just 1.1 second ahead of Abernathy. Paul Booth was last at 132.04 mph.

MIDGET RACE

Bill Falck and *Rivets* set a new high of 212.77 mph in qualifying for the midget races with Bob Downey and *Ole Tiger* doing 195.65 mph. Five ships qualified, with three others allowed to race without qualifying. Falck and *Rivets* were last off in the final event, a race-horse start for six midgets May 1st and, as usual, finished first from their high perch at 203.01 mph.

Steve Wittman, first off, was second in his trusty *Bonzo* with 196.01 mph. Bob Downey's *Ole Tiger*,

Howell "Nick" Jones and his new *Half Fast*, Roy Berry's *Miss Dallas* and Jim Wilson with his *Baby Cyclone* strung out rather evenly to finish in that order.

1966 Los Angeles National Air Races

The 1966 Los Angeles Air Races were again held on the Mojave Desert at Fox Field north of Los Angeles near Lancaster, Calif. May 27-30. As last year, a hard gusty wind blew dust and sand across the airport all four days, varying each day from hot to cold but blowing strong enough to allow racehorse starts for the midgets and biplanes off the one runway.

The meet proved to be almost an entirely local air show, with one aerobatic pilot after another displaying their wares. Margaret Ritchie, flying a rebuilt and lightened Taylorcraft, proved to be the best individual crowd pleaser by performing her graceful acrobatics just a few feet above the concrete runway.

The U.S. Air Force Thunderbirds, composed of six F-100 Super Sabre jets, completely stole the air show as they closed each of the four days' events with their extremely intricate and spectacular demonstration of dangerous 600-mph precision flying.

Air races were sandwiched between each day's acrobatic shows for what had now become three standard class races—small home-built biplanes, the wonderful little monoplane midgets and the unlimited class for big WWII surplus prop-driven fighters.

BIPLANE RACES

Eleven home-built biplanes showed up at Lancaster, one from Seattle (Bruce McIntire), two from Nevada—all others being from southern California. Four heat races, a consolation and final race were flown in the rough air for extremely low prize money—fifty dollars for 1st in heats and only four hundred for the final race winner. Bruce McIntire bounced his Pitts Special through rough air into first place on May 30th, averaging 139.93 mph, with Dr. Sid White and his Starduster battling with Bill Boland in a Mong Sport for second, with Sid finally taking over at 138.01 mph. Dr. Don Wickliffe in his Dollar Special, Don Jansen and his Miniplane followed in order, with versatile and busy Bob Downey last in a Starduster.

Start of final biplane event at Frederick, Maryland 1966, shows Jack Lowers in his Lowers Special, who finished 2nd, and Paul Booth and Pitts No. 6 which took 1st place. Lowers also took 2nd at St. Petersburg 1966, Booth 4th and last.　　Robert F. Pauley

Skeeter Royall in Pitts Special, No. 21 N6W, won Sport Biplane race at St. Petersburg 1966 with 148.76 mph.　　Robert F. Pauley

Lt. Col. Oliver Arquilla and Miss DARA at 1966 Washington races, Fredericksburg, aborted heat 1A take-off half way down runway with fuel trouble, dropped out of heat 2A with tail flutter, landed OK. Ollie crashed fatally on test hop that evening.　　Robert F. Pauley

Howell "Nick" Jones and new Half Fast at Lancaster 1966. Nick took 3rd in finals after finishing 4th at St. Petersburg. Half Fast was destroyed later in spectacular mid-air collision at Frederick, Md. with Jerry Quartons racer, both pilots safe!　　Kinert

Howell "Nick" Jones towed his little *Half Fast* all the way from Augusta, Georgia, to compete against ten Californians in the midget races. The useless qualification trials were dispensed with in favor of four heat races, a consolation event and the final race for the fastest six entrants. Ray Cote in beautiful little *Shoestring* took his heat race with ease and finished more than a country mile ahead of the field in the finals with 197.08 mph but was disqualified for running an illegal cam in his C-85 Continental. Strict rules for engines were, at last, being enforced by inspection.

Bob Downey, a Whittier, Calif. paint store owner, whose *Ole Tiger* is slow to take-off, was back in the pack but pulled out front to win the race at 189.48 mph and picked up $2,000. School teacher Art Scholl was 2nd in *Miss San Bernardino* at 187.97 mph, followed by Nick Jones and *Half Fast* in its second midget race. John Paul Jones in heavy *Miss Cosmic Wind* followed Howard Terrill in his new *Shushonik*, who was awarded 6th and last after cutting four pylons.

UNLIMITED CLOSED COURSE RACE

Seven North American P-51D's and two Grumman F8F-2 Bearcats appeared at Lancaster to battle for $5,000 first prize and a total purse in the final race of $12,700. Except for their paint jobs, six of the ex-fighter planes were stock in outward appearance. Darryl Greenamyer, Lockheed test pilot, had gradually modified and stripped down his F8F-2 Bearcat until it now looked like a different cat. First he had made a smaller canopy, then changed to a midget racer size bubble canopy that was affixed to a quick attach-release type hatch. He then put parts of four engines together to get about 500 hp more than his 2800 hp stock Pratt & Whitney R-2800-34W had delivered. An unusual two-speed CB17 supercharger was installed. Water injection from a 75-gallon tank was installed and used in all racing. To absorb this additional horsepower, it was necessary to affix a 13 ft. 6 in. four-blade prop like that used on the Navy Douglas AD aircraft, complete to spinner. It was now necessary to take-off and land 3 points to avoid prop damage. Darryl lightened his Bearcat 700 lbs. by removing the complete electrical system and all but a few feet of hydraulic line — to which was now fitted a nitrogen bottle for a one-time gear retraction. One drycell battery operated the little transistorized Bayside 990 radio.

Greenamyer cut 3½ ft. off each wing tip and 18 inches from atop the rudder and fin. He planned to go after the world's 3 km prop-driven speed record at Lancaster, but found his craft so unstable at 450 mph that it began to slide sideways and started to roll. Darryl also flew a few pylons later, found his rudder control inadequate to race!

No. 1 Bearcat is truly a "hot" airplane. Exhaust gases flow over the fuselage which can blister paint clear back to the tail surfaces. Darryl wears Alaskan mukluks to keep his feet from blistering. The throttle is heavily taped to dissipate some of the heat but gloves are still required. Once the throttle is set he lets go of it as it is too hot to handle!

Heat races for the unlimited's were flown on May 28 and 29 then, on May 30, six P-51 Mustangs and the remaining F8F-2 Bearcat was sent off from a flying start by Bob Hoover and his yellow Mustang. Walt Ohlrick in his Navy blue Bearcat immediately took the lead by dropping down to the desert floor and hugging the pylons like he wanted to take them home.

Clay Lacy, who had held pole position in his passionate purple No. 64, began to gain on Ohlrick and pull away from the five other Mustangs. Anyone who tried to pass Walt Ohlrick had to fly high and wide as Ohlrick continued to fly about three inches above the sage brush in the gusty winds to utilize boundary layer effect. Walt's Bearcat was wearing a strictly stock P&W engine so Clay Lacy, followed by E. D. Weiner, Ben Hall and Russell Schleeh, gradually worked their way around him.

Lacy's P-51, nicknamed "Purple People Eater" by one and all, proved to be the most souped-up Mustang in the race by establishing a comfortable half lap lead over the others. Then, with the race apparently all ribboned up, Clay's prop control malfunctioned and he zoomed high and out of the race on lap 8 of the 10 lap event.

E. D. Weiner in his bronze Mustang No. 49 assumed the lead and took the race with 375.81 mph, ahead of Ben Hall and his No. 2 *Seattle Miss*, who did 366.30 mph. Walt Ohlrick grimly held on to the desert floor and 4th place, behind Russell Schleeh and ahead of stock P-51's flown by Dick Weaver and Dave Allender who finished in that order.

Washington National Air Races

The Washington National Air Races were staged at the Municipal Airport, Frederick, Maryland from September 2 through the 5th and featured races for homebuilt biplanes, midgets and a Women's closed course race.

BIPLANE RACES

Only six home-made bips appeared at Frederick and the fastest, Frank Tighe in a Pitts Special, was flying an off spec ship that could only take last place money. All the little biplanes flew a qualifying lap and two heat races each day to fill in the program, all of which was quite confusing to the spectators who saw Tighe finish first in heats and final event but not win any race!

Jack Lowers in his Lowers Special qualified fastest at 129.5 mph, then finished second in the final race Sept. 5, behind Paul Booth, who won with 124.16 mph.

Judy G. Wagner flew a beautiful race on September 5th to win this event easily in her Beech Bonanza at a credible 178.5 mph, followed by Edna Whyte in an Aero Commander with 172.7 mph. Two Piper Comanche's and a Cherokee brought up the rear. This was the only race held in 1966 which could lead directly to aircraft improvement.

Twelve mighty midgets showed up to race at Frederic but two of these arrived too late to qualify.

Steve Wittman in *Bonzo* and, surprisingly, newcomer Nick Jones in *Half Fast*, tied for first in qualifying at 194.1 mph. Wittman threw several inches off a prop blade in a heat race and never could get going fast enough with his spare prop to make the final event.

Colonel Oliver P. Arquilla, USAF, aborted takeoff in his *Miss Dara* in the first heat race, pulled out of another with wing flutter and landed safely. Then, on Sunday evening Sept. 4 Arquilla experienced structural failure in a test dive in his midget and crashed fatally.

Bill Falck and *Rivets* were last off again in the final midget race Sept. 5 and again worked up front from their high altitude to win the event at 192.8 mph, just 5 mph faster than Bob Downey in *Ole Tiger*. Falck won $3,000 for first prize, the highest purse offered to date, also picked up $360 in heat races. Art Scholl in *Miss San Bernardino* and Tom Cooney in *Tom Cat* finished 3rd and 4th but no times were taken as a result of an incident that occurred before the race was completed. Howell (Nick) Jones, diving his No. 3 *Half Fast* on lap 11 of the 12 lap race to pick up a bit more speed, flew into Jerry Quarton's *Lil' Rascal! Half Fast* chewed and tore the tail of Jerry's ship off clear up to the cockpit. Occurring directly in view of thousands of spectators, this must go down as one of the most amazing and spectacular mid-air collisions ever recorded, for Quarton's ship, engine still wide open, shot up vertically then lowered easily to the ground, helicopter like! Jerry was pinned in the wreckage and had to be cut out but was intact except for three broken ribs and a few facial cuts and bruises!

Meanwhile, Nick Jones and *Half Fast* were slithering over the rolling landscape at 200 mph until the little craft finally slowed and stopped. Nick crawled out with a few cuts and bruises! Both pilots were awarded equal shares of 5th and 6th place money, $800 each and were glad to be there to accept!

1966 National Championship Air Races

The third big annual Reno Championship Air Races were held at de-activated Stead Air Base, Reno, Nevada September 21 through 25. For the third annual official National Aerobatics Championships, there were now two divisions—men's and women's. Bob Herendeen won his division with a beautiful Pitts Special biplane, while Margaret Ritchie and her Taylorcraft bested Mary Gaffney and Mary Aikens, in Pitts biplanes, to win her division.

There were 35 raceplanes at Reno; 10 unlimited; 10 190's plus one that arrived too late and another whose engine mount was declared unsafe to race— and 15 sport biplanes were there.

As so many homebuilt biplanes entered this year, it was necessary to eliminate 3 of the 15 in time trials. Leading the pack was Lancaster winner Bruce McIntire in an orange Pitts, at 151.261 mph, just 1/10 of a second over 1965 Reno winner Bill Boland in his red and white Mong Sport. Just 9/10 of a second, in 3rd, was Dr. Sid White, followed by Don Wickliffe, another MD, in his Dollar Special at 142.631 mph.

In the final biplane race, held September 25, Dr. Wickliffe took the lead, followed by Bill Boland, Bruce McIntire and Dr. Sid White. White passed McIntire on the first lap, while Boland closed on Wickliffe. They were in a dead heat at the end of lap 2, then Wickliffe, whose engine seemed to pick up as he raced, pulled away to a mere 20-foot lead by lap 4. Then Bill Boland and his Mong took over the lead on lap 5, several hundred feet ahead of Wickliffe.

White and McIntire fought over 3rd place with the Doc finally beating McIntire by only 15 yards. After the race it was learned that Boland had cut pylon 4 on the 3rd lap, so Don Wickliffe and his Dollar Special were declared the winner at 147.723 mph, Sid White taking 2nd and McIntire 3rd. Bob Herendeen's Pitts Special was 4th while Clem Fischer of Reno was 5th and last at 127.096 mph in his Mong Sport.

Ray Cote qualified his beautiful little *Shoestring* at 204.545 mph to lead the midget field, followed by Bill Falck's *Rivets* at 200 mph and Steve Wittman with *Bonzo* at 195.228 mph. Bob Downey's *Ole Tiger* wasn't ginning properly at the 5,046 ft. airport altitude, so qualified at a fairly slow 193.548 mph.

In the final race, held September 25, just after the biplane finals, Wittman was first off as usual and built up a commanding lead over Art Scholl and *Miss San Bernardino*, Downey, Falck, Roy Berry in his *Miss Dallas* and surprisingly slow starter Cote, in *Shoestring*. By the end of lap 2 Falck, flying his usual high race, had moved up to 2nd, Downey and *Ole Tiger* were still 3rd, Scholl had dropped to 4th and Cote worked up to 5th ahead of Berry.

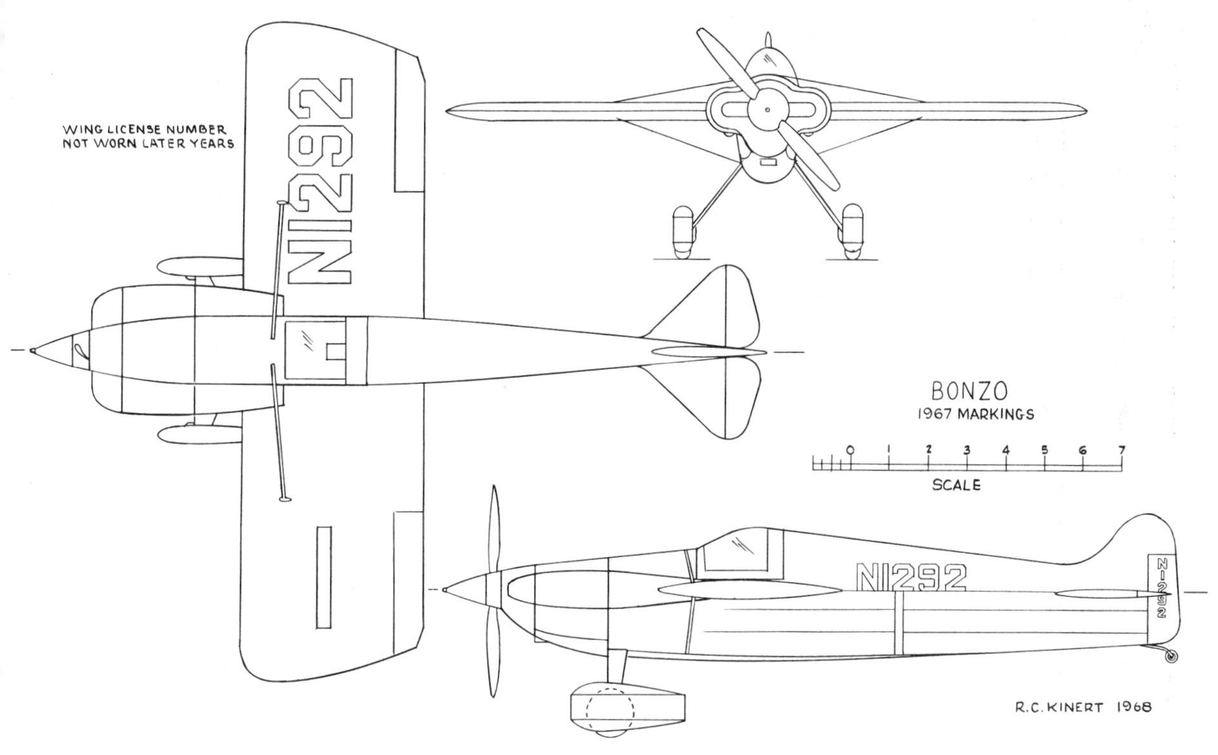

Steve Wittman and fabulous red trim and yellow Bonzo poised for take-off at St. Petersburg, Florida, 1966.
Bonzo is one of few midgets employing wire bracing. Bonzo is 2nd in midget wins with nine 1sts, sixteen 2nds
and five 3rd places.
Robert F. Pauley

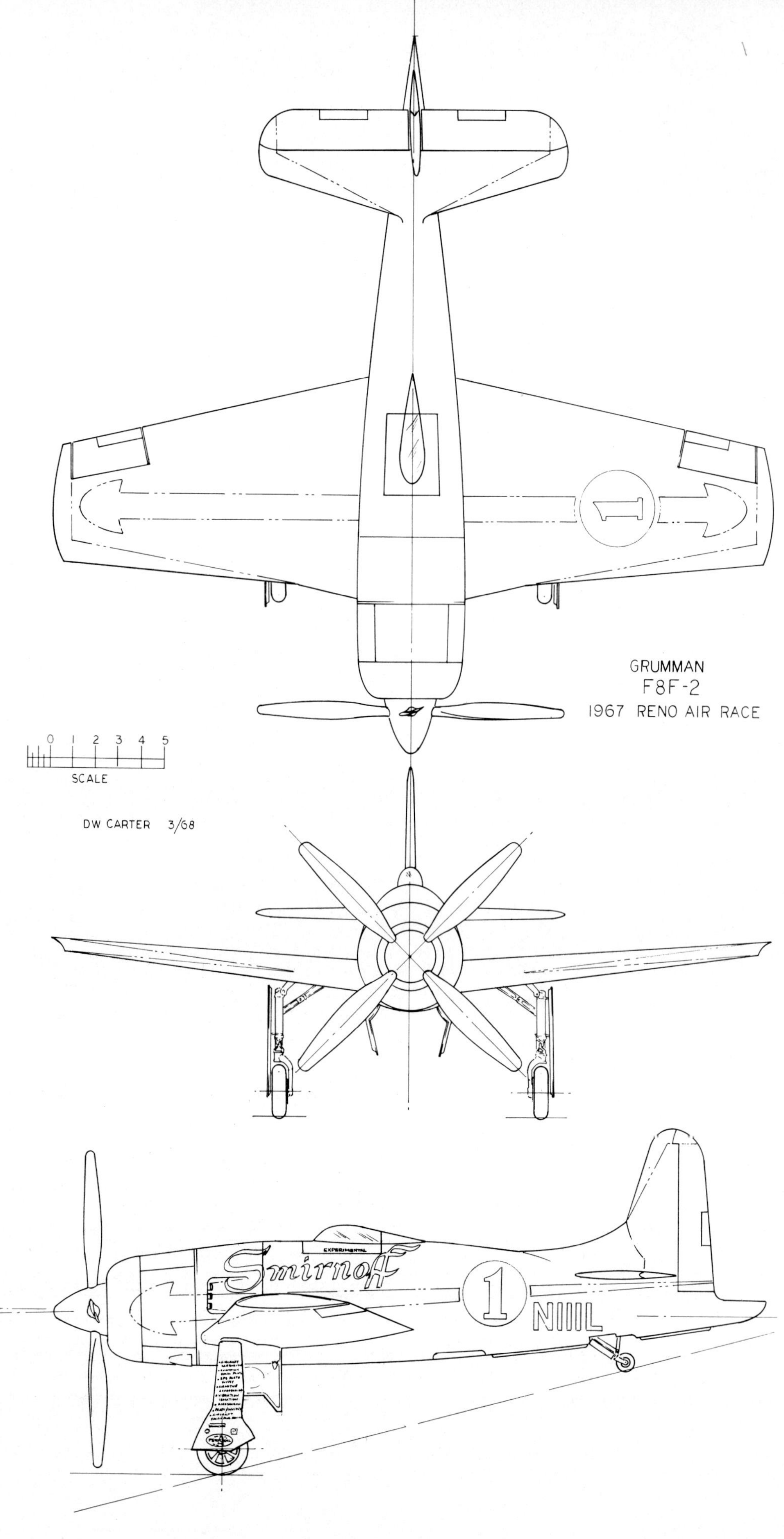

GRUMMAN
F8F-2
1967 RENO AIR RACE
SCALE
0 1 2 3 4 5
DW CARTER 3/68
Smirnoff
EXPERIMENTAL
1
N111L

Darryl Greenamyer appeared at Lancaster 1966 with his No. 1 Grumman Bearcat more extensively modified than any WWII fighter plane in the history of air racing. Wings had already been clipped to a fantastic 28' 6" and Hoerner tips added. Fuselage was only a shell, having been stripped inside to the last ounce. Huge prop, to absorb high engine power, required 3-point takeoffs and landings. Entire exterior had been filled at seams, painted white, and was highly waxed and polished.　　　　　　　　　　　　*Kinert*

View shows tail after Greenamyer had cut 18" off fin and rudder top, resulting in dangerous rolling character-istics at 450 mph, somewhat less than full throttle. Small midget-type canopy makes No. 1 seem larger. Rags, seen in this and 3/4 view, were stuffed into aileron gap at inside hinge lines to hold ailerons steady in strong, gusty winds at Lancaster. Trim color on Bearcat is medium blue.　　　　　　　　　　　　*Kinert*

Mr. Lucky, N6355T, Cassutt design built 1966 by LaMonte Snyder, seen at Fredericks-burg 1966. Tom Arnold cut 3 pylons in heat, was eliminated. Arrived too late to race at Reno. Snyder crashed fatally on XC flight to Cleveland races. Mr. Lucky?   Robert F. Pauley

Ohm Special, No. 15, built by Dick Ohm and Jamie Krapf in 1949. Ohm, at St. Pete, above, turned but 121.48 mph in 1st heat, never made finals. Qualified 9th at Fred-erick, took 5th and last in semi-finals, 157.7 mph.   Robert F. Pauley

Trans-Florida Aviation Executive P-51D Mustang appeared at Lancaster 1966, did not race. Jack Shaver flew this ship in Harold's Club XC races, 5th place 1964 and 6th place 1965, despite blowing tires both years landing at Oklahoma City!   Kinert

Darryl Greenamyer shows off markings and trim and normal-size rudder and fin on No. 1. Aggregate effect of so much trim paint on all surfaces adds undue amount of parasite drag and should be eliminated if try for world piston-engined speed record is ever made.   Smirnoff

Sid White and Starduster owned jointly with Lee C. Mahoney who set new qualifying record for sport biplanes at Cleveland 1967 with 157.618 mph then won finals. Built 1961 by John and Grady Day. Sid dropped 60 lbs., down to 160 lbs. for 1966 Reno races, lost out to Dr. Don Wickliffe. Sid barely lost 1st place to Bill Boland's Mong Sport at Reno 1967. Starduster grosses at 1,000 lbs, has 19' span, cruises 150 mph at 75% power, trues 185-190 mph.
Sidney G. White, M.D.

Cmdr. Walter Ohlrich Jr., USN, arrived at Lancaster 1966 with his blue and white Grumman F8F-2 Bearcat still stock except for added prop spinner, turned in his fastest pylon speed, 362.65 mph, in heat race, took 4th in finals. Ohlrich, who flies low enough to strafe ant-hills, has raced Tom Cat since 1964 except when on active war duty. Sandy Falconer took over for Walt at Reno 1966, placed 3rd in consolation with respectable 351.049 mph.
Kinert

On lap 3 Cote's *Shoestring*, which had a wing
well suited for the high altitude, passed Scholl and
really began to show its speed. Falck's *Rivets* was
again on its long and relentless chase after leader Wittman. By the end of lap 5, Cote and *Shoestring* had
passed Downey's *Ole Tiger* and was moving up on
Rivets, a rare thing indeed! Excitement mounted as
Shoestring closed in on *Rivets*, who was slowly gaining on Wittman's *Bonzo*. Then, as the three leading
contenders passed the starting line for lap 8, *Shoestring*
pulled up and out of the race because a 25 cent valve
spring keeper had broken!

Falck's chase after Wittman shortened when Steve
got caught in traffic at his lower level, while Falck
whizzed on by from his higher spot, midway through
lap 8. Falck finished 200 yards in front, averaging
193.098 mph, Wittman led Downey by at least 400
yards and Scholl was 4th. Roy Berry and *Miss Dallas*
finished 5th and last at 174.446 mph.

UNLIMITED CLOSED COURSE RACE

Seven North American P-51D's, three Grumman
F8F-2 Bearcats and, for the first time, a Hawker Sea
Fury turned up to do battle on the desert racecourse.
Also, for the first time since 1949, a Mustang appeared
with extensive external modifications.

Three unlimited's were favored. Darryl Greenamyer's record-holding No. 1 Smirnoff Bearcat appeared with the vertical tail restored to stock size.
Chuck Lyford's P-51D No. 8 was greatly modified.
The wing tips had each been clipped 3½ feet and
capped with modified Hoerner tips to bring the wing
span down to only 30 feet. The wing surfaces had been
carefully filled in at butt joints and painted to glossy
perfection and the horizontal stabilizer tips had been
clipped. The Rolls Royce Merlin was now modified
to deliver a wild 3600 hp as found on a test stand, a
full 1800 over stock. As the clipped wings might present a control problem, Lyford, in test flights, made
several intentional dead-stick landings and even performed acrobatics to feel out the controls of his hot
Mustang. Third of the most modified ex-fighter craft
was the Hawker Sea Fury, a British carrier plane,
owned by Mike Carroll and flown by airline pilot
Lyle Shelton. The strikingly painted big ship, the last
prop-driven fighter built, had 6½ feet clipped off each
wing tip, a tiny new canopy and extensive clean-up
of its entire outer skin. The engine cowl front was
painted white which faded into light and then dark
blue, which faded into a bright orange then red, as if
flames were licking back along the chrome yellow fuselage.

Time trials were held Wednesday, Sept. 21 and
the top qualifiers were assigned their starting positions
from the trial speeds, as had worked out so well at
Cleveland in the late 40's. However, for show purposes,
heat races, which burn up highly developed race engines, were held on Thursday and Friday, all partici-
pants receiving an equal $100 per' heat—so the lead-
ing contenders nursed their engines for the final race.

Darryl Greenamyer qualified his No. 1 Smirnoff
Bearcat at a fast 409.972 to gain pole position while
Lyle Sheldon in the beautiful Sea Fury did 364.075
mph but was dropped from the finals for cutting a
pylon. He had mistaken a checkerboard-roofed shack
on the course for a pylon.

Chuck Lyford took off for his time trial, turned
several fast warm-up laps then came down low for his
try. Nearing pylon 4 he turned on a secret power boost
and his P-51 fairly leaped ahead, spewing smoke and
actually roaring like no two Mustangs had ever roared.
After Chuck completed his lap he pulled up high then
quickly landed.

His white airplane was covered with black oil
and inspection disclosed that a connecting rod bolt had
snapped and pieces of the rod had torn a hole in each
side of the engine block. Despite turning part of his
lap at low throttle, Lyford averaged 390.081 mph!
Ben Hall of Seattle qualified his much raced Mustang
No. 2 at 378.848 mph, showing his craft to be far from
stock engined.

One Grumman Bearcat, Greenamyer's, and five
P-51D Mustangs took off Saturday afternoon, September 24 after the biplane and midget races had been
held and they flew in quest of a low $10,600 total purse.

Pacesetter Bob Hoover circled the field, herding
the six racers together in line abreast by radio from
his yellow Mustang. After a warm-up circle, Hoover
gave the go ahead as all six ships roared by the stands.

Chuck Lyford had replaced his broken engine with
another Rolls Royce Merlin and the crowd hoped his
engine was as powerful as the first for a great race
between Lyford and Greenamyer had long been
awaited. It was not to be, for on the back stretch Bearcat No. 1 had already taken a good lead over Clay
Lacy, Ben Hall and Lyford, with the latters engine
again beginning to stream oil and smoke. Chuck
dropped back to last place on lap 3 to be clear and
pulled out on lap 5, landing safely. The water injection system had failed and the resulting detonation
had burned a hole through the engine side!

Greenamyer maintained a comfortable lead while
Dick Weaver dropped out on lap 8 with bad spark
plugs; then, on lap 9, Wayne Adams was forced out
with a propeller pitch malfunction.

The remaining three racers finished well strung
out with Greenamyer averaging a fast 396.221 mph
and Ben Hall taking 2nd at 372.701 mph. Clay Lacy
and his lavender P-51D finished 3rd and last with
360.627 mph. Both Mustang pilots had eased their
hopped up engines back after they had established their
place in the race, saving their engines for yet another
year of big-bore racing.

Air races were held at Ft. Worth, Texas, Detroit, Michigan, and Reno, Nevada, to make 1967 another banner year for the sport. And there were no fatalities at any of the meets.

Texas National Air Races

The Texas Nationals were staged under very adverse weather conditions in an oversized bean patch called Luck Field, near Ft. Worth, Texas. Scheduled for May 12, 13 and 14, the 14th was rained out, forcing postponement until May 27 and 28.

The heavy rains turned the sod and dirt airport into a quagmire that made take-off and landing conditions the worst and most dangerous in air race history and the race course itself left much to be desired. Despite all difficulties, there was excellent flying and the race pilots put on a great show.

BIPLANE RACES

Eight sport biplanes made the long cross country flight to Texas from the west to compete for low prize money. To fill out the program, and because of postponement, each pilot had to qualify, fly four so-called elimination heats and then fly in the finals.

Finals were flown May 28, 10 laps over the 2½-mile course. Bruce McIntire, who had led all the others in qualifying and who took all four of his heat races, also led the field in the final race with his little Pitts, averaged 156.17 mph. Lee Mahoney followed at 155.93 mph in a Starduster and Dr. Don Wickliffe, who had made the Texas flight twice from Ramona, California, was 3rd in his Dollar Special with 144.97 mph. Clem Fischer of Reno finished 4th in his Mong, followed by Paul Booth (Pitts) and Joe Priblo in a Starduster.

McIntire, who had flown all the way from Seattle to compete, won only 260 dollars in his four heat races and 750 dollars for first place in the final race, proving this to be not a poor man's sport!

WOMEN'S STOCK PLANE RACE

Eight ladies showed up for their most important race since Cleveland days. Two Beech Bonanza's, three Aero Commanders and three Pipers, two of them Comanche's and one a Cherokee, flew qualifications and four heats to earn a place in either the consolation or final race. Judy Wagner, who had won last year's women's event at Frederick, Maryland, qualified her Bonanza fastest at 192.31 mph, took her two heat races. Then on May 28, she won the main event, 10 laps around the 2½-mile course, at 194.72 mph.

MIDGET RACES

Eleven gaily painted midgets flew or were towed into Luck Field from all points of the compass to fly four heats, a consolation race and the final event. Dauntless Howell "Nick" Jones came from Augusta with a newly built midget all eager to race again after his spectacular mid-air collision in Maryland the year previous. Nick took his little racer aloft for tests, later related the following:

"Since this was a new aircraft it had to pass the PRPA flight tests which calls for a dive speed of 1.3 times normal top. As this airplane would do almost 240 mph, over 300 mph would be required.

"May 10 was very windy but the racer was ready so I climbed to 5000 feet and entered a full-throttle shallow dive. Air speed quickly climbed to an indicated 285. (We later found the indicator used to calibrate the one in my racer was 20 mph slow, so I was actually doing 305 mph indicated.) I eased forward on the stick to pick up the 20 mph I thought was needed when suddenly the wings exploded!

"The forces were so great on me that I could not get my hand up to the quick-release canopy latch. The engine was wide open and the fuselage was going straight down. The sound of my engine as the prop blades went beyond the speed of sound was terrifying.

"I then decided to break the canopy out and, releasing my belts, butted it as hard as I could with my crash helmet. G loads from the spinning aircraft threw me back into the seat. I saw the canopy was loose and dived against it again. The canopy came completely off and I sailed out. The airstream force blacked both my eyes and flattened my body into a spread-eagle position.

"I could not bring my hand up to pull the ring until my fall slowed. Then I found the D-ring had blown from its pocket, so pulled the wire. The chute popped at once and I was looking through a set of

Red and white Mong Sport competed against 18 other bipes at Reno 1967 and pilot-owner Clem Fischer qualified 2nd with 149.502 mph, took 5th in finals. Best pylon speed 150.964 mph in heat race. Took 4th place at both Texas and Cleveland 1967. Kinert

C. Don Wickliffe, M. D. and Dollar Special at Reno 1967. Built and raced by Buck Dollar 1965, ship resembles Great Lakes. Don purchased and raced ship at L.A. 1966, won finals at Reno 1966 with 147.723 mph, his best pylon speed to date.   Kinert

Dallas Christian and black and white Mong Sport N33Z at Reno 1967. Qualified 4th with 147.3 mph, took 4th in finals. Qualified 5th at Cleveland, 144 mph even, took 5th in finals.   Kinert

Red and white Boo Ray was completed April 1967, had a busy year with builder-pilot Marion Baker. Took 1st in consolation at Texas, turned best speed qualifying 5th at Cleveland with 185.95 mph, took 5th in finals, also 5th in Reno finals.   Kinert

Here is wonderful Rivets and Bill Falck at Cleveland 1967, where they qualified 1st with 206.61 mph, ahead of Bob Downey and Ole Tiger, won main event. Rivets is top midget with 13 firsts, 6 seconds and 2 third places. Falck stated that Rivets has had many cowling changes, has used exhaust augmentation for 11 years. T-tail was made in 1954 and first used at Dansville that year. Turned up wing tips were done in 1958.   Al Chute/Falck

Bill Boland's red and white Mong Sport, seen at Reno 1967, is cleanest homebuilt to appear since smaller Knight Twisters were barred. Boland likes to fly high, Falck style, thrilled crowd with dive finish in finals to beat Sid White by fractions. Qualified 1st at 153.548 mph. Bill qualified 3rd at Cleveland 1967, finished 3rd in finals.

Kinert

Red and white Shushonik,·built in 1966 by Howard Terrill, as it appeared at Reno 1967. Dan Lawson qualified 8th at 172.414 mph, took 3rd in consolation with 166.852 mph.
Kinert

Lavender mist Snoopy and builder-pilot Jim Wilson at Reno 1967. Qualified 6th at 182.926 mph, 6th and last in finals. Snoopy first raced at Cleveland 1967, qualified 5th, 185.95 mph, took 6th and last in finals. Ailerons, rudder, black and white checkerboard.
Kinert

P-51D Mustang No. 2 had a cut down canopy for Reno 1967. Mike Loening, new owner, qualified 6th with 366.793 mph, finished 5th and last in final unlimited event to close air meet.
Kinert

Black and gold stock Grumman F8F-2 Bearcat No. 11 qualified 9th at Reno 1967 with 332.690 mph. Owner-pilot John Church, newcomer to racing, did a beautiful flying job to take 2nd in consolation race with 336.167 mph.
Kinert

power lines. The plane hit on one side of the lines and I hit on the other and was dragged about 4,000 feet in the strong wind before I could gain my feet and collapse the parachute."

Seventeen days later, dauntless Nick was back flying another midget as substitute pilot in the consolation race at the Texas Nationals. "Howell" about that!

Bill Falck had arrived in Texas too late with *Rivets* to qualify but took a 1st and 2nd in his heat races, then once again caught and passed Bob Downey in *Ole Tiger* to win the final race May 28 with 203.97 mph. Steve Wittman was only .39 fractions per hour behind *Rivets* over the finish line, but *Bonzo* had cut a pylon so Steve and Ray Cote with *Shoestring* were awarded a tie for 3rd. Roy Berry in *Miss Dallas* was 4th and Howard Terrill flew *Shushonik* in last at 173.24 mph. Terrill had been allowed to race without qualifying as all the other midgets had departed for home.

1967 Cleveland National Air Races

The Cleveland National Air Races held at the Burke-Lakefront Airport in downtown Cleveland Labor Day weekend, September 2-4, were the first air races seen in that city for 18 years and were a far cry from the earlier races. What was lacking in number of races held was much made up for in excellent competition in the three class events in the most beautiful three days of weather Cleveland had enjoyed in a long time.

Air race management had not planned a cross country race as there was no prize money available, so E. D. Weiner talked three other unlimited plane owners into each placing 1000 dollars in a pool, to race Palm Springs, Calif. to Cleveland. E. D.'s P-51D covered the 1961.2-mile great circle course September 3 in 5 hours to average 400 mph, followed by Mike Carroll and his yellow Hawker Sea Fury and Bob Guilford's P-51D. Guilford's Mustang was not fitted with wet wings so had to make three fuel stops along the way. Jim Ventura crashed his P-51D fatally near Minden, Nebraska, far off course and in very bad weather.

Ten homebuilt biplanes flew into Cleveland from all over the U.S. to compete in four heat races, a consolation and final heat. Two biplanes were found to have oversize engines so raced for last place in heat races.

All six of the fastest qualifiers flew in the finals September 4 and all six finished in the same order in which they had qualified!

Lee Mahoney and his *Starduster* qualified at a new high of 157.618 mph for the little bips and, on September 4, flew all ten laps of the 2½-mile course with an average 155.119 to win the finals. Bruce McIntire was close behind with his Pitts at 154.493 mph, followed by Bill Boland, Clem Fischer and Dallas Christian who were evenly spaced out in their *Mong Sports*. Mike DuPont was last with his *Pitts* at 134.529 mph.

WOMEN'S STOCK PLANE RACE

Six ladies qualified their 4-place private planes at Detroit and all six flew an exhibition heat race on Saturday and Sunday and then finals Monday, September 4.

Edna Whyte, who had cut a pylon at Ft. Worth earlier in the year, made no such mistake this time, qualified her Aero Commander in first position at 185.950 mph around the 2½-mile course. Edna was an old hand at air racing, having tooled AT-6's at Cleveland in the late 40's.

In the final race September 4, Pat Arnold and her Comanche took over to win at 181.542 mph after Whyte's engine faltered. Whyte did manage to take an easy 2nd, followed by Elaine Loening in an Aero Commander, Mary Knapp and Dorothy Etheridge in Mooney Super 21's and Dorothy Julick in a Comanche.

MIDGET RACES

Eleven sleek little midgets appeared at Cleveland, one arriving late but allowed to race, another being rejected due to faulty wing construction.

Again it was a replay of many previous midget races as *Rivets*, *Ole Tiger* and *Bonzo* were flown by their veteran pilots in 1-2-3 order in both the qualifications and finals. Falck and *Rivets* qualified with 206.61 mph and took his usual come-from-behind final with 202.893 mph. Bob Downey finished a heartbreaking .171 fraction per hour behind Falck, while Wittman finished 3rd at 196.757 mph.

Nick Jones was now renting out as a sky jockey and flew *Miss Dallas*, the old Denight Special, into 4th place, followed by Marion Baker in his new *Boo Ray* and Jim Wilson in newly built *Snoopy* who finished last to end the race meet.

1967 National Championship Air Races

The fourth annual Championship races again were held on big Stead Air Base, northwest of Reno, September 21 through 24. Huge cumulus ice cream clouds formed a beautiful backdrop all four days in the crystal clear but somewhat bumpy air.

There were acrobatics galore as 14 men and 4 women vied for top U.S. Championship honors. Charlie Hillard won the men's class and Mary Gaffney the women's division.

Grey and white ex-RCAF P-51D Mustang in which Dick Kestle took 3rd place in 1967 XC race to Reno. Raced in both 1965 XC events, turned in best average, 343.467 mph, to finish 2nd in St. Petersburg to Reno hop 1965. Race No. 13.
Kinert

Tan and white Hawker Sea Fury which Tom Taylor qualified 7th with 354.272 mph at Reno 1967, used just enough power to stay in front in consolation race to win at 336.754 mph. Fury was stripped down but stock. License N260X.
Kinert

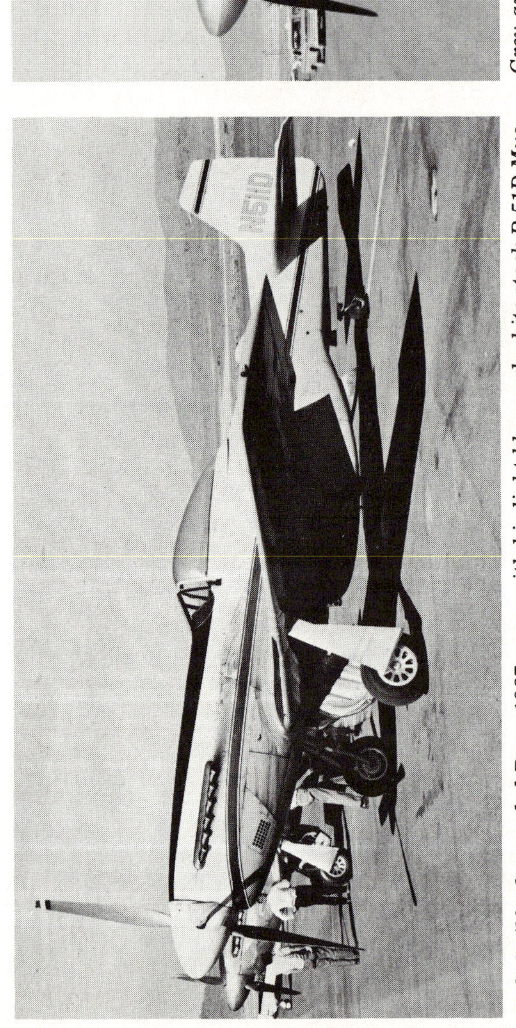

Bob Guilford attended Reno 1967 races with his light blue and white stock P-51D Mustang, did not race. Bob finished 3rd and last in 1967 Palm Springs to Cleveland XC race with slow 220 mph average after making 3 fuel stops, wore race No. 11.
Kinert

Cmdr. Walt Ohlrich Jr., USN, arrived at Reno 1967 with Tom Cat, his stock Grumman F8F-2, repainted a sleek red, white and blue. Walt qualified 8th with 333.841 mph, flew his usual beautiful race to finish 3rd in consolation race at 332.881 mph.
Kinert

There were closed course races for the home-built biplanes, the marvelous midgets and the big WWII fighters. To fill in the program there was also an exhibition race for stock North American AT-6 surplus trainers, won by Hank Otzen at 149.875 mph.

The third annual Harolds Club cross-country race for unlimited's was flown and 43 racing planes were there to dust pylons. The dazzling U.S. Air Force Thunderbirds, in their Super Sabre jets came by to fly breath-taking precision acrobatics just one day, having previous commitments elsewhere.

HAROLDS CLUB TRANSCONTINENTAL TROPHY DASH

Six surplus fighters took off from Rockford, Illinois, Sept. 21, to fly the 1606.2 great circle statute miles into Stead AFB. Only Mike Carroll's Hawker Sea Fury and E. D. Weiner's checkerboard P-51 Mustang were re-worked to carry extra fuel in their wings, the other four entries being stock, engines included.

Mike Carroll turned the table on E. D. Weiner this year, finished first at 417.346 mph, ten minutes and 8.014 mph ahead of E. D. Dick Kestle finished at a slow 304.736 mph, while Tom Kuchinsky was 4th and last at a creeping 278.349 mph. One Mustang pilot dropped out with engine problems and another, Jim Fugate, was fined and penalized for late arrival at race start and for a late start after he did show up! Some days it doesn't pay.

After the race E. D. Weiner was questioned about the race, said he had grown complacent and backed off his throttle a mite too much on the long flight.

BIPLANE RACES

A record 19 little homebuilts flew in the qualification trials and, for the first time, one was eliminated from the heat races because of the big turnout.

Veteran biplane pilots learned they were flying in faster company and former top contenders found themselves squeezed out of the finals and into the consolation race after six heat races had been flown.

Bill Boland and his extremely clean little Mong Sport led all others in qualifying at 153.584 mph, followed by Clem Fischer's improved Mong at 149.502 mph. The biplanes get faster each year and, with larger engines allowed than the midgets wear, 290 cubic inch as opposed to 190 for the midgets, 200 mph can expect to be approached in the near future as new designs appear.

In the final biplane race September 24, six pilots were flagged off in a race horse start and a ding dong battle ensued. Sid White and his Starduster was first off and around the scattering pylon west of the airport and was first past the grandstands, followed closely by Bill Boland's Mong and Bruce McIntire's Pitts. Sid elected to fly a varied race, higher on the downwind legs and lower on the up wind. Boland flew higher than all the other racers, in the same style Falck uses, while McIntire hugged the desert floor, taking the pylons very closely in an effort to catch the leaders.

Dallas Christian, Clem Fischer and Branch Smith began stringing out in that order with their Mong Sports to bring up the rear.

Dr. White began flying a lower groove race to hang onto the pylons more closely and prevent McIntire slipping by inside while Boland edged up high outside. White was first around the final pylon and onto the finish straightaway but Bill Boland, in a Hollywood finish, dived from his higher altitude to ease past Dr. White and take the race with 151.643 mph!

McIntire finished 3rd closely behind Dr. White at 151.311, while Christian and Fischer, who had vied for 4th place throughout the race, finished in that order. Branch Smith finished last at 139.462 mph.

MIDGET RACE

Thirteen midget racers qualified in the trials September 20-21 and, as usual, Falck and *Rivets* were tops with 203.160 mph. Ray Cote, who had reworked *Shoestring* after it had been damaged while towing it to San Diego after the Texas races, qualified at 201.793 mph, closely followed by Bob Downey and *Ole Tiger* with 200 even. Fred Wofford in his new *Gold Dust* was eliminated from all racing after turning but 145.396 mph in the trials. Four heat races and a consolation race, won by Roy Berry in *Miss Dallas* at 178.430 mph, were flown before the final race.

Six midgets lined up for the final starter's flag September 24 and Steve Wittman was a spectator! A big expansion program on Winnebago County Airport, of which Steve is manager, kept him from readying *Bonzo* for racing, so Steve hopped into one of his self-built Tailwind monoplanes and flew out to attend the last two days' events.

Four of the racers that took off were old timers and two were newly built in 1967. *Shoestring* was first around the scatter pylon and onto the racecourse, followed by Bob Downey in *Ole Tiger*, Smokey Stover in *Miss San Bernardino*, Marion Baker with his new *Boo Ray* and Jim Wilson in his clean new Cassutt *Snoopy*. And there was Bill Falck and *Rivets*, off last and easing up to his usual high spot. Nick Jones commented that Falck is the only midget pilot he knows who has the ability to fly high and not cut pylons.

Bob Downey gradually overtook Ray Cote and *Shoestring* to take a slim lead as *Rivets* began its relentless pursuit of the leaders. Downey, Cote and Stover were flying a low classic type race, taking the pylons with inches to spare, but Falck was closing in high. Baker in *Boo Ray* also flew quite low to hang onto 5th place while Jim Wilson and *Snoopy* was higher in last place.

No. 1 F8F-2 Bearcat at Reno 1967, with rudder and fin restored to original configuration. Note huge prop for hopped up 18-cylinder P&W engine. Darryl Greenamyer qualified 1st with 408.814 mph, took final event after Bardahl Special dropped out. Kinert

Sleekly finished white Bardahl Special at Reno 1967 had horizontal tail clipped and wings chopped to 30'! Huge paddle-bladed prop was installed to absorb added power of louder-than-ever Merlin engine. Three-point take-offs and landings were mandatory!
Kinert

E. D. Weiner taxies his P-51D in front of grandstands at Reno 1967 after finishing 2nd in Harolds Club XC race. E. D. thought he had race in the bag, held off on throttle all the way. Mustang has a 25 gallon methanol tank behind pilot's seat. Kinert

E. D. Weiner repainted his No. 49 in black and white zebra stripes for 1967, making it the wildest of Mustangs. Horizontal stabilizer was clipped and wing chopped to 30'. Bardahl had hopped up the engine. Qualified at 399.779 mph, took easy 2nd in finals.
Kinert

Mike Carroll taxies to grandstands after surprise 1st place finish in Harold's Club 1967 SC race. Mike flew high throttle setting all the way and a bit extra last few minutes. His huge Hawker Sea Fury, built as an English WWII carrier fighter had, with a lot of loving care and money, been converted to a flamboyantly beautiful cross-country racer. Wheel brakes, unsuited for long hot landing and taxi rolls, have been a problem, requiring fire-bottle application at rolls-end to prevent fire.
Kinert

Exquisite aerial of E. D. Weiner and his P-51D Mustang over southern California coast. Parasite drag of zebra stripes add considerable drag at 400+ mph but is certainly attractive! Entire ship has butted skin joints filled and smoothed, high gloss finish. E. D. pulls all the power he feels won't blow engine apart, admits to "well over 100 inches of manifold pressure." Hi Time has annunciator warning lights to display malfunctions. E. D. never looks into cockpit while racing unless light flashes.
E. D. Weiner

Rivets passed *Ole Tiger* as usual, and went on to win with 202.703 mph while *Ole Tiger* stayed ahead of Cote and *Shoestring* to finish 2nd at 201.192 mph. *Shoestring*, flying a beautiful race, was 3rd at 200.557 mph followed by Stover's *Miss San Bernardino*, Baker's *Boo Ray* and Wilson in *Snoopy*.

UNLIMITED CLOSED COURSE RACES

A record eleven big-bore unlimiteds qualified at Reno. There were three Grumman F8F-2 Bearcats, one Hawker Sea Fury, six P-51D Mustangs and a Vought F4U Corsair. Another Corsair had flown in to race but blew its engine while practicing.

The consolation race for the big boys was flown early in the afternoon of September 23 and was a beautiful event to watch. John Church said before the race that he had but two engines for his stock jet black Bearcat, and that he was not about to push too hard. But he decided after the race began that there was a chance to take Tom Taylor and his white Sea Fury. Taylor led by a slight margin and flew rather high and wide while Church, in his first major race, flew quite low and took the pylons closer.

Just in back of Church for the entire race was pylon duster Wal Ohlrick in his stock Bearcat which now sported a beautiful red, white, and blue paint job and was polished to a mirror finish. Jim Fugate, the only unlimited pilot to fly in both the cross-country and closed course races this year, was forced out with engine trouble in his Mustang on lap 9 of the 10-lap race.

Taylor grimly held on to the lead and finished with 336.754 mph with Church close behind with 336.167 mph, while Ohlrick had eased off on his throttle to be content with 3rd place.

There are not too many F8F Bearcats around anymore and their owners say they are such a dream to fly, especially in acrobatics, that they are not about to burn their scarce engines up for peanut race purses. Gene Akers, flying a shiny blue-nosed but unclean Corsair cruised in 4th at a leisurely 300.779 mph. Mike Loening had cruised his hot No. 2 Mustang in 4th but his role was that of fill-in, so took an automatic last place.

Six ex-fighter planes took off late afternoon of September 23 to be led across the starting line in company front by Bob Hoover and his yellow Mustang. And all six racers wore hopped-up engines.

Darryl Greenamyer, as usual, held the pole position with his cut-down hot F8F-2 Bearcat and Chuck Lyford in his hopped-up P-51D Mustang was right alongside. Darryl had qualified at 408.814 mph and Lyford at 400.332 mph. Lyford's Mustang had its wing clipped down to 30 ft. and his engine sounded louder than ever as he qualified, so the spectators were hoping that both pilots would have healthy engines for the long-awaited duel to the finish between the two hottest piston-engined aircraft ever flown together.

E. D. Weiner was third in line with his former bronze Mustang No. 49 clipped down to a 30-ft. span and now wearing a wild black and white zebra paint job. E. D. had qualified at 399.779 mph to show his engine was far from stock.

Clay Lacy was next to Weiner in his still stock-appearing purple Mustang No. 64, Chuck Hall was next in Mustang No. 5 and on the outside was Mike Loening in much-raced Mustang No. 2. Mike's racer had a lower profile canopy, the first attempt at reducing drag of the huge canopies on the D series Mustang since Ed Lunken's 1948 Bendix Mustang.

As Bob Hoover came over the starting line, the six big racers bellowed a crescendo of sound that was a joy to the ear. Bob gave the "go" signal. Greenamyer and Lyford leaped ahead of the pack like a couple of scalded cats. Darryl's Bearcat flew low with Lyford's white Bardahl Special just above and right. They passed pylon 2 on the NE corner with Lyford just a hair behind. On the backstretch, Lyford started to let down to the right of Darryl and really began to pour on the coal. Then it happened!

The Bardahl Special began emitting a huge black trail of oil and smoke and slowed as if tied to a giant rubber band. Lyford pulled up high, went outside the racecourse, then made a beautiful dead-stick landing on the runway. He had practiced such landings after each flight of his hot Mustang, so it came natural.

With the threat of *Miss Bardahl* gone, Greenamyer throttled back some with a ½-lap lead and sat there. Clay Lacy and his "Purple People Eater" No. 64 was wide-open and low in 2nd place, but E. D. Weiner and his zebra Mustang dropped down to challenge Clay. Midway in the race it was Greenamyer by ½-lap, E. D. Weiner had eased into second and was increasing his lead over Clay Lacy. Chuck Hall and Mike Loening battled the entire race for 4th position.

By lap 8 of the 10-lap 80.04-mile race, the final standings were established. Greenamyer and his white Bearcat cruised well back in maintaining a ½-lap lead over E. D. Weiner's wild zebra, who was gradually lengthening his lead over 3rd-place Clay Lacy and his lavender P-51. Chuck Hall finally pulled in front of Mike Loening long enough to finish 4th, Mike being last at 359.866 mph.

Although Darryl Greenamyer had turned in a respectable 392.621 mph average in winning the $5,000 first place, everyone who saw the race hoped Bardahl would give it a go again next year — and when were they going to see an attempt at the 469.220 mph piston-engined speed record set by Germany way back in 1939?

BENDIX TROPHY RACE 1946—49

YEAR	COURSE and PLACE		PILOT	RACE NO.	LICENSE NO.	AIRCRAFT	ENGINE AND DISPLACEMENT	HP	AV. SPEED		REMARKS
1946	2048 miles	1	Paul Mantz	46	NX1202	North American P-51C-10	Packard V-1650	2270	4:42:14	435.501	*Wet wing.*
	Van Nuys, Calif.	2	Jacqueline Cochran	13	NX28388	North American P-51C-10	Packard V-1650	2270	4:52:00	420.925	*Exterior tanks*
	to Cleveland	3	Thomas Mayson	60	NX1204	North American P-51C-10	Packard V-1650	2270	5:01:05	408.220	
		4	William Eddy	31	NX66851	North American P-51D	Packard V-1650	2270	5:29:18	373.252	
		5	James Harp	95	NX79123	Lockheed F-5G	Allison (2) V-1710	1700	5:31:47	370.447	
		6	Donald Husted	45	NX37482	Douglas A-26C	P & W R-2800 (2)	2100	5:34:06	367.889	
		7	Charles Tucker	30	NX63231	Bell P-63C-5	Allison V-1710	1325	5:34:46	367.149	
		8	Harvey Hughes	70	NX70087	Lockheed F-5G	Allison (2) V-1710	1700	5:44:50	356.428	
		9	Walter Bullock	50	NX70006	Lockheed F-5G	Allison (2) V-1710	1700	5:45:21	355.908	
		10	Harold Johnson	63	NX21765	Lockheed F-5G	Allison (2) V-1710	1700	5:57:57	343.380	
		11	John Carroll	22		Lockheed P-38J	Allison (2) V-1710	1475	6:03:46	337.880	
		12	H. L. Marshal	99	NX66108	Lockheed F-5G	Allison (2) V-1710	1700	6:05:52	335.938	
		13	Rex Mays	55	NX57492	Lockheed F-5G	Allison (2) V-1710	1700	6:15:16	327.526	*Famous race car driver.*
		14	William Lear, Jr.	71	NX66613	Lockheed F-5G	Allison (2) V-1710	1700	6:15:45	327.105	*18 year old pilot.*
		15	Thomas Call	90	NX63382	Goodyear FG-1D	P & W R-2800	2000	6:17:29	325.612	
		16	M. W. Fairbrother	58		Lockheed P-38J	Allison (2) V-1710	1475	6:17:53	325.295	
		17	Andrew Grant	82	NX33698	Lockheed F-5G	Allison (2) V-1710	1700	7:49:44	261.665	
		—	John E. Shields	36		Lockheed P-38	Allison (2) V-1710	1700			*Landed late.*
		—	Spiro Dilles	47		Bell P63C-5	Allison V-1710	1325			*Out near Winslow, Ariz.*
		—	Hermon Salmon	74		Lockheed P-38L	Allison (2) V-1710	1700			*Returned, mechanical.*
		—	Hasson Calloway	48		Lockheed P-38	Allison (2) V-1710	1700			*Out, Toledo, Ohio.*
		—	John Yandell	11		Lockheed P-38	Allison (2) V-1710	1700			*Out, Hutchinson, Kansas.*
1947	2048 miles	1	Paul Mantz	46	NX1202	North American P-51C-10	Packard Merlin V-1650	2270	4:26:57	460.423	
	Van Nuys, Calif.	2	Joe C. DeBona	90	NX33699	North American P-51D	Packard Merlin V-1650	2270	4:28:15	458.203	
	to Cleveland	3	Edmund Lunken	33	NX61151	North American P-51D	Packard Merlin V-1650	2270	5:00:43	408.723	
		4	Bruce Gimbel	13	NX28388	North American P-51B	Packard Merlin V-1650	2270	5:04:10	404.080	
		5	William Eddy	31	NX66651	North American P-51D	Packard Merlin V-1650	2270	5:26:25	376.549	
		6	Thomas Mayson	60	NX1204	North American P-51C-10	Packard Merlin V-1650	2270	5:26:49	376.084	
		7	Frank Whitton	99	NX63382	Goodyear FG-1	P & W R-2800	2400	6:24:04	320.025	
		8	William Lear	25	NX56687	Lockheed Lightning F5G	Allison (2) V-1710	1700	6:59:57	292.680	
		9	Jane Page Hlavcek	63	NX21765	Lockheed Lightning F5G	Allison (2) V-1710	1700	8:15:59	247.812	
		—	Jim Ruble	88	NX5101N	Lockheed Lightning P-38	Allison (2) V-1710	1700			*Bailed out over Arizona.*
		—	Dianna Cyrus	91	NX67807	Douglas Invader A-26	P & W (2) R-2800	2400			*Landed in Michigan.*
		—	Joe Kinkella	92	NX6282	Bell Kingcobra P-63	Allison V-1710	1700			*Landed at Pueblo, Colorado.*

Bendix Trophy Race (*continued*)

Year	Course and Place		Pilot	Race No.	Serial No.	Aircraft	Engine	Thrust Lbs.	Time	Av. Speed	Remarks
1948	2045 miles	1	Paul Mantz	46	NX1204	North American P-51C-10		2270	4:33:48.7	447.980	
	Long Beach, Calif.	2	Linton Carney	60	NX1202	North American P-51C-10	All powered by Packard built Rolls-Royce Merlins, V-1650	2270	4:34:57.5	446.112	
	to Cleveland	3	Jacqueline Cochran	13	NX28388	North American P-51B		2270	4:35:07.3	445.847	
		4	Ed Lunken	33	N61151	North American P-51D		2270	4:37:46.3	441.594	
		5	J. F. Stallings	81	N66313	DeHavilland Mosquito M-25		2270	5:59:35	341.120	
		—	Joe DeBona	90	N5528N	North American F-6C		2270			*Out of fuel near Cleveland.*
1949	2008 miles	1	Joe DeBona	90	N5528N	North American F-6C	Packard Merlin V-1650	2270	4:16:17	470.136	
	Rosemond, Calif.	2	Stanley Reaver	46	N1204	North American P-51C	Packard Merlin V-1650	2270	4:33:17	450.221	
	to Cleveland	3	Herman Salmon	60	N1202	North American P-51C	Packard Merlin V-1650	2270	4:28:13	449.214	
	First Race-Horse	4	Don Bussart	81	N37878	DeHavilland Mosquito MK-25	Packard Merlin (2) V-1650	2270		343.757	
	Start this year.	—	L. H. Cameron	24	N5546N	Martin B-26C	P & W Twin Wasp (2) R-2800	2400			*Arrived after deadline.*
		—	Vincent Perron	61		Republic AT-12	P & W Twin Wasp R-1830	1450			*Forced out Grand Junction, Colo.*

BENDIX TROPHY RACE JET DIVISION 1946—1951

YEAR	COURSE AND PLACE		PILOT	RACE NO.	SERIAL NO.	AIRCRAFT	ENGINE	THRUST LBS.		TIME	AV. SPEED	REMARKS
		1	Col. Leon Gray	PN465	485465	Lockheed FP-80A-5-LO				4:08:25	494.779	*All ships made one fuel stop.*
1946	2048 miles	2	Maj. Ruddell	PN347	485347	Lockheed P-80A	*All powered by*			4:18:51	474.836	
	Van Nuys, Calif., to		Maj. Barber			Lockheed P-80A	*Allison J-33 engines,*					*Landed in Kansas, engine.*
	Cleveland, Ohio		Maj. Loofburrow			Lockheed P-80A	*4600 lbs. thrust.*					*Landed in Kansas, engine.*
		1	Col. Leon Gray		485465	Lockheed FP-80-A5				4:02:18	507.255	
1947	2048 miles	2	Maj. Clay Albright			Lockheed P-80A	*All powered by*	*2nd, 3rd place planes landed at Dayton, O.*		3:55:40	486.280	*Speed entered is official.*
	Van Nuys, Calif., to	3	Capt. W. S. Patterson			Lockheed P-80A	*Allison J-33 engines,*			4:07:00	463.968	*All ships made one fuel stop.*
	Cleveland, Ohio		Lt. E. A. Klapel			Lockheed P-80A	*4600 lbs. thrust.*					*Landed in Kansas, engine.*
		1	Ens. F. E. Brown	116		All entries North American				4:10:34	489.526	*All ships made one fuel stop.*
1948	2045 miles	2	Comdr. E. P. Aurand	101		Navy FJ-1 Fury Shipboard	*All powered by*			4:13:04	484.674	
	Long Beach, Calif., to	3	Lt. E. R. Hanks	119		Jets. Span	*Allison TG-180 engines,*			4:15:53	479.358	
	Cleveland, Ohio	4	Ens. R. E. Oechslin	120		38"1'; length 33"7'.	*4000 lbs. thrust.*			4:20:44	470.439	
		1	Maj. Vernon Ford			Republic F-84E Thunderjets	*All powered by*			3:45:51	529.614	
1949	2008 miles	2	Capt. J. W. Newman			Span 36'5"; length 37'2";	*Allison J35-A-17 engines,*			3:47:00	524.620	
	Rosemond Dry Lake,	3	Lt. Col. L. E. Moon			empty 11,000 lbs.;	*5000 lbs. thrust.*			3:48:02	524.551	
	Calif., to Cleveland, Ohio	4	Capt. Harry M. Lester			gross 18,000 lbs.					514.747	
		1	Col. Keith Compton			North American F-86A	General Elec. J-47-GE-3	5200		3:27:56.4	553.761	
1951	1919.6 miles	2	Col. Emmett Davis			Republic F-84E	Allison J-35-A-17		5000	3:25:17.6	534.857	
	Muroc, Calif., to	3	Lt. Col. G. B. Thiebault			North American B-45C	Allison J-35-C-3 (four)	4000		3:36:11.2	532.637	
	Detroit, Mich.	4	Capt. B. W. Watts			North American B-45C	Allison J-35-C-3 (four)	4000		3:36:32.4	531.768	

SOHIO TROPHY RACE 1946

PLACE	PILOT	PLANE	RACING NUMBER	LICENSE NUMBER	ENGINE	DISPLACEMENT	SPEED
1	Dale Fulton	North American P-51D-30	61	NX-33685	Packard V-1650	1650 c.i.	352.781
2	William Ong	North American P-51D	44	NX-61151	Packard V-1650	1650 c.i.	345.867
3	Jack Hardwick	Lockheed F5G	34	NX-62828	Allison V-1710	1710 c.i.	322.625
4	Wilson Newhall	Bell P-63C-5	65	NX-69702	Allison V-1710	1710 c.i.	310.545
5	Earl Ortman	Lockheed P-38	2	NX-	Allison V-1710	1710 c.i.	303.909
6	James DeSanto	Lockheed F5D	51	NX-49721	Allison V-1710	1710 c.i.	303.682
7	Charles Bing	Bell P-39Q-10	12		Allison V-1710	1710 c.i.	276.135

WEATHERHEAD SERVICE JET SPEED DASHES 1946

PLACE	PILOT	PLANE	AIR FORCE NUMBER	ENGINE	SPEED
1	1st. Lt. W.J. Reilly	Lockheed P-80A-1	019	Allison J-33	578.360
2	Capt. J.L. Moutier	Lockheed P-80A-1	085	Allison J-33	572.792
3	Capt. D.E. Eberhardt	Lockheed P-80A-1	051	Allison J-33	569.801
4	1st. Lt. J.J. Hancock	Lockheed P-80A-1	334	Allison J-33	566.751
5	Lt. W.J. McAuley	Lockheed P-80A-1	044	Allison J-33	566.617
6	Capt. J.E. Sullivan	Lockheed P-80A-1	247	Allison J-33	547.570

SOHIO TROPHY RACE 1947

PLACE	PILOT	PLANE	RACING NUMBER	LICENSE NUMBER	ENGINE	DISPLACEMENT	SPEED
1	Tony LeVier	Lockheed P-38L-5	3	NX-21764	Allison V-1710	1710 c.i.	360.866
2	Charles Walling	Modified Lockheed P-38	14	NX-25Y	Allison V-1710	1710 c.i.	351.785
3	Ivis Hill	Lockheed P-38L	66	NX-4530N	Allison V-1710	1710 c.i.	347.391
4	John Thomson	Modified Lockheed P-38	27	NX-61121	Allison V-1710	1710 c.i.	328.739
5	Sonny Hlavacek	Lockheed F5G	63	NX-21765	Allison V-1710	1710 c.i.	270.197
	J. E. Saum	Lockheed P-38	64		Allison V-1710	1710 c.i.	Out 1st Lap
	Wm. Lear	Lockheed F5	25	NX-56687	Allison V-1710	1710 c.i.	Disqualified

TINNERMAN TROPHY RACE 1947

PLACE	PILOT	PLANE	RACING NUMBER	LICENSE NUMBER	ENGINE	DISPLACEMENT	SPEED
1	Ken Knight	Bell P-63A	51	NX-4699	Allison V-1710	1710 c.i.	352.168
2	Charles Tucker	Bell P-63C-5	30	NX-63231	Allison V-1710	1710 c.i.	347.657
3	S.J. Wittman	Bell P-63C-5	4	NX-69797	Allison V-1710	1710 c.i.	339.467
4	A.T. Whiteside	Bell P-63	87	NX-52113	Allison V-1710	1710 c.i.	313.513
5	William Bour	Bell P-63A	55	NX-69901	Allison V-1710	1710 c.i.	254.913

KENDALL TROPHY RACE 1947

PLACE	PILOT	PLANE	RACING NUMBER	LICENSE NUMBER	ENGINE	DISPLACEMENT	SPEED
1	Steve Beville	North American P-51D	77	NX-79111	Packard V-1650	1650 c.i.	384.602
2	Kendall Everson	North American A-36A	44		Allison V-1710	1710 c.i.	377.926
3	Woody Edmondson	North American P-51A	15	NX-4E	Allison V-1710	1710 c.i.	372.392
4	M.W. Fairbrother	North American P-51D	21	NX-65453	Packard V-1650	1650 c.i.	367.035
5	William Murray	North American P-51D	31	NX-66851	Packard V-1650	1650 c.i.	357.084
	Anson Johnson	North American P-51D	45	NX-13Y	Packard V-1650	1650 c.i.	Out 5th Lap
	Jack Hardwick	North American P-51C	34	NX-4814N	Packard V-1650	1650 c.i.	Out 3rd Lap

ALLISON TROPHY RACE 1947

PLACE	PILOT	PLANE	AIR FORCE NUMBER	ENGINE	SPEED
1	Capt. Bernor	Lockheed FP-80A	8384	Allison J-33	494.277
2	Capt. E. Bishop	Lockheed P-80A	8302	Allison J-33	480.425
3	Lt. Col. Schilling	Lockheed P-80A	5464	Allison J-33	478.227
4	Capt. Armstrong	Lockheed P-80A	355	Allison J-33	471.904
5	1st. Lt. Gw. LaRose	Lockheed P-80A	8355	Allison J-33	471.523
6	Capt. W. Wisner	Lockheed P-80A	8303	Allison J-33	457.588

SOHIO TROPHY RACE 1948

PLACE	PILOT	PLANE	RACING NUMBER	LICENSE NUMBER	ENGINE	TIME HANDICAP	SPEED [a]
1	R.I. Eucker	Bell P-63A	55	N69901	Allison V-1710	137.5 sec	320.220
2	H.S. Gidovlenko	Modified Lockheed P38	25	N68394	Allison V-1710	1.5 sec	317.952
3	C.C. Walling	North American P-51-D	37	NX-37492	Packard V-1650	180.2 sec	316.877
4	B.E. Raymond	North American P-51D	77	NX-79111	Packard V-1650	151.8 sec	315.623
5	Charles Bing	North American P-51A	15	NX-4E	Allison V-1710	188.3 sec	312.942
6	Jack Hardwick	Lockheed F-5	34	N67864	Allison V-1710	86.0 sec	312.655
7	Frank Singer	Bell P-63	53		Allison V-1710	.0 sec	308.347
8	Wilson Newhall	Bell P-63C-5	65	NX-69702	Allison V-1710	101.5 sec	302.962
	J.E. Saum	Lockheed P-38	64		Allison V-1710	52.1 sec	320.220 [b]

a - Includes Handicap.   b - Disqualified for low and hazardous flight.

TINNERMAN TROPHY RACE 1948

PLACE	PILOT	PLANE	RACING NUMBER	LICENSE NUMBER	ENGINE	DISPLACEMENT	SPEED
1	Bruce Raymond	North American P-51D	77	NX-79111	Packard V-1650	1650 c.i.	362.245
2	R. I. Eucker	Bell P-63A	55	N-69901	Allison V-1710	1710 c.i.	362.093
3	W. V. Newhall	Bell P-63C-5	65	NX-69702	Allison V-1710	1710 c.i.	314.123
	M. W. Fairbrother	North American P-51D	21	NX-65453	Packard V-1650	1650 c.i.	Out 6th Lap
	Frank Singer	Bell P-63	53		Allison V-1710	1710 c.i.	Out 7th Lap

TINNERMAN TROPHY RACE 1949

PLACE	PILOT	PLANE	RACING NUMBER	LICENSE NUMBER	ENGINE	DISPLACEMENT	SPEED
1	Ben McKillen	Goodyear F2G-1	57	N5588N	Pratt Whitney R-4360	4360 c.i	386.069
2	Wilson V. Newhall	North American P-51-K	65	N40055	Packard V-1650	1650 c.i	379.735
3	J. H. G. McArthur	Spitfire Mk. X1V	80	CF GMZ	Rolls Griffin 65	2239 c.i	359.565
4	Jack Hardwick	Lockheed F-5	34	N67864	Allison V-1710	1710 c.i	328.470
5	J. P. Hagerstrom	Lockheed P-38	14	NX-25Y	Allison V-1710	1710 c.i	311.598
	James Hannon	North American P-51A	2	NX-39502	Allison V-1710	1710 c.i	Out 7th Lap
	H. S. Gidovlenko	Lockheed P-38	25	N68394	Allison V-1710	1710 c.i	Out 3rd Lap
	Anson Johnson	North American P-51-D	45	N-13Y	Packard V-1650	1650 c.i	did not start
	Cook Cleland	Goodyear F2G-1	94	N5590N	Pratt Whitney R-4360	4360 c.i	did not start

SOHIO TROPHY RACE 1949

PLACE	PILOT	PLANE	RACING NUMBER	LICENSE NUMBER	ENGINE	DISPLACEMENT	SPEED
1	Wm. Odom	North American P-51C	7	N4845N	Packard V-1650	1650 c.i	388.393
2	Ron Puckett	Goodyear F2G-1	18	N91092	Pratt Whitney R-4360	4360 c.i	384.888
3	Charles Tucker	Bell P63-C-5	30	N63231	Allison V-1710	1710 c.i	381.529
4	Steve Beville	North American P-51D	77	NX-79111	Packard V-1650	1650 c.i	376.719
5	Ken Cooley	North American P-51D	37	N37492	Packard V-1650	1650 c.i	373.437
6	Frank Singer	Bell P-63C5	53	N73744	Allison V-1710	1710 c.i	359.060
7	M. W. Fairbrother	North American P-51D	21	N65453	Packard V-1650	1650 c.i	349.602
8	A. T. Whiteside	Bell P-63	87	N52113	Allison V-1710	1710 c.i	330.359
9	James Harp	Bell P-39	95	N13381	Allison V-1710	1710 c.i	329.596
	Dick Becker	Goodyear F2G-1	74	NX5577N	Pratt Whitney R-4360	4360 c.i	no start

THOMPSON TROPHY RACE 1946—49

YEAR	COURSE and PLACE		PILOT	RACE NO.	LICENSE	AIRCRAFT	ENGINE	HP	SPAN	LENGTH	EMPTY	GROSS	WING LOAD	AV. SPEED	REMARKS
1946	10 Laps—300 miles	1	Alvin "Tex" Johnson	84	NX92848	Bell P-39Q-10 Cobra II	Allison V-1710 E30	2000	34'	30'2"	5578	7886	37	373.908	*Airacobra with King Cobra Engine*
	Cleveland, Ohio	2	Tony Le Vier	3	NX21764	Lockheed P-38-L5	Allison V-1710 (Two)	1700	52'	37'10"	11000	15000	45.87	370.193	*Lockheed Lightning*
		3	Earl Ortman	2	NX66453	North American P-51D-30	Packard Merlin V-1650	2270	37'	32'3"	5752	8072	34.64	367.625	*Mustang*
		4	Bruce Raymond	77	NX79111	North American P-51D	Packard Merlin V-1650	2270	37'	32'3"	5752	8072	34.64	364.655	*Mustang*
		5	Robert Swanson	80	NX79161	North American P-51D	Packard Merlin V-1650	2270	37'	32'3"	5750	8072	34.64	362.052	*Mustang*
		6	Cook Cleland	92	NX69900	Goodyear FG-1D	P & W Twin Wasp R-2800	2400	41'	33'4"	8200	11390	36.2	357.465	*Corsair*
		7	Woodrow Edmundson	42	NX69406	North American P-51D	Packard Merlin V-1650	2270	37'	32'3"	5752	8072	34.64	354.395	*Mustang*
		8	Steve Wittman	4	NX69797	Bell P-63C-5	Allison V-1710	1700+	38'4"	32'8"	6000	8340	33.66	341.225	*King Cobra*
		9	Howard Lilly	64	NX69901	Bell P-63A	Allison V-1710	1700	38'4"	32'8"	6000	8341	33.67	328.154	*King Cobra*
		10	H. L. Pemberton	21	NX1719	Bell P-63F	Allison V-1710	1700	38'4"	32'8"	6000	8341	33.67	304.406	*King Cobra*
		—	Charles Tucker	28	NX62995	Bell P-63C-5	Allison V-1710	1700	25'	32'8"	5800	8141	45.2		*Out 1st lap, gear stuck*
		—	George Welch	37	NX37492	North American P-51D	Packard Merlin V-1650	2270	37'	32'3"	5752	8072	34.64		*Out 2nd lap, mechanical*
1947	20 Laps—300 miles	1	Cook Cleland	74	NX5577N	Goodyear F2G-1	P & W Major R-4360	4000+	41'	33'9"	8486	11676	37.18	396.131	*Vought Design Corsair*
	Cleveland, Ohio	2	Richard Becker	94	NX5590N	Goodyear F2G-1	P & W Major R-4360	4000+	41'	33'9"	8486	11676	37.18	390.133	*Vought Design Corsair*
		3	Jay Demming	11	NX92848	Bell P-39Q-10	Allison V-1710-135	2000	34'	30'2"	5578	7886	37	389.837	*Airacobra*
		4	Steve Beville	77	NX79111	North American P-51D	Packard Merlin V-1650	2270	37'	32'3"	5752	8072	34.64	360.840	*Mustang*
		5	Tony Le Vier	3	NX21764	Lockheed P-38L-5	Allison V-1710	1700	52'	37'10"	11000	15000	45.87	357.488	*Lightning*
		6	William Bour	55	NX69901	Bell P-63A	Allison V-1710	1700	38'4"	32'8"	6000	8341	33.67	327.280	*King Cobra*
		—	Ron Puckett	18	NX91092	Goodyear F2G-1	P & W Major R-4360	4000+	41'	33'9"	8486	11676	37.18		*Out 19th lap.*
		—	Woodrow Edmundson	15	NX4E	North American P-51A	Allison V-1710	1700	37'	32'3"	5700	8000	34.21		*Crashed 11th lap.*
		—	Paul Penrose	37	NX37492	North American P-51D	Packard Merlin V-1650	2270	37'	32'3"	5752	8072	34.64		*Out 6th lap.*
		—	Tony Janazzo	84	NX5588N	Goodyear F2G-1	P & W Major R-4360	4000+	41'	33'9"	8486	11676	37.18		*Crashed 7th lap. Fatal.*
		—	Joe Ziegler	82	NX300B	Curtiss P-40Q	Allison V-1710	1700	37'3"	33'3"	5780	8100	34.3		*Bailed out. Only P-40Q built.*
		—	Charles Walling	14	NX25Y	Lockheed P-38J	Allison V-1710	1700	52'	37'10"	11000	15000	45.87		*Out 2nd lap.*
		—	Jack Hardwick	34	NX4814N	North American P-51C	Packard Merlin V-1650	2270	37'	32'3"	5752	8070	34.64		*Out 1st lap.*
1948	20 Laps—300 miles	1	Anson Johnson	45	NX13Y	North American P-51D	Packard Merlin V-1650	2270	37'	32'3"	5750	8070	34.63	383.767	
	Cleveland, Ohio	2	Bruce Raymond	77	NX79111	North American P-51D	Packard Merlin V-1650	2270	37'	32'3"	5752	8072	34.64	365.234	
		3	Wilson Newhall	65	NX69702	Bell P-63C-5	Allison V-1710	1700	38'4"	32'8"	6000	8341	33.67	313.567	
		—	Charles Brown	11	N92848	Bell P-39Q-10	Allison V-1710F	2000	34'	30'2"	5578	7886	37.	392.407	*To 19th lap. 1 lap at 413.097 MPH.*
		—	Charles Walling	37	NX37492	North American P-51D	Packard Merlin V-1650	2270	37'	32'3"	5752	8072	34.64		*Out 18th lap.*
		—	Woodrow Edmundson	15	NX4E	North American P-51A	Allison V-1710	1700	37'	32'3"	5700	8000	34.21		*Out 14th lap.*
		—	M. W. Fairbrother	21	NX65453	North American P-51D	Packard Merlin V-1650	2270	37'	32'3"	5752	8072	34.64		*Out 13th lap.*
		—	Robert Euker	55	N69901	Bell P-63A	Allison V-1710	1700	38'4"	32'8"	6000	8341	33.67		*Out 6th lap.*
		—	Cook Cleland	94	N5590N	Goodyear F2G-1	P & W Major R-4360	4000+	41'	33'9"	8486	11676	37.18		*Out 4th lap. 2 laps at 410 MPH.*
		—	Richard Becker	74	N5577N	Goodyear F2G-1	P & W Major R-4360	4000+	41'	33'9"	8486	11676	37.18		*Out 3rd lap.*

(continued)

YEAR	COURSE AND PLACE		PILOT	RACE NO.		AIRCRAFT	ENGINE	HP	SPAN	LENGTH	EMPTY	GROSS	WING LOAD	AV. SPEED	REMARKS
		1	Cook Cleland	94	N5590N	Goodyear F2G-1	P&W Major R-4360	4000†	33′	33′9″	8390	11580	42.26	397.071	Clipped wings with tip plates.
1949	15 laps—225 miles	2	Ron Puckett	18	N91092	Goodyear F2G-1	P&W Major R-4360	4000†	41′	33′9″	8486	11676	37.18	393.527	
	Cleveland, Ohio	3	Ben McKillen	57	N5588N	Goodyear F2G-1	P&W Major R-4360	4000†	41′	33′9″	8486	11676	37.18	387.589	
		4	Steve Beville	77	NX79111	North American P-51D	Packard Merlin V-1650	2270	37′	32′3″	5752	8072	34.64	381.214	
		5	Charles Tucker	30	N63231	Bell P-63-C5	Allison V-1710	2000	29′	32′8″	5800	8141	40.7	378.340	
		6	James Hagerstrom	37	N37492	North American P-51D	Packard Merlin V-1650	2270	37′	32′3″	5752	8072	34.64	372.719	
		7	Wilson Newhall	65	N40055	North American P-51K	Packard Merlin V-1650	2270	37′	32′3″	5740	8062	34.63	372.320	
		8	James Hannon	2	NX39502	North American P-51A	Allison V-1710	1700	37′	32′3″	5700	8000	34.21	300.396	
			Anson Johnson	45	N13Y	North American P-51D	Packard Merlin V-1650	2270	37′	32′3″	5752	8072	34.64		Out 9th lap. Wing air scoops.
			William Odom	7	N4845N	North American P-51C	Packard Merlin V-1650	2270	37′	32′3″	5752	8072	34.64		Crashed 2nd lap.

THOMPSON TROPHY — JET DIVISION 1946, '47, '49, '51

YEAR	COURSE AND PLACE		PILOT	RACE NO.	AAF SERIAL NO.	AIRCRAFT	ENGINE	SPAN	LENGTH	EMPTY	GROSS	WING LOAD	AV. SPEED	REMARKS
		1	Maj. Gus Lundquist	PN123	Not	All identical Lockheed	All powered by Allison	38′10″	34′6″	8000	14000	59	515.853	Fastest lap 549 mph.
1946	6 laps—180 miles	2	Maj. Robin Olds	PN230	Available	P-80A-1 Shooting Stars	J-33 engines of 4600		All identical				514.715	Fastest lap 553.293 mph.
	Cleveland, Ohio	3	Capt. A. M. Fell	PN064			lbs. thrust.						509.382	
		4	Capt. J. E. Sullivan	PN247									470.048	
			Lt. Col. R. L. Petit	PN069										Cut a pylon, disqualified.
			Maj. R. O. Chilstrom	PN044										Out 3rd lap.
		1	Lt. Col. R. L. Petit	PN388	58388	Lockheed FP-80A		38′10″	34′6″	8000	14000	59	500.704	
1947	8 laps—180 miles	2	Lt. J. Howard	PN331	58331	Lockheed P-80A							497.943	
	Cleveland, Ohio	3	Lt. Col. Dunham	PN309	58309	Lockheed P-80A	All powered by Allison J-33						494.656	
		4	Capt. W. Gates	PN474	55474	Lockheed P-80A	engines of 4600 lbs. thrust.		All identical				484.878	
		5	Lt. Col. Preston	PN342	58342	Lockheed P-80A							443.169	
		6	Capt. L. Powers	PN334	58334	Lockheed P-80A							430.234	
		1	Capt. Bruce Cunningham	FU263	8263	North American F-86A	All powered by General Electric	37′1″	37′6″	9200	13715	50	586.173	All three were Sabre fighters.
1949	10 laps—150 miles	2	Capt. Martin Johansen			North American F-86A	J-47 engines of 5200 lbs. thrust.						580.152	Fastest lap 635.444 mph.
	Cleveland, Ohio		Capt. Vern Henderson			North American F-86A			All identical					Out 2nd lap, seat broke.
1951	1 lap—62.14 miles	1	Col. Fred Ascani	2		North American F-86E	GE J-47-GE-13	5400	37′1″	37′6″	9400	16000	58.39	628.698	Only one ship entered. Did 635.698 mph two days previous to set new 100-km world record.
	Detroit, Michigan														

UNLIMITED CLASS—CROSS COUNTRY 1964–67

YEAR	COURSE and PLACE		PILOT	RACE NO.	LICENSE	AIRCRAFT	ENGINE	NORMAL HP	TIME	SPEED	REMARKS
1964	2254 miles	1	Wayne Adams	9	N332	North American P-51D	Packard Merlin V-1650-7	1490	7:04:07	318.88	*Wet wing. 600 gallons.*
	St. Petersburg, Fla.	2	Charles Lyford	8	N2869D	North American P-51D	Packard Merlin V-1650-7	1490	7:19:32	307.78	
	to Reno, Nevada	3	C. E. Crosby	3	N35N	North American P-51D	Packard Merlin V-1650-7	1490	8:08:27	276.92	
Harold s Club Transcontinental		4	Dick Snyder	45	N651D	North American P-51D	Packard Merlin V-1650-7	1490	8:32:00	264.24	
Trophy Dash		5	Jack Shaver	69	N351D	North American P-51D	Packard Merlin V-1650-7	1490	9:12:06	245.00	*Blew tires Oklahoma City.*
		6	Stan Hoke	99	N551D	North American P-51D	Packard Merlin V-1650-7	1490	9:25:32	239.18	
			E. D. Weiner	14	N335J	North American P-51D	Packard Merlin V-1650-7	1490			*Landed Jacksonville, bad weather.*
			Howard Olsen	1	N5073K	North American P-51D	Packard Merlin V-1650-7	1490			*Landed Ocala, Fla., bad weather.*
1965	2260 miles	1	E. D. Weiner	14	N335	North American P-51D	Packard Merlin V-1650-7	1490	6:28:38	348.6	*Fueled 400 gal. Duncan, Okla.*
	St. Petersburg, Fla.	2	Clay Lacy	64	N182XF	North American P-51D	Packard Merlin V-1650-7	1490	6:36:07	342.4	
	to Reno, Nevada	3	Wayne Adams	9	N332	North American P-51D	Packard Merlin V-1650-7	1490	6:49:02	331.4	
Harold s Club Transcontinental		4	Dick Kestle	13	N6303T	North American P-51D	Packard Merlin V-1650-7	1490	7:48:02	289.7	
Trophy Dash		5	John Gower	11	N12064	North American P-51D	Packard Merlin V-1650-7	1490	8:04:32	279.7	
		6	Jack Shaver	69	N351D	North American P-51D	Packard Merlin V-1650-7	1490	8:22:29	269.7	*Again blew tires, Okla. City.*
		7	Doug Wood	7	N469P	North American P-51D	Packard Merlin V-1650-7	1490	8:47:36	257.1	*Self refueled, Hobbs, N. M.*
			Tom Green	6	N191R	Riley Rocket (Cessna 310)	Lycoming 10-540 (2)	290			*Out, engine.*
			Jim Fugate	83	N5077K	North American P-51D	Packard Merlin V-1650-7	1490			*Out, engine.*
1965	2037.9 miles	1	E. D. Weiner	14	N335	North American P-51D	Packard Merlin V-1650-7	1490	5:36	363.911	
	St. Petersburg, Fla.	2	Dick Kestle	13	N6303T	North American P-51D	Packard Merlin V-1650-7	1490	5:56	343.467	
	to Palm Springs, Calif.	3	Mike Carroll	87	N878M	Hawker Sea Fury	Bristol Centaurus	2450	6:16	305.685	*40 min. delay in engine restart San Angelo, Tex.*
1967	1961.2 miles	1	E. D. Weiner	14	N335	North American P-51D	Packard Merlin V-1650-7	1490	5:00	400	*Wet wing, 600+ gallons*
	Palm Springs, Calif.	2	Mike Carroll	87	N878M	Hawker Sea Fury	Bristol Centaurus	2450	5:20	375	*Wet wing, 600+ gallons*
	to Cleveland, Ohio	3	Bob Guilford	11	N511D	North American P-51D	Packard Merlin V-1650-7	1490	9:00	220	*3 refueling stops.*
(Times & Speeds approximate)		4	Jim Ventura	25	N2871D	North American P-51D	Packard Merlin V-1650-7	1490			*Crashed fatally off course near Minden, Neb.*
1967	1608 miles	1	Michael D. Carroll	87	N878M	Hawker Sea Fury	Bristol Centaurus	2450	3:50:55	417:346	*Wing span cut to 31'8"*
	Rockford, Illinois	2	E. D. Weiner	14	N335	North American P-51D	Packard Merlin V-1650-7	1490	4:01:20	399.332	
	to Reno, Nevada	3	Richard Kestle	13	N6303T	North American P-51D	Packard Merlin V-1650-7	1490	5:16:15	304.736	
Harold s Club Cross Country		4	Thomas Kuchinsky	18	N6165U	North American P-51D	Packard Merlin V-1650-7	1490	5:50:00	275.349	
Race		5	James R. Fugate	83	N5077K	North American P-51D	Packard Merlin V-1650-7	1490	5:36:00	286.821	*Penalized for late arrival and start.*
		6	H. F. Rupp	17	N5151M	North American P-51D	Packard Merlin V-1650-7	1490			*Out, engine trouble shortly after take-off.*

UNLIMITED CLOSED COURSE 1964—67

YEAR	COURSE and PLACE		PILOT	RACE NO.	LICENSE	AIRCRAFT	ENGINE	NORMAL HP	SPAN	LENGTH	SPEED MPH	REMARKS
1964	10 laps—80.19 miles	1	Bob Love	8	N2869D	North American P-51D	Packard Merlin V-1650-7	1490	37'	32'3"	336.82	2nd, points. Qualified at 395.46 mph.
	Reno, Nevada,	2	Mira Slovak	80	N9885C	Grumman F8F-2	P & W R-2800-34W	2800	35'6"	28'3"	355.52	Point winner.
	Sept. 20	3	Clay Lacy	64	N182XF	North American P-51D	Packard Merlin V-1650-7	1490	37'	32'3"	354.74	3rd, points.
		4	Ben Hall	2	N5482V	North American P-51D	Packard Merlin V-1650-7	1490	37'	32'3"	344.45	4th, points.
		5	Walter Ohlrich	10	N7827C	Grumman F8F-2	P & W R-2800-34W	2800	35'6"	28'3"	343.43	5th, points.
		6	E. D. Weiner	14	N335J	North American P-51D	Packard Merlin V-1650-7	1490	37'	32'3"	282.72	
		—	Darryl Greenamyer	1	N1111L	Grumman F8F-2	P & W R-2800-34W	2800	35'6"	28'3"	351.88	Qualified 2nd at 359.51 mph.
1965	15 laps—135 miles	1	Chuck Lyford	8	N2869D	North American P-51D	Packard Merlin V-1650-7	1490	37'	32'3"	390.61	Qualified 2nd at 380 mph.
	Lancaster, Calif.	2	Clay Lacy	64	N182XF	North American P-51D	Packard Merlin V-1650-7	1490	37'	32"3"	370.54	Qualified 1st at 383 mph.
	June 6	3	Mira Slovak	80	N9885C	Grumman F8F-2	P & W R-2800-34W	2800	35'6"	28'3"	369.64	
		4	Darryl Greenamyer	1	N138X	Lockheed P-38L	Allison (2) V-1710-111	1475	52'	37'10"	356.	
		5	E. D. Weiner	14	N335	North American P-51D	Packard Merlin V-1650-7	1490	37'	32'3"	346.89	
		6	Ben Hall	2	N5482V	North American P-51D	Packard Merlin V-1650-7	1490	37'	32'3"		Out 6th lap.
		7	Dave Allender	19	N5452V	North American P-51D	Packard Merlin V-1650-7	1490	37'	32'3"		No start, mechanical.
1965	10 laps—80 miles	1	Darryl Greenamyer	1	N1111L	Grumman F8F-2	P & W R-2800-34W	2800	35'6"	28'3"	375.10	Qualified 1st, 369.70 mph.
	Reno, Nevada	2	Chuck Lyford	8	N2869D	North American P-51D	Packard Merlin V-1650-7	1490	37'	32'3"	368.57	
	Sept. 12	3	Clay Lacy	64	N182XF	North American P-51D	Packard Merlin V-1650-7	1490	37'	32'3"	356.97	
		4	Mira Slovak	80	N9885C	Grumman F8F-2	P & W R-2800-34W	2800	35'6"	28'3"	356.00	
		5	Walt Ohlrich	10	N7827C	Grumman F8F-2	P & W R-2800-34W	2800	35'6"	28'3"	333.22	
		6	Lyle Shelton	12	N66111	North American P-51D	Packard Merlin V-1650-7	1490	37'	32'3"	331.99	
1965	10 laps—93.50 miles	1	Chuck Lyford	8	N2869D	North American P-51D	Packard Merlin V-1650-7	1490	37'	32'3"	391.62	Qualified 2nd at 418.14 mph.
	Boulder City, Nevada	2	Ben Hall	2	N5482V	North American P-51D	Packard Merlin V-1650-7	1490	37'	32'3"	363.30	
	Sept. 26	3	Mira Slovak	80	N9885C	Grumman F8F-2	P & W R-2800-34W	2800	35'6"	28'3"	322.23	
		4	Walt Ohlrich	10	N7827C	Grumman F8F-2	P & W R-2800-34W	2800	35'6"	28'3"	319.37	
		5	Clay Lacy	64	N182XF	North American P-51D	Packard Merlin V-1650-7	1490	37'	32'3"		Cut 2 pylons.
		6	Darryl Greenamyer	1	N1111L	Grumman F8F-2	P & W R-2800-34W modified	3300	28'6"	28'3"		Out 9th lap mechanical. Qualified new high of 423.40 mph.

(continued)

(*continued*)

YEAR	COURSE and PLACE		PILOT	RACE NO.	LICENSE	AIRCRAFT	ENGINE	NORMAL HP	SPAN	LENGTH	SPEED MPH	REMARKS
1966	10 laps—79.42 miles	1	E. D. Weiner	49	N335J	North American P-51D	Packard Merlin V-1650-7	1490	37'	32'3"	375.81	*Engine reworked, 2000+ hp.*
	Lancaster, Calif.	2	Ben Hall	2	N5482V	North American P-51D	Packard Merlin V-1650-7	1490	37'	32'3"	369.29	*Engine reworked, 2000+ hp.*
	May 30	3	Russell Schleeh	9	N332	North American P-51D	Packard Merlin V-1650-7	1490	37'	32'3"	366.30	
		4	Walt Ohlrich	10	N7827C	Grumman F8F-2	P & W R-2800-34W	2800	35'6"	28'3"	362.65	
		5	Dick Weaver	15	N713DW	North American P-51D	Packard Merlin V-1650-7	1490	37'	32'3"	360.27	
		6	Dave Allender	19	N5452V	North American P-51D	Packard Merlin V-1650-7	1490	37'	32'3"	343.51	
		7	Clay Lacy	64	N182XF	North American P-51D	Packard Merlin V-1650-7	1490	37'	32'3"		*Out 8th lap, prop control. Fastest entry, 2500+ hp.*
1966	10 laps—80.04 miles	1	Darryl Greenamyer	1	N1111L	Grumman F8F-2	P & W R-2800-34W modified	3300	28'6"	28'3"	396.221	*Qualified 409.972 mph.*
	Reno, Nevada	2	Ben Hall	2	N9885C	North American P-51D	Packard Merlin V-1650-7	1490	37'	37'3"	372.701	*Qualified 378.848 mph.*
	Sept. 25	3	Clay Lacy	64	N182XF	North American P-51D	Packard Merlin V-1650-7	1490	37'	37'3"	360.627	*Qualified 362.253 mph.*
		4	Wayne Adams	9	N332	North American P-51D	Packard Merlin V-1650-7	1490	37'	37'3"		*Out 9th lap, engine.*
		5	Richard Weaver	15	N713DW	North American P-51D	Packard Merlin V-1650-7	1490	37'	37'3"		*Out 8th lap, engine.*
		6	Charles Lyford	8	N2869D	North American P-51D	Packard Merlin V-1650-7	1490	30'	37'3"		*Out 5th lap, engine. Qualified 390.081 mph.*
1967	10 laps—80.04 miles	1	Darryl Greenamyer	1	N1111L	Grumman F8F-2	P & W R-2800-34W modified	3300	28'6"	28'3"	392.621	*Qualified 408.814 mph.*
	Reno, Nevada	2	E. D. Weiner	49	N335J	North American P-51D	Packard Merlin V-1650-7	1490	30'	37'3"	373.712	*Engine reworked, 2500+ hp.*
	Sept. 24	3	Clay Lacy	64	N182XF	North American P-51D	Packard Merlin V-1650-7	1490	37'	37'3"	363.207	*Engine reworked, 2500+ hp.*
		4	Charles Hall	5	N	North American P-51D	Packard Merlin V-1650-7	1490	37'	37'3"	363.071	*Engine reworked, 2500+ hp.*
		5	Mike Loering	2	N5482V	North American P-51D	Packard Merlin V-1650-7	1490	37'	37'3"	359.866	*Engine reworked, 2500+ hp.*
		6	Charles Lyford	8	N2869D	North American P-51D	Packard Merlin V-1650-7	1490	30'	37'3"		*Qualified 400.332 mph. Out 1st lap, engine.*

GOODYEAR TROPHY RACE, 1947

Pilot	Aircraft	Race No.	License	Speed
1. Bill Brennand	Wittman *Buster*	20	N14855	165.857 mph
2. Paul Penrose	Chester *Swee' Pea*	5	N8400H	165.393
3. Fish Salmon	Cosmic Wind Special	4	N67889	158.798
4. Tony LeVier	Cosmic Wind *Little Toni*	3	N67888	157.851
5. Warren Siem	*Loose Siem*	44	NX64573	151.270
6. B. F. Robinson	Modified Brown Special	19	NX83Y	143.865

GOODYEAR TROPHY RACE, 1948

Pilot	Aircraft	Race No.	License	Speed
1. Fish Salmon	Cosmic Wind *Minnow*	4	N21C	169.688 mph
2. Steve Wittman	Wittman Special	1	N1292	168.862
3. Art Chester	Chester *Swee' Pea II*	2	N4000K	168.201
4. Bill Brennand	Wittman *Buster*	20	NX14855	167.063
5. B. F. Robinson	Cosmic Wind *Little Toni*	3	N20C	165.106
6. P. C. Quigley	Pitts Special	21	NX52120	164.892
7. R. B. Downey	Cosmic Wind *Ballerina*	5	N22C	161.453
8. W. L. LeFevers	Falcon Special	10	NX-1E	156.584
David Long	Long LA-1 *Peashooter*	67	NX-5111H	Out 9th lap

GOODYEAR TROPHY RACE, 1949

Pilot	Aircraft	Race No.	License	Speed
1. Bill Brennand	Wittman *Buster*	20	NX14855	177.340 mph
2. Keith Sorensen	*Deerfly*	39	N24C	176.726
3. Steve Wittman	Wittman *Bonzo*	1	N1292	176.244
4. Vincent Ast	Cosmic Wind *Ballerina*	5	N22C	175.974
5. Fish Salmon	Cosmic Wind *Minnow*	4	N21C	175.728
6. Cliff Mone	Williams *Estrellita*	34	N44183	175.016
7. Bob Downey	Mercury Air *Shoestring*	16	N26C	171.359
8. Luther Johnson	Long LA-1 *Peashooter*	67	NX511H	167.308
9. James Kistler	Kistler Special	31	N31C	153.369
Al Foss	*Jinny*	94	N68732	Out 12th lap

CONTINENTAL MOTORS RACE
(All engines Continental C-85)
1948 at Miami

Pilot	Aircraft	Race No.	License	Speed
1. Bill Brennand	Wittman Special	1	N1292	166.473 mph
2. Fish Salmon	Cosmic Wind *Minnow*	4	N21C	158.532
3. Art Chester	Chester *Swee' Pea II*	2	N4000K	145.650*
4. Earl Ortman	Loose Special	44	N64573	127.339
W. L. LeFevers	Falcon Special	10	N1E	Out 4th lap

* cut scatterpylon

1949 at Miami

Pilot	Aircraft	Race No.	License	Speed
1. Steve Wittman	Wittman *Bonzo*	1	N1292	176.867 mph
2. Bill Brennand	Wittman *Buster*	20	NX14855	174.193
3. T. B. Heisel	Pitts Special	21	N52120	170.011
4. Dave Long	Long *Peashooter*	67	NX-5111H	166.763
5. Art Chester	Chester *Swee' Pea II*	2	N4000K	166.730
6. N. C. Van Tuil	Williams *Estrellita*	34	N44183	166.698

1950 at Miami

Pilot	Aircraft	Race No.	License	Speed
1. Steve Wittman	Wittman *Bonzo*	1	N1292	185.400 mph
2. Keith Sorensen	Cosmic Wind *Ballerina*	5	N22C	182.044
3. Bob Downey	Shoestring	16	N26C	181.334
4. Phil Quigley	Pitts *Li'l Monster*	8	N97M	175.885
5. Bill Brennand	Wittman *Buster*	20	NX14855	175.731
6. Eddy Custer	Cosmic Wind *Minnow*	4	N21C	175.000
7. Wm. Falck	*Rivets*	92	N60089	173.421
8. John P. Jones	Cosmic Wind *Little Toni*	3	N20C	170.768

1950 at Detroit

Pilot	Aircraft	Race No.	License	Speed
1. John P. Jones	Cosmic Wind *Little Toni*	3	N20C	187.785 mph
2. Steve Wittman	Wittman *Bonzo*	1	N1292	185.050
3. Keith Sorensen	*Deerfly*	39	N24C	184.576
4. Chester Black	Williams *Estrellita*	34	N441	181.971
5. Wm. F. Falck	Falck *Rivets*	92	N60089	181.933
6. Phil Quigley	Pitts *Li'l Monster*	8	N97M	178.144

1951 at Detroit

Pilot	Aircraft	Race No.	License	Speed
1. John P. Jones	*Shoestring*	16	N26C	197.218 mph
2. Steve Wittman	Wittman *Bonzo*	1	N1292	192.174
3. Keith Sorensen	Modified Foss *Little Mike*	94	N68732	187.476
4. Bill Brennand	Pitts *Li'l Monster*	8	N97M	187.053

1952 at Detroit

Pilot	Aircraft	Race No.	License	Speed
1. Steve Wittman	Wittman *Bonzo*	1	N1292	197.29 mph
2. Bill Falck	Falck *Rivets*	92	N60089	194.38
3. Bill Brennand	Pitts Special II	8	N97M	192.31
4. Bob Porter	Wittman *Buster*	20	N14855	180.72
5. Jim Kistler	Kistler *Skeeter*	31	N31C	
6. John P. Jones	*Shoestring*	16	N26C	

SAN DIEGO, CALIFORNIA, April 24, 1949

Pilot	Aircraft	Race No.	License	Speed
1. Fish Salmon	Cosmic Wind *Minnow*	4	N21C	175.27 mph
2. Steve Wittman	Wittman *Bonzo*	1	N1292	175.
3. Bob Downey	Cosmic Wind *Ballerina*	5	N22C	174.
4. Bill Brennand	Wittman *Buster*	20	N14855	171.
5. Bill Broadbeck	Chester *Skybaby*	7	N8400H	

Note: Bob Heisel (Pitts *Pellet*) killed during first heat. In second heat, Art Chester (*Swee' Pea II*) killed.

NEWHALL, CALIFORNIA, May 8, 1949

Pilot	Aircraft	Race No.	License	Speed
1. Bob Downey	Cosmic Wind *Minnow*	4	N21C	169.4 mph
2. Steve Wittman	Wittman *Bonzo*	1	N1292	163.3
3. Bill Brennand	Wittman *Buster*	20	N14855	159.
4. Bill Broadbeck	Chester *Skybaby*	7	N8400H	158.6
5. Billie Robinson	Cosmic Wind *Little Toni*	3	N20C	154.2

ONTARIO, CALIFORNIA, May 22, 1949

1. Bob Downey	Cosmic Wind *Minnow*	4	N21C	176. mph
2. Steve Wittman	Wittman *Bonzo*	1	N1292	171.8
3. Billie Robinson	Cosmic Wind *Little Toni*	3	N20C	171.
4. Bill Brennand	Wittman *Buster*	20	N14855	170.6
5. Keith Sorensen	*Deerfly*	39	N24C	169.

WHITE PLAINS, N. Y., June 24, 1950

1. Bill Brennand	Wittman *Buster*	20	N14855	175.97 mph
2. Luther Johnson	Long *Midget*	67	NX511H	161.12
3. Jim Miller	Miller *Little Gem*	14	N5623H	158.53
4. Steve Wittman	Wittman *Bonzo*	1	N1292	
5. Bart Denight	Denight Special	0	N9059H	

SAN JOSE, CALIFORNIA, June 25, 1950

1. Vincent Ast	*Shoestring*	16	N26C	175. mph
2. Bob Downey	Cosmic Wind *Ballerina*	5	N22C	174.3
3. Eddie Custer	Cosmic Wind *Minnow*	4	N21C	174.
4. John P. Jones	Cosmic Wind *Little Toni*	3	N20C	173.
5. Jim Kistler	Kistler *Skeeter*	31	N31C	160.5

CHATTANOOGA, TENNESSEE, July 16, 1950

1. Bill Brennand	Wittman *Buster*	20	N14855	176.69 mph
2. Phil Quigley	Pitts Special II	8	N97M	175.86
3. Jimmy Wilson	Pack *Li'l Rebel*	10	N1E	163.02
4. Art Beckington	Parks Alumni Special*	87	N90522	158.17
* Pusher-type				

READING, PENNSYLVANIA, Sept. 24, 1950 (REBAT TROPHY)

1. Steve Wittman	Wittman *Bonzo*	1	N1292	185.57 mph
2. Bill Brennand	Wittman *Buster*	20	N14855	183.71
3. Phil Quigley	Pitts Special II	8	N97M	179.25
4. Jim Miller	Miller *Little Gem*	14	N5623M	169.55
5. Bart Denight	Denight Special	0	N9059H	167.77
6. Bill Falck	Falck *Rivets*	92	N60089	167.09

CHATTANOOGA, TENNESSEE, May 20, 1951

1. Steve Wittman	Wittman *Bonzo*	1	N1292	178.36 mph
2. Bob Downey	Cosmic Wind *Minnow*	4	N21C	176.32
3. Jim Wilson	Pack *Li'l Rebel*	10	N-1E	165.86
4. Bob Porter	Wittman *Buster*	20	N14855	165.64
5. Joe Mangano	Pack *Johnny Reb*	46	N66319	

READING, PENNSYLVANIA, August 12, 1951 (REBAT TROPHY)

1. Steve Wittman	Wittman *Bonzo*	1	N1292	184.69 mph
2. Bob Porter	Wittman *Buster*	20	N14855	180.68
3. Jim Wilson	Pack *Li'l Rebel*	10	N-1E	179.18
4. Luther Johnson	Long *Midget*	67	N6V	169.55
5. Bill Brennand	Pitts Special II	8	N97M	164.45

CHATTANOOGA, TENNESSEE, May 18, 1952

1. Bill Falck	Falck *Rivets*	92	N60089	186.95 mph
2. Steve Wittman	Wittman *Bonzo*	1	N1292	186.79
3. Bob Porter	Wittman *Buster*	20	N14855	176.91
4. Bill Brennand	Pitts Special II	8	N97M	175.97
5. Jim Wilson	Pack *Li'l Rebel*	10	N-1E	174.60

(No races in 1953)

DANSVILLE, N. Y., July 4, 1954

1. Jim Miller	Miller *Little Gem*	14	N5623M	181.06 mph
2. Dick Ohm	*Shoestring*	16	N26C	180.94
3. Bob Porter	Wittman *Buster*	20	N14855	176.33
4. Phil Quigley	*Mammy*	9	N9M	166.6
5. Bart Denight	Denight Special	0	N9059H	166.09

DANSVILLE, N. Y., July 3, 1955 (FRANK E. GANNETT TROPHY)

1. Bill Falck	Falck *Rivets*	92	N60089	186.85 mph
2. Steve Wittman	Wittman *Bonzo*	1	N1292	185.33
3. Dick Ohm	*Shoestring*	16	N26C	181.82
4. Tom Cassutt	Cassutt Special	111	N20N	180.68
5. John Scoville	Scoville *Stardust*	50	N85N	157.26

SPRINGFIELD, ILLINOIS, May 27, 1956

1. Bill Falck	Falck *Rivets*	92	N60089	191.07 mph
2. Steve Wittman	Wittman *Bonzo*	1	N1292	190.02
3. Tom Cassutt	Cassutt Special	111	N20N	188.77
4. Marion Cole	*Tater Chip*	88	N31E	165.26
5. Mel Stickney	*Mammy*	9	N9M	

NIAGARA FALLS, N. Y., July 8, 1956 (FRANK E. GANNETT TROPHY)

1. Bill Falck	Falck *Rivets*	92	N60089	199.96 mph
2. Steve Wittman	Wittman *Bonzo*	1	N1292	199.15
3. Tom Cassutt	Cassutt Special	111	N20N	197.62
4. Marion Cole	*Shoestring*	16	N26C	191.42
5. Charlie Bishop	Pack *Li'l Rebel*	47	N66317	163.09
Note: Scoville crashed in first heat.		50	N85N	

OSHKOSH, WISCONSIN, August 5, 1956 (S. J. WITTMAN TROPHY)

1. Steve Wittman	Wittman *Bonzo*	1	N1292	196.84 mph
2. Bill Falck	Falck *Rivets*	92	N60089	196.72
3. Dick Ohm	*Shoestring*	16	N26C	188.45
4. Charlie Bishop	Pack *Johnny Reb*	46	N66319	178.19

OSHKOSH, WISCONSIN, August 11, 1957 (S. J. WITTMAN TROPHY)

1. Steve Wittman	Wittman *Bonzo*	1	N1292	192.76 mph
2. Tom Cassutt	Cassutt Special	111	N20N	187.04
3. Bill Falck	Falck *Rivets*	92	N60089	186.39
4. Dick Ohm	*Shoestring*	16	N26C	179.91
5. Don Tygert	Ohm Special			172.21

FORT WAYNE, INDIANA, September 1, 1957

1. Bill Falck	Falck *Rivets*	92	N60089	196.65 mph
2. Steve Wittman	Wittman *Bonzo*	1	N1292	196.29
3. Tom Cassutt	Cassutt Special	111	N20N	191.42
4. Charlie Bishop	Pack *Johnny Reb*	46	N66319	187.18
5. Dick Ohm	*Shoestring*	16	N26C	187.14
6. Jim Miller	Miller *Little Gem*	14	N5623M	175.98

FULTON, N. Y., July 6, 1958

1. Bill Falck	Falck *Rivets*	92	N60089	196.72 mph
2. Tom Cassutt	Cassutt Special	111	N20N	196.19
3. Steve Wittman	Wittman *Bonzo*	1	N1292	192.24
4. Don Tygert	*Shoestring*	16	N26C	189.27

FORT WAYNE, INDIANA, August 31, 1958 (FORT WAYNE INDUSTRIES TROPHY)

1. Tom Cassutt	Cassutt Special	111	N20N	195.8 mph
2. Steve Wittman	Wittman *Bonzo*	1	N1292	193.9
3. Bill Falck	Falck *Rivets*	92	N60089	193.15
4. Jim Miller	Miller *Little Gem*	14	N5623M	190.78
5. Mel Stickney	Pack *Li'l Rebel*	47	N66317	188.6
6. Charlie Bishop	Pack *Johnny Reb*	46	N66319	183.99

FORT WAYNE, INDIANA, September 20, 1959

1. Jim Miller	Miller *Little Gem*	14	N5623M	199.15 mph
2. Bill Falck	Falck *Rivets*	92	N60089	196.94
3. Paul Booth	Pack *Grey Ghost*	47	N66311	188.49
4. Tom Cassutt	Cassutt Special II	11	N111U	182.12
5. Charlie Bishop	Pack *Johnny Reb*	46	N66319	181.5
6. Mel Stickney	*Shoestring*	16	N26C	177.73

FORT WAYNE, INDIANA, July 4, 1960

1. Jim Miller	Miller *Little Gem*	14	N5623M	200.23 mph
2. Bill Falck	Falck *Rivets*	92	N60089	198.89
3. John Thomson	Jersey *Skeeter*	111	N20N	195.5
4. Steve Wittman	Wittman *Bonzo*	1	N1292	194.67
5. Jan Christie	Cassutt Special II	11	N111U	193.73
6. Mel Stickney	*Deerfly*	39	N24G	187.82

RENO, NEVADA, September 20, 1964

1. Bob Porter	Miller *Li'l Gem*	14	N74J	193.44 mph
2. Steve Wittman	Wittman *Bonzo*	1	N1292	187.42
3. Art Scholl	*Miss San Bernardino*	31	N31Z	171.76
4. Bob Downey	*Miss Cosmic Wind*	6	N36C	166.57
5. Jerry Quarton	Cassutt-Quarton	19	N190A	162.86

Biplanes (Homebuilt), September 14, 1964

1. Clyde Parsons	Knight Twister		N67P	144.57 mph
2. Tom Shannon	Knight Twister		N13N	143.41
3. James Nagle	Knight Twister		N1B	131.50
4. William Boland	Starduster		N354L	130.63
5. Fred Rechenmacher	EAA Special		N73639	120.44

ST. PETERSBURG, FLORIDA, March 28, 1965

1. Bill Falck	Falck *Rivets*	92	N60089	200.75 mph
2. Bob Downey	Miller *Li'l Gem*	14	N-14J	200.75
3. Bob Porter	*Miss Cosmic Wind*	6	N36C	185.98
4. John Martin	*Shoestring*	16	N26C	185.25
5. Roy Berry	*Mr. Zip*	27	N32C	168.62

Biplanes (Homebuilt), March 28, 1965

1. Pat Ledford	Pitts Special		N8L	137.7 mph
2. L. J. Royall	Pitts Special		N6W	136.7
3. Jack Lowers	Lowers Special		N57J	126.7
4. Allen Ruby	EAA		N12X	118.2
5. Hal Thompson	Knight Twister		N25C	No time

LANCASTER, CALIFORNIA, June 6, 1965

1. Bob Downey	Miller *Li'l Gem*	14	N74J	195. mph
2. Art Scholl	*Miss San Bernardino*	31	N36C	191.
3. Bud Jury	Pack *Grey Ghost*	2	N26C	190.6
4. Mike Dewey	*Little Mike*	94	N35C	189.5
5. Bill Stead	*Miss Reno* (Cosmic)	6	N36C	179.6
6. Howard Terrill	Terrill Special	5	N3622G	155.0
7. Steve Wittman	Wittman *Bonzo*	1	N1292	*

* Cut three pylons

Biplanes (Homebuilt) Race, June 6, 1965

1. Bob Herendeen	Pitts Special		N66Y	126.5 mph
2. Mike Strboya	*Little Toot*		N9193Z	124.2
3. Buck Dollar	Clar-Dollar Spl.		N3369G	123.7
4. Jack Wells			N9614Z	118.0
5. Alex Rantos	Miniplane		N74P	100.6
6. Don Jackson	Miniplane		N4077K	99.6

RENO, NEVADA, September 12, 1965

1. Bob Porter	*Deerfly*	39	N84G	202.14 mph
2. Bill Falck	Falck *Rivets*	92	N60089	196.19
3. Bob Downey	Miller Special *Ole Tiger*	14	N74J	194.44
4. Art Scholl	*Miss San Bernardino*	31	N31Z	190.06
5. Rick Townsend	Cosmic Wind *French Qtr. Spl.*	7	N20C	184.40
6. Bill Stead	*Miss Cosmic Wind*	6	N36C	Not taken

Biplane (Homebuilt) September 12, 1965

1. Bill Boland	Mong Sport	3	N354L	148.68 mph
2. Clyde Parsons	Knight Twister	11	N67P	146.06
3. F. C. Rechenmacher	EAA Biplane	22	N73639	118.81
4. Ralph Ormsbee	Miniplane	5	N215R	117.42
5. Clem Fischer	Starduster	7	N3410G	115.43
6. Sidney White	Starduster	1	N3635G	91.49

LAS VEGAS, NEVADA, September 26, 1965

1.	Bob Porter	*Deerfly*	39	N84G	202.4 mph
2.	Bill Falck	Falck *Rivets*	92	N60089	202.2
3.	John Paul Jones	*Shoestring*	16	N26C	198.0
4.	Art Scholl	*Miss San Bernardino*	31	N31Z	195.7
5.	Bob Downey	Miller *Ole Tiger*	14	N74J	195.2
6.	Paul Booth	Wittman *Bonzo*	1	N1292	Not taken

Biplane (Homebuilt) September 26, 1965
Exhibition race only, no times taken

PALM SPRINGS, CALIFORNIA, November 14, 1965

1.	John Paul Jones	*Shoestring*	16	N26C	202.17 mph
2.	Bob Porter	Sorenson *Deerfly*	39	N84G	201.64
3.	Steve Wittman	Wittman *Bonzo*	1	N1292	191.35
4.	Bob Downey	Miller *Ole Tiger*	14	N74J	190.27
5.	Art Scholl	*Miss San Bernardino*	31	N31Z	190.14
6.	Bill Falck	Falck *Rivets*	92	N60089	191.56*

* Cut pylon, speed for 12 laps.

ST. PETERSBURG, FLORIDA, May 1, 1966

1.	Bill Falck	Falck *Rivets*	92	N60089	203.01 mph
2.	Steve Wittman	Wittman *Bonzo*	1	N1292	196.01
3.	Bob Downey	Miller *Ole Tiger*	14	N74J	193.72
4.	Howell Jones	Jones *Half Fast*	3	N4762S	191.46
5.	Roy Berry	Denight *Miss Dallas*	97	N9059H	179.40
6.	Jim Wilson	Wilson *Baby Cyclone*	21	N121W	163.59

Biplanes (Homebuilt) May 1, 1966

1.	Skeeter Royall	Pitts Special	21	N6W	148.76 mph
2.	Jack Lowers	Lowers Special	33	N57J	140.68
3.	Bob Abernathy	Pitts Special	13	N113A	140.38
4.	Paul Booth	Pitts Special	6	N14T	132.04

LANCASTER, CALIFORNIA, May 30, 1966

1.	Bob Downey	Miller *Ole Tiger*	14	N74J	189.48 mph
2.	Art Scholl	*Miss San Bernardino*	31	N31Z	187.97
3.	Howell Jones	Jones *Half Fast*	3	N4762S	185.36
4.	John Paul Jones	*Miss Cosmic Wind*	6	N36C	151.46
5.	Howard Terrill	*Shushonik*	5	N302HT	*
	Ray Cote	*Shoestring*	16	N26C	197.08**

* Cut 4 pylons, not timed   ** Disqualified, illegal engine

Biplanes (Homebuilt) May 30, 1966

1.	Bruce McIntire	Pitts Special	17	N2997G	139.93 mph
2.	Sid White	Starduster	1	N3635G	138.01
3.	Bill Boland	Mong Sport	3	N354L	137.65
4.	Don Wickliffe	Dollar Special	11	N3369G	134.30
5.	J. Don Janson	Miniplane	4	N4077K	123.63
6.	Bob Downey	Starduster	14	N9614Z	No time

FREDERICK, MARYLAND, September 5, 1966

1.	Bill Falck	Falck *Rivets*	92	N60089	192.8 mph
2.	Bob Downey	Miller *Ole Tiger*	14	N74J	192.3
3.	Art Scholl	*Miss San Bernardino*	31	N31Z	No time
4.	Tom Cooney	*Tom Cat*	71	N311Z	No time
5.	Howell Jones	*Half Fast*	3	N4762S	*
	Jerry Quarton	*Li'l Rascal*	19	N190A	*

* Mid-air collision 11th lap.

Biplanes (Homebuilt) September 5, 1966

1.	Paul Booth	Pitts Special	6	N14T	129.5 mph
2.	Jack Lowers	Lowers Special	33	N57J	128.2
3.	Clemens Fischer	Mong MS-2	8	N563A	125.6
4.	Frank Fox	BERT II	20	N900F	118.0
5.	Norman Taylor	Miniplane	12	N412T	111.6
6.	Frank Tighe	Pitts Special	15		139.5*

* Engine did not comply to specifications.

RENO, NEVADA, September 25, 1966

1.	Bill Falck	Falck *Rivets*	92	N60089	193.098 mph
2.	Steve Wittman	Wittman *Bonzo*	1	N1292	191.897
3.	Bob Downey	Miller *Ole Tiger*	14	N74J	189.009
4.	Art Scholl	*Miss San Bernardino*	31	N31Z	185.249
5.	Roy Berry	*Miss Dallas*	97	N9059H	174.446
6.	Ray Cote	*Shoestring*	16	N26C	*

* Out 7th lap, engine

Biplanes (Homebuilt) September 25, 1966

1.	Don Wickliffe	Dollar Special	11	N3369G	147.723 mph
2.	Sidney White	Starduster	1	N3635G	144.723
3.	Bruce McIntire	Pitts Special	17	N2997G	144.665
4.	Bill Boland	Mong Sport	3	N354L	148.423*
5.	Bob Harendeen	Pitts Special	37	N66Y	133.062
6.	Clem Fischer	Mong Sport	8	N563A	127.096

* Cut pylon 3rd lap

FT. WORTH, TEXAS, May 28, 1967

1.	Bill Falck	*Rivets*	92	N60089	203.97 mph
2.	Bob Downey	*Ole Tiger*	14	N14J	200.41
3.	Steve Wittman	*Bonzo*	1	N1292	203.58*
4.	Ray Cote	*Shoestring*	16	N16V	187.70
5.	Roy Berry	*Miss Dallas*	0	N9059H	185.54
6.	Howard Terrill	*Shushonik*	5	N302HT	173.44

* Cut pylon to avoid collision, awarded tie with #16 for 3rd.

Women's Stock Plane Race, May 28, 1967

1.	Judy Wagner	Beech Bonanza	11	N5395E	194.72 mph
2.	Elaine Loening	Aero Comdr. 200	26	N670CE	186.80
3.	Mara Culp	Aero Comdr. 200	5	N960D	187.77*
4.	Edna Whyte	Aero Comdr. 200	1	N2910T	177.83*

* Cut pylon, penalized one lap, speeds unofficial.

Biplanes (Homebuilt), May 28, 1967   (FT. WORTH CONT)

1.	Bruce McIntire	Pitts	17	N2997G	156.17 mph
2.	Lee Mahoney	Starduster	1	N3635G	155.93
3.	C. D. Wickliffe	Dollar Special	11	N3369G	144.97
4.	Clem Fischer	Mong	8	N563A	142.68
5.	Paul Booth	Pitts	6	N14T	128.39
6.	Joe Pribilo	Starduster	2	N163G	126.10

CLEVELAND NATIONAL AIR RACES, September 4, 1967

1.	Bill Falck	*Rivets*	92	N60089	202.893 mph
2.	Bob Downey	*Ole Tiger*	14	N14J	202.722
3.	Steve Wittman	*Bonzo*	1	N1292	196.757
4.	Howell Jones	*Miss Dallas*	0	N9059H	181.330
5.	Marion Baker	*Boo Ray*	81	N8081	179.970
6.	Jim Wilson	*Snoopy*	34	N3421	175.810

Women's Stock Plane Race, September 4, 1967

1.	Pat Arnold	Piper Comanche 250	7	N8548P	181.543 mph
2.	Edna Whyte	Aero Commander 200	1	N2910T	176.861
3.	Elaine Loening	Aero Commander 200	26	N670CE	170.334
4.	Mary Knapp	Mooney Super 21	3	N3389X	164.571
5.	Dot Etheridge	Mooney Super 21	8	N2916L	159.116
6.	Dorothy Julich	Piper Comanche 180	4	N7400P	149.347

Biplanes (Homebuilt), September 4, 1967

1.	Lee Mahoney	Starduster	1	N3635G	155.119 mph
2.	Bruce McIntire	Pitts	17	N2997G	154.493
3.	Bill Boland	Mong	3	N354L	151.108
4.	Clem Fischer	Mong	8	N563A	147.978
5.	Dallas Christian	Mong	99	N33Z	136.034
6.	Michael DuPont	Pitts	69	N4773S	133.472

RENO, NEVADA; September 24, 1967

1.	Bill Falck	Falck *Rivets*	92	N60089	202.703 mph
2.	Bob Downey	Miller *Ole Tiger*	14	N74J	201.192
3.	Ray Cote	*Shoestring*	16	N26C	200.557
4.	Smoky Stover	*Miss San Bernardino*	31	N31Z	191.083
5.	Marion E. Baker	Baker *Boo Ray*	81	N2081	183.892
6.	Jim Wilson	Wilson *Snoopy*	34	N3421	Not taken

Biplanes (Homebuilt), September 24, 1967

1.	Bill Boland	Mong Sport	3	N354L	151.643 mph
2.	Sidney White	Starduster	1	N3635G	151.311
3.	Bruce McIntire	Pitts Special	17	N2997G	151.286
4.	Dallas Christian	Mong Sport	99	N33Z	147.686
5.	Clemens Fischer	Mong Sport	8	N563A	146.723
6.	I. Branch Smith	Mong Special	26	N1126	133.462

Index

About the Author...

As a boy, Reed Kinert washed airplanes and hitched rides until learning to fly at Richmond, Indiana in 1932 on an OX-5 Waco 10. He next purchased a LeBlond engined Aeromarine Klemm to build up his hours toward a commercial pilot license. He barnstormed while operating the Richmond Airport and acted as airways observer for the Weather Bureau. After teaching Indiana college students and Air Corps cadets to fly, Reed became a flight test and delivery pilot for Convair in California. At the end of World War II he again worked as an instructor and did charter flying, reverting to "Sunday pilot" status in 1948.

Mr. Kinert began drawing at 4, later combined his love for flying with aviation art, originated and produced advertising illustrations for Aeronca and Vought, and in 1943, published his first of 13 books, to date, all written and illustrated by him.

Reed has flown many types of aircraft from the 37 hp 2 place Aeronca through Ford trimotors and 4 engined Coronado flying boats. Between books Reed likes to paint, in watercolor or oils, Early Americana mechanical objects, mostly, of course, aircraft. He is a member of the American Aviation Historical Society and Professional Race Pilots Association.

Reed Kinert

This series presents a rare collection of photographs along with authentic drawings by the author covering the famous air races through 1971 beginning with the first International Air Meet at Rheims, France, in 1909. Author Kinert expertly captures the excitement and color of each race so that the reader literally becomes a co-pilot with such world-renowned men as Glenn Curtiss, Louis Bleriot, Roscoe Turner, Paul Mantz, and others who made the first wavering flights which have culminated in the jet age of today.

With research and experience of a quarter of a century, Mr. Kinert, a former racing pilot himself, describes in detail the plane types, names, engines, horsepower, wing span, length, weight, speed, time, and personalities who risked and sometimes lost their lives in an attempt to better that last record. The inclusion of fine scale drawings also add greatly to the value of the series.

These books will be a delight to the collector and invaluable to every racing enthusiast.

Volume I covers air races from 1909 to 1923
Volume II, 1924-1931
Volume III, 1932-1939
Volume IV, 1946-67
Volume V, 1968
Volume VI, 1969
Volume VII, 1970
Volume VIII, 1971

AERO PUBLISHERS, INC.

329 Aviation Road Fallbrook, Cal. 92028

ISBN-0-8168-7853-6